Aboriginal Slavery on the Northwest Coast of North America

Leland Donald

University of California Press
Berkeley / Los Angeles / London

University of California Press
Berkeley and Los Angeles, California

University of California Press
London, England

Copyright © 1997 by
The Regents of the University of California

Portions of chapters 7 and 11 appeared in an earlier version
in *Research in Economic Anthropology* 6 (1984):77–119.

Library of Congress Cataloging-in-Publication Data

Donald, Leland, 1942–
    Aboriginal slavery on the Northwest Coast of North America /
Leland Donald.
        p.   cm.
    Includes bibliographical references and index.
    ISBN 0–520–20616–9 (cloth : alk. paper)
    1. Indians of North America—Northwest Coast of North America—
History.   2. Slavery—Northwest Coast of North America—History.
3. Indians of North America—Northwest Coast of North America—
Economic conditions.   4. Indians of North America—Northwest Coast
of North America—Social conditions.   I. Title.
E78.N78D63   1997
979.5′00497—dc21   96–46162

Printed in the United States of America

1 2 3 4 5 6 7 8 9

Contents

Figures

Tables

Preface

The purpose of this book is to describe and analyze the practice and institution of slavery among the aboriginal inhabitants of the North Pacific Coast of North America. In ethnographic terms this is one of the most famous regions of the world: it is the Northwest Coast culture area, the locus of the potlatch, and the focus of the ethnological investigations of Franz Boas, a key figure in the history of anthropology.

Although slavery is mentioned in the earliest sources on the region and never completely ignored in subsequent ethnography, it has never received full and careful treatment. This book remedies this omission. More, it argues that slavery is one of the key culture traits that must be fully understood if the Northwest Coast culture area is to be properly appreciated. The importance of slavery is implied in A. L. Kroeber's significant but relatively neglected 1923 essay, "American Culture and the Northwest Coast." Despite continuing brief descriptions in subsequent ethnographic works and a few publications that aimed at more substantial treatment of the topic, neither Kroeber nor anyone else has followed up the problem of slavery in the culture area in the detail that it requires.

If this book is primarily an anthropological analysis of one domain of culture on the Northwest Coast, it is also intended as yet another contribution to the already voluminous literature on slavery. Slavery scholarship is dominated by works describing and analyzing New World plantation slavery, although slavery in the "ancient world," primarily Greece and Rome, is the subject of a considerable literature also. Discussions of slavery in other parts of the world or at other time periods are much less numerous. In particular, there is very little discussion of slavery and other types of servitude in nonstate or prestate societies. (See, for example, the paucity of entries relating to these types of societies in Joseph Miller's periodic bibliographies published in *Slavery & Abolition*.) Thus this book contributes to our understanding of human slavery and of slave systems by focusing on a usually neglected facet of the multifarious appearance of involuntary servitude.

I should make my relationship to the tradition of Northwest Coast scholarship clear. I was not trained as a Northwest Coast scholar or even as an Americanist. At the University of Oregon, where I received my Ph.D., my regional ethnographic specialty was sub-Saharan Africa, especially West Africa. I did my dissertation fieldwork in northern Sierra Leone and wrote my dissertation on one of the smaller ethnic groups in Sierra Leone, the Yalunka. As an undergraduate I had done two seasons of archaeological fieldwork in northern Georgia and learned some southeastern prehistory and ethnohistory but had decided to pursue cultural anthropology and non–North American ethnography in my graduate studies. Nevertheless, my first ethnographic fieldwork was done in North America, a summer among the Navajo in northern Arizona. At the time I thought of its importance primarily in terms of getting my feet wet as a fieldworker and not as Americanist experience to add to my previous archaeological work.

My introduction to the Northwest Coast came in a series of graduate seminars conducted at Oregon by David F. Aberle. The topic of the seminars was "cultural ecology," but wisely believing that a concrete focus was needed, Aberle chose to have us apply cultural ecological ideas to the Northwest Coast material. As a result of those seminars I learned a lot about cultural ecology and probably more than I realized about the Northwest Coast and then went off to "do" cultural ecological research in West Africa.

In 1969 I took a teaching job at the University of Victoria, where Donald Mitchell, who had also taken Aberle's cultural ecology seminars, was working. Mitchell was already a genuine Northwest Coast expert, actively working on both the prehistory and ethnohistory of the region. He wanted to pursue problems related to the resource base of Northwest Coast cultures and possible relationships between the resource base of various communities and other sociocultural variables. When the opportunity came to try to tie fluctuating salmon resources to other variables, I became involved because of my interest in quantitative methods. The information relating to salmon was an enormous data base of Canadian Department of Fisheries estimates of the annual escapement of salmon by species into most of the streams along the British Columbia coast. Mitchell and I teamed up on the salmon resources project and had a simple division of labor: he supplied the Northwest Coast expertise; I analyzed the salmon data. The result of our initial collaboration was "Some Correlates of Local Group Rank among the Southern Kwakiutl" (1975). Our findings in that paper led us into problems regarding the organization of work and the mobilization of labor. There is not much analysis of labor, work, or the organization of production in the Northwest Coast literature, but as we explored the ethnographic and historical material, we kept coming across slaves and slave labor even though Northwest Coast ethnographers themselves nearly always played down the value of slave labor. Since slaves were largely produced as captives resulting from intergroup fighting and were clearly traded from group to group, it was obvious that the topic of slavery led in a number of different directions. For this reason Mitchell and I began what we came to call the Northwest Coast Intergroup Relations Project. With the help over the years of a number of student research assistants, we began to systematically assemble all of the material we could find on Northwest Coast intergroup relations—trade, war, intercommunity feasts and ceremonies, intergroup marriages, patterns of leadership involved in intergroup relations of all types, and slavery.

In the context of the intergroup relations project, I began working on Northwest Coast slavery as a research topic in 1975. Since we began in 1975, Mitchell and I have published, together or separately, a number of papers on various topics relating to intergroup relations, especially slavery. Therefore the project has been a joint venture, although each of us has worked up some parts of our material independently and has maintained other research interests.

The salmon resources project has also continued so that, between it and the intergroup relations project, I became more and more involved in the Northwest Coast. In part this is because Victoria is such an ideal place to work on the culture area, and the problems and issues raised by Northwest Coast ethnology and ethnohistory are so fascinating that it was easy to become more and more taken up with them.

As an Africanist outsider, when I first began to work my way through some of the sources the lack of attention to slavery seemed odd to me. No one working in West African ethnology or history can ignore slavery even when, as in my own fieldwork in Sierra Leone, it is not a primary research interest. Thus my African experience and general materialist theoretical approach kept me looking and thinking against the grain of the orthodox approach to Northwest Coast cultures. This volume is the result.

All scholarly projects are a collective activity. This book is no exception, and there are many people and institutions to thank. For financial support I must thank the Social Sciences and Humanities Research Council of Canada for two research grants during the early phases of the research. The Province of British Columbia's Youth Employment Programme provided student assistants for several summers, and the Faculty Research Committee of the University of Victoria provided several small grants that facilitated progress on the research for this book.

All ethnohistorians owe much to librarians and archivists. I gratefully acknowledge the help of many who work (or worked) at the following institutions: Bancroft Library, University of California, Berkeley; Hudson's Bay Company Archives; Province of Manitoba Public Archives; McGill University Library; Museum of Anthropology, University of British Columbia; Province of British Columbia Archives and Records Service; Public Archives of Canada; Royal British Columbia Museum; University of British Columbia Library; University of Victoria Library; University of Washington Library; and Wellcome Institute for the History of Medicine.

A number of University of Victoria students helped to assemble and organize much of the source material used during the course of this research: Murray Davison, Rod Edwards, Bob Lawson, Ross McMillan, Paul Merner, Rebecca Murray, Margaret Rogers, and Gloria Ruyle. Three students deserve special mention: Brian Horne did much to organize the slavery material into manageable computer files at a time when this was a much more demanding task that it would be now, and Simone Decosse and Chris Morgan offered insights and comments on the material that went beyond expectations and contributed significantly to my thinking about Northwest Coast slavery.

Thom Hess and Barry Carlson made useful suggestions about linguistic matters. William H. Jacobsen, Jr., very kindly sent me information about Wakashan words for slaves. M. Dale Kinkade supplied me with material about Salish words for slaves, but he did more than that. His generous and full responses to my inquiries about Salishan linguistics and his careful critique of my attempts to deal with the linguistic history of the Northwest Coast were a forceful reminder that there is indeed a community of scholars.

I began research on Northwest Coast slavery in the late 1970s, but the preparation for this work goes back farther than that. Although many contributed to my development as an anthropologist and a Northwest Coast scholar, two teachers deserve special mention. Vernon Dorjahn encouraged me to study African ethnology and to do fieldwork in West Africa. Without his preparation and support I would never have gotten there and would thus have lacked some of the perspective I now bring to the study of slavery. David F. Aberle introduced me to Northwest Coast studies and in many other ways supplied me with the intellectual tools and perspective needed for my research. He also set a standard to which I still aspire.

Bruce Trigger very kindly read the first draft of chapter 12. His comments on it led to improvements. Beyond that, our conversations about equality and inequality in Native American societies have benefited me greatly, as have his publications on the Iroquoians.

Three friends and colleagues read the first draft of this book. Few authors can have had the benefit of such careful, scholarly attention to their work. I have been discussing Northwest Coast matters with Kathleen Mooney Berthiaume for about twenty-five years, and her labors over this manuscript are merely the most recent contribution that she has made to my knowledge of the region and its native peoples. Joseph G. Jorgensen's exacting standards of scholarship and his passionate commitment to Native Americans have been a goad to me since I worked with him as a postdoctoral student at the University of Michigan nearly thirty years ago. His comments on the first draft were as valuable as I knew they would be, but his enthusiasm for the book and his support and encouragement at a time when I wondered if I would ever complete it require my deepest gratitude. As noted earlier, Donald Mitchell and I have been working together on Northwest Coast problems since the early 1970s and on slavery and related matters since about 1975. There is no way that I can exaggerate the importance of his contribution to this book. Without Don's counsel and expertise I could not have written it. I look forward to many more years of fruitful collaboration with him.

An earlier version of the discussions of the slave trade and slave prices in chapters 7 and 11 appeared as "The Slave Trade on the Northwest Coast of North America" in *Research in Economic Anthropology* 6 (1984):77–119, published by JAI Press, Inc. (Greenwich, Conn.).

The names of indigenous communities and cultural, ethnic, and linguistic groups and groupings appear in myriad forms in the historical and ethnographic literature. It is frequently difficult to decide what is the appropriate form to use in a work such as this. My goal has been to make my reference to a group as clear as the sources allow. To that end, since this is not primarily a linguistic study, I have tried to use the most consistently and recently used anglicized version of names in local or scholarly use. In quotations I keep the author's original term and spelling. There are a few important exceptions to the principle of using the most consistent and recent term. Some contemporary aboriginal peoples have made it clear that they wish to be known and referred to by names of their own choosing, rather than by European labels or names first applied to them by other native groups. Where such usage has been requested by the political body currently representing the descendants of a group or where local usage has become consistent with a large body of local native feeling, I have used the preferred term rather than the term more commonly used in the scholarly literature. The principle invoked here is a simple one: people have a right to be called by a name of their own choosing rather than one affixed by outsiders, even if we outsiders must bear the burden of expanding our vocabularies. The most commonly invoked such native usages in this book follow. If through ignorance or oversight I have not used the preferred indigenous name for a group, I offer my apology.

For "Bella Coola," the preferred name is "Nuxalk." (Bella Coola is retained as a language name.)

For "Nootka," the preferred name is "Nuu-chah-nulth." (Nootka is retained as a language name.)

For "Southern Kwakiutl," the preferred name is "Kwakwaka'wakw." (Kwakiutl is retained for the four groups who resided near Fort Rupert in historic times. To minimize confusion, they are usually referred to in full as "Fort Rupert Kwakiutl.")

For "Thompson," the preferred name is "Nlak'pamux."

For "Shuswap," the preferred name is "Secwepemc."

For "Lillooet," the preferred name is "Stl'atl'imx."

Introduction

From phrases in North American English ("low man on the totem pole") to glimpses of spectacular wood carvings in museums throughout the world to images of the "Dionysian Kwakiutl" from Ruth Benedict's still in print *Patterns of Culture* (1934) there is widespread, if extremely fragmentary, awareness of the aboriginal cultures and peoples of the Northwest Coast of North America. Most of those who have taken an introductory anthropology course at university or college have heard a lecture or read in their course textbook about the Northwest Coast potlatch.

Within anthropology and related disciplines aspects of Northwest Coast societies and cultures are among the most familiar parts of the world ethnographic record. This is partly because this culture area was the principal geographic focus of research for Franz Boas, the founding father of American academic anthropology, and he and his students published widely on the ethnography of the region. But the Northwest Coast cultures themselves pose a number of challenging ethnological problems and puzzles that have engaged the continuing interest of Boasians and non-Boasians alike.

Complex Foragers

At the time of first contact with Europeans (in the 1770s) the cultures of the North Pacific Coast of North America were based on a foraging subsistence mode: they fished, hunted, and gathered, as domesticated plants and animals made no significant contribution to their diet. As hunter-gatherers, or non-agricultural peoples, they represented to the eighteenth, nineteenth, and even twentieth centuries examples of the earliest types of human societies—"primitive man" unspoiled by having to engage in agricultural labor. In aboriginal times the peoples inhabiting what came to be known as the Northwest Coast culture area lacked not only agriculture but also pottery, two critical prerequisites to cultural development in the view of nineteenth-century evolutionists. Yet as ethnographic information began to be systematically collected and compared, it quickly became apparent that the Northwest Coast peoples were not at all typical of other historically known hunter-gatherers.

Hunter-gatherers have come to be identified with "band"-type societies, in which settlement patterns are nomadic, communities are small (usually under one hundred people), and populations are scattered. The populations of historically known bands are small and sparse because they exploit environments with low potential productivity, lack storage technologies, and are not organized to maximize what productive potential there is. Being highly mobile, those living in bands tend to have little in the way of material goods. They lack political office and hierarchy. Their economic systems are based on sharing, pooling, and reciprocity. They tend to be egalitarian, often fiercely so with leveling mechanisms that ensure that no person or family becomes materially or socially superior to their peers. They do not have elaborate social organization based on descent groups, and they are not organized into secret societies. In short, people organized as bands lack social and cultural complexity.

Bands in this sense were not found on the traditional Northwest Coast. Although these peoples were hunter-gatherers, their modes of subsistence and environments supported one of the densest known nonagricultural populations. Many other Northwest Coast cultural and social traits are more usually associated with agricultural peoples: large wooden plank dwellings housing many people; an elaborate material culture based on wood carving; relatively sophisticated transport systems (i.e., large canoes capable of transporting thirty people and their goods); permanent community sites; unilineal descent groups (clans and lineages); elaborate public ceremonies complete with spectacular costumes, music, dance, and drama perhaps best described as ritual theater; a wealth of public art (totem poles, carved house posts, painted house fronts); wealthy leaders whose personalities and skill at trading impressed the first Europeans to meet them; and complex notions of property and ownership. In short, to continue to use the vocabulary that goes with the concept of band-type societies, the Northwest Coast peoples were "tribes" and not bands. Recent students of foragers take such differences into account by distinguishing between "simple" and "complex" hunter-gatherers.[1] The peoples of the Northwest Coast culture area are the most familiar and best described historically known complex hunter-gatherers.

The recognition that the Northwest Coast peoples were both hunter-gatherers and organized as tribes in terms of society and culture creates some important problems in the interpretation of Northwest Coast ethnology. Just how did the Northwest Coast peoples achieve such rich and complex cultures on a foraging subsistence base? The orthodox answers to this question have noted the rich environment of the North Pacific Coast of North America, especially in terms of a relatively accessible and very rich marine biomass—above all salmon but also seals, halibut, herring, whales, and shellfish. This was interpreted as providing a stable resource base that allowed Northwest Coast cultures to flourish without serious environmental limitations. This interpretation was challenged in the 1960s when it was argued that there was environmental variation that produced local shortages (both from year to year and from place to place) that had to be overcome. At that time Wayne Suttles and others suggested that the Northwest Coast feasting complex—the famous potlatch—provided one such mechanism for balancing resource variation and shortages. This interpretation was not accepted by all Northwest Coast specialists. And little systematic work was done by those supporting either position on the question of exactly how the rich resource base was exploited in a manner that led to surpluses and cultural complexity. Much has been written about the technology of traditional Northwest Coast food production but relatively little about the organization of work and only a little more about the organization and control of food distribution.

One of the principal themes of this book is how those who controlled access to resources on the Northwest Coast utilized the labor of slaves in the process of food production. Slave labor, almost completely ignored in earlier discussions, is shown to have been of critical importance in both food production and the control of its distribution by the elites who were the principal beneficiaries of Northwest Coast cultural complexity. By a thorough investigation of slave labor and its implications, this book considerably clarifies how the traditional Northwest Coast economies worked.

Social Inequality

From first contact European observers recognized that the Northwest Coast societies exhibited considerable inequalities. People whom they labeled chiefs and slaves were quickly recognized. By the mid-nineteenth century the presence of three strata, usually called social classes, was clearly established: a ruling elite, free commoners, and slaves. In the most influential late nineteenth-century analysis of the region's aboriginal societies, Boas discounted the importance of slaves, treating them as outside society, that is, of no standing in the decision-making or prestige systems of any Northwest Coast community. Although he used the term "classes" to describe the three Northwest Coast strata, Boas does not appear to have given the notion of class any particular theoretical meaning.

The Northwest Coast societies continued to be considered as divided into three classes until Philip Drucker published his very influential paper "Rank,

Wealth, and Kinship in Northwest Coast Society" in 1939. Drucker argued that although there was a sharp break between slaves and free people on the Northwest Coast, there was no clear division between nobles and commoners. Rather, he placed the emphasis on free people being ordered in a continuously ranked series of social positions. It was, he wrote, impossible to see clearly where the nobility ended and commoners began. The existence of slaves was certainly recognized by Drucker, but his entire discussion was concerned with inequality among the free.

In the 1950s some regional specialists began to argue again that classes were present on the Northwest Coast. The "rank not class" position remained dominant, but the possibility of true classes was more widely discussed among those working in the area. Finally most Northwest Coast scholars more or less accepted Wayne Suttles's argument that although there were classes in traditional Northwest Coast societies, the usual pyramid model of class was not applicable. Suttles suggested that a more appropriate model was that of an "inverted pear." That is, most traditional Northwest Coast societies were made up of a large nobility, a small number of lower-class people, and a slightly larger number of slaves. This interpretation has the advantage of conceding the existence of classes in the region's societies—something recognized in the vocabularies of all the indigenous languages—while saving the "rank is what is important" position. If Suttles's inverted pear model is accepted, the rank-not-class view remains essentially intact because the non-nobility are a very small proportion of any community's population and play no significant role in society and culture.

Everyone involved in the argument over the nature of inequality in the culture area appears to concede that slaves formed a class. If slaves are a numerically small group and play no important role, however, the puzzle of how a society works if its members are preoccupied with rank and contains two classes, one free but internally ranked and one held by members of the free class as slaves, does not have to be considered, much less solved. If slaves did play important roles in many Northwest Coast societies, then who benefited from their presence and who did not becomes an important issue. Perhaps all the free benefited, but if they did so, did all benefit equally? A full understanding of the nature of Northwest Coast slavery and the roles slaves played in their communities is necessary to progress on the Northwest Coast social inequality problem.

This book contributes to the ongoing discussion of the nature of Northwest Coast social inequality in two ways. Its full and detailed analysis establishes just what slaves contributed to their communities and what benefits their owners received. It then focuses on the problem of class on the Northwest Coast, taking specific account of the analysis of slavery and of the relationship between slaves and their masters.

Traditional Northwest Coast Economies and the Potlatch

The Northwest Coast peoples used fishing-hunting-gathering technologies to extract from their environments sufficient food and other material goods to enable them to create cultures and societies of much greater richness and complexity than are usually found associated with such extractive technologies. An important question in Northwest Coast ethnology is how they managed to do this. The North Pacific Coast of North America supports very rich maritime and riverine resources, and the Boasian answer to this question was to emphasize the richness of this resource base and to turn to discussions of society and culture. The link between environment and culture was assumed but not described or analyzed. The ethnographic writings of Boas and others certainly do contain a great deal of information about technology, but there is little analysis of the organization of work, or of other aspects of economics. Even in the post-Boas Northwest Coast literature little attention was paid to the organization of production and distribution (although the work of Kalervo Oberg, Viola Garfield, and Wayne Suttles are exceptions).

Everywhere in the Northwest Coast culture area members of the elite formally invited guests to feasts at which the host(s) gave wealth to the guests. These feasts are the famed potlatches. At times property was destroyed as well as given away. Large quantities of food and other goods had to be amassed for a successful feast/potlatch. Although potlatches have many aspects—social, religious, economic—the essential feature is public validation of the hosts' status before the invited guests, principally the hosts' titleholder peers. In his early analyses Boas mistakenly treated the potlatch as a means of *acquiring* rather than *validating* rank and as a form of interest-bearing investment: he believed that hosts gave away property to guests as a means of receiving return gifts that were mandatory repayments of the original gift at high rates of interest.

Boas developed his analyses as a result of his observations of Kwakwaka'wakw potlatches in the late nineteenth century. These same potlatches horrified missionaries and government officials because the large quantities of goods given away and sometimes destroyed seemed wasteful and harmful to the participants and because they offended the Protestant sensibilities of the observers. Such reactions led to the outlawing of potlatches by the Canadian government. In part, Boas's discussions of the potlatch were designed to show the positive sides of the activity (interest-bearing investment, etc.) to Euro-Canadians and Euro-Americans.

Since Boas, interpretations of the potlatch have been a major focus of anthropologists' (and others') interest in Northwest Coast ethnology. Much of the attention in these analyses has been on understanding the potlatching behavior of late nineteenth- and early twentieth-century potlatchers on the assumption that it would illuminate the workings of earlier versions of the potlatch. More recent interpreters (following or reacting to the work of Suttles) have sometimes considered how possible variation in the resource base and problems of production and distribution are related to or even explain potlatch behavior.

In our 1975 study of local group rank among the Southern Kwakiutl, Donald Mitchell and I showed that among the local groups that formed a feasting hierarchy, three variables were strongly associated: relative rank for quantity of salmon resources, relative rank for population size, and relative rank in the feasting hierarchy. Among other issues, these findings raised the question of just how a local group's leaders (who were in charge of the feasts) managed their group's resources in such a way as to produce the goods (both food and nonfood) that formed the basis of the feasts and property distributions that were the occasions at which the group rankings were demonstrated and validated.

Consideration of how these Kwakwaka'wakw groups transformed salmon swimming upstream to spawn into food revealed that salmon fishing sites were controlled by descent groups (one or, usually, more of which made up the local group); that the elites of these communities (descent group heads) controlled access to salmon; that the critical work organization problem was not sufficient labor to catch enough salmon but sufficient labor to process the caught salmon for storage; and that the gender division of labor meant that women did most of the work associated with salmon preservation. This meant that the most important problem facing resource production managers (i.e., descent group heads) was sufficient female labor. Examination of the sources for other Northwest Coast groups suggests that female labor was a critical problem for elites in most, if not all, Northwest Coast communities.

Slaves were present in nearly all Northwest Coast communities, sometimes in large numbers proportional to community size. Slaves were by and large owned by members of the elite. Many slaves were women and obviously available to supplement the labor of free women. In addition, male slaves were available for all forms of labor, including female labor, since their slave status had already demeaned and degraded them and prevented them from resisting performing tasks usually associated with women. There are other associations of slaves and women. For example, among the Kwakwaka'wakw slaves are frequently included as a part of the goods sent by the groom's family to the bride's family as a part of the transactions surrounding an elite marriage (see chapter 7 for more details). All of this strongly suggests that the role of slaves in Northwest Coast systems of work and production requires a much more thorough investigation than has previously been undertaken. Reporting the outcome of this investigation is a major feature of this book; see especially chapter 6.

Northwest Coast Slavery and Northwest Coast Culture

A major goal of this book is to assemble, describe, and analyze the range of available data both historical and ethnographic on slavery in traditional Northwest Coast cultures. But this study is also motivated by the hypothesis that a fuller understanding of slavery will show just how slavery fit into and contributed to other aspects of traditional Northwest Coast culture and society. The research on which this book is based began with the conjecture that a better understanding of how slave labor was organized and used would enhance our understanding both of traditional Northwest Coast economic systems and of how the resources used in the potlatch were amassed. The demonstration that slaves did make very important contributions, via their labor, to their masters' ability to function as elites does advance our understanding of how these economies worked. But slaves appear over and over again in many other aspects of Northwest Coast culture as well. Working out the place of slaves in the economic and social system brings new insights to our understanding of Northwest Coast ranking and inequality. Analysis of the frequent appearance of slaves as ritual victims clarifies our understanding of both Northwest Coast ceremonial activity and thought and belief systems. A fuller understanding of slavery does not answer all our questions about Northwest Coast ethnology, but in recognizing that slavery is a central and not a peripheral feature of Northwest Coast cultures we have taken important steps toward such answers.

Northwest Coast Slavery in Wider Contexts

The historical and ethnographic record contains examples of a wide range of forms of servitude, only some of which are appropriately labeled slavery given the definitions of slavery that are commonly used by scholars of the topic. By any of these definitions those held in servitude on the Northwest Coast can properly be called slaves. This places Northwest Coast slavery alongside slavery in classical Greece and Rome, in the early nineteenth-century American South and the Caribbean, and in eighteenth-century African societies, to name only a few. This placement is appropriate not merely because of the presence of slaves, properly speaking, in traditional Northwest Coast societies, but because of their proportionally large numbers in many Northwest Coast communities and because of the importance of the institution of slavery to Northwest Coast society and culture.

The existence of slavery as a major institution in Northwest Coast societies is another facet of the unique contribution that these cultures make to the historical and ethnographic record. Few students of slave societies and few of those interested in problems of sociocultural evolution would expect to find that slavery is a significant feature of any society based on a hunting-gathering subsistence technology. The Northwest Coast peoples were, it is true, complex hunter-gatherers, but even complex hunter-gatherers are small-scale societies and do not compare in complexity of social organization with the state and near-states found in the regions mentioned above.

A Brief Note on Methodology

A full discussion of the methods used in this book appears in chapter 3. Here I offer brief comments on two of the main methodological problems I faced and the solutions I adopted to overcome them. First, how does one establish generalizations about *the* Northwest Coast culture area and at the same time also uncover important variation *within* the region? Although Northwest Coast cultures were never static and unchanging, the pace and range of change increased dramatically from the time of first European contact. This gives rise to the second methodological problem: how does one take change into account but also document continuity where appropriate?

Establishing Generalizations

There is no cluster of traits and certainly no single trait that defines the Northwest Coast. Thus when generalizations about the culture area are advanced, they must be based on a systematic assessment of the range of variation present in the region. Many of the assertions in the literature on Northwest Coast cultures that are presented as generalizations are based on haphazard, although sometimes extensive, coverage of the source material, are not supported by any specific methodology, and are documented by example. In contrast, the generalizations advanced in this book are based on an explicit procedure.

Ideally one would generalize about a topic relating to Northwest Coast cultures by assessing the topic for each society in the culture area. This is impossible to do for the following reasons: for any potential unit of study (society, culture, community) the most common answer to a specific query about a topic of interest is "no information"; where information is available on the same topic for a number of different units, the information has often been collected at different times and, because of the continuous change since contact, may not be comparable; some sources give only very generalized information about a topic whose basis is uncertain while others describe concrete events and specific examples, although their typicality is rarely established.

For reasons described in chapter 3, the winter village community is the ideal unit of analysis on which to base generalizations about the Northwest Coast. The problem is to get a representative set of winter village communities. Such a representative set would cover the range of variation present in the culture area, have the same time focus for each community in the set, and have sources that are rich enough in quality and quantity to afford confidence in the accuracy of one's assessment of that community with respect to the variables of interest. Given that slavery is the primary topic of interest, it quickly became apparent that the time focus had to be as early as practicable. My goal was a reconstruction of the situation for the first third of the nineteenth century for each unit included in the sample. Not surprisingly I could achieve even an approximation of this goal for only a few winter villages. The initial sample was too small and had too many gaps with respect to geographic coverage and known variation. Therefore, I added some sets of winter villages where the available information approximated that for my original smaller sample. In the end I had what I call a "tribal unit sample" of twenty. The units are distributed over the northern, central, and southern part of the culture area in about equal numbers, although there are still some gaps in geographic/linguistic coverage because of poor information. Because of variation in topical coverage from group to group, a study of another topic would require a somewhat different tribal unit sample. No one sample is possible for all problems in Northwest Coast ethnology.

All generalizations about Northwest Coast slavery advanced in this book are based on codings of the relevant variables for the tribal unit sample. These codings reveal important subregional variation as well as overall patterns. The codings are not simply mechanical recordings of sources whose information is treated as "fact." All the sources used were assessed for their potential value, their biases, the time period they represented, the basis for their content, and so on. In addition, I have used many sources on groups not in the tribal unit sample to illustrate generalizations and for insight into slavery and other aspects of Northwest Coast culture.

Although the tribal unit sample is important to my ability to have confidence in my analysis of Northwest Coast slavery and its applicability to the entire culture area, other sources have also been important, particularly ethnohistorical ones. There is a great deal of published and unpublished writing about various parts of the culture area by observers who were on the scene between 1775 and 1850. For all their biases and misunderstandings, these records offer invaluable insights and information and I have used all those I could find.

Another important source of information is, of course, the native inhabitants of the Northwest Coast themselves. Of particular interest to me were statements from those who had been alive when slavery was still actively practiced in their communities. Although there appear to be relatively few direct or extensive comments about slavery from such people, often their comments and especially their telling of myths and folklore illuminate the practice of slavery. This kind of information is all the more important because its context makes it unlikely that the source is consciously trying to convey a particular image of slavery to his or her listener.

Recognizing Change

Slavery and related practices changed rapidly throughout the Northwest Coast from the 1780s until the late 1880s when slavery finally came to an end. The problem faced in a book such as this is to situate the material in its historical context. The strategy that I have adopted is to reconstruct slavery on the Northwest Coast as it appears to have been in the first third of the nineteenth century. I have described and documented this reconstruction on a topic-by-topic basis in Part II. Change is dealt with explicitly in Part III, chapter 11. In the discussion of change it is especially important to make the link between changes in slavery and the changing character of the fur trade, which in the first fifty years of contact was the major focus of interaction between the indigenous peoples of the region and Euro-Americans. After establishing this context I review the nature of change for the same topics that were treated more statically in Part II.

Separating the description of my reconstructions from the descriptions of the changes that were occurring has its risks. One may lose sight of the fact that change was continuously occurring or fail to realize that some features of mid-nineteenth-century slavery were at least in part an outcome of contact. Experimentation with mixing discussions of change with the topical description and analysis seemed to me to result in other confusions and a very blurred analysis of some important topics. Hence my decision to proceed with the current format.

A Brief Guide to the Book

My description and analysis of Northwest Coast slavery is divided into four parts. Part I begins with an overview of traditional Northwest Coast culture. It provides the cultural and social background to the practice of slavery and sketches my resolution of several of the key issues in Northwest Coast ethnology, such as the nature of stratification and political organization in the culture area. Also included in this part are a discussion and a critique of previous views and studies of Northwest Coast slavery. Finally, I describe the various methods used to establish the nature of slavery in the culture area, including my solutions to the problem of describing and documenting variation in both space and time.

Part II describes Northwest Coast slavery as reconstructed for the first third of the nineteenth century on a topic-by-topic basis. This is the heart of the book. The topical coverage is comprehensive and establishes regional generalizations and documents important variation within the culture area. Especially important topics are a consideration of whether, given a broad cross-cultural perspective on slavery, Northwest Coast "slaves" are usefully labeled as such; a linked discussion of both slaves and masters; a detailed consideration of the contribution of slaves to various aspects of traditional Northwest Coast economies; and an analysis of the roles slaves played in rituals.

Northwest Coast slavery is placed in its historical context in Part III. The evidence for the antiquity of slavery in the culture area is reviewed. Then changes in slavery that can be documented for the period 1780–1880 are described and the gradual end of slavery in the last half of the nineteenth century is discussed.

Part IV puts Northwest Coast slavery in perspective. The culture complex of slavery is considered in the context of native North America. Important in this discussion is the distinction between the status of slave on the Northwest Coast and the status of captive in most of the rest of aboriginal North America. The integration of slavery into Northwest Coast society and culture is also discussed, with particular attention to stratification and hierarchy in the culture area.

Part One

Background and Methods

1
An Overview of Northwest Coast Cultures

The distinctiveness of the indigenous cultures of the North Pacific Coast of North America has been recognized by anthropologists since Otis Mason (1896) published the first cultural geographic classification of North American indigenous groups. Since Mason the Northwest Coast culture area has been variously defined. As used here the Northwest Coast stretched down the Pacific Coast of North America from Yakutat Bay in Alaska south to the mouth of the Columbia River; to the east it was bounded by the complex Coast and Cascade ranges.[1] (See fig. 1.) Boas sometimes used the same boundaries for his North Pacific Coast region, and the definition used here is not uncommon. The other major approach to defining the area includes the peoples of the coast of Oregon, often down into northernmost California. The most recent classification, that of the *Handbook of North American Indians*, begins in the north with the Eyak (who are just north of the Yakutat Tlingit) and continues south to the Takelma at the northern border of California.

For the past hundred years differences in delimiting the culture area have largely involved its southern boundary. The eastern boundary (distinguishing the Northwest Coast from the Subarctic, Plateau, and Great Basin culture areas) has caused little controversy. I have chosen the Columbia River as the southern boundary of the culture area because the ethnographic and ethnohistorical record for the Oregon groups is very poor, especially for topics like slavery. A more southerly boundary would add little to the discussion of Northwest Coast slavery.

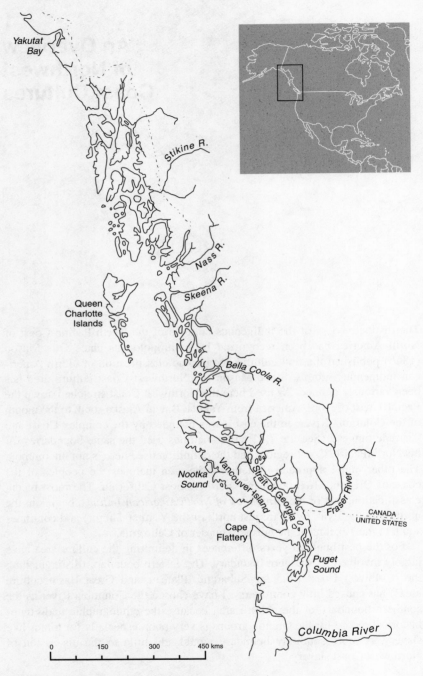

Yakutat
Bay

Stikine R.

Nass R.

Skeena R.

Queen
Charlotte
Islands

Bella Coola R.

Nootka
Sound

Vancouver Island

Strait of Georgia

Fraser River

CANADA
UNITED STATES

Cape
Flattery

Puget
Sound

Columbia River

0   150   300   450 kms

Figure 1.   The North Pacific Coast of North America.

The Northwest Coast Culture Area

The most distinctive characteristics of the Northwest Coast culture area are:

- a marine and riverine orientation that permeated not only subsistence practices but ideology and outlook;
- a subsistence pattern that places a heavy emphasis on fishing and marine mammal hunting and also involves considerable gathering of shellfish, other marine invertebrates, and plant foods;
- a highly developed woodworking technology whose most spectacular products are large plank houses, very large dugout canoes, and various carved and painted wooden art objects including, in the northern part of the region, "totem" poles;
- a tripartite system of social stratification that includes a bottom stratum of hereditary slaves;
- an emphasis on property, both tangible and noncorporeal, with the control of all types of wealth the principal criterion of social importance and success and with both individual and kin group ranking important;
- the lack of inter- or even intracommunity political organization and the absence of significant political office.[2]

The culture area was probably one of the most densely populated in native North America. The best recent estimate suggests a population possibly as high as 150,000 at the time of first European contact (Boyd 1990, 136). This would give an approximate density of 40.5 persons per 100 square kilometers, which is considerably higher than for most other parts of native North America, including some whose populations practiced agriculture.

In a 1923 paper A. L. Kroeber argued that the Northwest Coast culture area was the most distinctive of the aboriginal culture areas of North America. He suggested that those traits it shared with most other North American culture areas (such as the dog, the bow, the firedrill, woven basketry, shamanism, and life crisis rites for individuals, especially for adolescent girls) were a common inheritance from the earliest populations to settle in North America via the Siberia/Alaska landbridge route. He noted that it shared few, if any, of the traits that had diffused from Middle America to most other culture areas on the continent and that it had a number of traits that seem to have been local innovations and that had diffused to only a modest degree into closely neighboring culture areas. Kroeber also made the important point that traits absent from the Northwest Coast but common elsewhere in North America were as significant as those that were present.

Finally, the Northwest is substantially without officials, chiefs, government, or political authority. This may seem a strange statement about a culture in which a class of chiefs or nobles is recognized as distinct from commoners. Yet the very breadth of this class of chiefs argues that it is something different, in the main, from a group of officials constituting part of a political mechanism. The concept of such a mechanism is what seems to be foreign to the Northwestern culture. It knows privileges and honors, but not office; a status of influence, but no constituted authority. (1923, 9)

Kroeber thought that slavery was a key element in the cultural features that made the Northwest Coast distinct.

What counts among these people is possession; possession of property, of inherited or acquired use, of privilege, of ritual. Enough of such possessions, jealously maintained, give honor and influence and command. Custom law operates to guard and increase the possessions, prestige, and power of the wealthy. (1923, 9)

[There was] an active cultural focal center lying within the Northwest area and rather rigorously limited to it. There follows an impressive series of other elements, some of them of cultural weight and well known. These include first the so-called caste stratification of Northwestern society, the extensive development of slavery as a property institution, the prestige attaching to wealth, the potlatch and credit system—a formidable and distinctive economic complex. (1923, 14)

The Natural Environment

The physical space occupied by aboriginal populations was a long narrow coastal strip that ran roughly north to south for nearly 2,000 kilometers. At its widest point (in the Fraser River delta area) this coastal belt was about 300 kilometers, although it was usually nearer to 150 kilometers and in the far north of the region less than 50 kilometers wide. Except where major rivers had significant valleys that cut into the mountains (the Columbia, Fraser, and to a lesser extent the Skeena and Nass), mountain ranges formed effective barriers to the interior, focusing inland contact and influences along major river valleys and a small number of mountain passes. Except along some of the major rivers, arable land was in short supply, and it is not surprising that, except for the growing of tobacco by a few groups, agriculture was not practiced.

For the latitudes involved (approximately 60°N south to approximately 48°S) the climate is relatively mild, and most parts of the region receive considerable precipitation. This climate produced temperate rain forest in many sections. The dominant species were Sitka spruce and western hemlock in the north and western hemlock and Douglas fir toward the south. Western red cedar and yellow cedar were also significant species in many local areas. Large numbers of edible plants grew in or on the fringes of these great forests, so that there was a varied supply of bulbs, roots, rhizomes, tubers, and fruits and berries available for human exploitation.[3]

Important land fauna included blacktail deer, elk, mountain goats, black bears, beaver, and numerous fur-bearing carnivores such as mink and ermine. Land birds were not generally significant for native peoples, but waterfowl certainly were. Most of the exploited birds were of seasonal significance. Two species of swans, the Canada goose, the brant, and nearly thirty species of ducks were all abundant, some available at particularly favored spots in seasonal flocks of tens of thousands. Breeding colonies of seabirds provided eggs and easily caught nesting birds.

Marine and riverine fauna were particularly significant. A large variety of marine invertebrates were collected either from the intertidal rocky shores or the sandier beaches. These included various species of clams, mussels, cockles, abalones, sea urchins, oysters, crabs, and octopus. Local beach and shore conditions determined which species were available when and where. The dentalium deserves special mention. Collected in a restricted part of the west coast of Vancouver Island, its shells were highly valued and traded all over western North America in precontact times. Marine mammals were abundant and widespread. The harbor seal is found throughout the region, including in many rivers. Steller's sea lion and the California sea lion are also common. Several species of porpoise are also found, as are several species of whale, of which the orca, humpback, and California gray are culturally the most important. The sea otter was significant for its fur in precontact times and was the focus of early European/native interaction.

The most important marine resource was fish, particularly the anadromous species. The major anadromous fish were the five species of Pacific salmon, the eulachon, and the sturgeon. The Pacific salmon spawn in fresh water, go to the sea to mature, and return to their natal streams to spawn. Every year large numbers of these five species returned to spawn and were available for harvesting. Of the saltwater fishes, halibut, herring, the true cods, and smelt were particularly important, although many other species were also exploited and might be important in a local area.

Many observers have commented on the richness of the environment from the point of view of human use. The region appears to be a fisher's and hunter-gatherer's paradise, and the high population density of the aboriginal inhabitants bears out their successful exploitation of the area. But there was a great deal of variation from locale to locale. There was also considerable temporal variation. Not only were seasonal considerations important, but most animal populations were subject to longer-range cycles and fluctuations as well. Short- and long-term weather patterns also affected the success of those seeking to harvest particular flora or fauna. This temporal and spatial variation produced a complex picture that meant that each local territory had its own characteristics and that significant amounts of time and effort went into subsistence activities. The Northwest Coast was a forager's paradise, but it required effort and shortages did sometimes occur.

Subsistence and the Annual Round

The culture area's subsistence technologies were extractive, that is, based on fishing, gathering, and hunting. A few of the northern groups (some Tlingit and some Haida) probably grew tobacco in precontact times, but otherwise the only domesticate, plant or animal, was the dog. The available resource base varied from local community to local community, but for a majority of communities the most important source of food was the Pacific salmon. These were mostly taken when the adult fish returned to their natal streams to spawn; nets, scoops, spears, weirs, and traps were all common salmon fishing devices. The late summer and fall were particularly heavy work seasons for most people, for salmon were not only taken for immediate consumption but dried and smoked to preserve through the winter. Other fish that were taken during their spawning season and had great importance for some local groups were the eulachon and herring. Species like halibut, the cods, and many rockfish were also often important (the halibut in particular for the Haida of the Queen Charlotte Islands, for example) and were taken with hook and line and lures and spears.

The most important sea mammals from a subsistence perspective were seals and sea lions. Almost all Northwest Coast groups hunted them. Whales were hunted by only a few groups (Nuu-chah-nulth, Makah, Quileute, Quinault), but drift whales were taken wherever they turned up. Seals and sea lions were harpooned from canoes or clubbed on rocks where they hauled out to rest. Whales were harpooned from large canoes, and their capture was surrounded by much specialist knowledge and ritual.

Marine invertebrates were essentially gathered from their intertidal habitats. Shellfish were the major type collected (various species of clams, mussels, oysters, limpets, and others), but sea urchins, crab, and octopus were also significant. Local knowledge, baskets, and, for some species, digging implements were the required technology.

Waterfowl were taken in nets and snares and shot from blinds. Many parts of the region lie along important migration routes, so large numbers of swans, geese, and ducks were available at appropriate seasons.

Land animals were not nearly as significant as were marine resources for people in most communities. The most important food species of land mammals throughout the area were deer and bears. Elk, found along the Pacific Coast south of 51°N (the northern tip of Vancouver Island is just south of this latitude), were an important food and hide source in the southern part of the area. Mountain goats were also locally important.

Plant foods were also significant. Many varieties of berries were collected and eaten in the appropriate season. Several species of marine algae were collected and eaten, and algae associated with deposits of herring roe was especially prized. Nut-bearing trees were not important except for hazel nuts and Garry oaks in a few restricted local environments. Camas and wapato were the most important sources of starch where they were found. Clover, cinquefoil, and rice-root were among the many other roots, bulbs, and rhizomes that were also significant where they were available. Starchy carbohydrates seem to have been scarce in the culture area, which probably explains why rice and ship's biscuit rapidly became important trade items when they were introduced by Europeans.

A comparison of nine communities scattered over most of the area showed that freshwater-based resources were either the most important or tied as the most important resource type for eight of the sample groups. This is entirely due to the fact that salmon and eulachon were taken in fresh water.[4] Ocean-based resources were generally ranked second or tied for first. This would be true for most Northwest Coast communities, except for those that were well up a major river system or at the mainland ends of long fjords. The important ocean-based resources for most of the sample groups were herring, seals, halibut, and shellfish (Mitchell and Donald 1988, 309–312).

Most of the resources available in a territory were distributed in such a way that they could not be efficiently exploited from a single settlement. This led to a seasonal pattern of people moving from one resource locale to another. No single annual round was common to the entire culture area, although for almost all groups the winter village was considered the central residential focus of the cycle. Each community adjusted its shifts and movements to the local situation and to the personnel available. One common pattern was the occupation by the entire community population of a "winter village" during the winter and early spring, a late spring/summer move to an aggregation of several winter village communities, and a fall dispersal into fishing camps, each occupied by a kinship unit much smaller than the winter village community. This pattern was only one of many, and even within the same winter village community different kin groups might follow different patterns of dispersion and aggregation. For example, some Squamish kin groups moved as many as four times a year, while others remained in their winter village year-round. Thus the annual circuit for a Squamish kin group might range from zero to 320 kilometers. Kin units belonging to other cultures on other parts of the coast might move as many as 500 kilometers in a yearly round, while in yet other winter village communities the annual rounds involved total distances of about 8 or 10 kilometers for each of their kin units. Subsistence activities dominated all of the seasons except for winter, when such work was at a minimum and ceremonial and ritual activities came to the fore.

Material Culture and Technology

The most distinctive aspect of Northwest Coast technology was woodworking. Among the more spectacular manifestations of this technology were large plank houses, many types of canoes, and totem poles, but a wide variety of smaller items including oil-tight boxes and ceremonial masks were also skillfully and beautifully made. The preferred raw material was the red cedar. This tree was so important that stands of red cedar may well have been the most important plant resource loci. Red cedar is a very even-grained wood, soft and easy to work. It is easy to use wedges and chisels to split out straight long-grained planks from this tree, which could be up to 30 meters high and nearly 2 meters in diameter. Other even-grained trees such as the yellow cedar and the alder were also important. Hardwoods were used for small items and when hardness was important.

All trees, including the very large red cedars, were felled with stone adzes and chisels. Axes and saws were not in the aboriginal tool kit. Very small amounts of iron (whose source is still uncertain) were available before contact, but early contact saw a significant inflow of iron for tools of various sorts. Aside from ground and polished stone tools, shell, horn, bone, and beaver incisors were the principal materials for making cutting edges. The quality of workmanship should be emphasized. Symmetrical form was the norm and surfaces were carefully polished—usually beyond utilitarian need. The surfaces of many utilitarian objects were decorated with incised carving, and even the large roof beams, which might be over 25 meters long and 60 centimeters in diameter, had carefully treated and aesthetically pleasing surfaces.

At winter village locations the rectangular plank house was usual, and it was found at other important places as well. There were a number of regional variants on the basic pattern. The plank roof was supported by large ridge-poles, which were in turn supported by large, usually carved house posts at the gables and house corners. The walls were usually plank as well. In the north of the area the house plan was typically nearly square, and houses might be 12 meters by 12 meters or more. The Wakashan house was rectangular in plan and might achieve dimensions of 12 meters by 30 meters. Houses farther south were also large but not quite on the northern or Wakashan scale. House posts were permanently sited, but some of the roof and wall planks could be moved from dwelling site to dwelling site as families made their annual round.

There were over half a dozen major types of dugout canoes, all made of red cedar. The manufacture of the various types tended to be regional, although, as canoes were major trade items, popular canoe types had a wider distribution in use than in manufacture. Some types were mainly functional while other variants were probably ethnic or aesthetic in origin. Canoes ranged from small one- and two-person crafts up to large freight, open water travel, or "war" canoes that sometimes exceeded 15 meters in length.

Wooden containers were manufactured for a wide variety of purposes including food and other storage and food preparation (including cooking) and serving.[5] One of the more spectacular containers was the bent wood box. A single board was carefully thinned with the planing adze to the correct dimensions. Then kerfs were cut about three quarters of the board's thickness deep where the corners were to be. The kerfed portions were then steamed and bent until the four sides of the box were formed with only a single joint.

Twined basketry and other types of weaving were also important. The major materials used were spruce roots, the inner bark of red and yellow cedar, mountain goat wool, and dog wool. Twined basketry could be woven so tightly that the resulting containers could hold water and be used for the storage of liquids or cooking by stone boiling. Twined basketry hats were also waterproof and were very useful in the rainy climate.

Except for Tlingit men, who wore breechcloths, men went nude when the weather permitted, and women wore hide or shredded cedar bark skirts. Otherwise clothing consisted of skin, fur, or woven garments that were draped rather than tailored. One outstanding example of the weaver's art on the Northwest Coast is the woven goat's wool blanket decorated with elaborate designs known today as the Chilkat blanket.

Communities

For virtually all Northwest Coast people, the community was what will be called the "winter village." As already mentioned, the winter village was the settlement in which people resided during the winter season when subsistence activity was at a low ebb and ceremonial life more active. Physically, the winter village consisted of a number of large, permanent plank houses usually in a single or double row at the back of a beach. The location was in sheltered water, away from the open ocean, often up an inlet, in a protected bay, or along the lower reaches of a river. Each house was occupied by a kin unit under that unit's head. Several of the kin units in a winter village might recognize common descent, or a very large kin unit might occupy more than one house.

As typical house size varied so did the number of occupants. In the far north, for example, the typical Tlingit house probably had about fifty occupants. The larger Kwakwaka'wakw longhouses had even more occupants. Winter village communities also varied greatly in size, depending on their location along the coast. Estimates of typical community size for some cultural units are Chilkat (Tlingit), 375 persons; Lower Skeena Tsimshian, 500; Fort Rupert Kwakiutl, 1,500; Makah, 480; Saanich (Northern Straits Salish), 175; Twana (Southern Coast Salish), 85.

The winter village formed a face-to-face community. At other times of the year at least some of a village's inhabitants were away at other resource loci, and it was not unusual for all of a winter village's people to be dispersed at some point in the year, especially in the fall. Members of different winter village communities also regularly gathered together. For example, large numbers of people from many communities (usually speaking the same language) might come to a favored eulachon spawning spot to collect the prized fish. Such aggregations were usually in the spring or summer, and members of the same winter village might go to different summer aggregations, although in the majority of cases everyone from a community shifted to the same multi-community aggregation.

People identified themselves primarily with their winter village and not these larger aggregations, but not too much should be made of this as kin unit affiliations were often more important than winter village membership, and, as will be seen below, the winter village was not a highly coordinated political unit.

Social and Economic Life[6]

Northwest Coast households could be quite complex. The large dwellings were usually occupied by either lineal or extended families. The male heads of the individual families who composed these households were typically kinsmen of the male head of the entire composite household. In the northern part of the region the men were matrilineally related to the head and the ideal form of residence was avunculocal. In the central and southern parts of the region residence tended to be virilocal. Common additional members of such households were miscellaneous kin of core members and the household's slaves, if any.

In the north (among the Tlingit, Haida, Tsimshian, and Haisla) kin units were organized on the basis of matrilineal descent. The large households tended to be matrilineages, which were organized into clans and which in turn were grouped into moieties or phratries. The principal production, consumption, and resource control unit was the large matrilineage household. To the south kin units were organized on the basis of nonunilineal descent, although the leadership tended to be controlled by a patrilateral core (Heiltsuk, Oowe-keeno, Kwakwaka'wakw, Nuu-chah-nulth). Thus the large households of these groups might be thought of as quasi-lineages. They also tended to control production, consumption, and resources. Even farther south descent was much less important, and the kin units tended to be smaller and weaker and have a more bilateral emphasis. Independent family households were more likely to have some autonomy of action, although the complex household was still important.

Most adults were monogamously married, although a significant minority of men practiced polygyny. These men were usually members of the elite segment of the community. The matri-moieties of the north were exogamous, although the nonunilineal descent groups of the central region were not.

In both production and manufacturing tasks a fairly strict gender division of labor was observed. Fishing, marine mammal hunting, land hunting, and house and canoe building were predominantly male activities in all Northwest Coast societies, while gathering and weaving were predominantly female activities. Hide working was more evenly shared by the genders. Women played a more prominent role in subsistence activities than this brief summary might suggest, however. For example, although most of the work of catching salmon during the important fall spawning runs was done by men, women did most of the work that was involved in preserving the fish for consumption during the winter season. In a good locale salmon were normally abundant and the crucial problem facing the people trying to exploit the relatively short season was not that of labor to catch fish but labor to preserve it.

The typical winter village community consisted of a set of kin units in the form of large, complex households residing in plank houses. Some of these kin groups considered themselves related to some other similar units within the community, although frequently they considered themselves related to similar kin groups in other winter villages as well. Kin groups intermarried with some other units in the winter village and with some outside the winter village. We can therefore identify all Northwest Coast societies as kinship based. That is, the primary mode of social relations was based on ties of kinship. But there was another important division within and across Northwest Coast communities.

Each Northwest Coast community was divided into three ordered strata: "titleholders," "commoners," and "slaves." Membership in these strata was recognized between as well as within communities. Titleholders are commonly referred to in the Northwest Coast literature as "chiefs" and "nobles" and held rights to leadership positions in kin groups and communities. The right to hold a title and exercise its prerogatives was hereditary. Commoners did not hold or have inherited rights to titles, although they were full members of their kinship unit (descent group) and enjoyed the full privileges that this implied; of principal importance was access to productive resources and the expectation of the assistance and protection of other kin. Slaves, who had lost their rights to kin group membership and were human property, will be discussed more fully below. The rigidity of the barrier between titleholder and commoner status and the implications of the difference varied from group to group in the region.

Titleholders were the dominant stratum in all Northwest Coast societies. They tended to be endogamous, preferring to marry fellow titleholders from

other communities rather than commoners from nearer home. They monopolized leadership roles and controlled most of the resource locations and wealth
in many communities. These claims to control and their successful maintenance were significant, for ideas of property and ownership were highly developed throughout the culture area. Almost everything could be and often
was owned. From the indigenous point of view this included not only resource loci and material goods but also noncorporeal property such as songs,
myths, and knowledge of various types. A person needed to have rights of
access to fish for salmon in a particular spot, but he needed similar rights of
usage to sing a particular song or display a particular image on his house.

Most kin units controlled a variety of resource loci and aimed at self-
sufficiency in the necessities of life. In this sense we can speak of the various
Northwest Coast peoples as having subsistence economies. But exchange
and trade were also important activities. Extensive trade networks existed in
the early nineteenth century, and the earliest European visitors to the coast
noted the expertise of the locals and often bemoaned their ability to drive a
hard bargain. Archaeological evidence supports the existence of considerable
trading activity before contact. Some exchanges of food occurred, with the
most widespread item of exchange being eulachon oil—probably because of
the spatially restricted availability of eulachon spawning grounds. More commonly exchanged items were canoes, furs, hides, dentalia, and slaves.

Politics and Intergroup Relations

Although titleholders are usually referred to as "chiefs," these men and
women were not political officeholders as such. Indeed, one might say that
political office as we understand it did not exist on the Northwest Coast. Titleholders led or were important in their kinship and residential group. In many
winter villages the heads of the component kin units were ranked, but although this gave the "village chief" considerable prestige and some ritual authority, it bestowed little or no power or authority to command in what is
usually thought of as the political arena. Winter villages were social and ceremonial entities and usually cooperated for defense, but even in military matters
constituent kin groups might go their own way.

In no Northwest Coast society did the authority of a leading titleholder,
even a village chief, extend beyond his own winter village. Multicommunity
political units did not exist. As an apparent exception some Nuu-chah-nulth
winter villages gathered together into what have been termed confederations,
recognizing one of the village chiefs as the confederation chief. This was
done by the coming together of the various winter villages into a common
summer village. Although the kin group leaders were ranked in an overall
confederation hierarchy, this hierarchy was not an authority structure. The

Nuu-chah-nulth confederation is best thought of as an alliance of winter villages rather than a political unit. And even many (or perhaps most?) winter villages might also be described as alliances of kin groups that resided together for a part of the year.

Individuals expected to be and were protected by their kin group. It was the kin group that exacted vengeance for the killing of one of its members or demanded some other form of compensation for lesser offenses. The winter village was normally expected to be a peace group, and a kin group bent on vengeance against an outsider would probably call on those belonging to other kin units residing in the village for help. Help was usually forthcoming, but even the ranking titleholder of the village could not compel it.

Intergroup fighting seems to have been common in both pre- and early contact times. We know, for example, that many traditional village sites had a fortified sanctuary or strong point nearby. One motive for fighting has already been mentioned: retribution for the killing of a kin group or community member, especially if the victim was a titleholder. Other motives included territorial gain, especially of rich resource loci, and plunder, including slaves. Rights to perform certain ceremonies and other display prerogatives could be taken over from their original owners by success in war and formed a noncorporeal aspect to plunder. Indeed, one of the principal mechanisms for the diffusion of new ceremonial elements was capture in war.

The most common form of intergroup hostility was the surprise attack or raid. If victorious, the raiders returned to their home village with trophy heads, slaves, and other plunder and left the victimized village too weak for quick retaliation. Less successful raiders were pursued immediately and might easily suffer heavy casualties themselves or bring disaster to their home community in the form of a quick and effective retaliatory raid from the intended victims and their friends. Some attacks were so successful that the survivors of a group were forced to find refuge among friends and relatives in other local groups and their territory (and its resources) fell into other hands.

It should be emphasized that fighting was not the only, or even the most important, form of intervillage relations. Titleholders frequently married titleholders from other communities, and such marriages could cross linguistic and cultural borders. One marriage often established an ongoing series of marriages across the generations. Exchanges of gifts at such marriages frequently involved the transfer of various ceremonial prerogatives and sometimes even the rights to titles. Titleholders also traded with each other across community lines and attended, as witness and participant, ceremonies and rituals in other winter villages as well as their own. The relationships among titleholders thus tied large numbers of communities together at the top into social, economic, and ceremonial systems of considerable extent. These systems were not politically organized or centralized, and there was not a single system that encompassed the entire culture area, although overlapping ties certainly gave titleholders at least indirect connections over considerable portions of the region.

Religious and Ceremonial Life

As is true with most other small-scale societies, systematic theology was not a part of Northwest Coast religions. Nevertheless, there were certain common religious ideas or themes. The most important of these were beliefs about the immortality of the animals important to subsistence and the need to perform rituals to ensure continued return of these species, the concept of a personal guardian spirit who may assist a person throughout his or her life, and vague notions of a supreme being who is remote from and disinterested in human beings and their affairs.

A rich group of myths was present in the area. Indeed, it is probable that several different myth cycles were originally present, each gradually coming to influence and be influenced by the others. Even within a single community, every person did not share a single, unified set of myths, for myth, like many other intangibles, was the property of the kin group. Each kin group had its own version of a culture's myths detailing the role and experiences of its own ancestors in earliest times.

Beliefs and practices about the need to ensure the renewal of crucial animal species can be illustrated by first salmon rites, which, although varying in form, were practiced in the majority of Northwest Coast communities. Typically, salmon were conceived of as immortal beings who sacrificed their physical bodies for the benefit of human beings. Offending the salmon by not recognizing their sacrifice in appropriate ways could lead to their refusal to return the next year—with disastrous consequences for the food supply. Therefore, the first caught salmon of the year were given an elaborate ritual welcome. Only after a complex public ceremony involving a ritual specialist and the first caught fish did members of the community begin to fish for their own subsistence needs.

As they began to mature, boys and girls trained to seek what are usually termed in English "guardian spirits." The details and form vary from culture to culture, but in general youths sought to forge a relationship with a supernatural being that would enable the human to have access to some of the spirit's power. This power was often for a specific purpose (success in hunting or in war, for example) or it could be more general in nature. Although individuals sought guardian spirits, it was usual for the seeker to have an inherited right to the particular spirit relationship sought. Titleholders were more likely to seek guardian spirits than others. Among the main features of the myths that titleholders retold were the accounts of how their ancestors had obtained the supernatural privileges and relationships that the living were attempting to obtain. In many communities, public display and validation of the successful achievement of such a relationship was even more important than the quest itself. Thus relationships with guardian spirits were integrated into the rank system of the community.

One of the most important gifts that a spirit could bestow on its human partner was the knowledge and ability to cure (and cause) illness. Individuals who could do this, usually termed shamans, are of a type widespread in northeastern Asia and western North America. Shamans were usually commoners, men (less frequently, but not rarely, women) who achieved considerable public recognition for their abilities to cure illness. Because the power to cure illness also meant the power to cause illness, the esteem in which shamans were held was strongly mixed with fear and caution.

Shamanistic curing occurred during a public performance that was as much public drama as curing rite. The patient was usually very ill, "home remedies" already having proved insufficient. The ritual was done at night before an audience of the patient's family and friends. The shaman had already made an earlier examination and decided to take the case. Failure to effect a cure was often interpreted as unwillingness to bring about a cure because of bribery by the patient's enemies, so care in selecting patients was necessary. Illness was often thought to be caused by the intrusion of foreign objects into the body; and if this was the case, the climax of the cure came when the shaman sucked the object (or objects) out of the patient's body. Another major source of illness was "soul loss," or the straying of the soul. In this instance cures were usually placed in the hands of a shaman who specialized in such cases.

Ceremonies, aside from those of the first salmon rite type, tended to focus on the supernatural experiences of individuals. These were associated either with life crisis events (childbirth and especially puberty and death) or with supernatural quests. Particularly in the latter type, the ceremony typically enacted the acquiring of inherited privileges and validated their display.

Perhaps the center of ceremonial innovation on the coast was the Northern Wakashan winter villages. Here were found the "dancing societies" that put on elaborate ritual dramas. Over several nights during the winter, these dramas portrayed the hero's encounter with a supernatural being that kidnaps the hero and takes him or her out of the mundane world, then endows the hero with supernatural powers and, finally, returns him or her to the community. The central actor in such a performance normally reenacted such events as they had occurred to his ancestor, the performer having inherited from his ancestor the right to do so. There were many variations on this theme depending on the particular titleholder and kin group. These dramas were true multimedia events, involving elaborate costumes and masks as well as skillful dancing and singing performances and, frequently, elaborate technical tricks to simulate death and rebirth.

The cycle of ritual dramas was most coherently and elaborately organized among the Northern Wakashan, but similar performances were undertaken by neighboring cultures, probably at least partly as a result of borrowing. In the southern part of the culture area the performances were less well organized and tended to put more emphasis on individual experiences and less on the display of inherited prerogatives.

Art

The many high-quality works of art executed in a distinctive style are perhaps the aspect of Northwest Coast cultures most familiar to those without a professional interest in anthropology.[7] Given the development of woodworking technology in the area, it is not surprising that carving in the round or in relief is the principal art form.

Characteristic elements of the general style are known archaeologically from the Fraser River north for at least two thousand years before contact, suggesting a long development in situ of this distinctive art tradition. The examples of Northwest Coast art collected in the eighteenth century by James Cook and others show that the style was fully developed at contact. Although there was a style general to the culture area, there were important regional variants. In the north the Haida, Tsimshian, and Tlingit developed a version that was both highly conventionalized and standardized. Nearly abstract elements were arranged into elaborate rule-determined designs to decorate the surfaces of an array of objects. South of these peoples, the Wakashan speakers, especially the Kwakwaka'wakw, developed a more rounded three-dimensional style. The design elements of this variant were less abstract than those to the north, although many details were deleted from the representations of animals that formed the major themes represented in the art. South of the Kwakwaka'wakw and south and east of the Nuu-chah-nulth, the Salish groups produced works that often seem to be bolder, simpler versions of Wakashan work. Their designs also seem closer to some of the earlier, archaeological examples of the general regional style.

Although there are examples of highly effective naturalistic depictions of human faces in masks, the subjects of most of the artworks were supernatural beings—that might be depicted in the form of animals, monsters, or humans. These beings were associated with episodes in the kin group traditions present throughout the area. The current members of a kin group had inherited the right to display the symbolic representations of the beings that appeared in their ancestral traditions. The leading titleholders had the right to display the most important "crests" as a part of their title's prerogatives. Thus the content of the art reflected the social structure of the communities where it was made in terms of both its kin groups and its rank structure.

Drucker (1955, 181–185) has identified four major characteristics of the art style: (1) it is basically "applied" in that the design forms are usually adapted to the forms of the objects that are being decorated; (2) both form and design elements were highly conventionalized and followed a clear set of principles—symmetry and balance of design, emphasis on certain parts of the subject (the head and paws, for example), and standardization of certain elements allowing for ease of identification of the being represented (the long snout and teeth of the wolf, for example); (3) there seemed to be an aversion to blank spaces, leading to a tendency to fill in all vacant areas; and (4) design elements were organized so that the viewer's eye is readily drawn from one part of the design to another, creating movement.

Almost any useful object—tools, spoons, bowls, boxes—might be brilliantly decorated with relief carving. Most wooden items were decorated to some extent, but there was also carving of antler, bone, ivory, and stone. Many surfaces that were not carved, or only lightly carved, were painted. These included house fronts, boxes, and basketry hats. Among the larger carved items were house posts and totem poles. Ritual objects such as masks, frontlets, and rattles were also carved, painted, and decorated with abalone shell, fur, and feathers. Even workaday baskets might be decorated, and textiles might also be objects of art. This was especially true of Chilkat blankets, woven of mountain goat's wool by women according to designs done by men. The design principles followed were the same as those used in painting and relief carving.

Altogether, one has the impression of a high degree of development of the visual and decorative arts both for workaday and ritual objects. The distinctiveness of style and the high quality of artistic production give the Northwest Coast culture area one of the world's great regional art traditions.

The "Potlatch"

Life crisis rites have been briefly mentioned. Associated with many such rites and with other occasions when titles or names were taken up were feasts that have come to be known as potlatches.[8] At a potlatch a host gave away large amounts of property to his invited guests. When the guests accepted their gifts, they gave public recognition to some claim of the host. The host and the principal guests were normally titleholders. On some occasions all the guests were from the same winter village, but not infrequently the guests came from another village (or villages). Among the more important occasions for giving a feast were the death of an important titleholder (and validation of his or her heir's claim to the deceased's position), when a new house was built, when a totem pole was erected, and when a child came of age. At major feasts large amounts of food were consumed and given away and the scale of property dispersal could exhaust most of the material wealth of the host. Gifts included such major wealth items as canoes and slaves, but the mainstay of the property dispersal was furs, which were gradually replaced by blankets after trade with Europeans began.

Feasts were given by titleholders for other titleholders, whose major role was to act as witnesses to the host's display of privileges and taking up of particular titles. Commoners were invited to watch the proceedings and often received some of the less important property through the titleholders they followed, but feasting focused on titleholders. Titleholders had to demonstrate and validate their claims to a position; one of the most important ways to do this was to skillfully amass a large amount of property (with the help of commoner followers and other relatives) for distribution at a feast. Feasts could take on a strongly competitive atmosphere, with titleholders trying to outdo and shame other titleholders with the spectacular scale of their property giveaways. This aspect of feasting probably intensified during the contact period. In any event, rivalry over status and the scale of property dispersals that accompanied it have become synonymous with the Northwest Coast in the anthropological literature.

2
The Study of Northwest Coast Slavery

Every traditional Northwest Coast community contained at least a few slaves. A word translatable as "slave" is found in all languages spoken in the culture area, and in many communities outsiders could distinguish slaves from the other inhabitants because of special haircuts or other external markers. In all of the region's cultures slavery was regarded as shameful and degrading. Slave status was hereditary: the children of slaves were slaves. As they were without kin group membership, slaves had no rights or privileges. Masters exercised complete physical control over their slaves, and could even kill them if they chose.

Slaves were produced for the most part by war. Whatever the motive for a particular instance of intergroup fighting, slaves were a common outcome of warfare, but, in the northern part of the culture area especially, the desire for captives was itself a common motive for an attack on another community. Even though the children of slaves were also slaves, it is probable that the birthrate for female slaves was low. War and birth were the major sources of slavery, but there were several minor methods of enslavement. There was an active trade in slaves, with the result that many of a group's slaves had not been captured by members of the group but had been obtained in trade.

Almost anyone could become a war captive. We know of a few cases of enslavement by force of members of one's own local group. Enslavement of people from communities who spoke the same or a very similar language was widespread. Raids for slaves might range widely, but close neighbors—people with whom one had a number of other important kinds of relationships—were common victims. Where it is possible to consider the time period of a raid for slaves, the data suggest that in earliest contact times most attacks were relatively close to home and that longer-distance raiding arose later in the historic period.

The expressed preference was for women and children, and the general impression gained from the sources is that slaves were more likely to be women than men. Many of those captured in war were already slaves and merely changed owners. But members of the other two strata could be enslaved as well. Being a member of the titleholder class did not protect one from enslavement. And, although there were exceptions, many former titleholders were treated like other slaves. The victim's group sometimes tried to redeem or ransom the newly enslaved so that a member of a prominent titleholder family probably had a better chance of redemption, but many former titleholders spent their lives in slavery during the early historic period. During the late eighteenth- and early nineteenth-century maritime fur trade period, Europeans were also readily enslaved if the opportunity arose.

Most slaves were probably owned by kin groups, although the person who exercised control over the unit's slaves was its head. Other slaves were owned by individual titleholders. The number of slaves held by a kin group or an individual varied considerably. Maquinna, the famous Mowachaht leader who dealt with Cook and many other early European explorers and traders, was said to have owned about fifty slaves, while many masters undoubtedly owned only one or two. There was also considerable community-to-community variation in the proportion of slaves held. Neighboring winter villages might have very different percentages of slaves, although the proportion of slaves tended to increase from south to north in the region. For some winter villages a major segment of the population was slave, sometimes reaching 30 percent and ranges of from 15 to 25 percent were not uncommon. Other communities contained only 1 or 2 percent slaves.

The economic importance of slavery is controversial among students of the Northwest Coast. The orthodox view is that slaves were of no economic significance. In later chapters I will demonstrate that slaves were of considerable importance to the economy of many Northwest Coast communities, in two ways: they were a significant commodity in intergroup transactions, especially trade, and their labor power was important in many subsistence activities and other mundane tasks.

Slaves were also used in rituals. In both precontact and early historic times, especially in the northern part of the culture area, they were often killed during important ceremonies, in particular the funerals of important titleholders. Throughout the region, the funeral of a community's leading titleholder usually included the killing of one or more slaves. Slaves were killed both to accompany the deceased as servants in the next world and to show the power of the heir. Slaves might also be given away as a part of the large-scale property dispersals that accompanied many feasts and that were used to validate titleholders' prerogatives. In later historic times, slaves began to be freed rather than killed. This was partly in response to European pressures. From the point of view of the slave owner, freeing a slave and killing a slave both represented property destruction. Slaves were still sometimes ritually killed in a few communities at least as late as the 1870s. When slaves were killed it was usually in a ritual context, but the choice was often mundane: the old and sick, or those who failed to realize that slaves were expected to act like slaves, were frequently chosen for death.

The Traditional Scholarly View of Northwest Coast Slavery

The remarkable sculpture shown in figure 2 stands in the Museum of Anthropology at the University of British Columbia. It was carved sometime in the twentieth century by an anonymous Kwakwaka'wakw. It is described in the museum's records as "Chief carried on the back of a slave" (Hawthorn 1979, 69). This image is an almost perfect representation of the principal findings and argument of this book. Indeed, the entire book might be considered an extended gloss on this work of art. This is not the only carving with this theme. The same museum also holds various pieces from an early twentieth-century Quatsino house frame. One of these carvings, by George Nelson, is a large human ancestor figure with a platform placed in front of it. The platform is intended as a seat for important members of the family owning the house and is supported by two kneeling slaves. (See fig. 3; Hawthorn 1979, fig. 36.) Like all good works of art, neither of these sculptures is subject to a single, simple reading, but one compelling possible reading of both is "chiefs rise/stand-tall/hold-their-places on the backs of slaves."

In other words, slavery—the holding of slaves, the contribution of slaves—is vital to the other central characteristics of the Northwest Coast culture area. The ranking system, the fabulous feasts known as potlatches, the elaborate ceremonial performances, the prerogatives of chiefs, the elaborate material, social, and intellectual culture are all intimately interdependent with each other and with slavery.

This is not a view of Northwest Coast culture normally held by experts on the culture area. Most have barely mentioned slavery, and none treat it as an important aspect of Northwest Coast culture. We may begin a consideration of the standard view of Northwest Coast slavery with Franz Boas's brief remark, written toward the beginning of a discussion of Kwakwaka'wakw descent groups:

All the tribes of the Pacific Coast are divided into a nobility, common people, and slaves. The last of these may be left out of consideration, as they do not form part and parcel of the clan, but are captives made in war, or purchases, and may change ownership as any other piece of property. (1897, 338)

Figure 2. "Chief carried on the back
of a slave." Kwakwaka'wakw. (Courtesy University of British Columbia
Museum of Anthropology, A17154)

Figure 3. "Human ancestor figure with platform and kneeling slaves." Quatsino. (Courtesy University of British Columbia Museum of Anthropology, A50009)

Boas does not have much more to say about slavery elsewhere in his voluminous writings on the Northwest Coast, and those holding the orthodox view of
Northwest Coast slavery often take this passage as giving Boas's imprimatur
to their interpretation. The following is a sample of the statements of some
representatives of the usual position on Northwest Coast slavery.

> Slavery was firmly established among the Coast Salish. But the harrowing pic-
> tures which that word brings before our mind have little connection with the
> institution as it existed among the Indians of this region. Slaves were captives
> taken in war and traded from tribe to tribe, and almost always the prisoners
> were women or children. They wielded paddles in their master's canoes, fished,
> gathered wood, cooked, and made baskets and other utensils, but they labored
> no more strenuously than the free members of the lower class, and in return
> they were well treated as members of the household. . . . As concerns his labor
> the slave was no great asset, and the principal reason for the existence of the
> institution of slavery was that the possession of captives reflected honor and
> dignity upon their owners. A chief's influence was in direct proportion to the
> number of his slaves.
> . . . In general it may be said that slaves were very well treated. Instances
> of cruelty, such as slaying a captive at the funeral of a favorite child, were
> sporadic, and cannot fairly be charged against the institution itself. (Curtis
> 1913, 74)

> [In the context of the distribution of goods at potlatches:] The economic loss
> suffered upon occasions when slaves are murdered or emancipated is not great;
> in bondage they are as much of a liability as an asset and are useful primarily as
> an overt demonstration of the ability to possess them. (Barnett 1938, 352)

> That slaves were sometimes treated with kindness and given certain conces-
> sions made no difference in their class membership; they were still slaves, and as
> such belonged in a sphere apart from the free. . . . As a matter of fact, the slaves
> had so little societal importance in the area that they scarcely need to be consid-
> ered in problems relating to the social structure. "Society," in the native view,
> consisted of the freemen of a particular group. Slaves, like the natives' dogs, or
> better still, like canoes and sea otter skins and blankets, were elements of the so-
> cial configuration but had no active part to play in group life. Their participation
> was purely passive, like that of a stage prop carried on and off the boards by the
> real actors. Their principal significance was to serve as foils for the high and
> mighty, impressing the inequality of status on native consciousness. (Drucker
> 1939, 55–56)

Helen Codere has very little to say about slaves or slavery in her study of
Kwakiutl potlatching and warfare, 1792–1930, but at one point in the chapter
"Kwakiutl Warfare" she claims, "The economic value of the slave captured in
war was so slight as to be nonexistent" (1950, 105).
In his 1965 summary volume on Northwest Coast ethnography, Philip

Drucker devotes one and a half of his 231 pages of text to slaves. A number of his generalizations about slaves will be shown to be factually inaccurate in later chapters of this book. His overall assessment of slavery's importance in the region has been frequently quoted with approval.

> Possession of slaves was prestigeful since it implied success at war or great wealth. . . . It is difficult to estimate the slave population of the area, but it was certainly never large, for slave mortality was high. Slaves' economic utility was negligible. They gathered firewood, dug clams, and fished, but so did their masters. (p. 52)

In their student-oriented "case study" of the Kwakiutl, Ronald Rohner and Evelyn Rohner have the following to say about slaves.

> At one time the Kwakiutl also had slaves who were usually war captives from other tribes. Slaves contributed little to the traditional social system except to give prestige to their owners; we give them no further attention. (1970, 79)

Few Northwest Coast specialists have dissented from these views (see below), and most of those who have used Northwest Coast materials for more general theoretical purposes have either ignored slavery or followed the orthodox experts' view. Morton Fried's treatment of the subject in his influential *The Evolution of Political Society* is typical.

> The overall picture I would like to present of Northwest Coast slavery can be sketched briefly. . . . I believe that "slaves" should be better referred to as "captives" and that their numbers . . . must have been small at almost all times. . . . It is likely that in pre-European times, before the end of the eighteenth century, captives must have been quite few and comprised, with negligible exceptions, women and children. (1967, 220)

Fried goes on to suggest that the fur trade with Europeans led to an increase in the value of slaves, a growth in the numbers of captives, and changed captives into something more like slaves as they are usually known. This transformation may be in part due to "increased knowledge of slavery practiced elsewhere in the United States, although . . . this is merely speculation" (1967, 220). Fried then briefly reviews a little of the literature on Northwest Coast slaves, endorsing Drucker's 1965 views cited above, although he acknowledges that the picture presented by this material is "not altogether clear" (p. 221).

> It is my impression, subject to correction, that though chiefly status may have depended on "slaves," this dependence was not on labor power. That is, slaves did not spend their time producing commodities to enhance their master's wealth and improve his position as the giver of potlatches. It is explicitly stated that the

> highest value of a captive was as a sacrifice [no references]; he might be killed at the climax of various rituals, and it was for this potential moment that he was kept. (1967, 222)

> It should be clear by now that the status called "slavery" in the Northwest Coast cultures bears little resemblance to that associated with stratified societies. (1967, 223)

Later chapters will show that most of Fried's generalizations and speculations about Northwest Coast slavery are incorrect. Yet his views continue to be widely shared by both Northwest Coast specialists and others.

Among Northwest Coast scholars I know of only three who have given clear, if partial, dissent from the orthodox view: Julia Averkieva, Viola Garfield, and Wayne Suttles.[1] Averkieva's view of slavery will be considered below in my discussion of the few fuller treatments of Northwest Coast slavery. In 1945 Garfield published a short paper entitled "A Research Problem in Northwest Indian Economics" in which she succinctly but clearly pointed out the gaps in the then-current knowledge about Northwest Coast traditional economics. She was also very clear about what needed to be done about it. Her paper met with little response within or without the circle of Northwest Coast experts. It contains two paragraphs on slavery that she never, to my knowledge, followed up.

> The economic value of slaves in the productive system has also been neglected, and the tendency has been to consider slaves from the point of view of "prestige value" rather than as productive property and therefore basic economic assets. Yet it cannot be doubted that twenty-five or thirty slaves in a household, even in an economy based on food collecting, produced enough to make them highly profitable. Slaves made possible larger surpluses, more intensive exploitation of resources, and the release of many individuals for specialized work or art. Nowhere, least of all on the Northwest Coast, can slavery be adequately explained as just another device for acquiring prestige, nor dismissed as of little economic importance. (1945, 628)

> Many writers have described the killing, freeing, or giving away of slaves with other property, but none has considered the value of slaves as producers of potlatch wealth. (1945, 630)

Chapter 6 will substantiate in detail and flesh out Garfield's remarks. Suttles is the only Northwest Coast expert known to me to have continued to cite and take seriously Garfield's 1945 paper (1968, 66; 1973, 622; Suttles and Jonaitis 1990, 87). In his 1968 paper he reports the opposing views of Drucker and Garfield. He mildly endorses her position but does not explore its implications (1968, 65–66).

Previous Studies of
Northwest Coast Slavery

Although slaves and slavery are often mentioned in the historical and ethnographic sources for the Northwest Coast and are even discussed in passages of a few pages in some of the ethnographic works on specific cultures, there have been only a few previous studies that have taken Northwest Coast slavery as a primary or even significant interest. In order of publication date those known to me are H. J. Nieboer, *Slavery as an Industrial System* (1910); William Christie MacLeod, "Debtor and Chattel Slavery in Aboriginal North America" (1925), "Some Social Aspects of Aboriginal American Slavery" (1927), "Economic Aspects of Indigenous American Slavery" (1928), and "The Origin of Servile Labor Groups" (1929); E. F. Dennis, "Indian Slavery in Pacific Northwest" (1930); Julia Averkieva, *Slavery among the Indians of North America* (1941, English translation 1966); Bernard J. Siegel, "Some Methodological Considerations for a Comparative Study of Slavery" (1945); Eugene R. Ruyle, "Slavery, Surplus and Stratification on the Northwest Coast" (1973); and Robert H. Ruby and John A. Brown, *Indian Slavery in the Pacific Northwest* (1993). In this section I will discuss the work of Nieboer, MacLeod, Averkieva, Siegel, and Ruyle. Dennis's work is a descriptive assemblage of some of the material on Northwest Coast slavery in the then-available historical and ethnographic sources; Ruby and Brown's is a longer compendium of the same sort (see Donald 1995 for a review).[2]

Nieboer's book is a well-known and frequently cited classic in the field of slavery studies. It is usually cited for its definition of slavery and its theory of the conditions under which slavery arises. Most students of slavery have not shown much interest in the ethnographic material that Nieboer analyzes in an attempt to demonstrate the validity of his theories about the origin of slavery.[3]

Slavery as an Industrial System is divided into two parts, one labeled "Descriptive" and the other "Theoretical." Nieboer begins the descriptive section of his book with a definition of slavery and a discussion in which he attempts to distinguish slavery from what he terms "kindred phenomena" (such as "children subjected to the head of the family," serfs, or pawns), but the bulk of this part is a 129-page survey of non-European slavery around the world. This survey is typical of the comparative studies of the period, where snippets about the topic of interest are brought together from uncritically examined sources without much concern over their cultural or social context. Unlike many similar works written about the same time, Nieboer's organizational focus is geographic rather than evolutionary. About a quarter of his twenty-page section on North America is devoted to Northwest Coast groups or their immediate neighbors.

Nieboer (1910, 169–171) begins his theoretical analysis of the material he has assembled by rejecting classification schemes that are based on supposed evolutionary stages. Instead he opts for a "mode of subsistence" approach, arguing that mode of subsistence must obviously affect the division of labor, including the presence or absence of slavery, although he explicitly rejects "the materialistic theory of history" (1910, 171). The classification of modes of subsistence (or "economic states") that he adopts is, however, implicitly evolutionary: hunting and fishing, pastoral nomadism, first stage of agriculture, second stage of agriculture, third stage of agriculture (1910, 175). In his geographic survey Nieboer identifies 391 "cases" about which he feels he can say with certainty that they either do or do not have slavery. Of the 70 "hunting and fishing tribes" among them, only 18 kept slaves. Nieboer can easily suggest why hunters (hunter-gatherers or foragers in modern parlance) should not practice slavery, and in general the hunting cases support him. Of the 18 exceptions, 15 are from the Pacific Coast of North America "from Behring Strait to the Northern boundary of California" (1910, 165). Most of these are within what is here considered the Northwest Coast culture area; the others are near neighbors (such as the Aleut and Kodiak islanders). He regards most of these 15 as relying on fishing as their basic mode of subsistence (fishing includes sea mammal hunting), and he produces arguments that show that fishers would be expected to practice slavery.[4]

In the context of hunter-gatherers and fishers, Nieboer provides the following analysis:

living in "fixed habitations" is more favorable to slavery than "nomadism";

living in "large groups" is more favorable to slavery than living in small groups;

if food is "abundant and easy to procure," slavery is more probable;

food preservation makes slavery more likely;

"commercial tribes, especially those that carry on a trade in manufactured goods" are more likely to have slaves;

the development of industry favors slavery (note that Nieboer considers that the Eskimo are an "industrial tribe");

if "wealth" exists, slavery is more likely;

if subsistence is "dependent upon capital," there is no slavery;

if the need is only for "highly skilled labour," slavery is not practiced;

female labor may be a partial substitute for slave labor, but slaves are more likely when the status of women is relatively high;

if "militarism" prevails and warriors are more needed than laborers, slavery is unlikely;

a set of societies that form a "homogeneous group" and maintain continuous relations among the societies are more likely to practice slavery than an isolated society (1910, 255–256).

Nieboer argues that the major underlying cause of these various conclusions is "the general economic state of society," in particular, whether subsistence is "dependent upon capital" and is "easy or difficult to acquire" (1910, 256), and that therefore "slavery can only exist when subsistence is easy to procure without the aid of capital" (1910, 258). Basic to this last statement is the distinction, important to Nieboer, between "open" and "closed" resources. In the agricultural context open resources implies plentiful, unused agricultural land. Foragers generally live in conditions of open resources (1910, 386). If resources are open and significant capital is not required for the production of food, then the only way for an individual to persuade others to work for him is coercion, hence slavery. Nieboer thinks that the Northwest Coast groups in his study conform both to his basic hypothesis about open resources and the lack of capital needs and to most of the secondary causes of slavery previously discussed.

Nieboer's hypotheses about the conditions leading to slavery have been frequently critiqued and frequently revived, often in a vocabulary more obviously compatible with twentieth-century economic theories. Most subsequent discussions of his ideas in the economic and economic history literature are interested in explaining classical or, more usually, New World plantation slavery and pay little if any attention to Nieboer's ethnological materials or to his analysis of them (see, e.g., Domar 1970). His treatment of Northwest Coast material has received virtually no attention in mainline Northwest Coast scholarship.

MacLeod published a number of papers on various aspects of North American ethnology during the 1920s and 1930s, four of which (cited above) deal at some length with Northwest Coast slavery. Most of each of his four papers is a compendium of the then-available data about Northwest Coast slavery which draws on both the historical and ethnographic sources available to him.[5] The data accumulated by MacLeod are not presented in a highly organized format, nor is MacLeod particularly sensitive to cultural context. He tends to treat all of the Northwest Coast groups as an interchangeable set, showing little concern for possible intraculture area variation. If he can find an example or two from one or another Northwest Coast group, he usually assumes that the trait he is discussing or point he is making is well established for the entire culture area. He is only occasionally sensitive to problems of historical change and not always as critical of sources as he should be, although he unquestionably had much better control of the Northwest Coast material than did Nieboer.

Among MacLeod's principal conclusions about slavery on the Northwest Coast are the following.

Hereditary chattel slavery was a conspicuous trait of the culture of the nonagricultural North Pacific coast where it has been noted for a continuous area from the Aleutian Islands to northwestern California inclusive. An active intertribal slave trade was carried on. . . . The proportion of slaves to the total population

has been variously estimated at from one-twentieth to one-third, varying apparently, with the conditions of life of the villages along the coast; the proportion
decreased under the influence of European culture, and slavery disappeared altogether with Canadian and American prohibition. (1925, 375)

MacLeod also concludes that slavery was not hereditary in aboriginal
North America outside the North Pacific Coast area (1925, 375) and can see
"no economic or political reason for the nonexistence of hereditary slavery in
the agricultural southeast of North America" considering its existence on the
Northwest Coast (1925, 379). He suggests unspecified "psychological" reasons and intergroup trade as possible causes of Northwest Coast slavery, specifically noting that since both the Northwest Coast societies and the Southeastern societies had marked social stratification, the presence or absence of
social stratification will not explain the difference (1925, 379). In his 1925
paper MacLeod cites Nieboer in only a general way, but in his rejection of
economic and political causes of Northwest Coast slavery he is responding
negatively to Nieboer's theory. He is more explicit in his negative assessment
of both aspects of Nieboer's theory and some of his treatment of ethnographic
materials in other of his papers on slavery as well.

In his 1927 paper MacLeod suggests diffusion from Asia as an explanation
for hereditary Northwest Coast slavery. In this same paper he discusses the
killing of slaves at funerals and suggests that the manumission of slaves was
substituted for killing under European pressure and influence.

In "Economic Aspects of Indigenous American Slavery" (1928) MacLeod
deals at some length with the tasks to which Northwest Coast slaves were put,
discusses slave raiding and the indigenous trade in slaves, and briefly details
what little price data he had been able to find. MacLeod concludes that Northwest Coast slaves "produced enough for their keep and a surplus besides"
(1928, 648–649). His final conclusion on the economic aspects of Northwest
Coast slavery is that slavery was of "nearly as much economic importance to
them as was slavery to the plantation regions of the United States before the
Civil War. Incredible as this may seem, it seems very definitely indicated by
all the facts" (1928, 649–650).

In his final paper on the subject MacLeod goes over points he treated earlier
and then discusses at much greater length than before the killing of slaves at
funerals and under other circumstances. His chief interest in slave killing is
that it seems to him to show that hereditary slavery and its attendant practices
on the Northwest Coast diffused from Asia (1929, 106–111).

Averkieva's *Slavery among the Indians of North America* was her 1941
dissertation for the U.S.S.R. Academy of Sciences. A limited-circulation English translation was published in 1966. In the 1930s Averkieva came to the
United States, worked with Franz Boas in New York, and also did some fieldwork on the Pacific Coast of North America before returning to the Soviet

Union. In spite of her monograph's title, it is essentially a discussion of slavery in the Northwest Coast culture area, for Averkieva agrees with MacLeod that in aboriginal North America hereditary slavery was present only on the Northwest Coast (1966, 10). Not surprisingly, in spite of her work with Boas, Averkieva's theoretical perspective is that of 1930s Soviet Marxism of a fairly pedestrian sort. Marx and Engels, who are frequently quoted, are her ultimate authorities on the nature and origins of slavery, and Averkieva's brief analyses are principally concerned with showing that the Northwest Coast data fit into the framework provided by Soviet historical materialism.

About half of the monograph is a descriptive summary of Northwest Coast culture. The remainder is a series of largely descriptive chapters on aspects of Northwest Coast slavery: "The Circumstances of the Rise of Slavery" (which includes sections on the economic importance and number of slaves), "War as a Source of Slaves" (which includes sections on the slave trade, bonded slavery, and slaves as a measure of wealth), "The 'Without Rights' Position of Slaves" (which includes sections on the branding and punishment of slaves), and "The Reflection of Slavery in Ideology."

Averkieva's discussion of Northwest Coast slavery is based on many of the published historical and ethnographic sources available in the 1930s. She relies most heavily on published ethnographic material, and she also uses some of her own and probably Boas's unpublished fieldwork results. Her control of the material is much better than MacLeod's and she does add data from Russian sources on the Tlingit not covered elsewhere.[6] Although she is certainly aware that there is considerable variation within the culture area, her treatment of slavery does not consider systematically any possible variation. Her principal conclusions about the economic importance of the work of slaves echo MacLeod's, although she does not like his comparison with plantation slavery because she feels that he is comparing two social structures that are not parallel. Another criticism of MacLeod is the accurate observation that he tends to see all "primitive" culture traits as being rudimentary forms of current capitalist traits. She also shows that MacLeod's arguments about an Asian origin for Northwest Coast slavery are supported by data whose relevance is far-fetched at best.

Aside from supporting MacLeod's conclusions about the economic importance of slaves with fuller quotations from the literature, perhaps Averkieva's most important contribution is the observation that slaves appear in myths as a normal part of the social and cultural scene. Thus it appears to her that, as slaves were present at the beginning of mythical events, mythology is suggesting that "slavery already existed when the world was made" (1966, 116). This is treated as support for the antiquity of Northwest Coast slavery.

On a more theoretical level Averkieva is concerned to show that Northwest Coast slavery is a form of "patriarchal slavery" à la Marx. She argues, following Engels's general theory, that slavery rose on the Northwest Coast after a sufficient level of production had been attained and after at least some inequality was present, but she offers no detailed argument of how this might have occurred.

Siegel's study focuses "upon some fundamental methodological concepts as a basis for reevaluating the differential status of labor and servitude between the Creek and Northwest Coast Indians" (1945, 357). One of the questions that MacLeod raised was why Creek and other Southeastern groups did not practice hereditary slavery while Northwest Coast societies did. Conditions for slavery seem at least as propitious in the aboriginal Southeast as on the Northwest Coast. Siegel agrees with MacLeod that Nieboer's theory will not explain the lack of slavery among the Creek. He also notes that MacLeod's invocation of vague psychological reasons for slavery or its lack is not an improvement over Nieboer. Although he starts with the ethnographic problem of why slavery occurred on the Northwest Coast but not among the Creek, Siegel's concerns are principally methodological. In brief he is attacking Nieboer's "positivist" assumptions and seeking to replace that approach with one he describes as "functional" (drawing inspiration from Richard Thurnwald).[7]

Siegel's primary source of information on Northwest Coast slavery is MacLeod, supplemented by a few other ethnographic accounts and summaries of the culture area. He accepts all of MacLeod's empirical conclusions about slavery in the area including the comparison of the economic importance of slaves with plantation slavery (1945, 364–366). But Siegel's own emphasis in his summary is not on the economic side of Northwest Coast slavery; rather, he downplays the direct economic contribution and plays up the slave's role in the status system.

> The institution itself performed a most important function in the whole system of ranks and statuses. Slaves, in addition to being articles of value, were used to assist in getting other prized articles on fishing and trading expeditions, and the like. Whatever the provenience of slavery on the Northwest Coast, its significance can best be appraised in terms of social prestige within the highly complex system of wealth symbols, competitive relationships, and associated political organization. (1945, 366)

Hereditary rank on the Northwest Coast is crucial in Siegel's analysis, for he views Creek society as lacking social distinctions based on wealth or hereditary privilege; instead, social advancement is based on a man's achievements in war (1945, 368, 370). On the Northwest Coast, slavery is consistent with and supports the ranking system. True to his functionalist approach, Siegel is less interested in the origins of Northwest Coast slavery than with how it was integrated into other aspects of Northwest Coast culture.

Ruyle's 1973 work, "Slavery, Surplus, and Stratification on the Northwest Coast," continues Siegel's emphasis on Northwest Coast status and ranking, although from the very different perspective of the neo-Marxist functionalism popular in some circles of American anthropology in the 1970s. Ruyle does not cite Averkieva or Siegel but does cite both MacLeod and Nieboer. As is the case with the other authors discussed here, Ruyle does not show any systematic interest in variation within the culture area. He uses quotations about an assortment of groups to establish what he considers to be the character of slavery and stratification in the culture area as a whole. He uses a variety of ethnographic and historical sources but is quite uncritical of their value or reliability. Ruyle's method for establishing what Northwest Coast slavery was like is scarcely more sophisticated than Nieboer's.

Ruyle's primary interest is in explaining what he sees as the Northwest Coast class system. His discussion of slavery is primarily aimed at showing that slaves were indeed economically important and exploited by their owners, the ruling class. In this context, slavery is only one of the ways—albeit a very important one—in which the ruling class exploited other strata (or classes) in the culture area's communities.

All four of the scholars who have devoted special attention to Northwest Coast slavery agree that slaves were economically important even though their approaches and interests differ considerably. Neither separately nor together have they had much impact on Northwest Coast scholars' views about slavery in the culture area. In part this is because they themselves were not Northwest Coast scholars and their control of the relevant ethnographic and historical material was too weak and their methodology not adequate to the problems they set themselves.[8] Also contributing to their lack of impact is that anthropological theory throughout the twentieth century has had relatively little interest in and relatively little to contribute to an understanding of slavery and other forms of servitude.

3
Methods and Sources

This chapter describes the methods used to arrive at the statements and conclusions in this book and the types of sources on which the discussion is based. Although "methods" will be of greatest interest to the specialist reader, this chapter should alert all readers to the strengths and weaknesses of both my sources and my approach.

Although it deals primarily with institutions, practices, and events of the late eighteenth and nineteenth century, this book is not primarily history or ethnohistory. Rather, it is comparative anthropology or comparative ethnology, within the sphere of continuous area studies. It compares a group of culture units within a single geographic region, in an attempt to arrive at generalizations about a number of variables relating to culturally significant institutions and practices in the area of concern. Continuous area studies can be traced to the nineteenth century. Boas (1895b) published the first such study on North American native materials, and there has been a steady trickle of studies since (see Jorgensen 1974 for a discussion of such work and its context in wider comparative studies).

Generalized statements about Northwest Coast phenomena are common in the literature, but few of these generalizations are supported by a systematic consideration of the groups that constitute the culture area. Attempts to lend such generalizations credibility are often confined to citing a few examples that seem to be haphazardly rather than systematically chosen. Such a procedure implies an overall uniformity within the culture area that should be established rather than assumed. It also implies that the sources of the examples are equally reliable and useful and either that all statements cited apply to the same time period or that change has not been significant in the domain of culture being studied. It is easy to document that there is considerable cultural variation within the region, that change has been great in every aspect of Northwest Coast culture since first contact with Europeans in the later part of the eighteenth century, and that the possible sources of information about the aboriginal inhabitants of the region vary greatly in their detail, their reliability, and their bias. This chapter details how I deal with each of these three major topics.

I begin with discussions of cultural variation in space and the problem of change over time. Next I describe the approach developed to establish generalizations about Northwest Coast cultures: the tribal unit sample. Then, after a brief discussion of the problem of missing information and how it affects attempts to generalize, I describe the sources used for the book and consider the various kinds of bias found in them.

Cultural Variation in Space

The cultures of the Northwest Coast contrast sharply with those of neighboring culture areas (the Arctic, Mackenzie-Yukon, Plateau, and Oregon Coast–California). But there is also considerable variation within the culture area.[1] In any regional study, one must be able to describe and analyze this variation. Cross-cultural researchers typically compare "cultures" or "societies." Units of analysis for such comparisons need to be as concrete and readily identifiable as possible. It is also useful if the unit of comparison is recognizable by and meaningful to the people who participate in such units: "natural" units are preferable to artificial ones.

In any continuous area study the "community" immediately suggests itself as an ideal unit of analysis. Neighboring communities are usually very similar, so that by selecting communities widely distributed throughout the study area one can both describe and analyze regional variation. Communities also appear to be concrete, locally recognizable social and cultural units giving meaningful and appropriate comparisons. The community is, of course, like other human universals ("marriage," the "family"), easy to recognize in a general way but difficult to define adequately cross-culturally. Fortunately, all that I have to do here is arrive at a community unit valid for one culture area only.

As in every human society, the peoples inhabiting the Northwest Coast were organized into communities—sets of people who resided near each other and who interacted frequently in a variety of social and other contexts. On the Northwest Coast, however, the composition and location of such a residential unit was not constant throughout the year. As described in chapter 1, all of the peoples in the culture area followed an annual round that led to shifts in place of residence and changes in which people and how many lived together at any particular time. A few people did reside in the same locale year-round, but even in communities where some people did not shift about, some community members usually did move. Most people moved at least twice during the year, and many moved four or five times. For Northwest Coast people, the most significant community unit was the winter village, which was the focal point of the Northwest Coast local group. Members of a Northwest Coast local group shared a common winter village and acted as a social unit at least part of the year. At other times of the year the winter village community separated into its constituent kin and residential units, when members moved to exploit the various seasonal resource locations owned by their kin group. In some parts of the coast members of several winter villages might reside together for brief periods. The summer villages of the various Nuu-chah-nulth federations are the best known of these, although there were other village aggregations such as the Lower Skeena Tsimshian eulachon fishery along the Nass River. In addition, some Coast Salish winter villages were so close together that they could almost be regarded as continuous habitation sites. Nevertheless, whatever the congregation of people outside the winter village, individuals, kin, and residential units recognized and identified themselves with their winter village community and retained a loyalty to it. At times, however, especially in the central and northern portions of the area, descent group loyalties were stronger than winter community loyalties. This means that although the winter village is the most prominent and permanent Northwest Coast residential and social unit, winter village ties never completely overrode kin ties and groups within the village as major foci of loyalty, nor did winter village loyalty completely erode kin ties between those of different villages.

At the time of contact there were several hundred winter villages on the Northwest Coast. Neighboring winter villages often shared a language and were frequently virtually identical in culture, but each retained its social and political independence. Thus the winter village is the ideal unit of comparison for a continuous area study of any aspect of Northwest Coast culture. The realities of data availability make it impossible to simply list and then sample these communities, but the winter village should form the basis of any practical sampling methodology and of any sample actually employed in Northwest Coast areal research.

Change: The Problem of Time

Ideally, the major focus of this work would be the "traditional" practice of slavery on the Northwest Coast. Strictly speaking, traditional would mean cultural practices just before European contact, say, in the 1760s. This is impossible, of course, because virtually all of the available information is post-contact, beginning with Spanish observations in 1774 and continuing until the most recent ethnographic fieldwork of the 1980s. This is a very long time span, especially when the amount of culture change that has occurred is taken into account. Therefore, although my main focus is a reconstruction of the practice of slavery in the period 1770 to 1840, the book is also a study of change, especially in the nineteenth century.

Because culture change was rapid and ongoing throughout the period of the 1770s to the present, we need to know as exactly as possible to what date particular information applies. Our time controls need to be as precise as our geographic controls. Unfortunately, many of the sources are as vague about time as they are locale. Some historical sources date most of the observations that they record. This is especially true of ship's logs and journals and Hudson's Bay Company post journals. Other historical sources allow us to place observations as having occurred during the time that we know the observer was on the Northwest Coast or perhaps when he (more rarely she) was at a particular locale. In other cases, however, it is difficult to tell if an observer is reporting his own observations or reporting the observations someone else made at an unspecified earlier date.

The time period of ethnographic information is even harder to pin down. Most ethnographers working on the Northwest Coast were interested in "traditional" culture and more or less ignored (at least in their writings) contemporary native life. They either queried older informants about traditional culture or reported such contemporary practices as seemed "traditional" to themselves or their informants. In any generation the oldest informants (in their sixties and seventies) can tell us quite a bit about events and practices they observed about fifty years ago and something about what they have heard from a now-deceased older generation. Professional ethnography began on the coast in the 1880s. This means that our strongest ethnographic information applies to the 1830s at the earliest, although we should probably begin to be confident about information pertaining to the period from the 1850s on. Like informants everywhere, Northwest Coast informants not infrequently describe practices as long-standing and traditional when they are in fact relatively recent innovations. Unfortunately, Northwest Coast ethnographers have rarely been rigorous in considering the problem of time and change when describing and analyzing their informants' statements. Even in the early 1980s some ethnographers wrote up material that they had collected in the 1970s as if it described practices at all times for the past several hundred years.

Another problem is that data are not available for all groups for the same time period. We are often forced to compare different local groups at different times. For example, the sources for the Mowachaht are very rich for the period 1775 through 1805, the richest by far for the entire coast for this interval. After 1805 very little information is available about the Mowachaht until Philip Drucker worked on the west coast of Vancouver Island in the 1930s. There is only sporadic information in the historical sources for the Nuxalk before the 1880s, and, although the Jacobsen brothers and Boas did some Nuxalk research in the 1880s, it is not until T. F. McIlwraith did his fieldwork in the

1920s that adequate information about most aspects of Nuxalk culture for any time period was collected. These same patterns of intensive historic contact or ethnographic research alternating with relative neglect are repeated all over the coast, making systematic comparison with temporal control very difficult.

Many of the dating deficiencies of the ethnographic sources cannot be remedied. What is done here, however, is to attempt to pin down as firmly as possible the time period to which particular reports apply. Whenever it is feasible to date events and practices, this dating is used to consider culture change. Ethnographic and historical reports are both distinguished and compared so that, inasmuch as possible, we can establish the period in which particular practices occurred. For example, in chapter 7 when the trade in slaves is described, the datable historical records of transactions are categorized as pre- and post-1845 to determine if the pattern and character of the trade and trading partners changed during the nineteenth century.

The Tribal Unit Sample

As has already been observed, the ideal unit of analysis for Northwest Coast studies is the winter village community. What the researcher would like to do is compare a representative sample of winter villages with respect to the variables of interest. Unfortunately, it is rarely possible to do this. There is a vast amount of information available about various aspects of Northwest Coast culture, but only a very small portion of this can be assigned with great confidence to particular winter villages. And on many variables, even general information is missing for large parts of the coast. What is needed is a compromise that will approach the ideal of a representative sample of winter villages while accommodating missing information and problems of data that are general rather than specific.

The solution adopted here is as follows. All of the material collected on Northwest Coast slavery has been located as precisely as possible with respect to space, time, and the identity of the actors involved. This information was then organized into geographic files. The goal was to locate material as precisely as possible. The ideal geographic file is a winter village, but often much larger units had to be used. In all, within the "core" Northwest Coast area thirty-eight files were constructed. An additional fourteen files were constructed for groups peripheral to this core (i.e., inland from the coastal strip). Sixteen of the core area files had fairly full information on slavery and were focused on a winter village or a relatively small set of culturally homogeneous winter villages. These sixteen from north to south are Yakutat, Chilkat, Sitka, Stikine, Fort Rupert Kwakiutl, Mowachaht, Clayoquot, Makah, Saanich, Klallam, Lummi, Skagit, Puyallup-Nisqually, Twana, Quileute, and Quinault. There are some important gaps in regional coverage within the culture area. For this reason four broader files were added: Haida, Lower Skeena

Tsimshian, Nuxalk, and Chinook. Some of these files contain an entire ethno-linguistic grouping of winter villages (e.g., Haida), but the quality of the data is such that it is not possible to build usable slavery files on subgroupings of these larger units.

These twenty files can be divided into three regional sets:

1. North (6)—Yakutat, Chilkat, Sitka, Stikine, Haida, Lower Skeena Tsimshian
2. Central (5)—Nuxalk, Fort Rupert Kwakiutl, Mowachaht, Clayoquot, Makah
3. South (9)—Saanich, Klallam, Lummi, Skagit, Puyallup-Nisqually, Twana, Quileute, Quinault, Chinook.

Generalizations advanced in this book will depend primarily on the data in these twenty files that I shall call the tribal unit sample. Information from the other eighteen core area files is used, both in examples and as checks on the material in the sample, but the primary focus is on the twenty groups. This sample is not advanced as an all-purpose set for use in Northwest Coast studies. Different topics would allow and require somewhat different samples because of the distribution of available information on different sets of variables. But I argue that a systematic sample, based on the winter village as unit of analysis, that aims to be representative is necessary if one wishes to generalize about the culture area and to consider variation within the area.

The geographic location of the groups in the sample are indicated in figure 4. There are still some significant gaps in coverage. The major problems are that no Northern Wakashan (Haisla, Heiltsuk, and Oowekeeno) group is represented, that only one Kwakwaka'wakw group is represented, that no northern Gulf of Georgia or Halkomelem Salish group is represented, and that there are no groups in the sample from the area between the Twana and the Chinook. Less serious, but still a drawback, is the absence of either of the up-river Tsimshian-speaking groups (Niska, Gitksan) and the presence of only two Nuu-chah-nulth groups (it would be desirable to have at least one group south of the Clayoquot in the sample). All of these groups are omitted from the sample for the same reason: too little information on slavery.

In spite of imperfections, the sample does provide broad coverage of the area and allows consideration of regional variation since three regional sub-samples can be derived. The sample also offers representative coverage of the major cultural and linguistic variations found in the region.

Missing Information

As in all comparative studies, missing information is the greatest single problem encountered in Northwest Coast area research. No matter what domain of

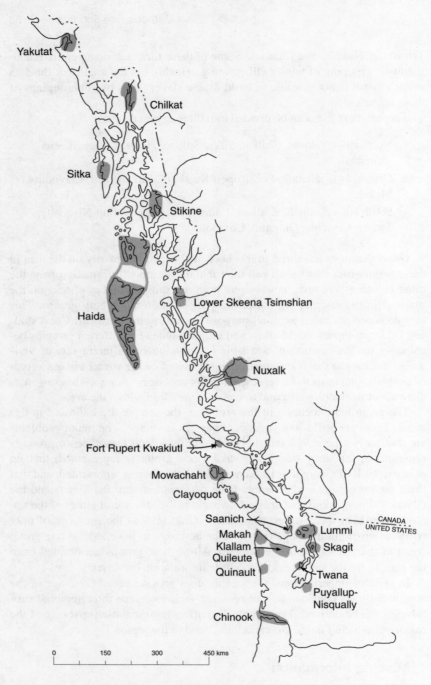

Yakutat

Chilkat

Sitka

Stikine

Lower Skeena Tsimshian

Haida

Nuxalk

Fort Rupert Kwakiutl

Mowachaht

Clayoquot

Saanich

Makah
Klallam
Quileute
Quinault

Lummi

Skagit

Twana

Puyallup-
Nisqually

Chinook

CANADA
UNITED STATES

0   150   300   450 kms

Figure 4.   Approximate Locations of Tribal Unit Sample.

culture is chosen, we simply do not know the traditional cultural practices for the majority of local groups. Indeed, we know little more than the name for many local groups (or the name by which they were known to their neighbors) and their general cultural and linguistic affiliations. Other local groups have been well studied. But all too often even detailed studies make generalizations about a fairly large set of groups presumed to be similar without providing any indication that information was collected on an individual group basis or even that the possibility of variation between close neighbors was considered.[2]

Quantitative information is particularly likely to be absent. But even information about the presence or absence of a particular trait is often unavailable. The problem of missing information is especially acute when it comes to assessing the absence of individual traits. If the sources do not mention a trait, does this mean that it was indeed absent or that it was merely overlooked or not thought important enough to mention? Very few sources more than occasionally state specifically that traits are not present.

The seriousness of missing information varies with the domain of culture of interest. Although missing data are serious everywhere, we do have a great deal of information about technology and material culture, for example. Slavery is one of the less favored domains.

The tribal unit sample that is the primary basis of the generalizations advanced in this book was chosen to represent the local groups (or small sets of local groups) on which information on slavery and related matters was best. In appendix 1 a number of tables give ratings on a total of fifty-eight variables relating to some aspect of slavery—mostly in the form of rating the presence or absence of a particular culture trait. For the tribal unit sample, this means a total of 1,160 ratings of variables. For 40.4 percent of these ratings the outcome is "missing information." These are variables that were chosen because information is often available. Other variables of equal or greater interest are relatively ignored either because there is information about them for only one or two groups or because there is virtually no information about them from anywhere on the coast.

Types of Sources

There are three major types of sources of information on Northwest Coast aboriginal society and culture, including slavery. These are the ethnographic, the historical, and the archaeological. Aside from the oral traditions of native people, archaeology is the only direct source of information about aboriginal practices before European contact. But archaeology has only a modest potential to tell us anything about the practice of Northwest Coast slavery and has made no direct contribution to the information on slavery used in this book. I delay discussion of the potential of archaeology until chapter 10, where the antiquity of Northwest Coast slavery is considered.

Ethnographic Sources

By ethnographic, I mean material collected by talking with or observing native people by someone who intends to use the information to produce a description of some aspect of native society or culture. The ethnographer may be professional or amateur, trained or untrained, European or native. The material collected may be published or unpublished. It is the goal of the person doing the work that counts. The ethnographer intends to describe the general situation. His or her report outlines the typical, the usual, the normal. Specific events or cases are of interest only as illustrations of the general. Examples of ethnographic sources used in this study range from general ethnographies of a group that aim to describe all or most domains of culture (e.g., T. F. McIlwraith's *The Bella Coola Indians*) to reports focusing primarily on one aspect of a culture (e.g., Leo H. Frachtenberg's "The Ceremonial Societies of the Quileute Indians") to brief reports that describe a single cultural element (e.g., Louis Shotridge's "Tlingit Woman's Root Basket").

Ethnographic sources vary greatly in quality and usefulness. In the sense used here, Northwest Coast ethnographic sources begin to appear in the last half of the nineteenth century. Probably the first professional ethnographer to work in the culture area was Franz Boas, whose first trip to the region was in 1886.[3] Boas's publications on Northwest Coast topics began in 1886, but some earlier publications deserve to be described as ethnography. Although as ethnography they do not bear comparison with Lewis Henry Morgan's *League of the Ho-de-no-sau-nee, or Iroquois* (1851), Gilbert Malcolm Sproat's *Scenes and Studies of Savage Life* (1868) and James G. Swan's *The Indians of Cape Flattery, at the Entrance to the Strait of Fuca, Washington Territory* (1870) should probably be regarded as the first book-length ethnographic studies of Northwest Coast peoples rather than as historical sources (these works do contain eyewitness accounts of specific events as well as generalized descriptions, but so do most good ethnographies). A work like Alexander C. Anderson's "Notes on the Indian Tribes of British North America and the Northwest Coast" (1863) is more problematic as to type for it still reports with something of a traveler's air and with as much interest in "quaint customs" as in scientific description. This suggests that the dichotomy of ethnographic and historical sources is somewhat arbitrary.

Historical Sources

A historical source is one that reports the observations of an eyewitness to the event(s) described. Most of the historical sources therefore report on events seen by their authors in the 1880s or earlier. Thus William H. Collison's *In the Wake of the War Canoe* is treated as a historical source when Collison is describing events that he witnessed while he was a missionary on the Queen Charlotte Islands in the 1870s even though he wrote at a later date and published his book in 1915. If a more recent ethnographer is describing an event witnessed by himself or herself (for example, Elizabeth Colson's [1953] account of the termination of a Makah man's political career in the 1940s when it was discovered that he was descended from slaves), then for that particular event we have a historical source as well.

Many important historical sources are the product of men and women who had no particular interest in reporting on the characteristics of native people as such. Even when valuable information can be obtained from such sources, it was recorded incidental to the keeping of business records or the reporting of "adventures." Especially rich historical sources of this type include the various journals kept at the Hudson's Bay Company trading posts (e.g., John Work's various journals kept at Fort Simpson and elsewhere), the logs of ships involved in the maritime fur trade (e.g., the log of the *Columbia*), the observations of mid-nineteenth-century visitors to the area (e.g., Richard Charles Mayne's *Four Years in British Columbia and Vancouver Island* [1862]), and the all too rare account of considerable firsthand contact with the area's aboriginal inhabitants (e.g., John R. Jewitt's *Narrative of the Adventures and Sufferings of John R. Jewitt* [originally published in 1815]).

Bias in the Sources

The merit of any comparative study depends heavily on the quality of its sources. Consideration of the weaknesses of and problems with any set of sources can easily lead to a lengthy catalog of deficiencies. Such a catalog is often so extensive that one may wonder why the researcher persisted. And yet, whatever the difficulties, if care is taken with sources and many sources are used, some confidence in the results can emerge. The deficiencies are a warning, however, that the results of such research are always tentative and in some sense hypothetical. The choice, however, is between such results and nothing, for there is no going back to collect more firsthand data to fill in omissions and errors.

From the perspective of a consideration of bias and similar causes of error in sources, there are three types of "sources" to consider here: the European observers (who were often also actors in the scenes they describe) who supply the historical sources used here;[4] the ethnographers (usually also European) who collected and wrote the ethnographic studies used; and the native actors and informants who supplied information about events and the native perspective on them to both historical observers and ethnographers. One problem common to all types of sources will be briefly described before each of these types is treated in turn.

Sometimes what appear to be two or more independent sources turn out to be partly or entirely a single source: although published or apparently recorded by different persons, the description of an event or practice has been taken in whole or in part from the same original source. This can mean that what appears to be corroboration by independent reporters is merely repetition. A good example of this comes from the literature on the Haida. Two frequently cited books on the late nineteenth-century Haida are William H. Collison's *In the Wake of the War Canoe* (1915) and Charles Harrison's *Ancient Warriors of the North Pacific* (1925). Collison was a member of the Church Missionary Society (CMS) who served with the Haida from 1876 to 1879; Harrison served in the same capacity from 1883 to 1890. Collison knew Tsimshian from earlier service on the mainland coast and learned some Haida; Harrison knew Chinook Jargon and learned some Haida. Although the two works are usually cited as two independent sources, a careful comparison of the contents reveals that many of the same incidents are described in both. In some instances events witnessed by Collison in the late 1870s are described by Harrison without mentioning Collison's presence. Since Harrison's book was published ten years after Collison's, the quickest inference to draw is that Harrison borrowed some material from Collison's book. This is reinforced if we are aware that Harrison left the CMS in some disgrace in 1890 (a drinking problem), that he hung around the Queen Charlottes off and on for the next twenty-nine years failing at several business schemes, and that he was careless over detail in his book (when one can check on the details, one finds they are often wrong). But Harrison published earlier versions of much of his Haida material from 1911 through 1913 in the *Queen Charlotte Islander*, before Collison's book was published. The two men knew each other and many of the same people (both Haida and European) in the Queen Charlottes and the nearby mainland coast. Without attempting to judge Harrison, it is clear that if material on similar incidents or topics appears in both books considerable care must be exercised before one can treat the material as coming from independent sources.[5]

Another kind of independence problem frequently arises in ethnography where several different ethnographers may work at different times with the same informant or informants. For example, a well-known study of a late nineteenth-/early twentieth-century Kwakiutl's life history is Clellan Ford's *Smoke from Their Fires* (1941). The subject of the book and Ford's principal informant was Charley Nowell. Nowell was a Kwexa, one of the four Kwakiutl groups that assembled at Fort Rupert in the last half of the nineteenth century. He was Drucker's principal informant for the information on the Fort Rupert Kwakiutl contained in both Drucker's Northwest Coast culture element distribution list (1950) and "Kwakiutl Dancing Societies" (1940). He was also a key informant for the Fort Rupert material published in Drucker and Robert F. Heizer's *To Make My Name Good* (1967). The Charley Nowell basis of all this material is easy to ascertain as all the authors are clear about who their informants were, but anyone using this material must remember to treat all of it as coming from a single source no matter who the ethnographer may be.

The Kwakwaka'wakw material offers a much more complex and difficult example of the "single informant" problem. With George Hunt as a very active collaborator, Boas produced several thousand pages of material on the Kwakwaka'wakw. Much of this material is based on texts dictated or written by Hunt for Boas. In addition, Hunt transcribed texts (and their initial translations) of other Kwakwaka'wakw for Boas. He also often acted as translator and assistant during Boas's field trips among the Kwakwaka'wakw. One may say that Boas's Kwakwaka'wakw are very largely Hunt's Kwakwaka'wakw, although Boas was not entirely dependent on Hunt. The most important late nineteenth-/early twentieth-century book-length work on the Kwakwaka'wakw other than those by Boas is Edward S. Curtis's *The North American Indian*, volume 10 (1915). Also significant is Curtis's film *In the Land of the Head-Hunters* (1914), probably the first full-length ethnographic film of Native North Americans. Curtis's principal Kwakwaka'wakw collaborator and assistant in both works was George Hunt.

The other important fieldwork-based reports on the Kwakwaka'wakw from this period are by George Mercer Dawson (1887) and Johan Adrian Jacobsen ([1884] 1977). Dawson's brief spell of Kwakwaka'wakw research was done with the assistance of Hunt, and Jacobsen's guide to the Kwakwaka'wakw was also Hunt. He was also important in the development of art and artifact collections for museums, playing a principal role in obtaining such material for the American Museum of Natural History (with Boas), the Canadian Museum of Civilization (with Dawson), the Field Museum of Natural History, Chicago (with Boas), the Milwaukee Public Museum (with S. A. Barrett), the Museum of the American Indian, Heye Foundation, New York (with G. Heye), the Museum für Völkerkunde, Berlin (with Jacobsen and Boas), and the Smithsonian Institution (with Boas).[6] It is fair to say that until Charley Nowell began assisting C. F. Newcombe with collecting for museums in 1899 virtually all of the ethnographic information on the Kwakwaka'wakw was filtered through George Hunt. Nowell's role as principal informant for a number of ethnographers who worked on the Kwakwaka'wakw in the 1920s and 1930s has already been discussed. Most of the vast corpus of Kwakwaka'wakw material collected before the Second World War was strongly influenced by the very small number of Kwakwaka'wakw who were the principal collaborators of ethnographers working in and around the Fort Rupert area. Although the George Hunt/Charley Nowell Kwakwaka'wakw case is perhaps the most extensive example of the single source problem in the

Northwest Coast material, it is encountered frequently in both the historical and ethnographic literature.

Historical European
Observers and Actors

European observations of the indigenous inhabitants of the North Pacific Coast of North America begin in the 1770s and continue to the present day. Because my topic is slavery, the observations of interest are primarily from the period before 1890. Throughout this period, but especially in the last half of the nineteenth century, Europeans were apt to come to the Northwest Coast with feelings of cultural, moral, and even racial superiority to the native inhabitants. Such views naturally colored what they thought they saw and what they wrote about those inhabitants.

First of all they came to the coast with certain expectations about "Indians." By the 1770s there had been nearly three hundred years of contact between Europeans and Native Americans. This contact had as one of its results a large and diverse literature purporting to be about the aboriginal inhabitants of the "New World." The complex European Enlightenment idea of the Noble Savage is only one of the most important stereotypes about Native Americans that grew up during the period from the 1490s until the 1770s. And if the observations of early travelers, settlers, and missionaries influenced the development of the Noble Savage and other concepts, it is also true that these concepts strongly colored perceptions of Europeans who came to various parts of North America somewhat later. Ideas about what natives were like and actual experiences of natives developed alongside each other and influenced each other.[7]

Virtually all of those who came later had some expectations based on earlier writings on the Northwest Coast's inhabitants, but even the earliest Europeans to visit the coast knew something of the real or imagined characteristics of Native Americans elsewhere and therefore had certain expectations. James Cook and his men, for example, had their recent experiences in the South Pacific as well as information from reading about the indigenous inhabitants of other parts of North America.[8] And the men from the North West Company and the Hudson's Bay Company who came to the coast from the 1820s onward had frequently had experience among the native inhabitants of other parts of North America first.

In addition to whatever general ideas about natives European visitors to the Northwest Coast may have brought with them, most also came with particular interests and attitudes that affected what they observed and the way they reported what they thought they had seen. There was often a lack of comprehension of aboriginal cultures and little, if any, understanding of native motivations and attitudes, although the role that language differences played was sometimes clear to visitors, especially to those who arrived before the lingua franca, Chinook Jargon, was well developed and widespread. Many Europeans failed to appreciate that different points of view and values existed. Many of the historical sources used in this study were not written with an eye to publication, but those that were often were shaped by the demands of a particular genre. There are, for example, travelers' accounts and captivity narratives. Many accounts also tended to frame events so that the writer's actions (or presence) are justified; such is frequently the case for missionaries, fur traders, government officials, and settlers. Finally, some accounts were written up long after the actual events were witnessed. The passage of time not only begets lapses in memory but also reinterpretation and reshaping in the light of subsequent events or experience.

Ethnographers

It is useful to distinguish two styles of ethnographic research on North American natives. One style, often associated with Bronislaw Malinowski but not in fact originating with him, emphasizes participant observation as well as interviewing and aims to describe and explain the ongoing cultural life of a particular community or group of communities. The other style emphasizes interviews with knowledgeable informants with the goal of obtaining information that will allow past cultural practices to be recovered or reconstructed. Brief and not too misleading labels for these styles are "community studies" and "memory ethnography."

Ethnography in the style that I have labeled community studies was almost nonexistent before 1900 and began to become common only after World War I. Until the 1950s virtually all ethnographic research done on Northwest Coast cultures was memory ethnography, and even the exceptions were mostly published in the 1950s or later (i.e., Barnett 1957; Drucker 1958). As the subject of this book means that our interest is in material from the nineteenth century or earlier, it is memory ethnography whose strengths and weaknesses must be considered here.

In memory ethnography the researcher seeks informants who are knowledgeable about the cultural practices of the past and who are willing to work with the researcher. Such informants tend to be elderly or at least middle aged with a keen interest in the past. Often they realize that knowledge of the older ways is being "lost" or forgotten, and one of their motives for working with an ethnographer is to preserve memories of "the way things were." The ideal informant is intelligent, has a good memory of what things were like and how they were done when he or she was a child or young adult, has knowledge of and interest in all aspects of culture, comes from a family or household that was culturally conservative when they were growing up, and remembers what their parents and grandparents told them of the old ways. Such an informant may seem an idealized paragon, but ethnographers have been able to find them surprisingly often.

Several assumptions underlie this description of the ideal informant. Perhaps the most important of these is that traditional North American native cultures were homogeneous and that any intelligent, interested adult participant "knew the culture." That is, the participant had a fairly complete knowledge of his or her culture and that specialization or conflicting versions of the culture were minimal if not nonexistent. Behind this assumption is an implicit idea from nineteenth-century evolutionary thought: that small-scale societies are simple and undifferentiated. Some heterogeneity was readily recognized—there was some gender specialization and different kin groups could be expected to have different genealogical and mythological traditions—but this variation was not seen as a major impediment to using a few informants or even a single good informant to acquire the information to produce a general ethnographic description of a culture.

Another important assumption is that there is not a sharp divergence between "ideal" culture (culture as people conceive of it or think it ought to be) and culture as it is actually practiced. But it seems clear that most people will remember and report the "rules of the game" much more clearly than they will actual instances of the game being played. For example, a person may well remember that the rule for marital residence was avunculocal but not be able to give more than an example or two of the actual composition of households—not enough to determine if the statistical norm in the society was also avunculocal residence. Good ethnography seeks to report and analyze both rules and practice.

A third assumption is paradoxical. Memory ethnography is undertaken because considerable cultural change has taken place and the researcher intends to reconstruct the past culture. But the researcher assumes that the informant is a repository of unchanged information about the past, perhaps even the past as it was for his or her grandparents or sometimes even great-grandparents. Great change may be recognized in technology and economic life while it is assumed that many aspects of ideology have been very stable.

Obviously each of these assumptions is open to attack, and even the best memory ethnography must be treated with some skepticism and used with care. At the very least we must recognize that some domains of culture are more suitable for this approach than others. Unfortunately, "slavery" is one of the less suitable topics.

Some specific features of Northwest Coast communities in both the nineteenth and twentieth centuries should also be considered in assessing the success and usefulness of memory ethnography in the region. By the end of the nineteenth century all Northwest Coast native communities were very small.

The precipitous population declines of the previous one hundred years had not yet begun to turn around. In most communities an ethnographer had only a very small number of possible informants. When the unable, unwilling, and unavailable were eliminated, the ethnographer often counted himself or herself lucky to work with even a single "good" informant. The high death rates also meant that many areas of specialist knowledge had either disappeared with its possessors or remained with only one or two potential informants. When persons were unwilling or unavailable to assist, the ethnographer's information on a particular topic might be sketchy at best. Traditional Northwest Coast communities were not homogeneous small-scale societies. Not only were there numerous specialists (mostly part-time it is true), but each community was divided into very clearly defined strata. In addition, many kinds of knowledge were "property" on the Northwest Coast, so it might be difficult to locate someone with the right to tell about or pass on particular information.

Most ethnographic work on the coast was done during the summer because travel was easier then and, for academics, it was the nonteaching or research season. The summer was also a season of intense economic activity for members of the native communities. Anyone able to contribute to their family's livelihood could not afford the time off to work with a researcher. The emphasis on summer research also meant that few Northwest Coast researchers gained significant competence in any Northwest Coast language. Even in the 1950s many of the most knowledgeable potential informants were virtually monolingual so that researchers were forced for the most part to rely on interpreters. Informants varied in knowledge, as did their ethnographers—who also varied in skills. Informants might or might not be available on schedules suitable to the researcher.

All ethnography tends to have something of a generalized, timeless quality, reflecting both the writing style usually adopted in ethnographic reports (the ethnographic present) and the goal of the ethnographer to produce an account that is general and describes first and foremost the usual and normal in belief and practice. Memory ethnography tends to emphasize these characteristics. Even when specific examples are given, they are often not clearly located in time or space. And even if the ethnographer is acutely aware of the difference between the culture and community as they exist when informants are being interviewed and as they might have existed in the reconstructed past (and even the most focused of interviewers must at least notice that now is not then), there is a tendency to write as if reports about previous practices represent a past that remained intact from "time immemorial" until contact. Customs of the recent past may have developed in the not quite so recent past and this can often be documented from the historical record, but Northwest Coast ethnographers rarely take up such possibilities.

As can be seen, memory ethnography is particularly poorly suited for cultures that were not homogeneous, especially where the variation is due to stratification. Members of the different strata within traditional Northwest Coast communities had very different opportunities to participate in many aspects of social and cultural life. This surely led to differences in knowledge about and views of many practices. For example, the active participants in many ceremonials seem to have been largely titleholders; commoners and slaves were merely a part of the audience. This sort of thing is rarely noted in the Northwest Coast ethnographic literature, but it gains in importance when one realizes that most of the informants who have supplied ethnographic information have come from the titleholder stratum.

The theoretical predisposition of the ethnographer might also be expected to play a role in the character of ethnographic reports, but theoretical differences have less of an impact in Northwest Coast ethnography than might be expected. This is because the great majority of ethnography produced about the region was done by persons under the influence, to greater or lesser degree, of Franz Boas, who remains the dominant figure in the anthropology of the culture area. Thus most reports reflect the strengths and weaknesses of Boas's approach to both theory and ethnographic method. The biggest gap results from the lack of interest in the economy. Technology and material culture are often described (especially in the earlier work), but the organization of production and work is neglected. This is unfortunate for a study of slavery. One of the few pre–World War II researchers in the area who had a background in economics was not strongly linked to Boasian anthropology. Kalervo Oberg's *Social Economy of the Tlingit Indians* pays particular attention to the organization of production and work and raises questions about labor (especially his distinction between ceremonial and other types of labor) not taken up elsewhere in the literature. It is unfortunate and representative of the indifference of Boasian anthropology to economic matters that this work, first written as a doctoral dissertation in 1933, was not published until 1973.

Related to the issue of the impact of an ethnographer's theoretical outlook is that of the ethnographer's attitude toward native people. Obviously those who undertook ethnographic research on the Northwest Coast were men and women of their times. It is easy enough to find indications of a patronizing attitude toward native people in the writings of some Northwest Coast ethnographers, but the work of professional ethnographers is free of the conscious racism that mars more than one historical source. Most ethnographers have been decidedly "pro-Indian" and usually have been personally concerned about the current situation and condition of native communities even when their scholarly publications are exclusively on arcane academic subjects. The earlier professionals (Franz Boas and Edward Sapir especially), for example, lobbied to overcome the negative image of the potlatch in the public mind, an image created largely by missionaries and government agents. Although their efforts met with little early success, in more recent times the educated general public has realized that the potlatch is not an irrational ceremony in which the participants beggar themselves. No one should criticize efforts to replace inaccurate, sensationalized accounts of the potlatch with accurate ones. But these have had some unfortunate effects on scholarship. Other elements of the traditional culture that Euro-Americans might disapprove of or view with distaste have been played down and little research has been done on them. These include head-hunting, cannibalism, slavery, and, to a lesser extent, warfare. Two brief examples must suffice: the Kwakwaka'wakw, like most Northwest Coast peoples, took heads in war, but although Boas collected or caused to be collected literally thousands of pages on a vast array of topics, there is no indication that he sought texts to explain or describe this culture trait from a Kwakwaka'wakw point of view. In 1914 Curtis made the first full-length ethnographic motion picture about a North American Native group. The subject was the Kwakwaka'wakw and the film was *In the Land of the Head-Hunters*. When the film was refurbished and rereleased in the 1970s it was shown under the title *In the Land of the War Canoes*.

Native Actors and Informants

Ultimately, of course, all information about the indigenous cultures of the Northwest Coast comes from the native participants in them. This is true whether they are acting as informants and describing and explaining some practice or event to an outsider or whether some non-native is observing and then describing the actions or artifacts of native participants.

It is a fundamental of good ethnography that one must always attend to and respect the statements of informants. But informants' statements are what one analyzes, not the result of analysis. Each informant has his or her own point of view and as often as not is trying to create an impression as well as convey information. This is not to suggest that informants do not tell the truth or that they misrepresent things; informants respond to inquiries from their own point of view, which is not necessarily the point of view of all or even most other members of their community. This is a commonplace warning, a repetition of what every experienced ethnographer knows, but this important point is often overlooked when some key controversies in Northwest Coast ethnography are discussed.

Because of whom within the various native communities Europeans tended to interact with during the eighteenth and nineteenth centuries and because of the way most ethnographic inquiry has been conducted on the Northwest Coast, the greater part of the information that we have about Northwest Coast cultures comes to us from members of one segment of Northwest Coast communities: the titleholder component. This may not have much impact on our information about domains of culture such as technology, but it is critical for a topic like slavery. To reemphasize the point: virtually all of our information about slavery and related topics comes from titleholders, not commoners or slaves. This means that an informant's statements about the nature and practice of Northwest Coast slavery cannot be taken at face value. The informant may be sincere, but if he or she was not a slave there is certainly another point of view. The same point would hold in reverse, of course. But, as in most societies, all of our information about the dominant group does not come from the most disadvantaged group in the community.

The dominant view held by most ethnographers and other scholars that Northwest Coast slavery was benign and economically and otherwise unimportant is based on the testimony of the descendants of titleholders. These views are highly colored by the informants' (and the informants' ancestors') position in their communities and by the knowledge (certainly present by the late nineteenth century when the ethnographic record began to be collected in earnest) that Europeans disapproved of slavery.

Part Two

Northwest Coast Slavery

Part Two

Northwest Coast Slavery

4
Slaves and Masters Described

Slavery is a contemporary moral and political concern as well as a topic for scholarly study. Not only does slavery continue to persist in a few places even today, but the aftermath of past slavery continues to affect the political and social life of many nations. The definition of slavery therefore remains a matter on the current international legal agenda as well as a subject for scholarly debate. For this reason, as G. E. M. de Ste. Croix argues, a good beginning point in defining slavery is the 1926 League of Nations Slavery Convention.

> Slavery is defined in the 1926 Convention as "the status or condition of a person over whom any or all of the powers attaching to the right of ownership are exercised." I accept this definition of "chattel slavery" (as it is often called) for the ancient as well as the modern world, the more willingly since what it stresses is not so much the fact that the slave is the *legal property* of another as that *"the powers attaching* to the *right of ownership* are *exercised over him"*; for the essential elements in the slave's condition are that *his labour and other activities are totally controlled* by his master, and that he is virtually without rights, at least without enforceable legal rights. In Roman law, enslavement was regarded as closely resembling death. (Ste. Croix 1981, 135)

The key idea, of course, is the notion of the slave as property. This has been fundamental to almost all definitions of slavery. The most important dissenter to the prevailing view is Orlando Patterson, who argues that the focus on property is misleading and not very informative as to what slaves actually are that is unique. Patterson accepts that slaves are property but says that this does not make them a distinct category of persons: "Proprietary claims and powers are made with respect to many persons who are clearly not slaves.

Indeed any person, beggar or king, can be the object of a property relation. Slaves are no different in this respect" (1982, 21). He offers his own definition, which does not depend on the notion of slaves as property: "Slavery is the permanent, violent domination of natally alienated and generally dishonored persons" (1982, 13).

Whatever the other merits of his argument, Patterson's distrust of the property definition of slavery reminds us that if we want a definition that will apply in the greatest number of cross-cultural comparisons, then we have to be very careful indeed of "property"—one of the most difficult notions to use precisely and carefully in cross-cultural comparisons. Concepts of ownership are particularly difficult to apply in kinship-based societies, which lack the state.

Ste. Croix is primarily interested in slavery in the ancient Greek world, and he is too careful a scholar to read modern concepts of property into the Greek situation. He explicitly notes that he likes the 1926 Convention definition because he can apply it to "the ancient as well as the modern world." But ancient Greek society is not aboriginal North American society, and we should remember that modern legal and sociological notions of property lean heavily on Roman law. In addition, Patterson is certainly right that in a very wide range of societies (especially modern ones) most individuals can be and are the "object of a property relation." But I think that Patterson goes too far when he attempts to deflect the definition completely away from the idea of the slave as human property. The 1926 Convention says that a slave is "a person over whom any or all of the powers attaching to the right of ownership are exercised." As Patterson argues, the exercise of *any* of the powers of ownership over persons who are definitely not slaves is commonplace in many societies. But surely it would be very difficult to find persons over whom *all* the rights of ownership are exercised that most of us would not describe as slaves. In addition, there are various forms of unfree labor of which slavery is only one. The exercise of some of the powers of ownership often means that another of these forms of unfree labor is involved.[1] Therefore, as a first approximation I will define a slave as a person over whom all the powers attaching to the right of ownership are exercised. It should be remembered that "all the powers attaching to the right of ownership" are locally defined.

We are not finished with Patterson, however, because—especially for kinship-based societies—his discussion contains many useful insights into the nature of slavery. Patterson's definition suggests that four things are always true of the slave:

1. His/her status is permanent;
2. The ultimate origin and maintenance of slave status is violent domination;

3. Slaves are alienated from their natal circumstances;
4. Slaves are dishonored persons.

Although the idea that they are natally alienated probably holds true for slaves everywhere, this is a key point when considering slavery in kin-based societies. For in a kin-based society, virtually all of one's social identity is determined by one's structural position at birth because the kin group is the dominant unit in society, the unit that undertakes most activities, whether they can be described as social, economic, political, religious, or whatever. To be alienated from the kin group is perhaps the most severe of fates in such a society. Furthermore, although in most societies that practice slavery slaves can be manumitted, the slave is permanently slave until the owner takes some voluntary action; there is no sentence to be served or term to expire. People become and are maintained as slaves by force. Many servile social relations are masked by ideologies that aim to justify servility in other terms, but with slavery, even where this is the case, the threat of force, often in its ultimate form—death—is always near at hand. Finally, the slave is a dishonored person. Slavery is a stigma. This is perhaps the most controversial part of Patterson's definition (see Blackburn 1988, 278 n. 13), but it fits nicely with the character of slavery on the Northwest Coast.

Northwest Coast Slaves
Were Captives "Slaves"?

One of the common consequences of intergroup violence throughout the Northwest Coast culture area was the taking of captives who were brought back to the home communities of their captors. Many of these captives never returned to their natal communities, and they (and their children, if any) spent the rest of their lives either in their captor's community or in another community where they shared the same status with other captives residing there. Although we could continue to speak of these persons as "captives," for comparative purposes we wish to apply a more specific label to this status, if we can find one that fits without too much distortion of the local situation. This is a fairly formal way of raising the question: Do Northwest Coast captives become slaves?

If we use the definition of slave discussed above, the answer is a clear yes: most Northwest Coast captives became slaves. The definition advanced was that a slave was a person over whom another person exercised all the powers attached to the right of ownership. In the Northwest Coast context, powers over an object owned would include the right to dispose of or to destroy the object. Also included would be the right to use the object in any practicable manner. If the "object" owned is a human being, these rights imply the following:

> disposal—the slave may be given away to another, exchanged for other objects, or otherwise included as an item in a property transaction;

> destruction—the slave may be killed or freed without reference to anyone else unless they share ownership rights;

> use—the slave may be put to tasks and duties of the owner's choosing, the slave having no rights of refusal, and the owner has rights to all products of the slave's endeavors;

> inheritability—an owner's heir enjoys all the above rights over inherited slaves and an owner enjoys all the above rights with respect to the offspring of a female slave.

In addition, we may note the following characteristics of slavery that are included in Patterson's nonproperty definition. The status of the slave is (1) permanent, unless it is freely altered by the master; (2) violent in origin (force is also the sanction that ultimately maintains the slave as slave); (3) natally alienated, that is, the normal social ties created in a society by birth are destroyed or not allowed; and (4) dishonored (there is a permanent stigma attached to slavery).

All these characteristics were probably true of captives held in virtually all Northwest Coast communities. Most of the criteria are present in almost all the groups in the tribal unit sample (see table A-1 in appendix 1 for ratings of the sample on these variables). Although these characteristics are found throughout the culture area, the data are better for the northern part than farther south. For the north the sources tend to make clearer, stronger statements that require less interpretation than do statements in sources for southern groups. But even so, the source for at least one southern group, the Twana, is explicit. William W. Elmendorf (1960, 331) is quite clear that among the Twana slaves could be disposed of by their owners in transactions; could be killed, even though this was not highly thought of by fellow titleholders (p. 345); labored entirely for their owner's benefit (p. 332); were inherited by the heirs of titleholder men (p. 363); were slaves if the children of slaves (p. 346); had permanent status as slaves and were never manumitted (p. 346); were war captives or their descendants (p. 561); were cut off from their former kin (p. 327); and were permanently stigmatized (pp. 326, 347). In brief, Elmendorf says that slaves were the negation of the four factors of Twana social evaluation: birth, wealth, personality, and spirit power (p. 327). For few other Northwest Coast groups are our sources as detailed or explicit, but Elmendorf's remarks are probably broadly true of all Northwest Coast communities.

On the Northwest Coast, captives, unless they were ransomed or otherwise re-covered very soon after capture, were slaves.

Living as a Slave

The passage below summarizes McIlwraith's view of the position of slaves among the Nuxalk. It is quoted here to reinforce the claim that Northwest Coast captives were slaves and to introduce my discussion of the conditions of life of Northwest Coast slaves.

> A master had complete power over a slave, unaffected by the force of public opinion, since the affairs of a slave, being without relatives, were of no conse-quence to anyone. Accordingly, the lot of a slave depended on the character of his master, and on his own ability and industry. An industrious slave was val-ued; such an one would not be traded or sold except through dire necessity, and in the course of years he became, as far as actual treatment was concerned, one of the family. Many masters gave their slaves *kusiut* dance prerogatives, ex-pending large sums for the purpose. In such a case the slave might become an influential member of the community, though the fact that he was not free was never forgotten. On the other hand, a master had not the slightest compunc-tion about beating a lazy slave, and could kill him if he so desired. None of the present Bella Coola has heard of such a case; it was considered more sensible to sell or give away an unsatisfactory slave. It was accepted as a matter of course that a master should provide his slaves with food and clothing, since anything produced or obtained by one belonged to him. A slave-owner had full rights to his female slaves, and unquestionably exercised them. The only restraints were the jealousy of his own wife or wives, and the feeling that it was undignified for a free man to demean himself. It was impossible to learn with even approximate accuracy to what extent intercourse took place between masters and slaves. Probably not a great deal, though there was considerable freedom of relations between slave women and the young men of the community, unrestrained by the pride of chieftainship. . . .
>
> To sum up, it may be said that the position of slaves in Bella Coola was not particularly onerous, though it depended entirely on the will of their masters. Without status in the community, a slave could have been abused by a cruel owner, though public life of the village, where all lived and ate together, tended to break down the unsystematically enforced differences of rank. (McIlwraith 1948, 1:160–162)

Note that, however favorable McIlwraith thinks a particular slave's situa-tion may have been, there is no suggestion that slaves ever became something else. His comments leave no doubt that Nuxalk slaves were indeed slaves in the terms discussed in the previous section. It is worth noting that McIlwraith begins his discussion with the observation that a slave was "without relatives" and that therefore the fate of a slave was of "no consequence to anyone."

Without denying their slavery or their masters' right to exploit and even kill them, McIlwraith takes a fairly favorable view of the situation of Nuxalk slaves, always allowing for a "cruel" master. We should note that there are descriptions in the literature on most slave systems that are similarly benign. They are particularly common where the main sources about the conditions of slavery are masters and former masters. As far as I can tell from McIlwraith's discussion of his informants (1948, 1:viii–xii), none of them were former slaves and most (probably all) were from the titleholder class. McIlwraith worked among the Nuxalk in the early 1920s and his major informants had been young adults in the 1860s and 1870s, early enough to have seen a few Nuxalk slaves but well after the heyday of traditional Nuxalk culture.

Informants from some other societies and the eighteenth- and nineteenth-century sources give us a harsher version of life as a Northwest Coast slave. One of Kaj Birket-Smith's Eyak informants, for example, described the following incident.

> Galushia told the following story to illustrate the power of the master. The incident occurred when he was a small boy, before he went to the United States: a party of Yakutat Tlingit were on a journey. They had not killed anything for a long time and were very hungry. Finally they secured some game and cooked it. One man had a slave with him but refused to give him any food. When they were ready to leave their camping place, the slave was picking the bones. The master beat him to death because he had kept the boats waiting. Galushia and his wife regarded the master's conduct with horror, and we understood that the other natives at the time had disapproved of the man's severity. (Birket-Smith and De Laguna 1938, 140)[2]

Both Eyak and (probably) Yakutat disapproval of such extreme behavior was most likely genuine, but no one questioned the master's right to deny his slave food or kill him. This incident again demonstrates the violent basis of slavery, but it also suggests another facet of slave life that was probably common throughout the culture area: in times of food or other shortages, it was not share and share alike. Slaves suffered first.

European experiences as slaves.   In the early years of contact, Northwest Coast people did not hesitate to enslave Europeans if the opportunity arose. Some Europeans were enslaved for short periods, but others spent long periods or even the rest of their lives as slaves. I know of three narratives that describe in at least some detail the life of European slaves: Charles Bishop's account of a sailor held by the Cumshewa Haida in 1794–1795 (1967, 95–98),[3] John Jewitt's account (with the help of a professional man of letters) of his captivity among the Mowachaht in 1802–1804, and Tarakanov's account of the captivity of a number of Russians by the Makah in 1808–1811 (Owens 1985, 39–65; Holmberg 1985, 107–125). Jewitt's account is the best known, having been reprinted numerous times since its first publication in 1815. All three accounts indicate that the life of a slave was quite strenuous and that treatment was often harsh. Bishop's diary suggests that the American sailor held by the Cumshewa received unusually brutal treatment, even for a slave. This may be partly explained by the fact that he was owned by the brother of the only Haida killed in the attack that resulted in the sailor's enslavement. He was kept naked, forced to work hard (collecting firewood is specifically mentioned), and treated badly by everyone, including other slaves.

The other two accounts also contain evidence of the difficult situation of slaves but are difficult to interpret because both center on "heroes."[4] That is, the narrators portray themselves as clever, resourceful, brave, and so on. Both admit to having been slaves but claim special treatment not normally the slave's lot (this may have happened, especially as both base their claims, at least in part, on their skill at making things useful to their owners); but strong elements of the theme of "the clever white man impressing the natives" are also present in these narratives. In any event, both the Russians held by the Makah (thirteen of about twenty survived and were freed by an American ship's captain) and Jewitt and his companion suffered from hunger and cold at times and were put to work. The Russians also changed owners many times: they were traded from group to group as well as passed from owner to owner among the Makah. Indeed, one young boy was not freed because he had been traded to a distant (unknown) group and another reached the Chinook at the mouth of the Columbia River where a different American ship's captain purchased him. Taken altogether these European accounts of life as a slave offer a picture of an often harsh and degraded situation, although indigenous as well as European slaves could sometimes receive better treatment. Jewitt's general description of Mowachaht slaves is not unlike McIlwraith on Nuxalk slaves.

> Their slaves . . . form their most valuable property. They are of both sexes, being either captives taken by themselves in war, or purchased from the neighboring tribes, and who reside in the same house, forming as it were part of the family, are usually kindly treated, eat of the same food, and live as well as their masters. They are compelled, however, at times, to labor severely, as not only all the menial offices are performed by them, such as bringing water, cutting wood, and a variety of others, but they are obliged to make the canoes, to assist in building and repairing houses, to supply their masters with fish, and to attend them in war and to fight for them. (Jewitt [1815] 1975, 65)

Once again, slaves are not badly treated, except that they are made to work very hard. In addition, no slave, not even Jewitt by his own account, lived as well as an important titleholder like Maquinna. The lives of slaves and commoners might at times be comfortably (or uncomfortably) similar, but titleholders, as can be seen from Jewitt and other sources, were distinctly better off than their fellow villagers.

External marks of slavery.   European observers never seem to have had trouble distinguishing titleholders, especially the more prominent ones, from the other members of a community. This was both because Europeans expected to find and deal with "chiefs" or "kings" and because, in their manner of interacting with outsiders and in their style of dress and deportment, titleholders "stood out from the crowd." But distinguishing commoners from slaves could be more difficult and required some experience, as C. E. S. Wood discovered among the Chilkat in 1877. Soon, however, some differences became clear. "The slaves hew the wood and carry the water and paddle the canoe. They cannot marry without the consent of their master, and are unpleasantly liable to be offered as sacrifice on their master's grave" (Wood 1882, 328). Although the details varied somewhat from community to community, the conditions of slave life were quite different from those of the lives of commoners. Underlying the difference, of course, was Wood's "unpleasant liability" to be killed.

Aside from the hard work and drudgery that they were put to, there were other features of slave life visible to the observant outsider. One of these lay in the treatment of the dead. We have information on the treatment of the corpses of deceased slaves for fifteen of the groups in the tribal unit sample (see table A-2 in appendix 1). In eleven of these groups the bodies of slaves were treated in a manner markedly different from those of ordinary members of the community. Most often the body was simply cast aside, tossed into the forest or into the water, and not treated in the same manner as the remains of other human beings. In the case of the Haida, Drucker (1950, 218) records a disagreement over the treatment of dead slaves: his Masset informant said that the bodies of slaves were not buried but simply thrown out, whereas his Skedans informant said that slaves were buried. This may reflect a difference between Haida local groups for although the various Haida groups were very similar, they certainly were not identical in culture. For three other sample groups (Nuxalk, Chilkat, and Clayoquot), Drucker's informants denied that slaves' bodies were simply thrown out and insisted that slaves were given a burial. As Drucker remarks, "It is to be understood that the burial of a slave was simple and unelaborate, but most informants insisted their bodies were put away decently, which sounds like more humane treatment than one would expect these unfortunates to have received" (1950, 280).

The other sources for the Nuxalk agree with Drucker and the other Clayoquot sources are silent as to the treatment of slave's bodies, so I have accepted the statements of Drucker's informants. But in the case of the Chilkat I have disregarded the claim of Drucker's informants that slaves were buried because two earlier sources state that they were not buried but thrown into the water (Jones 1914, 118; Muir 1915, 171 [based on observations in 1879]). Therefore, what appears to outsiders as degrading burials for slaves are recorded in sample groups from all three regions and, although it is true that in the 1920s and 1930s informants for three of the sample groups said that slaves were buried, overall I think it likely that dead slaves were ordinarily treated with what appears to have been disdain or disinterest in most Northwest Coast communities, typically by casting the slave's body into the water or the forest.[5]

There were, however, circumstances that led to better treatment of some deceased slaves. As will be discussed in detail in chapter 8, slaves were sometimes killed as a part of ceremonies. At least some of the time such slaves were given burial treatment more like that of other members of the community. Sources for the Tlingit (Krause 1956, 159) and Tsimshian (Niblack 1890, 356) suggest that slaves killed as a part of the funeral ceremony for a deceased titleholder would be cremated along with the titleholder. Albert P. Niblack also says that slaves killed on other ceremonial occasions might also be given burials like those of commoners. A ceremonial death may have led to better burial treatment in other groups as well, although the sources are not very informative at this point.

Slaves often lived under miserable conditions. In six of the sample groups, for example, the sources state that slaves slept in the least desirable parts of their master's dwellings, near the doors or other less comfortable or safe parts of the house. Nowhere do we find the suggestion that slaves were entitled to sleeping quarters as good as their masters'. Slaves also often had a different physical appearance from free members of the community. In seven of the groups in the sample the sources note that slaves wore their hair cut short.[6] Only in one sample group is a special haircut for slaves denied. And for six groups of the tribal unit sample, there is evidence that slaves were given special "slave" names. Some titleholders owned specific names for slaves, just as they owned names for themselves or members of their families. A Kyuquot titleholder, for example, owned in addition to many personal names four "war-chief" names, at least four names for dogs, several other names for pet birds, and "for male slaves he owned the name *tutuh*; for female slaves: *kwohaalitc, witspaiL, hahal,* and *hinitsaq*" (Drucker 1951, 258–259). The practice of special names for slaves was probably more widespread than the sources indicate.

External marks of titleholder status (or former titleholder status) sometimes clashed with a person's slave state. In the northern part of the culture area, titleholder women wore labrets, a special sign of prestige and a sign of feast participation. This was true of the six sample groups in the northern region of the culture area. Slaves are known to have been forbidden labrets in four of these groups, although the sources occasionally note that slaves sometimes bore the marks of previous labret wear; that is, they had been titleholders before enslavement.

A widespread practice in the southern and central regions of the culture area was cranial deformation—the artificial shaping of an infant's head by the use of binding. Feelings about the importance of cranial deformation could be very strong in some Northwest Coast communities. According to Ronald L. Olson,

> [Among the Quinault] every child of good birth had its [head] flattened. Persons with undeformed heads were called . . . flea face and were thought to be mentally inferior. Only orphans or the children of ne'er-do-wells grew up with heads not flattened. (1936, 102)

In spite of this Olson goes on to say that there "was no rule against the flattening of heads of slave children" (1936, 102).

Feelings were quite otherwise among the Chinook.

> This flattening of the head appears to be a sort of mark of royalty or badge of aristocracy, for their slaves are not permitted to treat their children thus. (Swan 1966, 168; see also Santee 1932, 274)

> A most inhumane practise existed here for some time after Fort George was established of the children of the whites by the Native Women being murdered by the mothers; this arose from the circumstance of the Fathers insisting that the heads should not be flattened and the Mother preferring to sacrifice the child to having it ranked as a slave. (Merk 1931, 101)

The deaths of these Euro-Chinook infants reveal very clearly the importance of rank and position in Chinook society and the degradation of slavery.

Of the fourteen groups in the tribal unit sample that practiced some form of head deformation, two did not allow a slave's child to have their head deformed, but in three at least some slave children were allowed cranial deformation. (For two groups the sources are contradictory.)

"These wretched slaves"?   Verne F. Ray, the principal ethnographer of the Chinook, after noting that slaves "may at times have been grouped in the less desirable parts of . . . houses" and that the "more arduous and disagreeable" tasks fell on slaves, goes on to say that "the domestic relations between masters and slaves seem to have been of a very healthy order. Intimate accounts are lacking but the indications are all in the direction of tranquil and unoppressive relations" (1938, 127–128). Ray's account of Chinook slavery is one of the most detailed in the Northwest Coast literature. Unlike many other ethnographers he does not downplay the importance or significance of slavery. And he was certainly familiar with many of the historical sources on the Chinook. But it is very difficult to reconcile his "very healthy order" with Sir George Simpson's account.

Slaves form the principal article of traffick on the whole of this coast and constitute the greater part of their Riches; they are made to fish, hunt, draw water and
wood in short all the drudgery falls on them; they feed in common with the family of their proprietors and intermarry with their own class, but lead a life of
misery, indeed I conceive a Columbia slave to be the most unfortunate wretch in
existence; the proprietors exercise the most absolute authority over them even
to life and death and on the most trifling fault wound and maim them sicken-
ingly. . . . These wretched slaves often change proprietors two or three times in
the course of a season and when they escape a violent death they are brought to a
premature end by Disease when they are left a prey to Dogs and Crows as they
are denied ordinary burial. (Merk 1931, 101)

Simpson's account is based on observations he made in the 1820s, and he
includes reassuring comments about slaves eating with their owner's families
and being able to marry other slaves. But the rest of his description bears no
resemblance to "tranquil and unoppressive relations." Simpson puts his case
very vividly. Is he exaggerating, playing to an audience, perhaps to justify his
own or other Hudson's Bay Company actions toward natives? Or is this an
accurate picture that reflects the demoralization of the Chinook and the impending destruction of their culture, rather than a description of traditional
master-slave relations? There must be something of the latter in this passage,
for the omitted portion describes the prostitution of their female slaves to
Europeans by their female titleholder owners. By the 1820s Chinook culture
was certainly reeling, but my reading of the eighteenth- and early nineteenth-
century sources leads me closer to Simpson's than to Ray's view of the condition of Chinook slaves. Ray himself acknowledges his lack of "intimate accounts," and once more his principal informants were of titleholder origin.[7]
James Swan's observations of the treatment of slaves by the Makah in the
early 1860s lends support to Simpson's view of the condition of slaves.

A [slave] woman used abusive language towards her master, till, finally, becoming exasperated, he struck her a blow on the head with a club, which stunned,
but did not quite kill her. She remained in that state all night, and toward morn-
ing partially recovered; but the owner's wrath was not appeased, and he killed
her with his knife. No notice was taken of this affair by the tribe. The owner,
however, for this and several other crimes, was taken to Fort Steilaccom and im-
prisoned for several months by order of the Indian Agent. The Indians say that
formerly when slaves were more numerous, and more easily obtained, they were
oftener punished. Instances are related which an offender has been bound hand
and foot, placed in a canoe and set adrift, while a strong east wind was blowing,
which could carry him out to sea and ensure a miserable death by starvation.
Others have been hung, and others tortured; but they are getting more moderate
of late years, and extreme measures are seldom resorted to. (Swan 1869, 54)[8]

There is definite or probable evidence that slaves were at least sometimes
beaten in ten of the groups in the tribal unit sample (Chilkat, Sitka, Haida,

Nuxalk, Fort Rupert Kwakiutl, Mowachaht, Clayoquot, Makah, Klallam, and Chinook). The sources imply that in three groups slaves were not beaten but that disobedient or "troublesome" slaves were sold to someone in another community instead (Saanich, Twana, Quileute). Male titleholders sometimes took sexual advantage of female slaves. This is reported in the sources for nine groups (Yakutat, Haida, Lower Skeena Tsimshian, Nuxalk, Mowachaht, Clayoquot, Puyallup-Nisqually, Twana, and Chinook). For the Saanich, Diamond Jenness (n.d., 86) says that titleholders had too much pride in upper-class prestige to involve themselves sexually with female slaves. But perhaps Elmendorf (1960, 346) is more realistic when he notes that although Twana titleholders were not supposed to have sexual relations with slaves, such relations did occur.

Taken altogether, the evidence suggests that throughout the culture area, although the treatment of slaves did indeed vary according to the master involved, overall slaves did have the "life of misery" that Simpson suggests.

The Killing of Slaves

We know that slaves were killed by their masters on many occasions. The most spectacular killings occurred during ceremonies, when it is often appropriate to speak of the ritual killing of slaves. The killing and other use of slaves in rituals will be treated in detail in chapter 8. Here I briefly discuss masters' rights to kill their slaves. They not infrequently exercised these rights, and not only in ritual contexts. Slaves were almost certainly killed in ritual contexts in all but one of the tribal unit sample groups. (Elmendorf [1960, 435] denies that slaves were killed in rituals among the Twana, although they were occasionally killed in rituals among other Puget Sound Salish groups.) Slaves were killed outside of rituals in at least ten of the sample groups (including the Twana). For the Saanich, there is a perplexing entry in Homer G. Barnett's culture element list: slaves were not "killed capriciously" (1939, 267). Does this mean that they were only killed for what their owners regarded as a "good" reason, or that the Saanich did not kill slaves? Taking all the available evidence into account, it seems likely that slaves in all Northwest Coast communities could be killed by their masters for whatever reason or caprice that suited them. Such killings might be disapproved of by community opinion but could not be prevented or interfered with.

The scale of slave killing was, relative to the size of Northwest Coast communities, quite large. A considerable number of slave killings are recorded in the historical sources. In one instance the data are complete enough over a long enough period of time to allow us to get some notion of the quantitative impact of slave killing.

The numerical data on slave killings is most complete for the Stikine for the period 1840 to 1848. Over this nine-year span there are reports of slave killings in four of the nine years, with a total of nineteen slaves reported to have been killed. It is highly probable that this is an underestimate for the period. We also have good (for the Northwest Coast) census data for 1845 for the Stikine. Comparing two census reports, we can estimate the number of slaves held by the Stikine in 1845 at 158.

To get a rough idea of the scale of deadly violence against Stikine slaves, let us assume that the Stikine held an average of 158 slaves for each year from 1840 to 1849. Nineteen slaves killed from 1840 to 1848 gives us an average of 2.1 slaves killed per year, almost certainly a conservative estimate. If we use 158 slaves as our population base, the annual death rate by ritual killing for Stikine slaves in the 1840s is approximately 1,329 per 100,000. Increasing the estimated number of slaves held by the Stikine to 300 (an unlikely number) only reduces the annual rate to 700 per 100,000.

In a paper on violence in simple human societies, Bruce M. Knauft (1987, 457, 462) notes that the Gebusi of New Guinea had one of the highest homicide rates ever reported: 568 per 100,000 per year. Homicide rates for most modern nation-states are well under 20 per 100,000 per year, although high-risk subgroups within such political units may have very much higher rates. Obviously the Stikine rate cannot be generalized to the entire culture area, but it is probably not unrepresentative for the north and north central portions of the region. Slaves on the Northwest Coast were not only worked hard and faced difficult living conditions, they lived under a threat of violent death that was unusually high for any segment of a human community.

The Character and Behavior of Slaves

Slaves were captives taken in war or were the children of captives. Most of the slaves held in any community had been obtained in war or in trade. The ethnic origins of slaves taken in war are discussed in detail in chapter 5 and trade patterns are treated in chapter 7. Here I discuss other characteristics of slaves, beginning with what is known of the gender, age, and status origins of slaves. Next I describe what might be called the "character," or psychological traits, of slaves.

The demography of slavery.[9]   When a community was attacked, anyone found there might be enslaved. Not surprisingly, however, when a preference is expressed in the sources, it is usually for women and children. Adult males were more difficult to manage and more likely to attempt to escape. They were also the prime opponents in battle and were more liable to be killed in the fighting. A preference for women and children as slaves was found in fourteen of the groups in the tribal unit sample (see table A-3). And the general impression gained from reading the source material is that slaves were more

likely to be women than men. For example, if one records the gender of a
slave where this is definitely mentioned in a source and calculates the sex
ratio for slaves who are identified by gender, for most groups the sex ratio of
slaves favors women.[10] For fifteen of the sample groups the sex ratio is well
under 100, for two groups it is about 100, and for only three groups is it over
100. Thus the implicit gender data in the sources support the explicit statements in the sources that women were preferred to men as slaves.

Although actual census data on Northwest Coast communities are very
poor, we do have six sets of census material in which the gender of slaves is
identified. If we examine the sex ratio for the earliest available census for
these groups, we find that for only one of the six groups is the sex ratio well
under 100 (see table A-3). The census data appear to contradict other data in
the sources: in both of the cases in which the census data show a sex ratio of
well over 100, the gender identifications in the sources produce sex ratios of
well under 100. Given such small populations and the poor reliability of the
data, not too much can be made of these figures. It is worth noting, however,
that the sex ratios for the free populations reported for these two groups (Chilkat and Chinook) are also well over 100—117 and 143, respectively.

Reactions to enslavement.   Although some of the captives taken in raids
were already slaves who merely changed masters, the reaction of those who
were suddenly transformed into property was considerable distress. A captured Sitka woman is quoted as saying, "It is just as well to die as to be enslaved" (Swanton 1909, 76). And in 1837 a recently captured Nawitti titleholder begged the Hudson's Bay Company trader at Fort Simpson to purchase
her and send her back home. Of this woman and those taken with her the
trader remarks, "Their looks, poor wretches, were pitiable in the extreme"
(Fort Simpson Journal 1834–1838, fol. 135d). Drucker's comments about the
feelings of Nuu-chah-nulth slaves probably apply to many slaves throughout
the culture area.

> All of this does not mean that a slave's life was a pleasant one. Even worse than
> the occasional mistreatment and possibility of violent death . . . must have been
> the galling consciousness of his low and shameful status. For a well-born per-
> son it must have been bitter medicine indeed to serve persons of no higher, or
> even lower, rank than himself. The fact that so many runaway attempts were
> made despite possible death or abuse if recaptured, indicates the unpleasantness
> of the situation. (1951, 272–273)

As Drucker suggests, slave escapes or escape attempts are not uncommon in
the literature. Escape is considered in detail later in this chapter.

But reactions to capture were not all so straightforward as desiring or attempting to escape. For example, some women recently captured by the Sitka

told their captors the locations of other villages and camps so that they, too, might be attacked (Swanton 1909, 72). And there are other accounts of slaves of longer standing leading their masters back to their home villages and lending assistance as spies to ensure a successful raid: see, for example, A. B. Reagan's (1929, 183–184) account of the use by the Quileute of a Chehalis slave as a guide for an attack on his own people.

The character of slaves.   The characterization of the personalities of slaves, leading perhaps to the question of whether or not there is a distinctive "slave personality," is a difficult task. For the Northwest Coast area one must be especially careful since virtually no direct testimony is available from slaves or former slaves. Most of our data on slave character come from the assessments of slave owners (or former owners) or from the reports of nineteenth-century European observers. Therefore, although we can say a good deal about what owners thought (or claimed) slaves were like, we must be cautious in accepting such characterizations as wholly indicative of the nature of slave character and behavior. Even if owners are reporting their observations in an accurate and disinterested manner (not likely since owners may well have an image of slaves they want to convey to themselves or to others), slaves are likely to dissemble about at least some of their thoughts and feelings. The testimony of European observers must also be treated with caution, for most of them certainly had fixed notions about the nature of slaves and slavery, influenced by slavery in the American South and the Caribbean.

Slaves were often loyal retainers. Masters traveled about with their slaves (reported for thirteen groups; see table A-4). There are frequent reports that masters went on journeys (sometimes long ones) accompanied only by their slaves. In a few instances masters were murdered and the slaves made good their escape. But in many more instances such journeys must have had a satisfactory outcome as the practice was widespread and there is no evidence of its being curbed.

Slaves are known to have accompanied their masters on war expeditions in nine of the groups in the tribal unit sample (these groups are from all three regions). As already indicated, sometimes these slaves had originated from the community being attacked. For only one group (the Saanich) is it explicitly stated that slaves did not accompany their masters to war (nor did Saanich slaves accompany their masters to ceremonies; Jenness n.d., 60).

Slaves sometimes were ordered to kill for their masters. They are known to have done this in eight groups in the tribal unit sample. Often they acted as instruments of social control for leading titleholders, but they also killed for their master's private revenge. But, of course, there is another side. For five groups instances of slaves killing their masters are recorded, and the danger was not simply from physical assault, for supernatural means might be resorted to as well since "slaves have nothing to restrain them from killing" (Stern 1934, 73–74, on the Lummi).[11] In addition, the sources for eight of the sample groups describe such minor rebellions of slaves against masters as talking back and breaking tools.

Other, more general characterizations of slaves and their behavior are not too common in the sources, nor are they evenly distributed throughout the study area. They are much more frequent in the southern part of the region, the reverse of the situation for most slavery topics.

Although they are not systematic evidence on the nature of slave behavior, the following statements reflect the complex behavior of slaves and the contradictory views others held of slaves (the order is geographic, from north to south).

1. Ordinary sexual morality did not apply to slaves: "They could have babies two or three times a day! Their owner would be proud of it" (Yakutat) (De Laguna 1972, 470).

2. A male slave who accidentally breaks an adze weeps for fear of his master's anger (Yakutat) (De Laguna 1972, 471).

3. When a woman is feeding a group of people and they never seem satisfied with the amount of food they are given, she remarks that they are like slaves (Haida) (Swanton 1905, 78).

4. A slave who fears the wrath of his master when a net is damaged lies about the cause (Haida) (Swanton 1905, 29).

5. An escaping slave is captured by another group and he immediately settles into life as a slave with the new owners (Lower Skeena Tsimshian) (Work 1945, 69–70).

6. When she discovers her master has been murdered, a woman slave begins to weep (Lower Skeena Tsimshian) (Barbeau 1950, 107–110).

7. In a myth, a slave is frightened in a supernatural encounter, but his master is brave (Nuxalk) (McIlwraith 1948, 2:115–116).

8. In a myth, people in difficulties are helped by a kindly slave (Nuxalk) (McIlwraith 1948, 1:633).

9. A slave is described as a "devoted guardian" of his master's child (Nuxalk) (McIlwraith 1948, 2:515–517).

10. A slave completely assimilates attitudes and values of his owner's group and becomes very upset when visitors ignore local customs (Nuxalk) (McIlwraith 1948, 2:373–375).

11. In a myth, a group of slaves traveling on their own aggressively seek to further the cause of their master (Fort Rupert Kwakiutl) (Boas 1935, 86–90).

12. Slaves are described as lazy and incorrigible (Saanich) (Jenness n.d., 61).

13. "Only slaves need to be ordered before they do any work" (Lummi) (Stern 1934, 73–74).

14. Freed slaves continued bad behavior they learned in servitude (Skagit) (Collins 1974b, 127–128).

15. If a man returned home from slavery, "he was great to lie now, when he came back, because he was a slave" (Skagit) (Collins 1974b, 127–128).

16. Within the family group, a pleasant and industrious slave was well off (Puyallup-Nisqually) (Smith 1940, 52).

17. Slaves are lazy (Twana) (Elmendorf 1960, 345).

18. Masters often regarded slaves with tolerant affection but never looked on them as really adult (Twana) (Elmendorf 1960, 346).

19. Slaves were stereotyped as "lackadaisical and childish" (Twana) (Elmendorf 1960, 346).

20. Slaves "enjoyed" playing with children (Twana) (Elmendorf 1960, 346).

21. Slaves might be "ambitious and enterprising" (Chinook) (Ray 1938, 53).

22. Only slaves drank to excess (Chinook) (Cox 1957, 173).

23. "Slaves go to the gambling ground as composedly to be played for as to their ordinary avocations" (Chinook) (Merk 1931, 102).

These statements come from a wide variety of sources. Some are from the accounts of contemporary European observers of slavery in the region (nos. 5, 22, 23), some are from twentieth-century informants' accounts (nos. 1, 9, 10, 12, 13, 14, 15, 16, 17, 18, 19, 20, 21), and others are from myths, tales, or other dictated texts (nos. 2, 3, 4, 6, 7, 8, 11). Neither the behavior of slaves nor the impression of them that others wished to convey was uniform, but many of these characterizations will be familiar to anyone who has read the literature on slavery in, say, classical Greece or the American South.[12]

Slaves are inferior and act this out. Slaves may try to escape, they may cause trouble, an individual slave may be potentially dangerous—but on the whole they are obedient and loyal, if somewhat lazy and childlike. Is this too benign a picture? Perhaps, for almost all our information, as already mentioned, comes from owners or former owners. But the ambiguity of the psychology of slaves can also be seen in the varied reactions of slaves to their role of ritual victim.

Over most of the Northwest Coast a basic part of many rituals was the destruction of property, which sometimes meant the killing of a slave. How did slaves react to the prospect of being killed? We have data on slave reactions from four groups.

> Sitka: A slave who is to be ritually killed flees to the Hudson's Bay Company post for protection (Krause 1956, 41); on another occasion a slave submits "philosophically" (Kotzebue 1830, 54);
>
> Stikine: Twelve slaves submit willingly to ritual killing at the death of their owner, preferring it to service under his heir (Gordon 1880, 69–70);
>
> Haida: A slave flees ritual death and seeks sanctuary with missionaries (Collison 1915, 139);
>
> Quileute: Slaves are not killed at a titleholder's funeral (the most common sacrificial occasion for ritual killing in the area) "unless the slaves asked to go with their master" (Pettit 1950, 17).

Slaves had quite different reactions to impending ritual death. Although some may consider it suspect, the last quote does reflect a common, albeit not exclusive, feature of the psychology of slaves everywhere: loyalty to the master and a desire to continue in the status of the ultimate dependent—that of slave—even after death.

Masters
Who Owned Slaves?

> None but the king and chief have slaves, the common people being prevented from holding them, either from their inability to purchase them, or as I am rather inclined to think, from its being considered the privilege of the former alone to have them, especially as all those made prisoners in war belong either to the king or the chiefs who have captured them. . . . There is probably, however, some little distinction in favor of the king, who is nearly always the commander of the expedition, as Maquina had nearly fifty male and female, in his house, a number constituting about one half of its inhabitants, comprehending those obtained by war and purchase; whereas none of the other chiefs had more than twelve. (Jewitt [1815] 1975, 65)
>
> He [Maquinna, the leading titleholder] has, in common with his chiefs, the right of holding slaves, which is not enjoyed by private individuals. (Jewitt [1815] 1975, 112–113)

Slaves were probably present in every Northwest Coast community, and so, since slavery was a relationship, were slave owners. Most of the owners of slaves were titleholders. For four of the groups in the tribal unit sample the sources state that only titleholders could own slaves (Mowachaht, Quinault) or contain statements that strongly imply this (Saanich, Twana). For only two groups does a source state that commoners were allowed to own slaves (Nuxalk, Chinook), and for the Nuxalk only titleholders are mentioned as slave owners. The other fourteen sample groups describe titleholders as owning slaves. But, while these do not explicitly deny that commoners could own slaves, they do not mention or describe any commoner slave owners. Few of the sources are as explicit as Jewitt on the subject of owners, but then few knew slavery as well as he did. It seems safe to infer that commoners rarely owned slaves anywhere and that in most communities they never owned slaves.

The reasons for this lie at the heart of Northwest Coast social and economic distinctions. One might say that only the wealthy could own slaves. But it would be equally accurate to say that only slave owners were wealthy. Wealth on the Northwest Coast was not simply a matter of possessions. The relationship between being an important titleholder and a slave owner is clear in the following passages.

> Quileute: Generally a good man was one who had many canoes, blankets, lots of food, beads, slaves, good common sense, a good talker, who did not steal, fight or quarrel. (Andrade 1928, 13)

> Quinault: The greatness of certain chiefs was measured *almost* as much by the number of their wives as by the number of slaves they owned. (Olson 1936, 108; emphasis mine)

> Chinook: Concomelly is the principal man of the Chinook tribe from the circumstance of his being the most wealthy, having a number of slaves and a large stock of Hyaques Beads and other property but he has little control over them, indeed every Flat Headed Indian who possesses a slave considers himself a chief. (Merk 1931, 97)

> Central Nuu-chah-nulth: Formerly almost every well-born native owned a slave, and some of the chiefs had five or six. A slave was considered a useful and honourable possession, and if sold or lost was replaced immediately by another. (Sproat 1868, 89)

Titleholders inherited their positions, especially in the northern part of the culture area, but although they inherited the rights to certain titles they had to validate them—the purpose of some of the more important potlatches. Slaves played an important role in amassing the wealth necessary to validate a title and were often an important part of the wealth given away or destroyed at a title validation. And their possession continued to be a significant marker of a man's importance and status. Possession of slaves also reflected spiritual worth or power: Yakutat informants told De Laguna that you know people are good when they have lots of slaves (De Laguna 1972, 471) and that a man was assisted by spirits because he was "a big rich man with lots of slaves" (p. 711), and among the Puyallup-Nisqually a man with a particularly powerful spirit would be one who owned slaves; "he was important" (Smith 1940, 68). It is also worth recalling that in the list of a Quileute "good man's" attributes, items of material wealth appear ahead of personal qualities. It is not that wealth is more important but that it is the tangible evidence of such qualities.

We must be careful about one aspect of "ownership": most of the sources appear to indicate that slaves were held by owners as individual property. This was not necessarily the case. Oberg (1973, 30) makes it quite clear that for the Chilkat, slaves were the common property of the house group and that the head of the house group managed all of the house group's property, including slaves, on behalf of and for the benefit of the entire group. Something like this is implied in Jewitt's remarks about Mowachaht slave ownership quoted above, when he says that slave ownership "is not enjoyed by private individuals" but by titleholders. By private individuals Jewitt means commoners, but he is also recognizing that titleholders represent, lead, and are responsible for their kinship group. It may very well be that Maquinna and other Northwest Coast titleholders held slaves on behalf of their kin groups rather than as individual owners.

Most of the references in the sources describe owners as adult, male titleholders. Female titleholders frequently have slaves assigned to them as servants and attendants. Most of the time we cannot be certain whether the woman owned the slave or slaves in question or merely had the use of her father's, mother's brother's, or husband's slaves. Kin group ownership would solve this problem, for, especially in the north, titleholder women had high status and would certainly have been able to claim the privilege of benefiting from the kin group's slaves.

Attitudes toward Slaves

The attitudes of owners toward slaves were probably often as contradictory as the sources themselves. For example, on the same page Boas says of Tsimshian masters and slaves: "The relationship between master and slave is often described as one of great friendliness, the master taking good care of the slave. . . . Slaves are described as standing in fear of their master" (1916, 435).

The material on the character of slaves obviously tells us as much about the master's attitudes. Slaves were not highly thought of and were known to be lazy, careless, and childlike. However, individual slaves might have good relationships with their owners. Masters who treated their slaves well were approved of by fellow community members, and harsh treatment often met with disapproval. This is clearly stated in the sources for four sample groups: kindness was approved among the Yakutat and Chilkat and harshness disapproved among the Saanich and Puyallup-Nisqually. There is no reason to doubt that these attitudes were widespread in the region. But whatever fellow community members might think about someone's treatment of his slaves, as has already been emphasized, no one denied the master's right to do as he pleased with his property. There were no codes to regulate or curb a master's acts. Even the most favored slave was still subject to his or her master's whims. The Stikine principal titleholder, Shakes, owned many slaves to some of whom he assigned other slaves. One even had the use of a canoe as well. When this slave bragged that Shakes would never do anything to him, Shakes had him killed during a ceremony (Olson 1967, 54).

Normally reasonable treatment of slaves is no more than prudence since slaves are valuable property and only a slave in good condition is a useful worker. Yet sometimes the sources do reflect a master's awareness that slaves are fellow human beings as well: among the Puyallup-Nisqually cranial deformation was practiced and a titleholder would have an infant slave's head deformed because he would be "ashamed to know that a child was growing up in his house without being properly cared for" (Smith 1940, 185). Slaves, however, could just as easily fall victim to their role as property in their owner's relations with other titleholders. In July 1838 two Kaigani women visiting Fort Simpson had a quarrel and fought: "They both hold themselves up as women of consequence and as is customary among them on such occasions proposed killing a slave on each side in order to make up the matter by showing who was the richest and could best afford the loss" (Fort Simpson Journal 1838–1840, fol. 33d). This was not an isolated incident, for in September of the same year some visiting Masset

> [had] a quarrel among themselves and as is customary with them on such occasions, they were going to kill a poor slave boy. . . . [The Hudson's Bay Company men interfered.] They then tore in pieces blankets, other articles and a large Copper, to the value of ten blankets on each side and gave them away or as they call it threw it away. These people are now poor and can ill afford such a sacrifice, but such is their pride to show who can afford to throw away most that they strip themselves and will be in want for their folly afterwards. Slaves are of high value and killing one on each side is reckoned a grand thing among them, when a quarrel is to be made up. The [Tsimshians] opposed killing the slave today and recommended giving away other property, no doubt expecting to come in for some share of the fragments. (Fort Simpson Journal 1838–1840, fol. 53)[13]

Slaves were also an extension of their masters. That is, just as their masters were the sole beneficiaries of their labor and other activities, they were responsible for their misdeeds as well. Slaves also often accompanied their masters on war expeditions (in at least eight of the tribal sample units), and we know for a number of these that any captives taken by the slave became the property of the master. Acknowledgment of the master's responsibility for the slave's other acts is less widespread in the sources, but we do know, for example, that in December 1840 Shakes paid the Kaigani compensation for a killing done by one of his slaves (Fort Stikine Journal 1840–1842).

As suggested by the quotations from the Fort Simpson journals and substantiated by numerous sources, pride of place or pride in rank was an important element in the typical titleholder's personality. Insults real or imagined were mortifying and titleholders had to avenge them or lose face. Even insulting a slave could have serious consequences, for a Gispakloats (Tsimshian) was killed "after having made insulting remarks about a slave in the owner's hearing" (Garfield 1939, 183). Some of the ramifications of an insult (for both master and slave) are brought out in the following account on an incident that took place at Fort Stikine in December 1840. Shakes, his wife, and a slave attempted to enter the fort to get some rum. Shakes scuffled with the gatekeeper and got two cuts on the face. He bled profusely.

> There was immediately a buzz amongst the Indians—Shakes called for a canoe and hastened to his lodge—where on arrival he immediately ordered five of his slaves to be murdered; they fortunately had rec'd notice of what had happened and had all run away with the exception of one poor wretch who concealed herself in his house—was found and immediately murdered. . . . [N]ot more than five or ten minutes after the affair occurred [we] saw the remains of the unfortunate slave hauled down by the hair of the head and thrown into the sea. Shakes harangued the Indians and called them all to come and attack the Fort with him but none listened to him. . . . Shakes is trying all he can to get up a party but few seems inclined to join him. . . . Shakes destroyed property including his slave to the value of about 25 Beavers to show his anger and grief. . . . Shakes' son has been here several times and says his father wants to hang himself sometimes and will neither eat nor drink and when he looks at his face he is like a madman. (Fort Stikine Journal 1840–1842, fols. 22–22d)

A little later Shakes is invited to come to the fort. He tells the factor that the natives are laughing at him and that he will need ten blankets to make them stop. The factor gives Shakes the blankets, obviously needing his goodwill for the sake of the trade. Shakes gives signs that he is not truly satisfied with ten blankets, but the affair then peters out.

It is probable that the four slaves that escaped immediate death were not killed. There are several statements in various Tlingit sources that indicate that if slaves scheduled for ritual killing could successfully hide until the ceremony was over, they simply resumed their lives as slaves. Sometimes titleholders even connived at such evasions, especially in the case of favorite slaves (Krause 1956, 280). But, as many sources makes clear, many slaves were killed.

One more account involving Shakes will illustrate the varying treatment of slaves by different masters and the reactions of slaves to this treatment. Sir George Simpson says of Shakes that he was

said to be very cruel to his slaves, whom he frequently sacrificed in pure wantonness, in order to show how great a man he was. On the recent occasion of
a house-warming, he exhibited as part of the festivities the butchery of five
slaves; and at another time, having struck a white man in a fit of drunkenness
and received a pair of black eyes for his pains, he ordered a slave to be shot, by
way at once of satisfying his own wounded honor and apologizing to the person
who he had assaulted. His rival (Qualkay) [the second-ranking Stikine title-
holder], on the contrary, was possessed of such kindness of heart, that on grand
holidays he was more ready to emancipate his slaves than to destroy them; yet,
strange to say, many bondmen used to run away from Qualkay, while none attempted to escape from Shakes; an anomaly which, however, was easily explained, inasmuch as the one would pardon the recaptured fugitives, and the
other would torture and murder them. (1847, 2:212–213)

Shakes was not motivated by "pure wantonness" as the occasions cited by
Simpson were among those when a titleholder of his importance was expected to kill a slave. Nevertheless, this quote does indicate both Shakes's attitude and Qualkay's response to pressure from Europeans to end slave killing.

We can sum up by saying that although owners did recognize that their
slaves were fellow human beings, their main attitude toward slaves was that
slaves were wealth. As the Sitka chief who obtained a magical box asked of
it, "Let me be wealthy, let me have five slaves" (Swanton 1908, 448).

The Shame of Slavery

"You are a great slave." This is their greatest term of reproach. (Said of the
Lower Skeena Tsimshian, *Church Missionary Intelligencer* 1858, 273–274)

The word "slave" is used commonly as a term of reproach. If a man acts meanly
or is niggardly in his distributions of property . . . , it is said that he has a
"slave's heart." Next to a "heart of water" which means a coward, the "heart of a
slave" is the most opprobrious epithet. (Said of the Central Nuu-chah-nulth,
Sproat 1868, 89)

Particularly in the northern part of the culture area, where matrilineal descent groups were the basis of social organization, people were often said to be
"ashamed" that fellow descent group members were slaves, and there seems
to have been some obligation to redeem such a person from slavery (see table
A-5). Sometimes this even extended to people from other linguistic units who
belonged to the same moiety.

This shame at having kin enslaved could also be exploited in the maneu-
vering and striving for rank that marked much of the activity of titleholders
as well. This can be seen in a case among the Lower Skeena Tsimshian, reported by Garfield (1939, 272), when a Gitandu titleholder employed the hu-

miliation of slavery to break a rich and powerful lineage in his local group. He told the head of the lineage that he wished to marry one of the women in the lineage. This request was granted, but as soon as the marriage took place he sold his wife as a slave to a Stikine titleholder. Her relatives redeemed her and the Gitandu titleholder asked to marry her again. Her maternal uncles felt that they could not refuse his request and, once more, she was sold as a slave. Her lineage redeemed her a second time. Her former husband announced once more that he wanted her for his wife. Before the third marriage her lineage gave a feast and announced that, for them, she was dead. If she was sold into slavery again they would not redeem her or use her name again. She was sold a third time and never returned to her family. Her kin have not used her name since her enslavement. The Gitandu titleholder was successful in ruining her family, since he forced them to use all of their accumulated wealth to obtain the woman's release from slavery and then left them with the permanent stigma of slavery in the family history.

Far to the south, the Lummi are said to have attempted to try to capture members of important families to humiliate them (Stern 1934, 98). And something similar may have been going on when a Haida man sold his new Tsimshian wife into slavery when they arrived back at his home after their marriage (Fort Simpson Journal 1838–1840, fols. 14–14d).

Even if a slave was successful in an escape attempt, a safe return home was not the end of his problems. For example, the Skagit refused to allow a Skagit man who had been a slave of the Duwamish to return to his natal community after he escaped (Suttles 1974, 396). Escaping and returning home or redemption by kin did not end a person's slavery. At least one additional step was needed to regain one's former status. In most, if not all, Northwest Coast societies it was necessary to validate one's return to free status by holding a feast and giving away property. The sources indicate that this was definitely or probably the case for fifteen of the twenty sample groups (see table A-5). Given that such feasts and property distributions were universally the method of publicly validating social status in the culture area, it is almost certain that the practice prevailed in all groups. For some of the northern groups and for at least some Central Coast Salish, this ceremony is explicitly described as "washing away" or "cleansing" the stain of slavery. Similar attitudes probably prevailed throughout the region. The necessity to mark one's departure from slave status with a distribution of property meant, of course, that only titleholders were likely to be able to regain a place in their natal community. Ordinary people and their relatives would have had a much more difficult time amassing the property necessary for such a ceremony. The case of a Fort Rupert Kwakiutl boy who escaped from the Haida and managed to get back to Fort Rupert gives us insight into both attitudes and the costs of restoration. Some at Fort Rupert wanted to keep the boy in slavery, but his father came forward and gave out fifty blankets to wash off the shame (Boas 1916–1931,

65, A720). Although Boas does not date this incident, fifty blankets was probably the price of a slave.

In most, if not all, Northwest Coast societies former slaves were stigmatized. This is clearly the case in sixteen of the sample groups and probably the case in three others. In the remaining case (Klallam) the data are ambiguous; some sources suggest little or no stigma, while others indicate that there was the usual stigma. Dawson's comments about Haida slaves probably apply to many held all over the coast: "Slaves sometimes regain their freedom by running away, but should they return to their native place they are generally so much despised that their lives are rendered miserable" (1880,132).

The poor welcome sometimes afforded such returning slaves is illustrated by the following newspaper account.

> Two Somenos [Halkomelem Salish from southern Vancouver Island] Indians, who, when very young had been carried off as slaves by the Stekin [Stikine Tlingit] Indians, lately found their way back to the place of their nativity, to the great astonishment of their friends. The captives had been so long away, that they had lost all remembrance of their home, but being informed by an old Stekin woman that they had belonged to the Somenos tribe, they determined to escape, and at length succeeded. On their arrival at Somenos, however, the Indians having a custom that a man once a slave had lost caste, and can never again be recognized as a freeman, they were treated with the greatest contumely and neglect, and would probably have been re-expatriated, had not a noble-hearted savage named Louis, who had been a slave once himself, taken pity on them, and given them shelter in his wigwam. (*Daily British Colonist*, 2 July 1864)

As described previously, in all Northwest Coast societies there was a permanent stigma attached to having been a slave. Former slave status seems always to have been remembered by one's fellows, and even those who had feasted their way back to acceptability seem always to have been in danger of disgrace. There is much evidence, which will be discussed in chapter 11, that even in the recent past former slave status has adversely affected people's lives. In aboriginal and early contact times this was also the case. For example, one Kwakwaka'wakw family history tells us that one descent group was originally descended from slaves. When one of its titleholders had three Coppers broken against him in a feast, he did not have the wealth to respond to such a large-scale property destruction. Because of this he reverted to slave status and was too ashamed to attend any more feasts (Boas 1921, 1094–1116).

It was very hard to escape a slave past. There are accounts of slave children being "adopted" by titleholders and of slave women of formerly high rank becoming the "wives" of their owners. There is good reason to believe that most, perhaps all, of these adoptions and marriages occurred in the last half of the nineteenth century when population decline and social change combined to force titleholders to seek heirs, spouses, and supporters in new and

unusual places. But even then marriage and adoption did not completely re-
move slave status: "A man now living at Metlakatla is the son of a Tlingit
woman who was captured by the Tsimshian and who became the chief's wife.
While the woman lost her captive status by this marriage, her son is still spoken of as of slave origin" (Garfield 1939, 272).

All of this suggests that to describe slavery as a stigma is appropriate to the
meaning of that term. It is true that there is little evidence that enslavement
literally involved the permanent physical marking of a slave. Averkieva (1966,
108) does speculate that at times slaves were actually branded; she cites no
evidence to support her speculation, however. But it is certainly the case that
slavery marked the slave with an invisible stain, a sort of birthmark (or rebirth
mark) acquired at the time of the slave's natal alienation from her or his kinship group.

The intersection of slavery and the practice of artificial cranial deformation is also of interest in the context of slavery as stigma. Cranial deformation
was widely practiced in the culture area.[14] A number of historical and ethnographic sources note that slaves often had a different shape of head than did
their masters: "roundheads" are said to have been the slaves of "flatheads"
and vice versa. Since there is good evidence that adherence to a particular
style of head shape marked the boundary of a multicommunity, multicultural
social system that involved, among other things, elite intermarriages, those of
different head shape were easily marked as outsiders and hence, in the way
stigma seems to work, easy to despise. Unfortunately for this view, as will be
shown in chapter 5, most slaves whose ethnic origins can be identified came
from communities relatively close to their masters' communities. Thus it is
probable that master and slave shared the same head shape. Certainly this was
frequently the case. The problem is compounded by the fact that some form
of cranial deformation was practiced from the Haihais and Heiltsuk south to
the Chinook (and beyond along the Oregon coast). To identify a slave as a
"flathead" only tells us that he was probably born in the large portion of the
culture area that followed the practice of head deformation (or was from one
of the groups that bordered the culture area that also practiced head deformation). To identify a slave as a "roundhead" says that he came from the far
north of the region (Tlingit, Haida, Tsimshian, Haisla) or from outside the
culture area. Identifying slaves as "roundheads" or "flatheads" is not a description of who was or was not actually a slave but is both the European observers' and the native informants' reaction to the stigma of slavery. The despised, stigmatized person is different, and if some physical indication of this
difference can be found, so much the better. Difference in head shape, which
probably did define who did and did not belong to the local regional social
system, was taken up as a mark of slave status even when many slaves had
head shapes that revealed that they had once belonged to the local social network. This use of a physical marker of slave status, even though it was a false

one, and speaking of the "stain" of slavery and of washing away the stain reveal how profoundly stigmatizing it was to be a slave.

The complexities of freeing slaves, ransoming a relative from slavery, and the permanent stigma of having been a slave can all be seen in the following Tsimshian example reported by Garfield: a Gilutsau (Lower Skeena Tsimshian) titleholder owned a woman who had been of titleholder rank and was from the nearby Coast Tsimshian village of Kitasoo. At the naming ceremony of his daughter the titleholder freed this slave. He did not free her daughter but sold her into another community. She was eventually bought by a woman of her own clan, although the slave did not belong to her purchaser's lineage or even local group. Her purchaser "adopted" her. The woman who adopted her felt that it was a disgrace to her clan for a clan relative to be in slavery. But "the older people at Port Simpson remember this girl and say that no one would marry her because of her former slave status. She died a spinster, a very rare occurrence for a Tsimshian" (Garfield 1939, 274).

Paths Out of Slavery

As already described, slavery was a permanent status in all Northwest Coast societies. War captives became slaves, and neither they nor their children (if any) could normally expect amelioration of this status. Neither captives nor their children could expect to be adopted into their master's kin group or to be gradually transformed into commoners. But few cultures are completely rigid about such practices, and those on the Northwest Coast were not exceptional in this regard. From time to time at least a few slaves were able to leave slavery: some were ransomed by their kin, some escaped from their masters and attempted to return home, and some were freed by their masters.

Ransom

One way out of slavery was to be ransomed by one's kin. All of the twenty sample groups either definitely or probably ransomed group members from slavery. But it is clear that no attempt was made to ransom every group member taken in war. The available data suggest that the cost of ransoming a prisoner could be as much as ten times the usual value of a slave and that other slaves were often a part of the ransom. The sources suggest that in most instances only titleholders had any hope of being ransomed. Jenness (n.d., 64–65) indicates, for example, that only titleholders were ransomed by the Saanich, and where the status of a ransomed slave is mentioned for other groups it is nearly always that of titleholder. As former titleholders were held as slaves in at least thirteen of the sample groups, many titleholders were not ransomed either.

Titleholders could fail to be ransomed because their kin could not locate them, because their kin were indifferent to their fate, or because their price was too high.

> Chief of the Fort Ruperts [Kwakiutl] was waited on by a Stickeen tyhee [Sti-kine Tlingit titleholder] who came for the purpose of redeeming two of his tribe held in captivity by the Fort Ruperts. Chief of the latter tribe offered to give them up in exchange for 100 blankets, two muskets and keg of powder, but ransom considered exorbitant and declined. (*Daily British Colonist*, 15 April 1861)

In the northern area prices for slaves ranged from thirty-five to sixty blankets in the 1850s and 1860s. The price asked here was a bit over this in blanket equivalents. We also know the size of a ransom paid by the Saanich to recover a titleholder girl captured by the Nanaimo of the central eastern coast of Vancouver Island. Sometime in the nineteenth century the Saanich paid one older female slave, several goat's wool blankets, several baskets of camas roots, and one or two guns (Jenness n.d., 66). Clearly, this was not simply the purchase of a slave.

The ransoming of captive titleholders was but one part of the complex relationships within the titleholding stratum of the various Northwest Coast communities. Titleholders from different communities were linked to each other in various ways: they intermarried, hosted each other at feasts, and so on. They also fought with each other. The various communities involved included those speaking the same or different languages as well as belonging to the same or different "tribes." Tribes on the Northwest Coast were not political entities and are in many ways the invention of Europeans, including scholars. The most important ties were descent group allegiances, and not even common community residence could break these down. Class allegiances were also important: titleholders did support each other even as they engaged in the fiercest rivalries.

The capture of a titleholder brought shame to the person and his or her descent group. The fullest discussion of descent group shame and how it motivated titleholder ransom is found in Olson's (1967) Tlingit monograph. Olson points out that one's family has an obligation to ransom any person taken captive. But he also makes it clear that it was usually titleholders who were ransomed, although a family might lack the wealth to do so. If this was the case, they sought help from other segments of the matriclan, for the enslavement of a titleholder reflected badly on the entire clan. Even if a person was ransomed, the fact of their former captivity might be brought up by nonclan members, even in later generations. To prevent this the clan redeeming the slave might pay a higher ransom than was asked. This would probably keep the captor's clan and their descendants quiet, but people in other clans might still bring the matter up in the event of a quarrel (Olson 1967, 53–54; for the Sitka, see Niblack 1890, 249, and for the Lower Skeena Tsimshian, Garfield 1939, 273–274). Apparently the only thing that kept early twentieth-century Tlingit from continually bringing up the shame of the past slavery of others was that virtually every clan had lost some members to slavery.

One aspect of the rivalry between titleholders was the use of enslavement to shame and even destroy rivals. Disgracing rivals by capture seems to have been a regular part of the tool kit of rivalry among the northern groups. The actions of the Gitandu Tsimshian titleholder against a rival lineage when he repeatedly sold his wife into slavery are described above. But this use of the shame of slavery could be turned on the captors. When an enslaved Oyalidox titleholder was ransomed from the Q!uanal (a Nuxalk village), the ransom that was paid was so heavy that the Q!uanal feared that they would be considered the Oyalidox titleholder's slaves. To prevent this they gave him a box containing dancing paraphernalia "in order to equal him and to avoid being considered his inferiors" (Boas et al. 1923, 165–166). Farther south the data are less full, but we do know that the Lummi attempted to capture members of important families in other groups in order to humiliate them (Stern 1934, 98). Among the neighboring Saanich, Jenness (n.d., 64–65) notes that titleholder males who were captured by nearby Salish-speaking groups were nearly always ransomed, although even a brief enslavement was a blot on the man's record. Saanich titleholder girls who were captured by nearby Salish-speaking groups often escaped slavery because they became the wives of titleholder men in the captor's group. This suggests a connection between war and marriage among the Coast Salish not unlike that described by Boas (1966, 53) for the Kwakwaka'wakw among whom the term for "war" (*wi'na*) is also associated with marriage between members of different communities or even different descent groups.[15] Boas writes as if he were describing the traditional marriage practices for all segments of Kwakwaka'wakw society when he talks about wives being spoken of as "obtained in war," but it is clear from his description that he is talking about titleholder marriages. The link between war, titleholder marriage, and slavery is stronger among the Kwakwaka'wakw than so far suggested here.

In Kwakwaka'wakw titleholder marriage arrangements, prestations were made by the groom to his father-in-law, who was expected to make return prestations of greater value at a later date. According to Drucker,

> The essential idea of the repayment . . . was that a man "bought his daughter back from her husband." After this payment had been made the woman might stay with her husband or not, as she pleased; if she left him, he had to buy her all over again (though for a smaller amount than the first time) to get her back. If a woman were not redeemed, informants say, it would be a great shame to her family, for she would be little better than a slave. Conversely, a redeemed wife was highly honored. Women boasted of the number of times they had been redeemed. And with the proceeds of the payment the husband gave a potlatch (often the greatest of his career), thereby "raising the names" of his father-in-law, his wife, and himself. (1950, 279)

Drucker's comments apply to the Fort Rupert Kwakiutl and to the other Northern Wakashan-speaking groups he studied (Koskimo, Oowekeeno, Heilt-suk, Haihais, and Haisla). He also applies them to the Salish-speaking Nuxalk. McIlwraith's discussion of Nuxalk marriage certainly emphasizes the importance of the father-in-law's "repurchase" of his daughter. Indeed, title-holder marriage among the Nuxalk even as recently as the 1920s seems to have been unthinkable without it. Unfortunately, McIlwraith does not say anything directly about the status of the wife if she is not "repurchased." He does, however, note the use of the vocabulary of warfare in marriage arrange-ments and ceremonies. The relationship among warfare, slavery, and marriage established for the Northern Wakashan speakers probably holds for the Nu-xalk as well (see McIlwraith 1948, 1:392, 406–416).[16]

The need for bride repurchase reinforced the tendency toward strata en-dogamy. A poor or low-ranking man could not afford to have his daughter marry into a titleholding family. Boas (1946, 199–200) reports from the Kwakwaka'wakw that when one low-ranking man's daughter married a title-holder, the man was unable to make a return of the blankets that the title-holder had given him at the marriage. He was thus thought of as a slave of the titleholder until he could repay them.

North of the Wakashan-speaking area, bride repurchase was not practiced, but we still find connections among warfare, marriage, and slavery. Some-times captured titleholder women are made wives, and sometimes wives are made slaves. In the first instance, the shame of slavery is avoided by a woman and her kin group because a titleholder in her captor's group finds an advan-tage in making her a wife rather than a slave. Perhaps he desires peace with her group or she has inherited prerogatives and titles so important that he deems it wiser to marry her. In the second instance, enslaving a wife can be used to humiliate rivals in an especially effective way. Selling a woman into slavery in a matrilineal society attacks the descent group at its core, by re-moving the people who recruit new members to the group.[17]

Escape

Attempted slave escapes are found in fourteen of the twenty groups in the tribal unit sample (see table A-4). Only for the Puyallup-Nisqually does a source suggest that slaves did not attempt to run away (Smith 1940, 52). It is impossible to know how common such escape attempts were or how success-ful they were. The sources for seven of the sample tribal units suggest that es-cape attempts were not common, whereas the sources for five other sample groups indicate that they were. Masters do not appear to have been greatly concerned about escape in most instances: seven of the fourteen sample units that report escape attempts also report that masters traveled alone with their slaves. One reason for this is that escape attempts were not likely to succeed. First of all, masters often pursued escaped slaves. And the escaping slave had to make his or her way not merely to another community but to his or her natal village. For, as numerous sources for many groups make clear, a slave attempting to return home was fair game and if caught would be kept as a slave by the captor. John Work, the Hudson's Bay Company man, remarked of slaves in the Skeena River area in 1835, "These poor wretches desert frequently, but as they have little chance of escaping, and are mostly taken by some other tribe, they seldom better their case, and as they have seldom an opportunity of providing themselves with arms, they are unable to defend themselves" (1945, 69–70).

Slaves attempting to return home could be a lucrative source of additional slaves, and for a few groups magical rituals to entice runaway slaves into one's hands are reported. In one reported instance among the Tsishaat, the objective of the ritual was more specific and particular slaves were targeted to be lured into running away to a new master (Sapir and Swadesh 1939, 185–209).

Even where escape attempts were not common, some slaves were determined enough to return home to kill their masters in order to do so. Five of the sample units report slaves killing masters, usually in the context of escape attempts. And as masters could be alone, away from the community, with some of their slaves, such a strategy might minimize the chance of pursuit. For example, a Nuxalk woman was held as a slave by a Tlingit group. She and a male Heiltsuk slave were taken out halibut fishing by their master. While he slept, the slaves killed him and hid the body, hoping that it would be assumed that all three had drowned. The woman eventually made it back to her natal Nuxalk village. She had been captured as a girl and returned past childbearing age (McIlwraith 1922–1924, 34). And one Saanich man escaped from his captors on northern Vancouver Island, was enslaved again as he attempted to return home, and succeeded in another escape that finally enabled him to reach his home village. Both times he had killed his master while alone with him on a hunting trip (Jenness n.d., 62).

Even though some escape attempts were successful, escape was a very uncertain way to end one's slavery for the stigma of slavery meant a poor or at least ambivalent welcome in the escapee's natal community.

Manumission

Owners had the right to free their slaves. Virtually all known manumissions occurred in ritual contexts or as a result of the termination of slavery by Canadian or American political authorities. The one exception known to me occurred among the Central Tlingit where a tradition relates that a slave girl provided food for guests during a time of famine and so saved her titleholder the embarrassment of not being able to feed his guests. The chief ordered his other slaves to bathe her to wash away her slavery. He then gave away a great deal of property and announced that he would marry her (Olson 1967, 13). The rarity of such accounts suggests that freeing slaves outside of rituals was extremely unusual. Of equal interest is the fact that the forms of washing away slavery are carefully adhered to: the person whose slave status is being terminated is washed and property is given away to validate her claim as a free person.

Because virtually all manumissions made more or less voluntarily by owners (i.e., not forced by Europeans) occurred on the occasion of ceremonies, manumission is best treated as a part of ritual and changes in ritual. Some attention is given to manumission and change in ritual in chapter 8 and fuller treatment of the topic is given in chapter 11.

Northwest Coast Slavery as a "Closed" Slave System

James L. Watson (1980, 9–13) has distinguished two major types of slavery, "open" and "closed." These are ideal types that represent the end points on a continuum. Open systems of slavery (which are common in Africa but found elsewhere as well) are characterized by the gradual absorption of slaves into the kinship and family system of their masters. It may happen that over the lifetime of the slave he or she will gradually be absorbed into the master's family, often as a junior kinsperson. Or it may be that over several generations the slave's descendants are treated more and more like junior kin until they are absorbed into the kin group of the former master as a cadet branch of the kin unit. Closed systems of slavery (which are common in Asia but found elsewhere as well) are characterized by the failure of slaves to be absorbed or adopted into the family or kinship unit of the master. Slaves are excluded from participating in the kin group. The only way out of slavery is by formal emancipation, and even then the slave is not taken into a local kinship unit but remains marked as a former slave or "freedman." Obviously these are extreme cases designed to give definitional clarity to Watson's idea. But, as he notes, many actual slave systems did conform very closely to these characterizations.

Watson explains the presence of an open or closed slave system by the suggesting that "the differences between the dominant modes of slavery that emerged . . . correspond to different concepts of property" (1980, 11). He goes on to argue that "the open mode predominated in Africa where land was plentiful and control over people was the main avenue to wealth and power. The closed mode, prevalent in Asia, is clearly a reflection of the high premium placed on land which, in turn, affects attitudes towards outsiders" (1980, 12).

All the Northwest Coast societies practiced a form of slavery that falls very near the closed end of Watson's continuum. Watson's explanation of the type of slavery practiced is designed to apply to agricultural societies. Where agricultural land is plentiful but people are scarce, resource-exploiting groups (kinship units) will need to acquire and retain people; hence open slavery. Where agricultural land is in short supply, resource-exploiting groups (kinship units) will need to restrict the people who have access to support from their lands. To see if Northwest Coast slavery supports Watson's hypothesis, we must translate his argument for agricultural societies into a more general one that will include extractive societies like those studied here.

In agricultural societies the key resource for food production is land (although we must not overlook water). Where good agricultural land is in limited or circumscribed supply, access to land will be the key to a kin group's agricultural success. Where good agricultural land is relatively easy to come by, but where people to work the land are in short supply, a sufficient and reliable labor force will be the key to a kin group's agricultural success. We can generalize this by substituting the characteristics of the key resource base exploited by a kin group for agricultural land. Land becomes an instance of the resource base.

All Northwest Coast groups exploited (by fishing, gathering, or hunting) a wide range of resources. But for most groups the most important resource was the Pacific salmon. Because salmon are anadromous and because they follow fairly predictable cycles, they are both plentiful and easy to obtain *at certain places and at certain times of the year.* This means that although the resource base offers great opportunities, it does so under quite circumscribed conditions. Most of the other resources of great importance to one or another local group are also either spatially or temporally (often both) circumscribed. Northwest Coast resources thus conform to the "scarcity" type, which, if Watson is correct, leads us to expect closed slavery, and this is what we have found.

As my subject is the Northwest Coast, another scarce resource must also be considered. Property in the form of prerogatives was a major interest of Northwest Coast titleholders: they claimed ownership, usually as family property, of songs, dances, ritual paraphernalia, myths, and names. All of these things were in short supply, and titleholders' careers were significantly motivated by the desire to validate claims to such property and by the desire to obtain additional property of this noncorporeal type. If Watson's argument is extended into this domain, closed slavery is also consistent with the scarcity of this resource. I am reluctant to go quite this far because, while salmon streams and similar natural phenomena have an existence independent of their exploiters (even though these exploiters do manipulate and otherwise act on the resource), the noncorporeal resource is produced and reproduced by the same persons who are producing and reproducing slavery. But even if the resource that forms the basis of food production is independent and can be a "cause" and noncorporeal resources are part of the same system as slavery and cannot be a "cause" of slavery in this sense, the two *are* consistent with each other. Closed slavery of the Northwest Coast type and the Northwest Coast style of ownership of and emphasis on noncorporeal property are mutually supportive parts of the same cultural system.

5
The Production of Slaves

Owners obtained their slaves in a number of ways, some much more common than others. Almost all slaves had been nonslaves, either commoners or titleholders, who were seized by force. Such seizures usually occurred in the context of intergroup fighting. The children born to a female slave were also slaves. Many slaves came to their owners by means of transactions with other owners. Such transactions included trade, the receipt of slaves as gifts at feasts and ceremonials, the inclusion of slaves as parts of marriage prestations, and the use of slaves in the prestations that normally concluded the successful negotiation of peace between two groups (see chapter 7). Slaves might also be included as a part of wergild payments, and slaves could be inherited as part of the estate of their deceased owner. Some people enslaved themselves because of extreme poverty or indebtedness. And finally, titleholders sometimes seized and enslaved members of their own local group; in some groups this may have been the common fate of orphans without close relatives. However an owner obtained a slave, that slave was ultimately the product of forcible seizure.[1]

Production by Capture

Although it has not been the focus of much attention in the anthropological literature on the region, intergroup violence was widespread and common on the Northwest Coast. Extensive reading of the historical and ethnographic literature gives the impression that whenever members of more than one group were together, there was always the danger of fighting. Even potlatches could be the occasion of violence. Such feasts and ceremonies were supposed to be free of physical strife, a peaceful time when other types of intergroup relationships prevailed. But this was not always the case. For example, on one occasion some Kwakwaka'wakw killed Heiltsuk potlatch messengers even though they were supposed to be under a universal safe conduct (McIlwraith 1948, 2: 370). Members of one group attacked another group for a variety of purposes and with various motivations. Both the ethnographic and historical record contain numerous accounts of specific incidents as well as more general traditions of fighting. A very common outcome of fighting was the taking of captives. The fate of prisoners was that they almost always became slaves, either kept as such by their captors or traded to other groups where they were kept as slaves. Capture during intergroup fighting was the most important means of slave production. This section deals first with the production of slaves as a by-product of "war" and then looks at intergroup fighting whose stated primary motivation was the taking of slaves.

Captives Taken in "War"

The term "war" has no consistent definition in the anthropological or any other literature. To some it means any sort of intercommunity violence, others confine the use of the term to armed conflicts between political units that are states, and still others fall somewhere between these two poles in their usage. The definitional problem merits careful discussion but would lead too far from the topic of slavery. I will use the term "war" here but will mean by it simply what I take to be the usual sense of the word for native informants when they spoke of war in English to outside inquirers.

The only good description of a word for war in a Northwest Coast language that I know of comes from Boas's Kwakwaka'wakw work: "*wi'na* includes not only fights between tribes or clans but also deeds of individuals who set out to kill a member or members of another group" (1966, 108). Such an all-inclusive view of intergroup violence was probably widely held in the culture area. And in this context it is quite likely that "another group" could refer not only to different communities but also to different descent groups within the same village community. Relations between descent groups and between communities were very complex and embraced a wide range of activities that larger-scale societies tend to separate and treat as economic or religious or political or military or something else. But both communities and kin groups had all of these kinds of relationships and more with each other simultaneously. The Northwest Coast societies are a classic example of and indeed one of the principal inspirations for Marcel Mauss's (1967, 1–5, 31–45) notion of the system of "total prestations" that characterized traditional kinship-based society. For example, in his discussion of the meaning of the term "wi'na" Boas goes on to note that "the same term is also used for the procedure customary in the marriage of a young man to a woman of another tribe or clan. The bride is 'obtained in war.' In tales, it is often said that she is given in order to avoid a warlike attack by visitors" (1966, 108).

Although, as noted above, intergroup violence could break out on almost any occasion when two or more groups got together, the organized military expedition was a common feature of most, probably all, Northwest Coast societies. These expeditions generally had as their object a surprise attack on another community and featured a mixture of ritual and practical precautions, a dawn assault, as much killing and looting as raider strength and victim weakness and bewilderment allowed, and a rapid retreat at the end, with the danger of pursuit by the surviving victims or their kin.[2]

The motivations for these attacks were complex. The most commonly stated reason was to revenge the death of a kinsperson. The attacked group was usually held to be responsible for the death, but this was not always the case. Economic motives, such as acquiring new territory with valuable resources, were also sometimes important.[3] Whatever the motive for a particular attack, a common outcome, in addition to any deaths, was the taking of live prisoners. Most of these captives were not killed but were taken back home by the successful raiders to become slaves.

Unfortunately, most of the sources tell us very little about how captives were transformed into slaves. The one significant exception to this suggests that captives were not regarded as slaves until several months or even a year after their capture. This was to allow enough time for their relatives to ransom them (Olson 1967, 53). As Olson implies, the possibility of ransom was largely confined to high-status captives of Tlingit origin. Such a captive's ransom would be from three to five times a slave's value. None of the other Tlingit sources known to me confirms Olson's statements on this point, but, given that it was a considerable dishonor for a titleholder family to have a member taken slave and the scant interest taken in slavery by most ethnographers of the Tlingit, such a waiting period before a captive titleholder was considered a slave is plausible. In many instances, however, it is probable that by the time successful raiders got back to their homes their captives were almost all regarded and treated as slaves. This is suggested, for example, by the fact that captives might well be quickly traded to someone from a community different from that of either the captor or the captive.

The sources are silent about any rituals or any other procedures that may have been used on the journey home to transform new captives into slaves. The torture of prisoners so familiar in eastern North America seems to have been absent. Forcible seizure itself may well have been all that was necessary under most circumstances to make a person a slave. If this was the widely accepted view in the culture area, then both captors and victims would have viewed the new prisoners as slaves and so perhaps little ritual or other reinforcement of slave status was necessary. And, as will be seen, virtually all those enslaved in such fighting were from groups that did share the same general views of the nature of slavery and its origins in capture in war.

Where were captives obtained?   Reading some of the historical sources and secondary accounts of the Northwest Coast culture area leaves the impression that long-distance military expeditions were fairly common. Drucker (1965, 75), for example, speaks of Tlingit and Haida from the northern part of the region attacking groups of Salish speakers in the Gulf of Georgia and Puget Sound, specifically asserting that such raids probably took place in pre-European times. The distance involved in such a journey is considerable. From Tlingit country south to the heart of the Gulf of Georgia/Puget Sound Salish region it is more than 1,000 kilometers. In precontact times, such a journey would also have involved Tlingit or Haida canoes passing through territories controlled by a number of groups that were both militarily strong and aggressive toward outsiders. A source's claims about the origins of captives taken in attacks must be assessed carefully. To assist in this, the sources are divided into the three categories that are used whenever problems of change may be at issue: ethnographic, pre-1845 historic, and post-1845 historic.

Almost all groups took slaves whenever possible from their relatively near neighbors. Since it is common for neighboring communities to speak the same or a very similar language and to have very similar cultures, people very often attacked and enslaved those belonging to the same language and culture as themselves. Among the twenty groups in the tribal unit sample, the sources state that for fourteen of the units there was enslavement within own language area. This includes all of the northern and central groups in the sample as well as the Klallam, Quinault, and Chinook from the southern groups. For the Quileute, Lummi, Skagit, and Puyallup-Nisqually the sources are silent on the subject. There is no record of Saanich taking slaves from fellow speakers of Straits Salish, but there is an ethnographic account of the Saanich enslaving some Cowichan, who spoke Halkomelem Salish, another cluster of Salish languages closely related to the Straits Salish language cluster (Jenness n.d., 60). Finally, Elmendorf (1960, 478–479) reports that the Twana definitely did not take slaves within the Twana speech community, but this does not rule out the possibility that they did take slaves from other non-Twana Salish speakers. We can conclude that although there may have been a few local groups who were exceptions, most groups within the culture area did enslave members of communities that were very similar to themselves in language and culture.

Northwest Coast people did not confine their enslavements to those of similar languages and cultures. They took slaves wherever and among whomever they could. But the data indicate that in the pre-European and early historic periods, intergroup fighting that led to the capture of slaves normally

Table 1.   Origin of Slaves Taken in Warfare by Tlingit Groups

	Source Type	
Group	*Ethnographic*	*Post-1845*
Yakutat	Chugach, Yakutat, Tlingit	
Chilkat	Henya, Tlingit	Coast Salish, Columbia River
Sitka	Tongass	Stikine, Nawitti
Stikine	Tsimshian	Haida, Vancouver Island, Gulf Islands, Puyallup, Makah, Cowichan
Henya	Chilkat, Stikine, Huna	
Tongas	Kitkatla	Tlawitsis
Central Tlingit	Tlingit, Tsimshian, Haida, Columbia River	
Southern Tlingit	Northern Tlingit, Southern Tlingit, Tlingit	
Tlingit	Auk	

NOTE: Nomenclature and spelling follow sources.

happened relatively close to home. Documentation of this assertion can begin with an examination of the sources of slaves for the three northern sets of local groups, the Tlingit, Tsimshian, and Haida.

The various Tlingit local groups occupied what is today the coast of the Alaska panhandle. Table 1 assembles all the available information on the origins of slaves taken in warfare by the various Tlingit groups. The relative specificity of the entries reflects the sources: where a source gives a local group as captor or victim the local group is identified; if only a broader identification is given, that is what is entered in the table. Most of the entries that come from ethnographic sources show Tlingit as having taken other Tlingit as slaves. One entry indicates that the Yakutat even enslaved members of their own local group by force (see De Laguna 1972, 469, 472, 592). The Stikine and unidentified Central Tlingit (Chilkat or Sitka?) groups held "Tsimshian" slaves, and the Tongas held slaves who originated in Kitkatla, a Coast Tsimshian local group. Both the Stikine and Tongas are Southern Tlingit groups who were relatively close to Tsimshian country and who had long-standing relationships of various kinds with one or another Tsimshian group. In addition to Tsimshian slaves, Central Tlingit groups are also recorded as having taken "Haida" slaves. The Haida, like the Tsimshian, occupy territory adjacent to some Tlingit groups. The Chugach are just north of Yakutat territory. Thus all but one of the non-Tlingit entries come from societies located not far from Tlingit country. The exception is a considerable one, for the Columbia River is more than 1,300 kilometers south of Central Tlingit territory.

Innokentii Veniaminov (1972) included a number of observations on the Tlingit (probably those around Sitka) in a report on the condition of the Russian Orthodox church in Russian America in 1840. He claimed that the Tlingit held slaves from the Columbia River region that they had taken in war. Veniaminov's work is generally well regarded as a source of information about the Tlingit of early nineteenth-century Russian America. Nevertheless, I am extremely skeptical of this particular claim. It is possible that some slaves were obtained by trade from this area prior to 1840, but there is no other evidence that any Tlingit war party went south of Coast Tsimshian territory before the 1840s.

The historical sources from the post-1845 period suggest that by this time some Tlingit warriors had begun to go farther afield in their quest for slaves. For this period there are some well-documented cases of northern groups raiding down into the Puget Sound area, although it is doubtful that Tlingit warriors actually traveled as far south as the Columbia River to capture slaves. The Puget Sound and Gulf of Georgia region had attractions for Tlingit and other northerners other than slave raiding: Fort Victoria was built on the southern end of Vancouver Island in 1843 and quickly became more than just another Hudson's Bay Company post. When slaves were taken by northerners in the south it often seems to have been as a sideline to a trip to Victoria, something to do at the end of a visit to add to the profits.

A look at the origins of slaves taken in warfare by the various Haida or Tsimshian local groups about which we have information reveals the same pattern. Tables 2 and 3 assemble this information for the Haida and Tsimshian, respectively. The ethnographic records show that Haida groups enslaved members of other Haida local groups and persons belonging to the closest blocs of non-Haida, the Tlingit to their north, the Tsimshian to the east, and various Wakashan speakers to the southeast and immediate south. The same pattern holds for the pre-1845 sources. It is only with the post-1845 sources that we find long-distance raids. The Lequiltok are the southernmost of the Kwakwala speakers and occupied territories at the extreme southern end of Johnstone Strait along the route that the Haida and others took to reach Victoria. The Cowichan were on southern Vancouver Island near present-day Duncan and the Nisqually in Puget Sound. Again I am not certain that "Columbia River" literally means that; it is more likely that it means

Table 2.   Origin of Slaves Taken in Warfare by Haida Groups

| | Source Type | | |
Group	Ethnographic	Pre-1845	Post-1845
Kaigani	Henya	Tsimshian	Ninstints
Skidegate	Haida	Tongass, Lower Skeena Tsimshian	
Masset	Ninstints, Tsimshian	Tongass	Cowichan
Ninstints	Masset	Sanya, Nawitti	
Haida	Kaigani, Skidegate, Haida, Tlingit, Niska, Gispakloats, Gitxala, Tsimshian, Kitlope, Kokoyet, Bella Bella, Northern Kwakiutl, Fort Rupert Kwakiutl, Kwakwaka'wakw	Ninstints, Sitka, Sanya, Kitkatla, Fort Simpson Tsimshian, Tsimshian, Milbanke Sound	Ninstints, Tsimshian, Nakwakto, Lequiltok, Nisqually, Columbia River

NOTE: Nomenclature and spelling follow sources.

from the south, that is, Puget Sound and environs. The Tsimshian data also reveal a pattern of war and slave taking fairly close to home. Again neighbors (including other Tsimshian) and near neighbors constitute the list of source groups. This is true not only for the ethnographic sources but for both historic periods as well. The new feature here is the appearance of Athapaskans in the record. With the exception of one group, the various Athapaskan speakers lived inland, not on the coast. Thus the taking of Athapaskan slaves would have meant expeditions on foot rather than by canoe. The Kitwankool are an upriver Gitksan Tsimshian group; the Carrier were their eastern Athapaskan-speaking neighbors. The "Athapaskan" entry probably includes many Tsetsaut, an Athapaskan group that once occupied the Upper Nass River and some adjacent small rivers and saltwater inlets. They were overwhelmed by Niska and Tlingit expansion and the few remaining individuals absorbed by the Niska in the 1880s (Boas 1895a; Emmons 1911).

The pattern is the same for the other groups in the region. Table 4 assembles the information on slaves taken in warfare by the various Salish-speaking groups. Except for the Nuxalk, the list is not very extensive. This reflects both the quality of Nuxalk ethnography (McIlwraith) and the fact that in this, as in many other features of culture, the Nuxalk exhibit a "northern" pattern rather than a Salish pattern of Northwest Coast culture. But like other

Table 3. *Origin of Slaves Taken in Warfare by Tsimshian Groups*

	Source Type		
Group	Ethnographic	Pre-1845	Post-1845
Lower Skeena Tsimshian	Kitwanga, Klemtu, Kitlope, Bella Bella, Haida, Tlingit	Skidegate	Niska
Kitkatla	Nakwakto, Nakomgilisala, Tlatlasikwala, Kwicksutaineuk, Fort Rupert Kwakiutl, Kwakwaka'wakw, Nuxalk	Oyalitoch, Goasila, Nawitti, Skidegate	Nuxalk
Kitselas	Kitwanga, Kitlope, Bella Bella, Haida		Niska
Kitwankool	Carrier		
Tsimshian	Kokyet, Nawitti, Kwakwaka'wakw, Haida, Tlingit, Athapaskan, Tsimshian		

NOTE: Nomenclature and spelling follow sources.

northern and central groups, the Nuxalk were fighting and taking slaves from their neighbors and near neighbors. I have not reproduced similar tables for the various Wakashan speakers or for Chinook, Quileute, or Quinault, for the pattern is the same for all of these groups.

As a final way to consider the problem, table 5 assembles data on two groups, Kitkatla Tsimshian and Nuxalk, that show both the groups from which they took slaves and the groups who took slaves from them. Once again, we can see that fighting is between neighbors and near neighbors. It should be remembered that neighbors and near neighbors also intermarried, traded, and feasted with each other. Warfare and its accompaniment, enslavement, were merely another facet of the complex relationship between neighboring communities in this region.

The preceding analysis shows that the ethnographic and historical data overwhelmingly support the earlier generalization that Northwest Coast fighting and enslavement occurred primarily between neighbors and near neighbors and that the more spectacular long-distance journeys from the north to the south were relatively late in time and were not a major source of slaves. Furthermore, if we divide the datable records of slave raids in pre-1845 and

Table 4. *Origin of Slaves Taken in Warfare by Salishan Groups*

	Source Type		
Group	Ethnographic	Pre-1845	Post-1845
Nuxalk	Nuxalk, Oyalitoch, Bella Bella, Kitkatla, Kwicksutaineuk, Fort Rupert Kwakiutl, Lequiltok, Kwakwaka'wakw, Chilcotin		Kwakwaka'wakw
Comox	Comox		
Sechelt	Lequiltok		
Cowichan	Lequiltok	Chilliwack, Pilalt	
Island Halkomelem	Comox, Kwakwaka'wakw		
Musqueqm		Chilliwack	
Klallam	Sooke		
Satsop	Chehalis		
Chehalis	Satsop		

NOTE: Nomenclature and spelling follow sources.

Table 5. *Warfare Resulting in Enslavement, by and against Kitkatla and Nuxalk*

Group	Take Slaves from	Slaves Taken by
Kitkatla	Nuxalk, Kwakwaka'wakw, Skidegate, Fort Rupert Kwakiutl, Nakomgilisala, Nawitti, Tlatlasikwala, Nakwakto, Kwicksutaineuk, Goasila, Oyalitoch	Nuxalk, Kwakwaka'wakw, Haida, Tongas
Nuxalk	Nuxalk, Kitkatla, Oyalitoch, Bella Bella, Fort Rupert Kwakiutl, Lequiltok, Kwicksutaineuk, Kwakwaka'wakw, Chilcotin	Nuxalk, Kitkatla, Nakwakto, Carrier

NOTE: Nomenclature and spelling follow sources.

post-1845 periods, we find that in the earlier period almost all groups raided within their own geographic region (86 percent) while after 1845 the proportion of raiders and raided who fell within the same region was much lower (41 percent). (These proportions are significantly different by the χ^2 test, $p < .01$.)

What types of people were enslaved?   When a war party attacked a settlement, it is clear that their initial efforts were concentrated on killing or driving into retreat the men of the community who were of fighting age. Others might very well be killed, but adult men were the primary targets for at least three reasons. They were the members of the community most dangerous to the attackers. It was they who might turn the raiders' victory into defeat and who would form the initial pursuit of the attacking party. In addition, the heads of adult men were probably the most desirable to take back home as trophies of success (most, if not all, groups in the culture area took heads in war; scalping although known was not widespread) and adult men were also the most likely to own important prerogatives, songs, dances, or rituals. The killer of the owner of such noncorporeal property might claim it for his own. By contrast, where the sources indicate a preference, women and children were preferred as slaves. For fourteen of the twenty groups in the tribal unit sample this is the case (see table A-3). The sources for the other six groups do not indicate a preference. A preference for enslaving women and children is not surprising. They were less dangerous to their captors than men, both on the journey home and after the return of the raiders to their home community. This does not mean, however, that adult men were always killed rather than enslaved. Some previously free men were enslaved, and it seems clear that often many of the slaves taken in a successful raid were already slaves. This is both because slaves were much less likely to fight and because slaves frequently slept in the most exposed parts of the community or house and were thus the most likely victims of a lightning raid.

But if a likely outcome of an attack on a community was that slaves would change owners by force rather than by peaceable transaction, this does not mean that other members of the settlement were immune from enslavement. Not even titleholders were safe. For thirteen of the sample groups the sources explicitly state that titleholders were enslaved, and for no group is the possibility denied (table A-3). Indeed, there are frequent references to slaves bearing the marks of former titleholder status. Among the most easily noticed of these marks by contemporary observers were the signs that the slave had formerly worn labrets, a titleholder privilege. Nor were former titleholders likely to get better treatment than other slaves. The plight of such slaves is vividly portrayed in the following passage from the Fort Simpson Journal for 24 August 1837.

Sieux and Quatkie [Stikine] returned from Sabassas [Kitkatla] with a number of the poor Naweitie [Nawitti] women whom the scoundrel Sabassa men took Slaves during the summer. The poor wretches, one of them in particular, the daughter of a Chief and the wife of a chief imploring Capt. McNeill whom she knew from seeing him down at Naweitie frequently, to trade her and take her back to her friends. When she and another were ordered to carry up some boxes from the canoe and another who had probably been a slave before, showing them how to do it, their looks, poor wretches were pitiable in the extreme. (fols. 135–135d)

The indigenous inhabitants of the region were not the only potential slaves. On a number of occasions Europeans were enslaved by one or another local group. The best-known European slaves were John Jewitt and his companion John Thompson who survived the Mowachaht attack on the *Boston* in March 1803 and were enslaved by the leading Mowachaht titleholder, Maquinna (Jewitt [1815] 1975). But Europeans were enslaved by other local groups as well; examples may be found in Bishop's (1967, 95–98) account of the enslavement of a sailor in 1794 by the Cumshewa Haida and the treatment in 1810 of some Russian captives by the Makah (Owens 1985, 39–65). The relative rarity of European slaves is almost certainly due to the general military strength of European ships and trading forts and not to any local awe of Europeans.

Captives Taken in Deliberate Raids for Slaves

Slaves were a common outcome of Northwest Coast warfare. This was almost certainly the most important method of producing slaves, whatever the motive for a particular episode of intergroup fighting. But, at least in historic times, some attacks on other groups had as their primary motive the capture of slaves. Such attacks can justifiably be called "slave raids." Because of their unusual motivation, such raids deserve separate consideration from other types of intergroup conflict.[4]

On 14 July 1840, James Douglas observed that many war expeditions in the northern part of the culture area were being undertaken for the sole purpose of taking slaves to sell for profit. Many others observed much the same thing during this time period, and in 1862 R. C. Mayne described indigenous fighting in the area as a "cruel system of predatory warfare" (p. 74). By at least the 1830s slave raids had become relatively common in the northern part of the culture area if not elsewhere.

The use of the distribution of wealth at feasts to validate titles and thus to maintain or enhance one's position in the prestige system is a very well known feature of Northwest Coast cultures. As Donald Mitchell (1984) has shown, during the first half of the nineteenth century some titleholders increased their store of wealth for such distributions and perhaps even hastened the accumulation process by means of slave raids and trades.

How slave raiding entered into a titleholder's feasting activities can be seen by examining a sequence of events recorded in the journal of the Hudson's Bay Company's trading post at Fort Simpson in 1837. (See fig. 5 for locations of places mentioned in these events.) In December of that year two journal entries tell us of a feast given at the village of Kitkatla, somewhat to the south of the fort:

> Dec 4 A party of Chimsyans [Lower Skeena Tsimshian] headed by Elgegh the Chief [Legaic, the leading Gispakloats titleholder] arrived with a few furs. They are going by special invitation to a great feast at Sabassas [Tsibasa, the leading Kitkatla titleholder] that has been talked of for the last two months, it is expected to be a grand affair. (fol. 157d)

> [Dec.] 14 The men [Lower Skeena Tsimshian] are mostly all off at Sabassas to the feast which has been so long talked of. (fol. 159d)

Tsibasa was giving a major feast (or potlatch) and had invited the important men from the Lower Skeena Tsimshian villages to witness and participate in the feast. No doubt they were among the chief beneficiaries of the property given away, for they returned the invitation to Tsibasa and his people and feasted them in early January 1838 (Fort Simpson Journal 1834–1838, fol. 163). We can find the first evidence of Tsibasa's preparations for his "great feast" in the journal entry for 11 August 1837, when it is noted that the company's steamship, the *Beaver*, has a disappointingly small trade at Nawitti, a Kwakwaka'wakw village on northern Vancouver Island. The reason for the poor return of furs is that the Nawitti are afraid to go out and hunt because they have recently been attacked by the Kitkatla who killed several men and carried off twenty women as slaves (Fort Simpson Journal 1834–1838, fols. 130d, 131). We have encountered some of these women in a quotation in the previous section; they are the Nawitti titleholder's daughter/wife and her companions who are now slaves of the Stikine. The Fort Simpson Journal notes that some Stikine Tlingit titleholders are off to Kitkatla to trade for slaves on August 16, that they are back on the 24th with a number of the newly purchased Nawitti women, and that on August 25 and 26 they leave Fort Simpson to return home (1834–1838, fols. 132, 135, 135d, 136). On October 18, Tsibasa and his Kitkatla arrive at the fort with a large load of furs to trade for various goods. The journal notes that "some of the beaver are known to have come from the Stikeen Indians when they were down there some time ago trading slaves" (1834–1838, fol. 149). We can be certain that the goods obtained for the furs were used in the great feast mentioned in the journal in December of that year.

This is almost certainly the best-documented sequence of slave raiding,

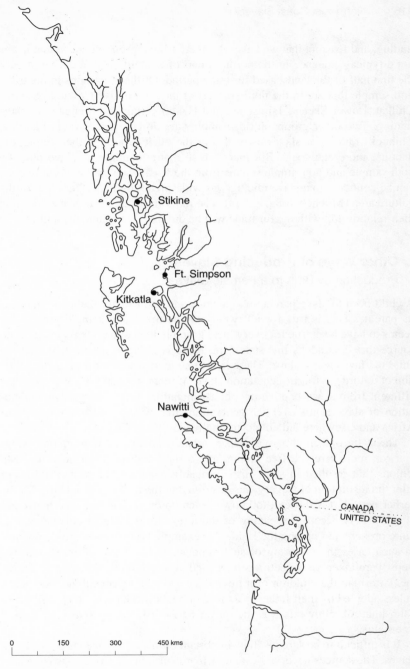

Figure 5.   Locations of Kitkatla Slave Raid and Feasts, 1837–1838.

trading, and feasting that we have. But there is no reason to believe that it was not a typical sequence in the northern part of the culture area during at least the first half of the land-based fur trade period. Of the six groups in the tribal unit sample that are in the northern part of the region, five (Yakutat, Stikine, Chilkat, Lower Skeena Tsimshian, and Haida) certainly did engage in slave raiding. Two other groups in this sample (the Fort Rupert Kwakiutl and the Chinook) raided for slaves as well. For the other groups in the sample, the data are more equivocal. But there are so many mentions of slave raids by both sample and nonsample groups from the Kwakwaka'wakw north that we can be confident that slave raiding was widespread in the northern half of the culture area (Mitchell 1984, 42–45). The fuller implications of slave raids and their relationship with the fur trade will be discussed in chapters 7 and 11.

Other Ways of Producing Slaves
Production by Birth to a Female Slave

A child born to slave parents was a slave and had exactly the same status as its parents. This is true for all twenty of the tribal unit sample groups and seems to have been true for every local group in the culture area. I know of no source that contradicts this statement. More is being said here than that the child of slaves was a slave. There is also no evidence that the status or situation of a third- or fourth-generation slave (if there were such) was in any way different from a war captive or a first-generation slave. The gradual amelioration of slave status over the generations that was fairly common in West Africa and elsewhere did not occur on the Northwest Coast.

The status of a child born to a slave mother and a free (often titleholder) father (or, more rarely, a free mother and a slave father) is not quite as clear. Unions that resulted in such births probably occurred before and did occur after the institution of slavery was destroyed in the region. Particularly for the earlier period, it is difficult to know if such unions could be called marriages in the locally accepted meaning of the term. Some form of concubinage is more probable, as among the Haida, for example (Harrison 1925, 55, 69–70). In such cases the offspring of such unions would be slaves unless unusual steps were taken, as sometimes happened at least among one group: among the Tsimshian the children of a titleholder and a slave concubine were slave unless adopted by their father as a niece or nephew (Garfield 1939, 29); given Tsimshian matriliny this was the only way for a father to give such a child free status.

It is difficult to be sure just how important birth was as a means of obtaining slaves. The sources never indicate how many birth or captive slaves were held by any group, nor do they have much to say about the frequency of births to slave women. All that we can be sure of is that from time to time children were born to slave mothers and this probably happened at least occasionally in every group where there were slave women of childbearing age. I infer, however, that birth was not an important originator of new slaves. No source suggests that it was, and the closest I can find to such a suggestion is the comment for the Central Tlingit groups that "many" were born into slavery also (i.e., in addition to capture in war) (Jones 1914, 116–118). Capture and trade are everywhere treated as the major sources of a local group's slaves. It was said, for example, that "there were no Quinault slaves because the Quinault had not engaged in war for a long time" (Olson 1936, 97).

One might also hypothesize that the rigors of a female slave's life would reduce both her fecundity and the chances of any child that she bore while a slave living past infancy. The source material is silent on either point. One reference does, however, suggest two other possible reasons why female slaves might have had a low birthrate.

> Infanticide is common among the slaves only, and for which they pretend two excuses. The first is the command of their mistress; the other, that their poor mothers have no wish that their wretched children should undergo the sufferings, which they have themselves experienced. (Green 1915, 31)[5]

Self-Enslavement

The sources tell us that in some groups individuals sometimes enslaved themselves. This could happen as the result of gambling, the inability to pay off a debt, or the threat of starvation.

Gambling was a widespread pastime, and a man could become so caught up in trying his luck that he not only risked and lost all his possessions but his own freedom as well. In the tribal unit sample this possibility is clearly reported for the Nuxalk (McIlwraith 1948, 1:159) and the Chinook (Ray 1938, 51–54) and is implied for the Haida (Swanton 1905, 58, 79). Outside the tribal unit sample gambling oneself into slavery is also reported as a possibility among the Heiltsuk (Boas 1928, 71). For no other groups is self-enslavement by gambling reported. Although self-enslavement by this means is not denied by any of the sources, it is unlikely that it was a regular or widespread Northwest Coast pattern, even though it probably did occur at least occasionally.

In the Nuxalk case it is stated that a man could lose his children as well as himself, but the most detailed account is that given by Verne Ray for the Chinook.

> A desperate gambler sometimes wagered his own body, beginning with hands, then limbs, and finally head, and with its loss came slavery. Sometimes a specified number of years was involved after which the person regained his former status. . . . In other cases a quantity of goods was named which should be considered the equivalent; if, then, by a lucky chance at gambling or through the

aid of his friends the enslaved man was able to amass that amount he might immediately gain his freedom. (1938, 51)

The possibility of eventually buying oneself out of this "slavery" suggests that for the Chinook at least, the self-enslaved gambler did not have quite the same status as the enslaved war captive and perhaps more closely resembled the debt pawn commonly found in West Africa.

Enslavement because of debt (nongambling), extreme poverty, or starvation is somewhat more widely reported in the region. It is reported for five of the twenty groups in the tribal unit sample (Yakutat, Chilkat, Sitka, Stikine, and Chinook). It is possible that debt enslavement also occurred among the Nuxalk, but the only case cited involves the enslavement of the son of a non-Nuxalk (Haihais) debtor by a Nuxalk creditor so that it is quite possible that such an enslavement occurred only because the debtor/creditor relationship crossed a group boundary. The only other case of debt enslavement reported is among the Kitimat (Lopatin 1945, 30) where the poor are said to have sometimes sold themselves into slavery to avoid starvation. Thus all the reports of debt enslavement are for the north (mostly the Tlingit) and for the southernmost group in the region, the Chinook. Again, although the silence of the sources does not necessarily mean the absence of a practice, it is probable that debt or starvation slavery was rarely found except in the extreme northern and southern parts of the culture area.

Ray's discussion of Chinook debt slaves makes their status appear to have been similar to that of Chinooks who became slaves through gambling. For the Yakutat Tlingit, Frederica De Laguna (1972, 245, 469) offers a special term for those who had sold themselves into slavery because of the fear of starvation: "dried fish slaves." She says that these "dried fish slaves" did not work like other slaves and that they might be redeemed either by their own efforts or by clan relatives. This again makes them different from those enslaved by war. But De Laguna's (1972, 245) informants also told her that even dried fish slaves might be killed at ceremonies, in which event one informant remarked, "Too bad! Too bad!" Chilkat debt slaves could also work until the debt was paid off or else they might be redeemed by their clan relatives to save the honor of their house. Such debt slaves should not be sold or given away unless they belonged to a different clan (Oberg 1934, 151). Speaking of the southern Tlingit in general, Olson (1967, 11) says that there was no debt slavery as such but that a "ne'er-do-well" could become so obligated that he was almost a slave. In discussing the Stikine, however, S. Hall Young (1927) describes what he calls the "self-surrender" of a man who got so deeply in debt that his only recourse was to enslave himself and sufficient of his children to make up the debt to his creditor. Young specifically makes the point, however, that while such debt slaves always had hope that they would serve out their time, war captives had no such hope (Young 1927, 127). What all of this material suggests is that among the Tlingit self-enslavement produced a status analogous but not identical to the slave by capture or birth. But, as De Laguna's Yakutat informants remind us, these debt slaves could be treated exactly like slaves and killed, and when that happened it was just "too bad."

Enslavement of Own Group Members

The taking of war captives as slaves from neighbors who belonged to the same language group and shared much the same culture was common. For thirteen of the twenty groups in the tribal unit sample, the sources show that this happened. For another group (the Fort Rupert Kwakiutl) there is a strong inference that they did so (many of their Kwakwala-speaking neighbors certainly did so). This leaves only five of the Salish groups (Saanich, Lummi, Skagit, Puyallup-Nisqually, and Twana) and the Quileute for whom there is no clear indication of raiding linguistically and culturally similar neighbors. It is worth noting that the Salish groups are in the part of the culture area that probably had the least warfare aboriginally and that, nevertheless, some of their Salish-speaking neighbors did raid linguistic confreres.

But some groups went further: we know that they enslaved people who belonged to their local group. At least four of the groups in the tribal unit sample sometimes enslaved orphans (Clayoquot, Lummi, Chinook, and Puyallup-Nisqually). Orphans were also enslaved among the Songish and Squamish. The Lummi had a special term for those enslaved because they were orphans. According to Bernhard J. Stern (1934, 73), orphans who had been enslaved could redeem themselves at adulthood by hosting a large ceremony and distributing much property. But even if they did this the shame of their childhood status remained. For four Salish groups (Songish, Squamish, Lummi, and Puyallup-Nisqually) we know that orphans were enslaved. Thanks to Barnett's (1939, 267) culture element survey trait list we also have denials for five other Salish groups: the Comox, Klahuse, Sechelt, Cowichan, and Nanaimo.

A person might also be enslaved because of an injury he or she had done someone or some group. For the tribal unit sample, this is explicitly stated in the sources for the Sitka, Chilkat, Klallam, and Chinook. The cited causes of such enslavement vary: among the Klallam a murderer could become a slave as an option to paying wergild (Gunther 1927, 266); among the Chinook the murderer of a titleholder automatically became a slave and any poor murderer might become a slave if he lacked the wealth to pay wergild (Ray 1938, 52); among the Chilkat low-ranking adulterers might become slaves as a part of their compensation for adultery (Oberg 1934, 149); and among the Sitka the need for payment for unspecified injury claims could result in slavery (Glass 1882, 28). In some southern Tlingit groups an accused witch might choose slavery over death (Knapp 1896, 135), and Boas (1889, 832) says that among the Tsimshian (group unspecified) serious mistakes in performing ceremonies could result in enslavement.

This miscellany of causes for enslavement within one's own local group suggests that in many (most?) Northwest Coast local groups the very poor might easily find themselves in a position where they could not meet some imposed financial obligation and, lacking the protection of powerful kin (probably the definition of very poor in the culture area), were then subject to enslavement. The sources also suggest that it is probably the case that such slaves were usually not quite the same as war captives and that either their own efforts or those of their relatives might very well redeem them from slavery. The sources also imply that all these methods of producing slaves taken together can be correctly described, in Ray's term for such methods among the Chinook, as "minor."

Enslavement by "Treachery"

A final method of producing slaves must be mentioned. It was probably not important as a source of slaves in terms of numbers, but it is important as an indicator of the nature and complexity of relationships between groups and as a measure of the impact of slavery as a moral force. I will call this enslavement by "treachery." By this I do not mean simple trickery or other gambits of war. These certainly occurred often enough. So too did violations of the principles of feasting hospitality. For example, in March or April of 1852 six canoes of Stikine went to Sitka where they had been invited to a feast and dance. After the Stikine were inside the feast house, they were attacked by the Sitka who killed four of the principal Stikine titleholders and most of the rest. The survivors, a few women, were enslaved (Fort Simpson Journal 1852–1853, fol. 15).

What I have in mind as treachery may be even more surprising to outsiders. This is the deliberate humiliation of one's affines by selling one's wife into slavery. Such an event was a part of the complex struggles for power, prestige, and influence that went on continuously within and between Northwest Coast communities. Its use and impact is illustrated by Garfield's (1939, 272) account of such an enslavement among the Lower Skeena Tsimshian, which has been discussed earlier (see pp. 91–92). The practice of selling one's wife into slavery is also recorded among the Haida (Fort Simpson Journal 1838–1840, fol. 14–14d).

6
Slave Labor

The Organization of Work
on the Northwest Coast

The organization of work and its impact on production are not well-studied topics for traditional Northwest Coast societies. To my knowledge, no systematic work on the subject on an areawide basis has been published. Some ethnographic accounts are much stronger than others on these topics (Garfield's Tsimshian studies are among the better ones, for example), but even those that are outstanding in most other respects are usually weak in the area of work and production (McIlwraith's Nuxalk monograph, for example). There are several reasons for this. Most of the ethnographic information collected was essentially "memory ethnography," transcribed well after native societies had been seriously disrupted by European conquest and dependent on older informants' memories of the cultures of their youth or even the memories of these informants about what they had been told by their elders. Also, most of the earlier ethnographers were interested in ritual, mythology, and the more spectacular aspects of Northwest Coast cultures. Finally, patterns of work organization were among the first aspects of culture to be disrupted after contact when new trading partners and demands for new types of goods required a reorganization of economic activities, including work and production. In spite of these difficulties, one ethnographer did collect and analyze a considerable body of data on work and production. Kalervo Oberg did fieldwork among the Chilkat Tlingit in the early 1930s. He had been trained in both economics and anthropology (probably the only one of the first or second generation of Northwest Coast ethnographers with a significant background in economics)

121

and produced a 1937 doctoral dissertation entitled "The Social Economy of the Tlingit Indians." It is a sad reflection of the lack of interest in Northwest Coast economics (in spite of all the ink spilled about the potlatch, the interest-bearing loans associated with the same, and so on) that this fine study was not published until 1973. Most of the prominent students of the region appear to have known of Oberg's work long before it was published, but it had little impact on their own investigations.[1]

Recent overviews of the Northwest Coast continue to reflect the lack of attention to these topics. In a recent summary of "Northwest Coast economies" Donald Mitchell and Leland Donald (1988) have little to say about the organization of work or production. This omission was due to the lack of readily available studies and the thinness of the easily accessible ethnographic record on this subject. These weaknesses in the record extend beyond the Northwest Coast. In his study of western Native North American cultures, Joseph G. Jorgensen's (1980, 150–155) discussion of the organization of work and production is mostly about the gender division of labor and the presence or absence of craft specialists. Again, this does not reflect a disinterest by Jorgensen in work but the poor quality of ethnographic material available.

This chapter is about slave labor and the ramifications of such labor for the various societies in the region. But it must be written in something of a vacuum, since overall studies of work and production are not available. Although such a study is badly needed, it cannot be undertaken here. What I will do is present a brief, and provisional, overview to give some context to the material on slave labor that is, of course, my primary concern.

The most important production activities to be organized were those that procured food. But other important tasks that had to be organized included the manufacture of clothing, shelter, transport, and, equally important, the manufacture of the tools needed to accomplish all these tasks. Of comparable importance to many of those living in traditional Northwest Coast communities was the production of objects and paraphernalia for use in ceremonial activities and having the time to undertake these important ceremonies.

Although there was significant variation within the culture area, all of the Northwest Coast economies were based on extractive subsistence activities. Because of the temporal and spatial patterning of resources, all production was based on an annual round of shifting production and residential locales. Food was produced by a combination of fishing, hunting, and gathering. Although some subsistence activities were done on an individual basis, most were undertaken by cooperative task groups. Sometimes this was necessary because the job at hand could not be accomplished by an individual working alone, but at other times group work was more pleasant or even safer.[2] The basis for most work groups was kinship. Kin units owned the rights to exploit most resource locales and the task group was usually drawn from members of the owning unit (Jorgensen 1980, 406–410, 435–440).

As in most kinship-based societies, the most fundamental aspect of work organization was the division of labor by gender. Most work was assigned primarily to one gender or the other, although some tasks could be done by either (Jorgensen 1980, 426–438). Some complex sequences of work involved both sexes, but usually different tasks within the sequence were assigned to different genders. The most important example of this was salmon fishing. For most groups, men were responsible for catching the fish and transporting them to shore. Then women prepared the fish for preservation and carried out the tasks of drying or smoking. The entire sequence was important and involved a good deal of organization, for the right amounts of labor were needed to both procure and preserve the catch, which was the single most important food source for most (although not all) winter villages.

Some tasks were undertaken by skilled specialists. Complex tasks that required many hands might be directed by specialists, or specialists might carry out the most important elements. Other tasks were largely done by specialists, at least in some communities (Jorgensen 1980, 427–440). Even fishing might involve specialists: there might be particularly skilled practitioners in some aspects and for some species, but most males in each community could and did fish.

It will be recalled that every Northwest Coast local group was divided into three strata. An important issue is the extent to which there was a division of labor by strata. Few of the ethnographic sources contain explicit statements that certain tasks were done by slaves or by titleholders. There is, however, a good deal of less explicit evidence that there was some strata-based division of labor in at least parts of the culture area. One ethnographer does address the issue explicitly. Oberg (1973, 79–90) describes what he calls ceremonial and common labor among the Chilkat. Because this distinction is potentially very important and because Oberg's description of the organization of labor is the most thorough and best organized in the ethnographic literature, it is worth recapitulating in detail.

The basic Chilkat unit of production was the "house group" which consisted of three or more generations of the male members of a matrilineage and their wives and unmarried children, plus their slaves, if any. The fundamental food production activities were collectively carried out by members of the house group under the supervision and direction of the unit's male head. There was a gender division of labor in food production. In general men hunted and fished, and women gathered plant foods and shellfish and preserved the products of male labor. All of this is common labor. The gender division of labor was marked, and men were very reluctant to do women's tasks for fear of ridicule. Age itself was not a significant factor in work organization.

Ceremonial labor included house building and burial. This work was performed by specified kin, sometimes of the opposite moiety. Other ceremonial work involved ear, lip, and septum piercing, tattooing, and the carving of poles and masks.

Status also played a major role in labor organization. The house group head oversaw and initiated all important activities, but he rarely did the more arduous forms of common labor. Especially, he would never carry water or gather wood. His position was primarily ceremonial and his major economic role was managerial. He also did the house group's trading.

If the house group head was also a member of the titleholder class, he was even less involved in common labor. Oberg says of all members of this category:

> A high-born Tlingit does little outside ceremonial activities other than amuse himself. He will scarcely speak to anyone but his equal. Common labor is quite impossible if he wishes to maintain his prestige. *Anyeti* [titleholder] women are not taught the common art of weaving but cultivate only mannerisms of speech and movement. In fact girls who have never worked are considered special prizes to be won in marriage. (1973, 87)

Chilkat slaves, in contrast, were not allowed to carry out ceremonial tasks. Slaves collected firewood, fetched water, cleaned fish and game, and generally did all household chores. On ceremonial occasions, however, food preparation was done by the young men and women of the house group.

No other ethnographer makes a clear distinction between ceremonial and common labor, but there are some indications in the data that Oberg's distinction is relevant beyond the Tlingit. Among the Makah and Nuu-chah-nulth, sea mammal hunting, especially whaling, seems to have been the prerogative of titleholders. Indeed, one passage in Swan's (1869, 10–11) account of the Makah implies that leading titleholders, at least, did as little common work as their Chilkat counterparts. And there are various other indications that titleholders up and down the coast did not expect to work in the same way and at the same tasks as did commoners and certainly not as did slaves. One final quote can probably be taken as summing up the attitudes of titleholders over much of the culture area. The speaker is a Chinook woman who was the daughter of the group's leading titleholder. The date is circa 1844 and she is speaking to her European husband, a Hudson's Bay Company trader named McDougall.

> "You profess to be a great chief; but I see you hard at work every day, behind the counter and at the desk, and your time is so fully employed that you have scarcely time to eat your food, or to enjoy the society of your wife a moment"; upon this she pointed to the swine in the puddle, and said, "See there, that is a true chief; he has no labour to perform, like a slave; when hungry, his food is served up, he fills himself, he then lies down in the soft mud, under the influence of the warming rays of the sun, sleeps and takes his comfort." "That," she repeated, "is the true chief." (Lee and Frost [1844] 1968, 64)

So far the difference between ceremonial and common labor has been emphasized, but one other aspect of Oberg's description also requires attention. Among the most important of a titleholder's activities was that of manager. Titleholders who headed households or larger descent groups were responsible for managing their units' productive and other economic activities. It should also be emphasized that the amassing of wealth and other goods for a feast also involved considerable managerial skill. This managerial role was probably an important aspect of titleholder duties and prerogatives throughout the culture area (see Drucker 1983).

Garfield's Tsimshian ethnographies contain some of the clearest descriptions of titleholders as managers of work and work groups.

> Chiefs [titleholders] delegated work to their immediate relatives, wives, children and slaves. . . . They supervised men's work while their senior wives supervised the labor of younger women and female slaves.
>
> . . . [T]ribal chiefs [lineage heads?] moved to their own fish camps with retinues of relatives, retainers and slaves.
>
> [A tribal chief] had patronage to distribute, and slaves and young men at his command to work for him. (1951, 15–16, 35)

Leaving aside slaves for the moment, it is clear that everywhere in the culture area the primary basis for the mobilization of labor was kinship. Ties of kinship entailed obligations that varied from village to village, but everywhere individuals and groups could call on other individuals and groups for assistance with a range of productive tasks. The basis of this call was some sort of kin tie, consanguineal or affinal, and the prevailing ethic was one of reciprocity.[3] Commoners might find it more than usually difficult to ignore the requests (demands) of titleholders, but even where status was unequal the differences were masked by the vocabulary of reciprocity. And, indeed, titleholders had to recognize their own obligations to their followers or face the possibility of desertion.

The conventional view of the Northwest Coast emphasizes kinship and reciprocity as the basis of the mobilization of all kinds of assistance, including work (except in the case of potlatch goods where interest-bearing loans are said to have occurred). The importance of reciprocal ties and kin group membership in uniting the efforts of titleholders and commoners should not be ignored, but the ideology of kinship should not cause us to overlook the fact that in many instances commoners acted as a kind of dependent labor for titleholders. If for no other reason, they were dependent because generally titleholders controlled access to resources. Titleholders certainly needed commoner followers, and this need did restrain titleholder actions toward commoners, but this did not mean that titleholders did not dominate commoners.

Work and other demands of titleholders, however, could not always be

satisfied by the labor power of their commoner followers, particularly since
in their struggles for glory with other titleholders they might have very great
needs indeed. Group esprit might well not be enough to mobilize the all-out
efforts sometimes required to build up wealth for a major feast and contest
with a rival. In addition, if more labor was needed, it might be very difficult to
obtain quickly. Kinspeople must be reproduced, not produced, and the natural
time frame is difficult to overcome. Adoption does not seem to have been a
widespread alternative. The other alternative source of labor was the slave.
Hence the importance of the issue of slave labor and its role on the Northwest
Coast. We shall return to these issues after examining, in detail, just what kind
of work and how much slaves did.

Tasks Performed by Slaves

A great range and variety of tasks were undertaken by slaves. Many of the
sources aptly describe these tasks as "drudgery" and sources for some groups
invoke the biblical "hewers of wood and drawers of water" to describe the
situation of slaves. Ratings for seventeen of the most frequently mentioned
slave tasks for the tribal unit sample can be found in tables A-6, A-7, and A-8
in appendix I. With the possible exception of one variable (go on raids and
participate in other aspects of warfare), it is probable that slaves in virtually
all local groups performed all of these tasks at one time or another.

Slaves worked in all of the most important areas of food production (table
A-6). In every instance nonslaves participated in these activities as well. It
seems to have been the case that slave and free person usually worked together. Within some of these clusters of variables, though, there were some
tasks that slaves did not usually perform or that were forbidden to slaves. The
clearest example of this is sea mammal hunting. The killing of whales seems
to have been the prerogative of titleholders alone among the Mowachaht,
Clayoquot, and Makah (Drucker 1951, 48–56).[4] Among the Twana, slaves did
not hunt sea mammals (Elmendorf 1960, 345). And among the Fort Rupert
Kwakiutl, Boas's (1921, 174–178, 451–464, 607–608, 750–751, 1093–1104)
discussion of seal hunting strongly suggests that harpooning seals was usually
a titleholder activity, although a lower-status man, even a slave, might act as
the steersman in the two-man team that formed the basic work unit in the seal
hunt. But slaves did participate in much hunting activity among many local
groups, including the Chilkat, where we have the best treatment of the division between ceremonial and common labor.

Slaves also performed most, if not all, household tasks and duties (table
A-7). Slaves are reported to have collected and carried firewood in sixteen
of the sample groups. This is the most widely reported slave activity. Maintenance of a household's firewood supply should not be dismissed as an unimportant task. A great deal of wood was needed for cooking and heat and,

especially in the winter, a good deal of labor had to be expended on keeping up the supply.

> Keeping the house supplied with firewood is a constant task which is performed collectively by the young men of the house, and which used to be delegated to slaves if the house was fortunate enough to possess some. . . . Every other day or so men can be seen going into the forest for dry branches and trunks of dead trees. (Oberg 1973, 79)

In addition to the most frequently mentioned tasks listed in the tables, other activities noted in a few local groups include making spruce chewing gum (Lower Skeena Tsimshian), making huts and temporary shelters when accompanying a party traveling away from the winter village (Lower Skeena Tsimshian), helping to make a fish dam or weir (Nuxalk), dressing skins (Fort Rupert Kwakiutl), assisting in building and repairing houses (Mowachaht), making canoes (Mowachaht, Saanich), making and mending baskets and mats (Mowachaht, Makah, Saanich, Klallam), making and mending nets (Klallam), and collecting cedar bark and rushes (Saanich). In some groups it is also noted that the daughters of important titleholders were always accompanied by female slaves who acted as their personal maid(s) (Chilkat, Lower Tsimshian, Chinook). In addition, specific note is taken of slaves as attendants during the seclusion of a titleholder's daughter at her puberty rites among the Chinook, Puyallup-Nisqually, and Klallam.[5]

Slaves might also play minor, menial roles on ceremonial occasions. For example, they brought in the food and gifts at Lower Skeena Tsimshian feasts and brought out and distributed food on similar occasions among the Haida. Slaves also assisted in property distributions at Nuxalk feasts. Haida slaves also tended fires at feasts and on one occasion were observed to run out into the water to some visitors' canoes as a part of greeting ceremonies for feast guests. They also acted as funeral attendants among the Mowachaht. But among the Chilkat, slaves did not serve food at feasts. The manner and degree of utilization of slaves at feasts and ceremonies was probably one of the more variable aspects of slave activity in the region.

Titleholders also used their slaves as tools and assistants in enforcing social control. For example, in cranberry season a slave might be stationed at Chilkat cranberry bogs to see that no one picked the fruit early or gained an unfair advantage over others (Shotridge 1921, 172–175). Less benign examples of masters using slaves are even more common.

Slaves were often used by titleholders to destroy an enemy. Not only did slaves frequently accompany their owners on war expeditions (among at least eight of the sample tribal units), but they are also recorded as having killed for their masters among eight groups (Chilkat, Stikine, Lower Skeena Tsimshian, Fort Rupert Kwakiutl, Mowachaht, Makah, Quinault, and Chinook). Often these killings were a part of intralocal group quarrels, not warfare. The

Makah had two types of poison: one that killed and one that destroyed the victim's ability to influence others. As one of Elizabeth Colson's Makah informants explained, "Long ago the best people used to have that done. They wouldn't handle the stuff themselves because a chief wasn't supposed to have anything to do with things like that or touch it. But the chief would have a slave to fix it for him and give it to the people he disliked or that he thought was getting too big" (Colson 1953, 226).

Traditional Assessments of the Value of Slave Labor

There is no doubt that slaves were put to a wide variety of tasks in most Northwest Coast communities. But the hard question is, What was the economic value of slaves to their owners? The answer to this question in most of the secondary literature and in the ethnographic sources is, in Drucker's (1965, 52) words, that "slaves' economic utility was negligible." Even those ethnographers who document most thoroughly the work done by slaves in the cultures they studied seem to agree with this assessment. Both Oberg (1973) and Garfield (1939) published statements in their ethnographies in line with Drucker's assessment and, when they comment on the value of slave labor, the historical sources often seem to agree. The very knowledgeable James Douglas (1841, 45) wrote of the Stikine that their slaves "in many cases are kept for the mere purpose of display." This phrase of Douglas's might serve as a motto for the usual assessment of the economic value of slaves in the culture area, for slaves are often described as being items of nonproductive wealth that seem to have been regarded as expensive pets, a drain on their masters' resources but necessary to maintain prestige—much like the chocolate-fed poodle so necessary to the cliché of the fat rich lady in North American culture.

One of the main purposes of this book is to show that this assessment of the value of slaves is wrong. Slaves made an important contribution to the Northwest Coast economies as they were organized aboriginally, and their masters needed their labor to maintain their positions, not simply for the prestige that ownership conferred. The task here is to argue against the grain of most of the previous literature on the subject.[6] This must be done using the same ethnographic sources previously used to reach the opposite conclusion. For although unpublished ethnographic notes and the historical sources do add some details to our knowledge, my conclusions about the value of slave labor are based on a reanalysis of the source material, not new discoveries of data.

My disagreement with the orthodox interpreters of Northwest Coast slavery cannot be resolved with a quantitative analysis of work done by slaves. There are no quantitative data on the work done by slaves or by any other members of any traditional Northwest Coast society. Nevertheless, a careful reading of both the data and the previous assessments of "negligible" economic value can give useful results.

There are sources that contain quite contradictory statements about the value of slave labor. One of the earliest of these is *Tlingit Indians of Alaska* by Aurel Krause.[7] Krause himself notes that "in regard to the treatment given slaves by their masters, diverse reports have been given" (1956, 111). He goes on to quote statements typical of the "slaves as prestige items only" view of Northwest Coast slavery.

> Lütke said that they were treated practically like children of the household; Veniaminof also finds that their position is not unfavorable since, he explains, a slave, even though a possession, is an expensive one. (1956, 111)

And he cites views of slaves similar to the interpretation presented here.

> In contrast to Lütke, Schabelski, who visited the Northwest coast a few years earlier, described the condition of slaves as a very sad one. He related that they were forced to perform the hardest labor and lost their lives at the slightest whim of their masters. (1956, 111)

Much more recently De Laguna (1972) states quite clearly, in her important monograph on the Yakutat, that the contribution of slaves to their owners' domestic economy was uncertain (p. 472) and that there is no indication that slaves worked harder than freemen (p. 471). This seems to contradict the data from other Tlingit groups, but on the same page she quotes an informant as saying that slaves often had snarled hair because "slaves can't brush their hair (they don't have time)." Other material in this monograph also strongly supports the view that the Yakutat were like the other Tlingit and worked their slaves long and hard and successfully extracted considerable surplus from them (see esp. pp. 309–310).

How are we to resolve the contradictions described in the last two paragraphs, which only make explicit the contradictory views of the meaning of slave labor implied in most Northwest Coast ethnographic work? The resolution lies in recognizing the objectives and perspectives of traditional Northwest Coast scholarship and that these objectives and perspectives largely ignored slavery. There are three major types of reasons why the economic importance of slaves has been neglected and denied for so long. First, all aspects of Northwest Coast slavery have been quite peripheral to the main interests of Northwest Coast scholarship, as have questions of the organization of work and productivity. (The same statements might be said to hold true to only a slightly lesser degree for anthropology, even economic anthropology, in general.) No one has thought much about how productive work was accomplished or about slaves, so that the contradictions attracted little attention.[8]

Second, no students of the Northwest Coast brought to their work any explicit theory about the organization of work or production or any systematic ideas about the relationship between work and production and other aspects of society and culture. The implicit interpretive framework was that of how kinship-based societies worked, a strongly egalitarian, reciprocity-based model that prevailed even as ethnographers described striving for rank. This is a model with no role for exploitation, domination, or slavery in the societies it purports to describe. Third, ethnographers have been largely dependent on the titleholders' own views, descriptions, and analyses of their societies. Most informants were of titleholder origin and by the late nineteenth century, to say nothing about the time when ethnographers like De Laguna came along, these individuals certainly knew what the dominant Europeans thought of practices such as slavery. But I am not simply saying that titleholders wished to put themselves in a good light and so implied that somehow the keeping of slaves was almost a charitable act (a claim that makes them not unlike slave holders elsewhere). Their own view of Northwest Coast society and how it worked emphasized their ceremonial and ritual role and the importance of ceremonials in traditional life. They placed little emphasis on the material underpinnings either of ceremonial life in general or of their role in this activity. Northwest Coast scholars appear to have adopted this view without much reflection. The evidence and the arguments that will be presented below should make the importance of slave labor clear.

The Value of Slave Labor

As remarked earlier, Oberg is the most economically sophisticated ethnographer to work in the region, so I will begin my reconsideration of the value of slave labor with him. It is worth quoting him at length.

> Slaves' work, formerly, consisted of the menial tasks of collecting firewood, fetching water, cleaning fish and game, and generally taking care of household duties. Food preparation and service on ceremonial occasions, however, were delegated to the young men and women of the house-group. As has already been mentioned, food and the food animals and plants were not sacred among the Tlingit so that slaves could participate in all the major food collecting activities such as hunting, fishing, and plant gathering. Slaves, likewise, participated in all the handicrafts, except the making of ceremonial objects, which they were only allowed to do under supervision when they possessed great talent. While the Tlingit possessed slaves, it would be erroneous to think of Tlingit economy as a slave economy, using this term to imply that the slaves were exploited solely for their labor power. The Tlingit slave was a piece of property, an instrument for certain social purposes, which were more important than the use of a slave as a means for producing wealth or providing services. (1973, 88)

The first problem here is that the phrase "slave economy" or "slave society" as used by analysts of such does not imply that slaves are exploited "solely for their labor power," nor does it mean that all the work is done by slaves. There have been very few, if any, societies in which these conditions prevailed, although slave labor has been crucial in many societies and in some has been so important that they have been termed "slave societies" or "slave economies." Oberg is insisting on a standard for the Chilkat that would apply to few, if any, slave societies anywhere.[9]

Second, it must also be recognized that slave labor can be important *and* slaves can be instruments "for certain social purposes." That slaves can be both is not a contradiction or impossible, or even unlikely. Most cultural objects are loaded, even overloaded, with meanings and purposes. Too many students of the Northwest Coast seem to assume that if a slave is a prestige object he or she can be nothing else and certainly not a valuable worker. Such an assumption seems to me to have no basis in Northwest Coast cultural realities.

Douglas's remarks about the roles of slaves also require further examination. After his comment about slaves being held merely for display, Douglas goes on to say that slaves

> are also exceeding useful as hunters and fisherman, while they constitute a bodyguard of generally faithful adherents, ready to protect their master or murder his enemies at the slightest intimation of his will without question or scruple. In fact, Shakes, the most influential Stikine chief, has no followers of his own tribe and merely a retinue of 24 slaves, who paddle his canoes, fish, hunt and perform for him every menial office, live under the same roof, and in short, uphold his cause with their ever ready swords and spears. The ladies too, slovenly as they are in their general habits, cannot condescend to exercise their tender hands at any kind of work, and must also have their train of attendants to relieve them of domestic drudgery, which in their opinion is degrading and would involve the loss of cast. (1841, 45)

The importance, in 1840, of slave labor to Shakes is clear. But Shakes's situation was certainly not that of the usual titleholder, neither in early historic nor in precontact times. Very few titleholders had only slave followers (and it is to be doubted that this was the situation for Shakes for very long).

For the general problem considered here, Douglas's last sentence is the most important. Stikine titleholder women do not wish to engage in "domestic drudgery," because it is unsuitable to their status as titleholders. This is strongly reminiscent of Oberg's discussion of the reluctance of Chilkat titleholders to perform what he called common labor. For Tlingit titleholders, at least, owning slaves meant that they did not have to engage in common work and thus slave labor directly supported their style of life as titleholders.

Although the data are not as detailed as for some of the Tlingit local groups, there are indications that slaves relieved titleholders, or at least the most prominent of them, from much ordinary work in some of the other groups in the tribal unit sample. Among the Lower Skeena Tsimshian, slaves "do the principal drudgery" (Dunn 1844, 284; see also Niblack 1890, 253). A Rose Spit Haida woman was treated badly by her own family, "almost like a slave," and was sent down to the beach to bring up pieces of a beached whale—implying that only slaves normally performed such labor (Swanton 1905, 101). Among the Mowachaht only slaves were employed at such menial tasks as carrying water (Meares [1790] 1967, 194). John Jewitt (1974, 65), speaking from personal experience, confirms that among the Mowachaht "all the menial offices are performed by" slaves. Among the Makah, "formerly it was considered degrading for a chief, or the owner of slaves to perform any labor except hunting, fishing, or killing whales" (Swan 1869, 10–11). In describing the Saanich, Jenness (n.d., 60, 64) says that slaves and commoners did most of the work involved in subsistence activities. Among the Klallam, Gunther (1927, 214, 264) says that slaves do the same type of work as their masters, noting, for example, that masters and male slaves fish together. But she also says that slaves did most of the menial tasks (1927, 214). Among the Lummi slaves are said to do the drudgery of the household (Stern 1934, 73–74), and among the Puyallup-Nisqually slaves did the routine and heavy work that otherwise would have fallen on some member of the family (Smith 1940, 52). The sources for the Chinook are more detailed.

> To them fell most of the laborious and disagreeable work though they often worked side by side with their masters. Emma Luscier said that there was no distinction in general type of work but that the most difficult tasks in oyster gathering, wood cutting, and fishing were assigned to slaves. (Ray 1938, 51–54)

> The women here are not generally subject to that drudgery common among most other Indian tribes. Slaves do all the laborious work; and a Chinooke matron is constantly attended by two, three, or more slaves, who are on all occasions obsequious to her will. In trade and barter the women are as actively employed as the men, and it is as common to see the wife, followed by a train of slaves, trading at the factory, as her husband. (Ross 1966, 92)

> Slaves are made to fish, hunt, draw water and wood; in short all the drudgery falls on them. (Merk 1931, 101)

Altogether, I have been able to cite evidence that slaves relieved their masters of significant amounts of what Oberg called common labor for eleven of the twenty groups in the tribal unit sample. All three of the area's regions are represented by these eleven units. Given the ever-present problem of missing information, this is a very strong indication that titleholders did benefit from their slaves' labor because it freed them from "drudgery" and enabled them to do other things rather then spend their time collecting firewood or carrying water. It is important to keep in mind that the "other things" titleholders did probably often included "nothing." To be at leisure while one's slaves labored must have been a principal feature of titleholder life. The reader is reminded of the Chinook titleholder and her "pig in a puddle" example cited earlier in this chapter.

I have established that the work of slaves enabled their masters to live free or at least partially free of "drudgery." The keeping of slaves contributed to their owners' prestige both by the fact of ownership of important objects of wealth and by freeing them from at least some common labor.

But what was the economic cost to titleholders of this freedom from drudgery? As in all societies with slaves, masters had to feed, clothe, and house their slaves up to a standard that enabled them not only to exist but also to perform their required duties. Was the cost of this a drain on the owners' resources? Could masters afford to keep slaves for the privilege of not doing so much common labor? The implication of the "slaves as pets" interpretation of Northwest Coast slavery is that it was expensive to keep slaves and that they were a significant drain on their owners' resources. If this interpretation is correct, it means that slaves did no subsistence labor or that any subsistence labor done by a slave was not productive enough to maintain him or her, much less produce a surplus over his or her basic material needs. Productivity in any Northwest Coast community cannot have been this low.

The natural environment of the North Pacific Coast of North America supports a considerable biomass, especially in its rivers and surrounding ocean areas. The subsistence technologies of traditional Northwest Coast cultures were well suited to exploiting these resources. The orthodox interpretations of Northwest Coast culture pay little attention to this environment and its exploitation beyond claiming that production of more than adequate amounts of food was easy and secure. These same scholars' interpretation of slavery as noneconomic implies either that production was low and slaves were a drain on their masters or that slave labor was unneeded because large surpluses were easy to extract. Beginning in the 1960s and following the lead of Wayne Suttles, some scholars began to reexamine the nature of the Northwest Coast resource base and the way in which it was exploited. This was done largely in the context of revising explanations of the potlatch.[10] Briefly, this research shows that there was considerable spatial and temporal variation in resources. At some places and times people could be very well off, but there were also shortages—even periods of starvation. Successful survival on the Northwest Coast required considerable skill at managing available labor power, organizing the preservation and storage of food, and managing its distribution and redistribution. The peoples on the Northwest Coast did not simply reap nature's abundance.

Many of the characteristics of different Northwest Coast communities reflected, in part, the characteristics of the resource base that they were able to control and exploit. For example, it can be shown that the relative abundance of salmon in a Kwakwaka'wakw winter village territory is a good predictor of a group's population size, which in turn predicts the village's position in the intergroup feasting hierarchy (Donald and Mitchell 1975). The strong correlation between group size and size of salmon resource (variation in rank on salmon resources accounts for about 80 percent of the variation in rank on population) is not surprising. The ethnographic record indicates that throughout the culture area, for the majority of local groups salmon was the most important resource (see Mitchell and Donald 1988, 301–305). Salmon, however, are also the preeminent seasonal resource, chiefly available when they return from the ocean to their natal stream to spawn. This means that if salmon are to make an important contribution to a group's food supply outside the main spawning runs, preservation of salmon is as important as catching salmon. In fact, preservation may well be the most important subsistence problem a descent group manager may have to make decisions about. Labor sufficient to preserve an adequate supply of salmon may be more critical than labor sufficient to catch this supply. This is partly because it seems likely that salmon fishing techniques were usually not as labor intensive as preservation techniques.[11] The gender division of labor is also important here: men caught the salmon, but women cleaned and preserved the catch. For many titleholder leaders of resource-exploiting kin units, the most important work allocation problem must have been the need to assure adequate labor to preserve the annual salmon catch. Given the gender division of labor, this meant an adequate number of female hands. Slaves, of course, could also be put to cleaning and preserving salmon, as they could be assigned other "drudgery." Some of the previously cited material has suggested this possibility, but the following passage is clear evidence of what was common among some Central Nuu-chah-nulth groups:

> When the canoes return to shore from fishing the men fill the baskets with the fish and place them on the women's shoulders. The latter, assisted by slaves, immediately cut off the heads, open, and wash the fish, press out the water, and afterwards hang them up to dry. (Sproat 1868, 53–54)

What Sproat observed for himself in the middle of the nineteenth century on the west coast of Vancouver Island was probably common throughout the culture area. Sproat's observation suggests that slave labor offers a solution to any shortages of female labor power due to the gender division of labor. If there were not enough women available for the job—and the reasons for this shortage could be many; for example, titleholder women not willing to do such work, or too few adult women (the small population size of any descent group made random fluctuations in the sex ratio frequent)—slaves of *either* gender could be utilized. Slaves are humans and can be made to do the work of humans, but they are also property. They cannot choose the role they are asked to fill in any particular situation. In this context they are not "men" or "women" but "slaves"—undifferentiated labor power. It is not inappropriate to demand that a male slave do "women's work," because a male slave is not a "man" in the fullest cultural sense. Here we may take note of Fred Lockley's (1928, 81–82) comment that the Chinook might not put a male slave to work normally done by men and so they " 'made a woman of him,' making him perform menial tasks." A further indication of the "gender flexibility" of slaves is the fact that at least some male slaves among the Nuu-chah-nulth were given female names (Sapir and Swadesh 1955, 177). Olson (1967, 54) describes an Angoon titleholder whose nursemaid when she was an infant and child was a male slave of Yakutat origin, so that there are instances of child care by slaves of the normally inappropriate gender. There are other clear indications of the connection between slave labor and the gender division of labor—for example, the quote in Averkieva from Archimandrite Anatolia (whose book, published in Russian in 1906, probably refers to mid-nineteenth-century Alaskan experiences), "The [Tlingit] Indian himself considered it humiliating to have to concern himself with unskilled work around the house; this was the responsibility of slaves, or, at least, women" (1966, 65). Thus slaves can be used as needed without the kind of consideration for the appropriateness of the demands made on them that are necessary with followers (commoner members of the descent group).

Slaves thus could contribute economically to their titleholder masters' well-being in at least three ways: they relieved them of at least some household drudgery, freeing their time for titleholder activities including leisure; their subsistence labors were a substitute for their masters' subsistence labors so that communities did not suffer a loss in food production when titleholders curtailed their own subsistence activity; and the surplus of their productive labors contributed to the stock of food and goods used by titleholders in feasts and ceremonies. Slaves certainly had the potential to make these contributions, but did they actually work hard enough to make important contributions?

Although some statements in the ethnographic literature imply that they did not, the suggestion is often found that masters and slaves worked equally hard. If this was true, it could easily mean that owners had the surplus of both their own and their slaves' efforts to exploit—for no one suggests that slaves could control the fruits of their own labor. But there is plenty of evidence that slaves frequently did work harder than their owners. Aside from the citations about slaves and drudgery introduced previously, note can be made of additional examples of how hard slaves worked. To begin with, the Tlingit: Wood (1882, 328) wrote that in 1877 it was at first hard to distinguish slave and free among the Chilkat, "but the slaves hew the wood and carry the water and paddle the canoe." And a little later Frederick Schwatka (1893, 38–39) noted that while Chilkat slaves were formerly kept at the severest tasks, in 1890 the demands on them were much more lax. Elizabeth Healey (n.d., 18) says that among the Kwakwaka'wakw the lot of slaves was hard; they had to provide food for the family who had charge of them and only got the leftovers. And among the Halkomelem Salish, "every family of distinction had its own body of slaves, male and female. These did all the rough, dirty work, such as keeping the house clean, fetching water, and carrying firewood" (Hill-Tout 1907, 163). Among the Makah, Francis Densmore (1924, 121) notes that the possession of slaves relieved women of much arduous work.

The Significance of Slave Labor

There is little reason to doubt that any healthy slave could, in most years, produce more food than was necessary to keep himself or herself alive. In many years and in many groups, such a slave could produce a considerable surplus. At the very least, such production would compensate the descent group for the titleholder's productive work time that was taken up in being a titleholder. Perhaps more important, the slave's work and the product of that work was even more at the disposal of titleholders than was commoners' work. Thus the slaves contributed directly and often importantly to the descent group's surplus—the surplus that titleholders required to free themselves from at least common labor and to be able to plan and give feasts. The previous sections of this chapter have demonstrated these points by focusing on the tasks performed by slaves and on the value of the labor that slaves performed. Below I discuss the qualitative significance of slave labor.

The key to understanding the significance in qualitative as well as quantitative terms lies in the fact that titleholders controlled slaves and their labor in ways that they could not control commoners and their labor. All Northwest Coast societies were strongly stratified with the top stratum (titleholders) controlling access to resources and organizing ceremonial feasts and performances that were a focus of much attention in all these communities. To put on a successful feast considerable amounts of wealth—surplus to ordinary subsistence requirements—were necessary. Titleholders managed their kin unit's resources and labor supply largely with goals of feast giving in mind.

Titleholders gained the cooperation of commoners through the twin means of appeals to kinship reciprocity and kin group solidarity and by the fact that they controlled access to the kin group's resource base. In spite of the ethic of kin group solidarity and reciprocity, this meant that commoners were to some extent dependent labor. And in spite of the egalitarian ethic of kinship theory, many kin-based societies contain elements of dependent labor of just this sort. (Dependent labor based on gender and age—wives working for husbands, young men working for lineage elders—is even more widespread in such societies.) But in Northwest Coast communities there were two types of dependent labor: commoners and slaves. This fact should not be overlooked, but the differences in the kind of dependent labor involved were even more important.

Commoners labored for titleholders within a framework of kinship solidarity and reciprocity. The dependence of commoners and the exploitation of their surplus by titleholders was masked by the ideology of kinship. Titleholders did exploit commoners but not without offering some return; the ethic of reciprocity was real enough, and commoners benefited by belonging to the kin group of a successful titleholder, sharing in his ceremonial, military, or other successes. The dependent nature of slave labor is easier to see, although most Northwest Coast scholars have avoided doing so. Like slavery everywhere, the slave's very life was dependent on the master. In addition, no one doubted the owner's right to all the produce of the slave's efforts.

The essential point is that if someone in a traditional Northwest Coast community wanted to mobilize the work of others he (or less usually she) had two ways to do so: invoke kinship ties or issue orders to slaves. Kin were obliged but not required to go along with the request (especially the request of a titleholder), but slaves were both obliged and required to obey. In modern societies there are many ways to mobilize labor, the most important of which we call "wage labor." To understand the Northwest Coast situation one must remember that wage labor did not exist. There were only three sources of labor: one's self, one's kin, or one's slaves. Some comments in the sources remind us of the difference between kin and slaves and of the fact that these are the only kinds of labor available. For example: "An active female slave, however, is more valued than any wife who does not bring riches or powerful connections, *for the slave cannot leave the master's service*" (Sproat 1868, 95, writing of the Central Nuu-chah-nulth; my emphasis).

Even fairly long exposure to Europeans and their ways did not necessarily bring an acceptance of new working relationships. On the west coast of Vancouver Island in 1894 a Nuu-chah-nulth man was rescued at sea during a storm. On the journey back to land he was asked to carry a bucket of water. He replied that he was not a slave but a passenger and refused (Public Archives of Canada, RG10, vol. 3614, file 4105).

An important aspect of slaves from a titleholder's perspective was that their labor could be controlled and utilized without the inconvenience of reciprocal demands likely to be made by commoners. Slave labor was one of the most dependable ways of preparing for a feast or of assuring other aspects of the titleholder's desired style of living. As a Kaigani titleholder told John Dunn in the 1840s, the man "considered we were slaves—even our chiefs—who were always doing something from necessity, and as we were always working for a living. 'I have slaves,' said he, 'who hunt for me, paddle me in my canoes; and my wives to attend me'" (1844, 193).

7
Transactions in Slaves

This chapter considers the transfer of slaves from one local group to another by means other than warfare and violence. The primary focus of the chapter is on the trade in slaves, which was extensive. Other types of transactions that will be considered are the inclusion of slaves as a part of marriage prestations and the use of slaves as ceremonial gifts. The ideal way to study transactions is to analyze a large series of transfers of slaves from one group to another, noting who was involved in the transfer (slave, former owner, and new owner), where and when the transfer took place, the "price" of the slave, and the context of the transfer (sale, marriage prestation, ceremonial gift, etc.). No existing record of a slave transfer known to me gives us all of this information. Nevertheless, the nearly eight hundred sources used in this study were combed for information about the transfer of slaves, and this information was recorded in as much detail as possible. More than two hundred records of nonwar slave transfers were found. A record may be based on a general account in an ethnographic or historical source (a statement that the Haida traded slaves to the Tlingit, for example) or on a report of a particular transaction in an ethnographic or historical source (a statement that a Masset Haida gave ten slaves to a Gispakloats Tsimshian in exchange for a Copper, for example). Because conditions were changing so rapidly in the area throughout the nineteenth century, the records have been divided into three groups: ethnographic records (essentially undated), pre-1845 historical records, and post-1845 historical records.

The Trade in Slaves
Geography of the Slave Trade

In this section I use the trade records to reconstruct the aboriginal slave trade network. During the maritime fur trade period, some Europeans participated directly in the slave trade. At least four American ships are known to have engaged in the slave trade on their own behalf and occasionally a native trader hitched a ride with his human goods on a European vessel. But my concern is with the aboriginal trade, so these incidents are not considered here. There is no evidence that direct European involvement in trading native slaves was ever important enough to have had much of an impact on aboriginal trading patterns.

There are 173 usable slave trade records. (A usable record in this context is one in which both the source and the recipient group are known.) Most of these records are from ethnographic sources, but 25 percent are from pre-1845 historical records and 5 percent are from post-1845 historical records. Some records identify the local groups involved quite precisely (Taku trading with Stikine); others specify only that slave trade relations existed between two broadly identified linguistic or ethnic units (Haida trading with Tsimshian). In addition, the records tend to be clumped in space and time rather than evenly spread throughout the culture area, reflecting the interests and diligence of particular ethnographers and the presence of contemporary observers whose records have survived. For example, over half of the historical records fall into the period 1834–1841, the result of the quality and quantity of a few of the surviving Hudson's Bay Company trading post journals. The records also rarely mention the numbers of slaves involved. This, combined with the uneven coverage of the area by the records, means that no attempt to gauge the intensity of the trade accurately is possible. What the records do allow us to do is identify basic sets of groups that we know traded slaves with each other. Once these networks have been described, some additional inferences about aboriginal slave trading patterns can be made.

Mapping the available records reveals two major networks that are not connected to each other by the slave trade data. One is focused on the Columbia River, in the extreme south of the culture area. The other involves the northern part of the area and stretches from Prince William Sound in the north, southward to the northeastern part of Vancouver Island.

The Columbia River network.   This network stretches from the west coast of Vancouver Island in the north to the present-day Oregon/California border in the south. I call it the Columbia River network because the recorded movement of slaves was largely *toward* the Columbia River from both the northern and southern parts of the trading system. Figure 6 is a schematic diagram showing the main groups involved in this network. The arrows indicate the recorded direction of movement of slaves.

Late historical and ethnographic sources indicate that slaves were traded from the Klamath and Shasta of southern Oregon and northern California to Upper Chinook groups, especially in the region of The Dalles (a famous early

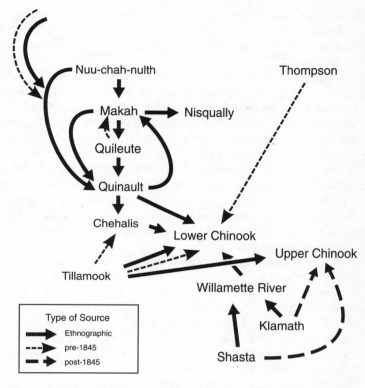

Figure 6.   Schematic Diagram of Columbia River Slave Trade Network.

historic trading center). Trade in slaves also came from these two groups via groups along the Willamette River to the Cowlitz and the Chinook at the Columbia River mouth.

From the north, ethnographic sources indicate that slaves were traded down the coast to end up among the Chinook. This trading chain probably began among the Nuu-chah-nulth on the west coast of Vancouver Island and, moving south, included the Makah, the various villages of Quileute and Quinault, the Lower Chehalis villages of Gray's Harbor, and, finally, the Chinook. Most of the records suggest that the most common pattern was trade between neighboring local groups. There was, however, some slightly longer-distance trade. For instance, occasionally some Nuu-chah-nulth groups bypassed not only their more southerly Nuu-chah-nulth neighbors but also the Makah at Cape Flattery (who were the major link in this chain with the west coast of Vancouver Island) and traded slaves directly to the Quinault. Similarly, the Quinault sometimes bypassed the Lower Chehalis and traded directly with the Chinook. North of the Columbia River the only movement of slaves other than north to south is an ethnographic indication of slaves being traded north to the Makah by the Quinault, which is reinforced by the circa 1809 trades by the Quileute to the Makah of the Russians who survived the shipwreck of the *Sv Nikolai* (Owens 1985, 64–65).[1]

The available records do not report any trade in slaves from the Salish-speaking groups in the Puget Sound region into the Columbia River network, although such trade would be expected. The journal of the Hudson's Bay Company post at Fort Langley tells us that in 1828 a Chinook traveled to this Fraser River post and purchased a slave from a Nlak'pamux who had traveled to Fort Langley from the interior (Fort Langley Journal 1827–1830, 53). Presumably, this Chinook returned to the Columbia with his purchase. This transaction did not directly involve any of the Lower Fraser River or Puget Sound groups, but it is probable that unrecorded transactions involving these groups did occur. Similarly, although there are no records of a trade in slaves between the Upper Chinook and the various Chinook groups near the mouth of the Columbia, it almost certainly did occur.

The Fort Langley transaction suggests that the construction of land-based fur trade posts created new opportunities for the slave trade by providing a recognized meeting place for would-be traders from considerable distances. It seems unlikely that direct trade would have occurred between the Nlak'pamux and Chinook without the development of an appropriately placed European post. It is also quite possible that the long reach of the southern portion of the Columbia River network (Shasta, Klamath) is a result of post-European contact conditions stemming from the fur trade.

The Northern network.   The northern network stretches from the Lequiltok of east central Vancouver Island north to the Chugach of Prince William Sound and includes some interior Athapaskan groups as well. In the southern part of this network, slaves tend to be traded north. Unlike the Columbia River network, there is a good deal of trade in several directions; a number of pairs of groups are recorded as trading slaves in both directions. The drift of slaves is, however, toward Tlingit territory, especially toward the Stikine, Chilkat, and Taku. These seem to have been the main points where slaves left the northern coastal network and were traded into the interior. Figure 7 is a simplified schematic diagram showing the main groups involved in the northern network. As can be seen from even a simplified diagram, the data available to reconstruct this network allow for a much more complex picture than is possible for the Columbia River network. One simplification is that all post-1845 records have been omitted altogether, as they make no significant new linkages. The most important simplification, however, is that all information about local or regional group transactions between Haida, Tlingit, and Tsimshian has

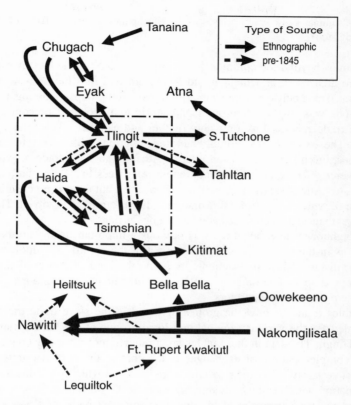

Figure 7.   Schematic Diagram of Northern Slave Trade Network.

been omitted. This information would make the diagram so complex as to be virtually unreadable.

The core region of the northern network is that occupied by various local groups of the Haida, Tsimshian, and Tlingit. Although only one record links the various Wakashan-speaking groups to the south to this core, other material, to be discussed later, suggests that additional links did tie these more southerly groups into the core. And the one record that does tie some Wakashan-speaking groups directly into the northern network is both clear and convincing about how the trade worked in the 1830s.

Thursday, December 25 [1834]: . . . Boston [a Heiltsuk titleholder] says they [the Lequiltok] barter their prisoners directly with the Quaghcuils [Fort Rupert Kwakiutl] & Nawity [Nawitti], who again dispose of the slaves to the Haeelt-zook [Heiltsuk] from whence they spread over all parts of the coast. At Stikine this summer I saw several slaves of the Kawitchin [Cowichan] Tribe. (Tolmie 1963, 299)

Groups beyond the commonly accepted boundary of the Northwest Coast culture area (such as Chugach and Eyak) are tied into the network via the Yakutat. Trade between various interior and coastal groups involving a number of goods was important throughout historic and probably precontact time. Slave trade records link only the Tahltan and Southern Tutchone with the coast. These two groups certainly had trade relations with other interior Athapaskans, but no evidence of an interior Athapaskan slave trade network was uncovered. (There are also ethnographic references to "Tsimshian" trade of slaves to "Athapaskans" [see Niblack 1890, 252], but there is no clear identification of which groups of Tsimshian or Athapaskan were involved. The most likely Athapaskan candidates are Tahltan or Carrier.)

Neighbor-to-neighbor trade was obviously important in the northern network as in the Columbia River network. But the records also indicate more longer-distance slave transactions. In the north, the distribution of water and land opens up a wider range of contact with both neighboring groups and more remote potential trade partners.

Tables 6 and 7 show the groups involved in the slave trade transactions recorded for the various regional and local groups of the Haida, Tsimshian, and Tlingit. The data in these tables are a reflection of what must have been a very complex pattern of exchanges in the core of the northern network, for almost certainly many local groups were involved who are not mentioned in connection with the slave trade in the sources. These data suggest that slaves tended to move from the Haida and Tsimshian to the Tlingit and also that Haida and Tsimshian were more likely to trade slaves with Tlingit than either Haida with Haida or Tsimshian with Tsimshian. It is also probable that, although there was some Haida-Tsimshian slave trading, the trade with the Tlingit was more important for both.

Other networks. The trade records reveal two small networks that the available data do not connect to either of the major networks. One of these connects the Nuxalk with the Chilcotin and through them to the Carrier. The available trade records do not connect the Nuxalk to the northern network, although we would predict such a connection through either the Heiltsuk or Haisla. Nor are the Carrier linked to the upriver Tsimshian (Gitksan and Niska), although trade between these groups in other goods is very well documented.

A Salish network involves both interior and coastal Salish-speaking groups. Three interior Salish groupings (Stl'atl'imx, Secwepemc, Nlak'pamux) are tied to four coastal Salish groups (Klahuse, Nanaimo, Sechelt, Squamish). The available records for this small network come largely from James A. Teit's

Table 6.   Haida and Tsimshian Transactions in Slaves

	Groups Traded from	Groups Traded to
Haida Group		
Haida	Tsimshian, Kitkatla, Central Tlingit, Southern Tlingit, *Tsimshian*	Central Tlingit, Southern Tlingit, Chilkat, Sitka, Stikine, Kitmat, *Stikine*
Kaigani		Southern Tlingit, *Sitka, Taku, Kitkatla*
Masset	Tsimshian, Gispakloats, Kitkatla	
Skidegate		*Stikine*
Ninstints		*Kitkatla*
Tsimshian Group		
Tsimshian		Haida, Masset, Tlingit, Central Tlingit, Chilkat, Athapaskan, *Haida, Stikine*
Kitkatla	Bella Bella, *Kaigani, Ninstints*	Haida, Masset, Tongas, *Southern Tlingit, Stikine*
Gispakloats		Masset
Fort Simpson		*Stikine, Tongas*
Lower Skeena	*Tongas*	*Stikine*

NOTE: Groups in italics from pre-1845 sources; all other groups from ethnographic sources. Nomenclature and spelling follow sources.

Stl'atl'imx monograph (1906). Teit reported fairly full information on slave trading for the Stl'atl'imx although unfortunately his data on slave trading are not equally detailed in his other Interior Salish monographs. Teit recorded slave trading in both directions between the Stl'atl'imx and the Secwepemc and Nlak'pamux. He recorded slaves as being traded from the Klahuse, Sechelt, and Squamish to the Stl'atl'imx. It is difficult to say whether the pattern suggested by these data reflects the overall flow of the slave trade in this part of the culture area, although it is consistent with the tendency for slaves to move from the coast to the interior noted among groups farther north. Other records show the Cowichan of Vancouver Island trading slaves to the Klallam, Lummi, Kwantlan, and Katzie. The available data do not tie these two

Table 7.   *Tlingit Transactions in Slaves*

Tlingit Group	Groups Traded from	Groups Traded to
Tlingit	Tsimshian	Tutchone
Southern Tlingit	Yakutat, Kaigani, Haida, Kitkatla	Yakutat, Haida, *Central Tlingit*
Central Tlingit	Haida, Tsimshian, *Southern Tlingit*	
Yakutat	Chugach, Southern Tlingit	Southern Tlingit, Sitka, Eyak
Taku	*Stikine, Angoon, Kaigani*	
Chilkat	Haida, Tsimshian	Tutchone, Auk
Sitka	Haida, *Kaigani,* Yakutat	Angoon
Henya		Auk
Angoon	Sitka, Taku	
Stikine	Haida, Tsimshian, *Kitkatla, Fort Simpson Tsimshian, Skeena River Tsimshian, Haida, Skidegate, Tongas*	Tahltan, Taku, *Tahltan*
Tongas	Kitkatla, *Fort Simpson Tsimshian*	*Stikine, Lower Skeena Tsimshian*

NOTE: Groups in italics from pre-1845 sources; all other groups from ethnographic sources. Nomenclature and spelling follow sources.

sets of groups together, but it is quite likely that all the groups mentioned belonged to a more general Salish trade network. It is certainly possible to establish trade in a range of other goods between many Salish groups. It is also almost certain that the various Puget Sound and Strait of Georgia Salish-speaking communities were tied into the Columbia River network, although we have no trade records to substantiate this.

Connections between networks.   Where the slave trade links are reported, we can be confident that trade in slaves occurred. But when our sources are silent—and they rarely explicitly deny trade links—we often cannot choose between the alternatives of no slave trade and missing information about slave trading that did go on. The problem of missing data leads to a consideration of two major problems posed by the network mappings: Were the northern and Columbia River networks connected? And to what extent did the Salish-speaking groups of Puget Sound and the Gulf of Georgia participate in the slave trade? These two problems are connected because the Coast Salish occupy most of the territory between the two networks and important links between the two would almost certainly have been through the Coast Salish.[2]

The general data on slavery imply that slavery was less important among the Puget Sound and Gulf of Georgia Salish than it was either to the south or north of that region. As there are only six trade records for the core Coast Salish area, the relative rarity of slave trade records supports this view. The Hudson's Bay Company journals from Fort Simpson in the north are full of references to slaves and slave trading during the 1830s. The comparable journal from Fort Langley on the Fraser River contains few such references. One must be cautious because of the missing data problem, but I suggest that there was little connection between the two networks until relatively late in historic times.

The Origins of Slaves Traded

In this section I consider what light the ethnic origins of the slaves obtained in trade by various local groups throws on the slave trade. Unfortunately, we have to rely on largely undatable ethnographic records for most of the ethnic identifications of traded slaves. The ethnic origin of slaves taken in war has already been discussed in chapter 5.

For the northern network almost all of our information on the identities of traded slaves comes from the three core ethnolinguistic groupings. Therefore, we will concentrate on those groups here. Table 8 assembles the available data on ethnic origins of slaves traded to or from one or another Haida, Tlingit, or Tsimshian group. Most of the slaves identified come from groups within the northern network or from groups on its periphery. The Salish almost certainly were Coast Salish from the Gulf of Georgia or even Puget Sound region. In early times these might well have been northern Gulf of Georgia Salish obtained in war by Kwakwaka'wakw who were on the southern edge of the northern network. In later historic times, northern groups from the Haida and Tsimshian are known to have taken some slaves from the heart of Coast Salish country as a sideline to trips to Victoria (see chapter 5) and some of these probably got into the trade. The "interior" Indians were almost certainly Athapaskans from groups bordering on the northern network. This leaves the "flatheads" unidentified. "Flathead" refers to the practice, widespread on the Northwest Coast, of artificial skull deformation. There being several distinct ethnic styles of head "flattening," this designation might refer to Kwakwaka'wakw speakers (within the northern network) or to more southerly non-network groups such as Coast Salish or even Chinook. The term is too vague for certain identification, but, as Olson (1967, 92) notes, the Tlingit called the

Table 8.   *Ethnic Origins of Slaves Traded from or to Core Groups of Northern Slave Trade Network, by Data Source*

	Data Source		
Group	Ethnographic	Pre-1845	Post-1845
Tlingit	Niska, Huna, Henya, Yakutat, Southern Tlingit, Haida, Tsimshian, Coast Tsimshian, Flatheads, Salish, Nakomgilisala, Tlatlasikwala, Kwakwaka'wakw	Skidegate, Chugach, Sitka, Kodiak, Cowichan, Nawitti	Tahltan, Columbia River
Haida	Salish, Interior, Kwakwaka'wakw		Columbia River
Tsimshian	Salish, Interior, Kwakwaka'wakw, Nakomgilisala, Tlatlasikwala, Nuxalk, Chilkat	Nawitti	Tahltan

NOTE: Nomenclature and spelling follow sources.

Kwakwaka'wakw by a term that translates as "flathead." Because of this, the common tendency to identify "flatheads" with people from the extreme south of the culture area should be resisted.

The only identified slaves traded in the northern network who clearly did not come from the network or its periphery are those from the "Columbia River" mentioned in post-1845 sources as being traded among some Tlingit and Haida groups. By this date slaves from this far south are consistent with the known journeys of some northern natives to Victoria and even into Puget Sound.

Turning to the Columbia River network, few of the traded slaves whose ethnic identities are known are from outside this network. For the groups around the mouth of the Columbia River, the focal point of this network, only two traded slaves are outside the already established network. One of these is a Lequiltok (the southernmost Kwakwaka'wakw group) obtained by a Chinook while on a trip to the Hudson's Bay Company post at Fort Langley in 1838, and the other is a Nisqually orphan who was sold to a Chinook in 1875 by another Nisqually (Ray 1938, 51–54). Neither of these instances does much to tie the Gulf of Georgia and Puget Sound areas into the Columbia River network.

According to the trade records, the west coast of Vancouver Island was a somewhat marginal part of the Columbia River network. The ethnic identities of slaves known to have been traded by or to Nootkan speakers (Nuu-chah-nulth and Makah) confirm this view. Except for some Quileute traded by the Makah (the Quileute and Makah are neighbors), all belong to Nuu-chah-nulth local groups. Except for one record involving a Lummi, the slaves traded by Quileute and Quinault are all from groups involved in the Columbia River network and most are from groups relatively near to the Quileute and Quinault.

The data on the ethnic identity of traded slaves support the hypothesis of the last section that the two major networks were probably not connected in a significant way. If important linkages did occur, they almost certainly happened in relatively late historic times. The ethnic identity records also suggest that although the Coast Salish were probably not important participants in the slave trade, they were involved as slaves, especially in the northern network.

Prices of Slaves

Scattered throughout the ethnographic and historical records are a number of references to prices paid for slaves. Altogether, 146 records containing price or value data were located.[3] The records are about evenly divided between the ethnographic and historical. The disparate nature of the data on prices paid for slaves makes it very difficult to compare one sale with another. The following examples will give some idea of the problem: in 1828 a Chinook buys a slave from a Nlak'pamux for a gun, a blanket, and two yards of copper wire (Fort Langley Journal 1827–1830); in the 1830s a Heiltsuk sells a slave for 10 3½-point blankets, 50 balls, 20 leaves of tobacco, 1 secondhand pint pot, 3 gallons of mixed rum, and 1 much-worn trading gun (Tolmie 1963, 310); in 1857 some Masset Haida pay 30 blankets and 1 gun "besides a number of other articles" for each of six slaves (Fort Simpson Journal 1855–1859, 59–99).

The price data include records of two types of transactions that should be kept distinct: the exchange of slaves for what may be called ceremonial or prestige items and the exchange of slaves for more mundane goods, especially furs and European trade goods. Although there are some "mixed" transactions in the records, the two types of exchange will be discussed separately. Some attention will then be given to the information that is available about differential prices paid according to the age and sex of slaves.

Eighteenth-century prices.   All but one of the seven eighteenth-century records deal with the sale (or attempted sale) of slaves to Europeans. Most of these records involve Spanish purchases of children who were to be taken to Mexico for Christian education and the exchange of metal (usually sheets of copper) for slaves. These records serve mainly to indicate the strong desire for metal in the early contact period. Prices are usually one to several "sheets" of

Table 9.   Value of Coppers in Slaves

Number of Slaves Equivalent to One Copper	Group	Date	Reference
9	Chilkat	Ca. 1840	Dunn 1844, 288
8	Yakutat	Ethnography	De Laguna 1972, 231
8–10	Yakutat	Ethnography	De Laguna 1972, 323
3	Yakutat	Ethnography	Hrdlicka 1930, 34
6	Chilkat	Ethnography	Oberg 1973, 117
8	Chilkat	Ethnography	Olson 1967, 19
2	Sitka	Ethnography	Swanton 1909, 332
10	Sitka	Ethnography	Swanton 1909, 347
1	Stikine	Ethnography	Swanton 1909, 133
4–6	Central Tlingit	Ethnography	Swanton 1908, 437
3–5	Huna	Ethnography	Olson 1967, 50
6–10	Southern Tlingit	Ethnography	Swanton 1905, 145
20 or 40	Tlingit	Ethnography	Emmons 1991, 42
6 or 7[a]	Kaigani	1838	Fort Simpson Journal 1838–1840, 62
1 (plus canoe, 90 boxes oil, ?)[a]	Skidegate	1852	Fort Simpson Journal 1852–1853, fol. 26d
2[a]	Masset	1855	Fort Simpson Journal 1855–1859, fol. 9d
4 (plus 2 slaves worth of property)[a]	Haida	Ethnography	Swanton 1905, 145
4–10	Haida	Ethnography	Curtis 1916, 131
10	Haida	Ethnography	Dawson 1880, 135
10	Haida	Ethnography	Harrison 1925, 213
2[a]	Masset	Ethnography	Swanton 1905, 70
6[a]	Skidegate	Ethnography	Sanger 1970, 156
9	Tsimshian	1840s	Dunn 1844, 283
10[a]	Masset/ Gispakloats	Ethnography	MacKenzie 1892, 53
10 (plus 2 canoes and 1 dance headdress)[a]	Masset/ Gispakloats	Ethnography	MacKenzie 1892, 53

Table 9 (continued)

Number of Slaves Equivalent to One Copper	Group	Date	Reference
8 (plus 1 canoe, 100 elk skins, 80 boxes of grease)[a]	Tsimshian	Ethnography	MacKenzie 1892, 53
15	Fort Rupert Kwakiutl	Ca. 1866	Lord 1866, 257
20 (plus other goods)[a]	Nimpkish	Ethnography	Boas 1910, 85
2 (plus 40 sewed blankets, 120 cedar bark blankets, 2 canoes)[a, b]	Mamalilikula	Ethnography	Boas 1921, 1024
4 (plus 80 skin blankets, 240 cedar bark blankets, 4 canoes)[a, b]	Nakwakto	Ethnography	Boas 1921, 1026
10–15	Nuxalk	Ethnography	McIlwraith n.d., 74

NOTES:
   [a]Actual transaction; all unmarked entries represent reported "value" of Coppers in slaves or what a Copper was reportedly "worth" in slaves.
   [b]The same Copper is involved in both transactions.

copper for a slave (Wagner 1933, 19; Howay 1941, 196). Also indicated is a ready supply of slaves available for sale to Europeans in the area of earliest intensive contact in the eighteenth century, the west coast of Vancouver Island, especially Mowachaht and Clayoquot.

Prices involving prestige items. The Copper is the most commonly recorded "ceremonial" item involved in slave transactions. Coppers are a special class of wealth object associated with ceremonial presentations during feasts. Large sheets of hammered copper of distinctive shape, they range from one and a half to three feet in length.[4] Table 9 shows the values of various Coppers in slaves. Coppers were northern phenomena, probably never used south of the Kwakwaka'wakw (Drucker 1955, 143), and these records reflect the relative richness of the Tlingit and Haida sources (13 and 9 respectively of 31 cases). Only twelve entries record actual exchanges of Coppers for slaves. The other entries reflect the custom of valuing Coppers in terms of slaves and are consistent with the substitution of Coppers for slaves in some ceremonial events. The value of each Copper depended on its size (as is explicitly indicated in some of the sources, e.g., Swanton 1905 for the southern Tlingit) and for some groups, at least (especially Kwakwaka'wakw), also depended on its potlatch history (Drucker 1955, 143). Particular Coppers ranged in value from one to forty slaves. The number of slaves involved in the seven known transactions (1 + other goods, 2, 2, 2+, 4+, 4+, 6, 6, 8+, 10, 10+, and 20) suggests that the values claimed for the other Coppers realistically reflect actual transactions.

Slaves were also part of the valuation of both material and nonmaterial ceremonial and prestige items other than Coppers. Table 10 shows the value in slaves of other types of ceremonial and prestige items. As with Coppers, most of the fourteen records deal with values claimed for slaves, although five do relate to transactions. The range in values is from one to forty slaves and, like the data for Coppers, is confined to the northern part of the culture area.

For the southern part of the culture area, the value of slaves is sometimes expressed in terms of the traditional shell "money" that was an important prestige item. Slaves are known to have been valued in terms of shell money among the Puyallup-Nisqually, Snohomish, Twana, and Nlak'pamux, although this practice was undoubtedly more widespread.

The price of slaves is also sometimes stated in terms of canoes. Canoes were major value items, important in travel, production, and warfare. But their ownership, much like the ownership of slaves, was a mark of importance and power and conferred prestige on the owner. As this was especially true of large seagoing canoes, I have included canoes in the prestige exchange section, even though they are also "practical" items. This practice existed among the Quinault, Klallam, Puyallup-Nisqually, Kitimat, Haida, and Tsimshian.

Prices involving furs and trade goods.   Slave transactions involving ceremonial and prestige items were probably important in both pre- and postcontact times. But, in addition, in the nineteenth century many slave transactions involved payment in furs, European trade goods, or even cash. Prices for slaves are expressed in a wide variety and mixture of goods, but a number are expressed in terms of the standard of exchange of the fur trade, the "blanket," or in the near-equivalent of the blanket, the beaver pelt. To facilitate analysis, I have attempted to translate all prices into a blanket equivalent. This is difficult because the available data on the value of blankets, furs, and so on, are very sketchy. The fur trade on the North Pacific Coast is not very thoroughly studied; almost all the enormous fur trade literature deals with the region east of

Table 10. Value of Ceremonial and Prestige Items in Slaves

Number of Slaves	Ceremonial/ Prestige Item	Group	Date	Reference
1[a] (?)	Carved figure for canoe	Yakutat	1820s	Krause 1956, 128
5	Cape with dentalia	Yakutat	Ethnography	De Laguna 1972, 349
1	Song	Chilkat	Ethnography	Olson 1967, 19
1	Copper spear	Sitka	Ethnography	Swanton 1909, 332
1 + 200 blankets[a]	Shark crest carving	Sitka	Ethnography	Olson 1967, 43
3[a]	Iron hammer	Sitka	Ethnography	Olson 1967, 53
5	Copper labret	Huna	Ethnography	Olson 1967, 48
1 + 50 blankets[a]	Wolf hat	Auk	Ethnography	Olson 1967, 43
40	Copper parts of crest hat	Stikine	Ethnography	Swanton 1909, 332
3	Highly decorated hat	Tlingit	Ethnography	Veniaminov 1972, 26
1 or 2	Hair ornament	Haida	Ethnography	Niblack 1888, 261
2	Pair of abalone shell ear ornaments	Gispakloats	Ethnography	Boas 1916, 378
10[a]	Figure on post	Nakomgilisala	Ethnography	Boas 1897, 381

NOTE:
   [a]Actual transaction; all unmarked entries represent reported "value" of items in slaves or what an item was reportedly "worth" in slaves.

the Rockies. The secondary literature does not supply much information about the prices paid to Natives for furs or other goods. For example, the price demanded for a beaver pelt varied over time and also from place to place, but there are no systematic data available on this in the published literature. I have used scattered data to estimate price equivalents, but these estimates are obviously subject to considerable possibility of error. To take one example, the "blanket" was not a single item; there were, for instance, 2$\frac{1}{2}$-point blankets, 3$\frac{1}{2}$-point blankets, and so on. These had different values, but the sources only sometimes indicate which grade of blanket is involved in a particular transaction. The major sources of the value equivalents of trade goods used here are Mayne (1862) and the letters of John McLoughlin (1941, 1943).

Most of the available price data are shown in tables 11 through 15. The tables are for individual ethnolinguistic groupings or regions and are organized chronologically. There are not enough data in any one table to allow confident statements about prices, but at least one trend can be identified: shortly after 1850 there was a significant jump in the price of slaves calculated in blankets. Before 1850, the price was usually in the ten- to twenty-blanket range. After 1850, the price was over, usually well over, thirty blankets. In the pre-1850 period, the price seems to have been somewhat higher in the north than in the south. What interpretations can be placed on these apparent trends? The price increase after 1850 may be due to a decline in the value of blankets that is independent of slave transactions. But if it is not, then it is probable that either the supply of slaves decreased or the demand for slaves increased. Both probably occurred, but it is likely that a decrease in the supply of slaves was a major cause. By the 1850s and certainly by the 1860s, European control of the coast was becoming more and more complete and, although some intranative fighting continued, the suppression of the raids that produced slaves was more successful. Fewer slaves were being produced, but the population declines both on the coast and in the interior, which might increase the demand for slaves, continued unabated throughout the mid-nineteenth century. Higher prices in the north also reflect what was probably a higher demand for slaves in the north. This would be consistent with the flow of slaves to the northern interior through such Tlingit groups as the Stikine, Chilkat, and Taku.

Prices according to age and sex. Too few cases in the price records detail the age and sex of slaves sold to allow for calculations to determine the relative value of male versus female or young versus mature slaves. A few statements do suggest some relative values. Five sources state that women were worth less than men: Chinook, ca. 1840 (Lee and Frost 1968, 103); central Tlingit, in the 1860s (Tikhmenev 1978, 407); Chilkat, ethnographic (Olson 1967, 80); Yakutat, Angoon, Sitka, and Stikine Tlingit, ethnographic (Emmons 1991, 42); and the Quileute, ethnographic (Singh 1966, 81–84). Three sources state that gender made no difference to the value of slaves: Nuxalk, ethnographic (McIlwraith 1948, 1:159); Quinault, ethnographic (Olson 1936, 87); and Saanich, ethnographic (Jenness n.d., 60). One ethnographic source states that women were worth more than men (Kitimat [Lopatin 1945, 30]), and one historical source states that, whereas men were formerly worth more, in the 1860s women were more valuable because of their potential as prostitutes (Nuu-chah-nulth [Sproat 1868, 89–92]). This last source is a reminder that the relative value of men and women undoubtedly varied over space and time and that other European demands in addition to the fur trade affected the course of the slave trade, for example, the demand for prostitutes in and around such growing centers as Victoria on southern Vancouver Island. In the 1860s

Table 11.   Chinook Slave Prices

Date	Price	Equivalent in Blankets	Reference
1828[a]	Gun, blanket, 2 yards copper wire	10 plus	Fort Langley Journal 1827–1830, 57
1836–1837		8 to 15	Slacum 1912
Ca. 1840		8 to 12	Lee and Frost 1968, 103
1843		4 to 5	Ruby and Brown 1976, 191
Ca. 1850	$100–$500	20 to 100	Swan 1966, 166
1875[a]	$200 + considerable property	?	Ray 1938, 51

NOTE:
[a]Actual transaction.

Table 12.   Coast Salish Slave Prices

Date	Price	Equivalent in Blankets	Group	Reference
1827[a]	7 or 8 blankets + minor trade items	7 to 8+	Klallam	Fort Langley Journal 1827–1830, 20
1828[a]	10 beaver	15	Cowichan	Fort Langley Journal 1827–1830, 79
1829[a]	10 beaver	15	Pilalt	Fort Langley Journal 1827–1830, 101
1829[a]	4 skins	6	Kwantlen	Fort Langley Journal 1827–1830, 164
1860[a]	$200	40	?	*Daily British Colonist*, 13 October 1860
1863[a]		50	Songish	*Daily British Colonist*, 26 September 1863
1860s[a]		80	Lummi	Brown 1869, 304
Ethnography	5 beaver	7 to 8 (?)	Snohomish	Haberlin and Gunther 1930, 29, 39

NOTE:
[a]Actual transaction.

Table 13.   Nuu-chah-nulth Slave Prices

Date	Price	Equivalent in Blankets	Group	Reference
1810[a]	5 blankets + many other trade goods	10+ (?)	Makah	Owen 1985, 64
1850s		50–100	Makah	Swan 1869, 32
1860s		30	?	Sproat 1868, 89
Ethnography[a]	gun	10–15 (?)	Nitinaht	Sapir and Swadesh 1955, 422
Ethnography[a]		200	Seshart	Sapir and Swadesh 1939, 227
Ethnography		400–500	Nitinaht	Mooney n.d.

NOTE:
 [a]Actual transaction.

Sproat (1868, 89–92) wrote that, while female slaves brought thirty blankets on the west coast of Vancouver Island, an area remote from white settlement, in Victoria female slaves brought fifty to sixty blankets apiece.

George T. Emmons (1991, 42) specifically states that for the Tlingit the value of a slave depended on his or her age and sex. He further suggests that, while a man was worth more than a woman, a pregnant woman or one of childbearing age was worth more than a young girl or an older woman. He cites values given by informants who had witnessed slave trading from four Tlingit local groups.[5] In two groups women were said to have been worth about half the value of a male slave and in two groups about two-thirds the value of a man.

Even less information is available about price differentials due to age, but, as would be expected, sources for three groups (Makah, Upper Chinook, Nuxalk) state that adults were more expensive than children.

Other Transactions involving Slaves

Although it is the best-documented transaction type involving slaves, trade was not the only way that slaves changed owners. Slaves might be included as a part of the goods that were exchanged at a titleholder marriage. Ceremonials almost always involved the host's giving away of at least some property, and on important ceremonial occasions even slaves might be distributed to some of the guests. Slaves were sometimes included in the settlements made at peace ceremonies and were sometimes a part of wergild payments to settle a claim for murder compensation. And occasionally a slave would be given away as a present for reasons not clear in the source. This final section will discuss such

Table 14.   *Tlingit Slave Prices*

Date	Price	Equivalent in Blankets	Group	Reference
1820s	25 beaver	10–15 (?)	Yakutat	Krause 1956, 128
1827	15–20 skins	8–10 (?)	Sitka	Litke 1987, 90
Ca. 1835	25 beaver	12–13	Sitka	Wrangel 1980, 32
Ca. 1839[a]	8 beaver	4	Stikine	Fort Simpson Journal 1838–1840, 27
Ca. 1839[a]	16–21 beaver	8–10	Stikine	Fort Simpson Journal 1838–1840, 79d
1840[a]	18–20 skins	9–10	Stikine	Douglas 1840, 36
1840[a]	16–20 skins	8–10	Killisinoo	Douglas 1840, 36–38
1840[a]	16–20 skins	8–10	Taku	Douglas 1840, 37
1860s	40–60 blankets + goods	40–60+	Central Tlingit	Tikhmenev 1978, 407
1860s	$200	40	Yakutat	Abercrombie 1900, 395
1860s	$200	40	Stikine	Emmons 1991, 42
Ethnography	6 sea otter	36	Yakutat	Emmons 1991, 42
Ethnography	10 moose hides	250 (?)	Angoon	Emmons 1991, 42
Ethnography	15 moose hides	375 (?)	Sitka	Emmons 1991, 42
Ethnography	Several hundred dollars	?	Southern Tlingit	Knapp and Childe 1896, 43
Ethnography	5–10 dressed moose hides	250	Chilkat	Olson 1967, 80

NOTE:
[a]Actual transaction.

transactions in slaves in as much detail as the sources allow. Only a handful of actual transactions of these types are described, although there are also many general statements in the sources indicating that such transfers took place.

The Use of Slaves in Marriage Arrangements

Throughout the Northwest Coast marriages were matters of arrangement between the families of the prospective bride and groom. Often complex negotiations were involved. This was especially the case if the proposed marriage was between titleholders. Everywhere in the culture area material gifts were

Table 15. *Northern Slave Prices*

Date	Price	Equivalent in Blankets	Group	Reference
1811[a]	15 elk hides, 4 otter, 2 blankets	50–60 (?)	Kwakwaka'wakw	Ruby and Brown 1976, 116
1811[a]	5 skins	2$\frac{1}{2}$	Skidegate	Reynolds 1970, 29
1811[a]	8 skins	4	Skidegate	Reynolds 1970, 37
1834	9 blankets, gun, + other goods	20–25+	Fort Simpson area	Dunn 1844, 183
1835[a]		10+	Owiltoch	Tolmie 1963, 310
1835[a]	15 elk skins + other goods	?	Tsimshian	Tolmie 1963, 313
1840[a]		10	Tsimshian	Fort Simpson Journal (Nass) 1840, 22d
1841[a]	Sea otter skin	12	Haida	Fort Simpson Journal 1841, 10
1842[a]	7 beaver, 4 guns, 1 blanket	16	Tsimshian	Fort Simpson Journal 1842–1843
1857[a]	30 blankets + 1 gun	35	Masset	Fort Simpson Journal 1855–1859, 99
1857		35	Fort Simpson area	Fort Simpson Journal 1855–1859, fol. 90d
1861[a]	50 blankets + 1 gun	55	Fort Rupert Kwakiutl	*Daily British Colonist*, 15 April 1861
1866[a]		55	Kitkatla	*Church Missionary Intelligencer*, PABC, file F 498 21
1870s		200	Haida	Dawson 1886, 132
Nineteenth century	$200–$1,000	40–200	Tsimshian	Garfield 1951, 29
Ethnography		10–20	Nuxalk	Boas 1892, 10
Ethnography		25	Kitimat	Lopatin 1945, 30
Ethnography	$500–$600	100–120	Kitimat	Lopatin 1945, 30
Ethnography		100	Nakwakto	Curtis 1915, 238

NOTE:
[a]Actual transaction.

exchanged between the kin of the two spouses. In some groups the value of the goods moving in each direction was about the same, in others the value of the gifts to the bride's kin was considerably greater, and we may speak of "brideprice" in these cases.[6] Where titleholders were concerned, the scale of wealth items involved in these marriage prestations could be considerable. Consider the following brideprice presented to an important Chinook principal titleholder on the marriage of his daughter in 1795: 20 slaves, 20 sea otter skins, a canoe, and 20 leather war dresses (Bishop 1967, 126). All of the items listed here were high-value items, and it is not surprising to find slaves on the list. This may appear to be an exaggerated report, but the Chinook were becoming wealthy from the maritime fur trade and Charles Bishop was an astute observer, so I think he is a reliable source. All the values are twenty except for the canoe. We might note that elsewhere on the coast canoes were sometimes described as holding twenty slaves, so that the consistency of the list is maintained for all items.

Slaves appear as a part of marriage prestations throughout the coast. Table 16 assembles the available information. Of the twenty groups in the tribal unit sample, ten are reported to include slaves in at least some of the wealth transfers associated with titleholder marriages. The Snohomish also appear on the table although they are not a sample group. This is because there is no information about the use of slaves in marriage prestations for any of the Puget Sound Salish in the sample and the Snohomish information serves to indicate that at least one Puget Sound Salish group transferred slaves in this fashion. This means that all three of the area's regions are well represented among the groups reporting positively on this variable. We can regard the inclusion of slaves in wealth transfers associated with marriages as a Northwest Coast–wide phenomena, although not every titleholder marriage in every local group included slaves in marriage prestations.

The data on the various Nuu-chah-nulth groups (represented by the Clayoquot in table 16) require some clarification. Curtis describes a particular instance among the Clayoquot when a slave was sent to the family of the bride, but both Drucker (1951) and Sapir and Swadesh (1955) indicate that among most Nuu-chah-nulth groups the families would send slaves in both directions. Drucker also noted that the Chickliset titleholder family owned an unusual prerogative: they had the right to "buy a husband." Instead of the groom's family coming to the prospective bride's family and offering them a brideprice as a part of the negotiations, the Chickliset principal titleholder had the hereditary right to reverse the usual pattern and "make an offer" for a prospective husband for one of his daughters. This included giving a slave to the groom's parents (Drucker 1951, 273).

Table 16 also records all the non-Kwakwaka'wakw instances when the number of slaves involved in a marriage prestation is stated in the sources,

Table 16. The Use of Slaves as a Part of Marriage Prestations

Group	"Direction" of Slaves	Number of Slaves	Reference
Chilkat	to wife	?	Olson 1967, 19
Sitka	exchange between families	8 [to wife's kin], 5 [to husband]	Olson 1967, 43
Stikine	to wife	10	Barbeau 1958, 129–142
	to husband	?	Swanton 1909, 112
	to husband	8	Swanton 1909, 133
Haida	with bride	?	Curtis 1916, 120
	to wife's family	?	Swanton 1905, 52
	with bride	10	Harrison 1925, 166
Lower Skeena Tsimshian	to husband	2	Boas 1916, 207
Nuxalk	to wife's family	?	McIlwraith 1948, 1:396
Fort Rupert Kwakiutl[a]	to husband's family	3	Boas 1935, 182
Clayoquot	to wife's family	?	Curtis 1916, 64
	exchange between families[b]	?	Drucker 1951, 147–148, 273
	exchange between families[b]	?	Sapir and Swadesh 1955, 176–177
Makah[c]	exchange between families	5 [to wife's family], 3 [to husband]	Olson 1936, 110
Saanich	with bride	?	Jenness n.d., 83
Snohomish	to wife's family	2	Haeberlin and Gunther 1930, 51
Chinook	to wife's family	20	Bishop 1967, 126

NOTES:
[a]For additional Kwakwaka'wakw examples, see text.
[b]Other Nuu-chah-nulth groups; see text.
[c]Makah titleholder groom; Quinault titleholder bride.

although many of the blank entries probably involved a single slave. On the whole the numbers seem likely. Bishop's report of twenty slaves as part of a Chinook bride price in 1795 was accepted above and the other numbers are all considerably smaller than this one.

The largest series of marriage prestations available is that for the Kwakwaka'wakw. This series is drawn mostly from the family histories in Boas's *Ethnology of the Kwakiutl* and is made up of seventeen different marriages, all involving leading titleholders. Kwakwaka'wakw titleholder marriage prestations are fairly complex. In the first instance, the prospective groom journeys to his proposed bride's community and makes a payment that Boas translates as the "marriage payment." When this is accepted the bride returns with her husband to his village. As they are ready to leave, the bride's father makes a gift to the groom that Boas variously translates as the "marriage gift" or the "marriage mat." Later, as children are born, the father-in-law will make additional gifts that will have a total value greater than the husband's original gift and that are considered repayment of the marriage debt. The father-in-law's various prestations usually include both material objects and important names and ceremonial prerogatives. All the prestations involving slaves occurred as a part of the bride's father's marriage gifts. The median number of slaves involved in these prestations is four and ranges from two to seven. Altogether the family histories list the material contents of thirty-two marriage gifts. This means that one-half of the known marriage mats included slaves. In addition, the family histories mention when the Hudson's Bay Company post at Fort Rupert was built, so we can date the impact of the first major European intrusion directly into Kwakwaka'wakw territory and examine its possible influence on the inclusion of slaves in marriage prestations. One-third of the post–Fort Rupert marriage gifts included slaves, and 57 percent of pre–Fort Rupert marriage gifts included slaves. Since this difference is not statistically significant (by Fisher's exact test), we cannot say with great confidence that the inclusion of slaves in marriage gifts declined after the building of Fort Rupert in the heart of Kwakwaka'wakw country, although the reported drop is considerable. The following are two typical examples of the makeup of Kwakwaka'wakw marriage gifts (the first pre– and the second post–Fort Rupert):

After the marriage [he] gave to his son-in-law . . . as a marriage gift two slaves, four large canoes, forty dressed elk-skin blankets, one hundred deer-skin blankets, forty lynx blankets, seven marten blankets, and twenty mink blankets, and also a name. (Boas 1921, 865–866)

[The father-in-law] made ready to give a marriage gift to his son-in-law. . . . They launched eight canoes, and loaded them with twenty woolen blankets, and forty mountain-goat blankets, two hundred cedar-bark blankets, and four slaves. (Boas 1921, 882)

The Use of Slaves in Wergild
and in Peace Ceremonies

In common with many kinship-based societies, in a number of Northwest Coast groups when a person was killed his or her relatives expected and sought compensation. This is often referred to as "blood money" or wergild. Historically, in European wergild the size of the compensation due to the relatives was dependent on the rank of the victim; the higher the rank, the higher the payment. It is an appropriate term for the Northwest Coast practice because here too the victim's rank determined the scale of the compensation. Wergild was widespread in the northern region of the area and among the Salish, but the Nuu-chah-nulth and at least some Kwakwaka'wakw groups did not practice the custom. In these last communities revenge by means of killing the murderer or one or more of the murderer's relatives was the approved way of settling a homicide. Such revenge killing also occurred where wergild was practiced. The sources tell us that slaves could be included as a part of wergild payments among at least six of the tribal unit sample groups (Sitka, Haida, Lower Skeena Tsimshian, Klallam, Twana, and Quinault) and perhaps among a seventh (Fort Rupert Kwakiutl) (Drucker 1950, 221; Boas 1916–1931, 218, A291). Elmendorf (1960, 477) says that among the Twana the usual wergild for a man of "good family" was two slaves, three canoes, twenty blankets, and "lots of beads and shawls." Quinault wergild included from one to three slaves (Olson 1936, 116). Among the Tongas Tlingit, Olson (1967, 91–92) records one instance of four slaves being included in a wergild payment and eight in another such payment; in another instance the murderer's kin offered five and then ten slaves, but the victim's kin demanded the life of the killer in addition to the payment of slaves. At Sitka, in the 1850s a slave was given in compensation for the death of a woman (Jones 1914, 200–201). Wergild payments could cross ethnic as well as local group boundaries as when, in 1832, a Kaigani offered ten blankets and a slave to the Henya in compensation for the accidental killing of a Henya (Simpson 1831–1832).

In the northern part of the culture area, hostilities between groups were sometimes concluded by a formal peace-making ceremony. At these ceremonies prestations were made by both sides. Slaves were often (usually?) included in these exchanges of gifts. The sources state this clearly for the Yakutat, Chilkat, Tongas, Haida, and Lower Skeena Tsimshian. The practice was probably universal among the Tlingit, Haida, and Tsimshian, but it is not certain how far south the custom occurred. There are a number of detailed accounts of the prestations involved in these peace ceremonials available in the literature.

One such account in Boas's *Tsimshian Mythology* (1916, 380–388) details the ending of a war between the Gispakloats Tsimshian and a Haida group. The Haida made a successful large-scale attack on the Gispakloats during which they killed a large number and took many women and children captive. Among these were the principal Gispakloat titleholder's sister and her son. The title-holder, Legaic, soon organized a retaliatory attack in which many Haida were killed or enslaved and Legaic's sister recaptured. But his sister's son (and heir?) remained with the Haida. The next year the Haida came to make peace, bring-ing with them Legaic's sister's son. As part of the peace settlement prestations were made by both sides. Along with many other items, the Haida titleholder, Sditala, gave Legaic ten slaves and various of Legaic's close matrilineal kin (or affines) gave Sditala a total of thirty-five slaves.

Slaves as Feast Gifts

Among the tribal unit sample, we know that the Chilkat, Sitka, Stikine, Haida, Lower Skeena Tsimshian, Nuxalk, Mowachaht, Clayoquot, and probably the Fort Rupert Kwakiutl used slaves as part of the gifts dispersed at feasts (pot-latches). Thus slaves were probably feast prestations (at least at very impor-tant occasions) throughout the northern and central parts of the culture area. I know of only one reported case of a slave being given away at a feast in the southern part of the culture area. This happened in 1863 when a Songish gave away a slave in a feast held near Victoria. But this potlatch was attended not only by people from other Salish groups (both from what was then Washing-ton Territory and from the Nanaimo) but also by Nitinat and Tsimshian, so it may well not reflect traditional Salish practice (*Daily British Colonist*, 26 September 1863).

The gifts presented to the invited guests by the Gitwilgyots hero of "The Prince Who Was Deserted" when he took a new name at the end of his tribula-tions are typical of the accounts of such distributions in myths and tales:

> [The hero] invited all the chiefs [i.e., the principal titleholders from all the Lower Tsimshian winter villages]. . . . When all the chiefs were in his house, he took ten costly coppers, ten large canoes, fourscore and ten slaves, elk skins, twenty score of sea-otter garments, marten garments, dancing blankets, and many horn spoons and horn dippers and many costly abalone shells, and earrings of killer whale teeth and many boxes of grease and crab apples mixed with grease, and all kinds of provisions. Before he gave away all of this, he took one of the costly coppers. They placed it on his chest, and he took his new name, Deserted One. After that they proclaimed his new name. Then he took the costly coppers and gave one to each chief, and he gave away the rest of his goods. (Boas 1916, 232)

The following account of a feast distribution among the Nakwaktak after the successful sale of a Copper by the feast's host offers more detail. The guests are the other heads of the Nakwaktak descent groups.

He gave all the four slaves to the holders of the first seat in each of the nu-
mayms [descent groups]. He gave one slave to the holder of the first seat of the
GexsEm, another one to the holder of the first seat of the sisnL!e, one slave to
the holder of the first seat of the TsetsEmeleqala, and another slave to the holder
of the first seat of the TEmltEmlEls; and he gave in addition to the slave a large
canoe to each, for he gave the canoe to the same men to whom he had given the
slaves. After he had given away the slaves and canoes to the holders of the first
seats, [he] took the eighty sewed blankets and gave them away to the chiefs of
second rank and their children; and after doing so, he took the two hundred and
forty cedar-bark blankets and gave them away to the people of lower rank. After
these had been given away, the guests went out of the house. This is another
kind of great feast, which is called "giving away at the time of the great feast."
This was done by [him]. Very few give this kind of feast, although they may be
head chiefs of all the tribes. (Boas 1921, 1027)

Slaves as a Part of Shamans' "Fees"

Shamans were found in all Northwest Coast communities. Among other
things, they were the principal medical practitioners in their societies. They
are known to have received slaves as part of their reward for curing titleholders in several groups. These are the Haida, Tsimshian (groups not identified),
Niska, and Fort Rupert Kwakiutl. Usually these slaves are described as a part
of the shaman's payment, but one source describes the slave as a "present"
(Swanton 1905, 42). The nature of the shaman's "fee" on the Northwest Coast
is not clear, so it may not be appropriate to describe them as being "paid" for
services as if they were practicing in a money economy. But in any event, important titleholders did sometimes reward a successful shaman with slaves.

8
Slaves and Ritual

The peoples of the Northwest Coast are famous for their rich and complex ceremonial life. In this chapter I examine the role of slaves in these ceremonies, focusing on both the use of slaves in ritual contexts and the participation of slaves in ceremonial life. As with other topics, ceremonial practice was not uniform throughout the culture area, and neither was the role of the slave in ceremonial activity. The chapter begins with a discussion of the use of slaves in rituals, first addressing their most widespread use—in the burial feasts of titleholders—and then looking at the use of slaves in other feasts and ceremonies. Next I consider slaves as participants in ceremonies and other religious activities. The chapter concludes with a description of the tie between cannibalism and slavery and a discussion of the possible symbolic association of slaves, Coppers, and salmon.

The Destruction of Slaves at Funeral Feasts

Throughout the Northwest Coast, among the most important occasions were the celebrations surrounding the death and funeral of a titleholder. These were events of religious, economic, political, and social significance. Not only was the deceased titleholder remembered, honored, and sent to the next world in glory, but the heir, the replacement of the deceased, was publicly recognized and undertook his or her first performance in a new role. Although there were variations in content from group to group, I will label all of these events "funeral feasts."[1] At many titleholder funeral feasts, especially if it was a feast for the leading titleholder of a community, it was not uncommon for one or more slaves to be killed. Usually the deceased's own slaves were the ritual victims.[2] These killings were part of a sequence of property distribution or destruction.

There are many statements in the sources that slaves were often or even usually killed during the feasts and ceremonies that marked the death of an important titleholder. There are several accounts of actual occurrences of such deaths. Among these, the Russian Orthodox priest Anatolii Kamenskii's (1985) account of the ritual slave destructions associated with a series of titleholder deaths at Sitka is probably unique. His report makes clear the nature of the killings and shows how they changed over time with economic and political circumstances.

As Kamenskii notes, certain regalia were associated with the office of clan chief. These regalia had known histories and were passed from officeholder to officeholder. The events that concern us here relate to the Huna Tlingit, although for most of the history recounted the Huna clan concerned, the Kaa-gwaantaan, were residing at Sitka. Two pieces of ceremonial regalia were involved, a "chief's" staff and a ceremonial hat.

Our account begins when a man named Kunanek became clan chief. Before he took up the staff and put on the hat, he gave a large feast and invited guests from several other villages. (Chilkat and Yakutat are mentioned; guests from Sitka were almost certainly invited and probably from other local groups as well.) The feast opened with the strangling of four male slaves. This was done in honor of the staff and hat.

Kunanek's heir was his sister's son, who moved to Sitka and gave an even larger feast to honor his regalia. Again guests from at least Chilkat, Huna, and Sitka were present. Once again the feast opened with the destruction of property. But this feast occurred in Sitka in the 1850s, by which time there was considerable Russian pressure to stop the killing of slaves. In this instance four male slaves were freed. The next heir (also a sister's son) freed two slaves. The one who followed him freed one slave. (All of these events are summarized in table 17.) When the man who had freed a single slave died, he had no living sister's son to be his direct heir. The closest heir was the woman marked "E" on the diagram in table 17. From the account it is not clear which of the two genealogical positions labeled "E?" she held. In any event, she inherited the regalia and the right to transmit them to her sons. By now slaves were becoming rarer and were difficult to obtain, so she gave away blankets to the value of two slaves. Her eldest son also gave away blankets worth two slaves when he took up the regalia. This man, marked "F" in table 17, assumed the regalia after 1867 and the coming of the Americans. He was the last to hold both the staff and the hat. When he died, the second and third brothers each got one of the chiefly artifacts, but whether or what they gave away to mark their coming into possession of them is not recorded. Sometime in the 1890s the youngest brother inherited the staff alone. (The hat went to

Table 17.   The Transmission of Ceremonial Regalia Associated with the Huna Kaa-gwaantaan Clan Chieftainship

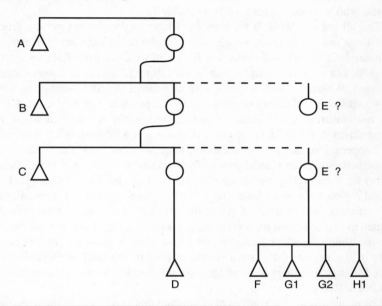

Chief	Action at Succession Feast	Approximate Date
A	kills 4 male slaves	?
B	frees 4 male slaves	post-1850
C	frees 2 slaves	?
D	frees 1 slave	?
E	gives away blankets worth 2 slaves	?
F	gives away blankets worth 2 slaves	post-1867
G1/G2	?	?
H1	gives away blankets and calico	1890s

another Kaagwaantaan clan member, whose relationship with the others is not discussed.) This man, "H1," did give away property at a feast to mark his taking up of the staff, but the value of the "blankets and calico" given away is unknown. Thus a feast to mark the passing of a titleholder and the taking up of the position and regalia by the heir was maintained throughout a period of considerable change. The association of the destruction/dispersal of valuable property with this feast was also maintained. What changed was that the freeing of slaves was substituted for the killing of slaves and, finally, the giving away of property to the value of slaves was substituted for the freeing of slaves, who were no longer readily available.[3]

The killing of slaves at funerals (and later in the contact period, freeing them) was present from the northern edge of the area (Yakutat) to its southern boundary (Chinook) (see table A-9 for ratings on the use of slaves in ceremonies). For only one sample unit is the killing of slaves at funerals denied (Twana). Where we have no information (most of the Salish-speaking units), Salish-speaking neighbors of these units did practice funerary slave killing. The northernmost Coast Salish, who bordered on the Kwakwaka'wakw, also killed slaves at titleholders' funerals (Comox and Klahuse). What was probably happening in late precontact times, then, was that most titleholder deaths in northern and central local groups (and around the mouth of the Columbia River) were marked by the killing of slaves, while in the Gulf of Georgia/Puget Sound region only some local groups killed slaves at some of their titleholders' funerals. The pattern of the distribution of this culture trait thus conformed to that observed for a great many Northwest Coast cultural attributes: it is most highly developed and intensely practiced in the northern and central parts of the region, the pattern is less intense in the Gulf of Georgia/Puget Sound region, and there is some increase in intensity around the mouth of the Columbia River.

For many groups the sources also indicate that slaves might be given away or freed as a part of funeral feasts. It was a widespread Northwest Coast practice to give slaves to titleholder witnesses as a part of the distribution of property to guests at important feasts, and it probably occurred more often and in many more groups than the sources indicate. But the freeing of slaves was almost certainly a substitute for the killing of slaves.

In the sequence of Huna feasts described above, we have already seen a shift from killing to freeing. In his account of these events Kamenskii suggests that the Kaagwaantaan heirs began to free rather than kill slaves because of Russian intervention. But as Sergei Kan (Kamenskii 1985, 97) points out in his editorial comment on this passage, this pressure did not always work and some ritual slave killings occurred even after 1867, when the much more militarily powerful Americans took over in Sitka.

As happened at Sitka, among many of the northern groups the sources indicate that during the middle part of the nineteenth century a gradual transition was made from killing slaves on important ceremonial occasions to freeing them. As suggested above, it is likely that some slaves had always been given away, although freeing slaves was probably an innovation. But during this period slave killing became increasingly rare. It did not, however, cease altogether for some time. As will be shown in chapter 11, there are reports of slave killings even in the 1880s. As the nineteenth century wore on ideally many titleholders would have preferred to kill some slaves, but they were able to do so less and less both because of the decline in the availability of slaves and because of the pressure from Europeans to discontinue the practice. The Huna Tlingit example shows this transition. And the following Tsimshian example suggests that the old forms were often closely followed even if slaves were no longer literally killed.

About 1866, Legaic, the leading Gispakloats titleholder, erected a totem pole called Legyarh's Eagle at Port Simpson. Titleholders were present from other Lower Skeena Tsimshian groups as well as from the Kitkatla Tsimshian, Niska, and Haida. Some of the more important guests brought slaves who were supposed to be killed and buried under the pole when it was erected. A Haida woman slave was held by her owner at the foot of the pole, ready to be killed. Her owner (a Lower Skeena Tsimshian) had his knife ready to perform his task. Another titleholder said, "This is enough. She has been killed, she is now dead. Let her go back to her people." She was then given to another titleholder who took her back to the Nass when he went home.[4] Other slaves were treated in the same fashion. (See Barbeau 1950, 90–91, for this ceremony.)

Titleholder motivations for killing slaves at funerals were complex, and the sources do not offer nearly enough information about them. At least four themes are clear: the destruction of property, the association of blood and human life and the taking of human life with power, the need for consolation over the death of a kinsperson, and the provision of servants in the deceased's afterlife.

The idea of providing one or more slave servants for the deceased titleholder was widespread. A Chinook source notes that

> the wife of Calpo, a very influential chief of the Chinook village near Cape Disappointment, on losing a daughter in the year 1829, killed two female slaves to attend her to the world of spirits, and for the particular purpose of rowing her canoe to the far off happy regions of the south. (Parker 1967, 245)

Other tribal unit sample groups for which the same motive is reported are the Sitka (Kotzebue 1830, 54), Stikine (Gordon 1880, 69–70), and Lower Skeena Tsimshian (Jackson 1880, 275–281). Another source discussing the Kwakwaka'wakw in general also states that the slaves who were killed would be servants in the afterlife (MacFie 1865, 448). This motivation was probably common among groups for which the sources are silent, as some idea of an afterlife was widespread in the culture area (Barnett 1939, 265–266; Drucker 1950, 229). Obviously, when slaves were freed rather than killed, deceased titleholders lacked servants in the afterworld.

According to Drucker (1951, 333–334), among the Nuu-chah-nulth slaves were killed to be the "death companions" of a deceased titleholder. This sounds much like the idea of the slave as servant in the afterlife. But it turns

out that an alternative method of providing a death companion was to attack
a neighboring group and kill one of its members. The most important conscious
motivation for warfare on the Northwest Coast was to avenge the death of
a fellow group member. Revenge was desirable not only when the attacked
group was responsible for the death; sometimes revenge was sought for deaths
that were not the result of intergroup violence. What was wanted was another
death to balance out and ease the pain of one's own group's loss.[5] A slave's
death would also "even up" the tally of deaths. This is especially so when it is
remembered that most slaves were originally members of another group. Revenge against outsiders could be accomplished with a victim already available
close at hand. The probability that this kind of generalized vengeance was
often involved in slave killing is increased when note is taken of the fact that
among some Tlingit groups slaves were sometimes killed in the same manner
in which the titleholder died: a slave was drowned if the titleholder drowned; if
the titleholder died of an illness, the slave was strangled by a log laid over his
or her neck (Krause 1956, 163–164).

The destruction of property is a common theme in the literature on Northwest Coast ceremonies and feasts. Property destruction showed the power
and wealth of the destroyer. Such destruction may have asserted one's strength
even more than the giving of valuable gifts to fellow titleholders. Heirs were
not only honoring the dead but were also validating their claim to the title
they were inheriting. As slaves were among the greatest and most important
wealth items, the killing of slaves was property destruction at its most spectacular. Freeing slaves, of course, destroyed them as property as well. This is
perhaps why Europeans had as much success as they did in the middle part
of the nineteenth century in persuading some to free rather than kill slaves at
ceremonies such as funeral feasts.

If killing a slave destroys property, it also destroys human life. Slaves
were literally killed. There are definite associations on the Northwest Coast
between power (mundane and spiritual) and blood and the taking of life,
especially human life. By killing slaves, titleholders not only demonstrated
that they had power, they obtained power as well. This must have been an
attractive prospect at any time, but it would have been particularly attractive when an heir was succeeding to a title. This, in conjunction with the
motivations discussed before, may explain why funerary ritual killing was so
widespread.

Other Slave Ritual Killings

A number of other important ceremonies also occasioned the ritual killing of
slaves (for ratings, see table A-9). Although there is a good deal of missing
information, from the northern Gulf of Georgia Salish south the sources indicate that slaves were rarely used in ceremonies except at the funerals of title-

holders. North and west of these Salish speakers, slaves were killed (or freed or given away) on the occasion of numerous important ceremonies. There are data to suggest that slaves were killed or given away at some "potlatches" (which are not identified more precisely) in all these northerly groups.

The killing or freeing of slaves should be distinguished from the giving away of slaves. I have already argued that freeing slaves developed out of killing slaves as a response to pressures from increasingly powerful Europeans. Thus the contrast is between the destruction of property at a feast (killing, freeing slaves) and the transfer of property from one owner to another at a feast (what is usually referred to in the sources as "giving away" slaves). As was briefly noted in the section on funeral feasts, the bestowal of gifts on other titleholders was an integral part of most Northwest Coast feasts and ceremonial occasions. During the most important of these events, titleholders, especially important ones, included among the property presented the most valuable types of property such as canoes and slaves. Thus the giving of slaves on these occasions is another reminder that slaves were property. Indeed, they were among the most valuable property that a person could control. When given away in a ceremony the slave played the same role as any other of the major property items that might be involved.

Major property items were often destroyed on the occasion of important feasts. To the outsider, slave killing is the most spectacular example of such property destruction. Also, the killing of slaves was not "mere" property destruction. The taking of human life, "killing," had a wider significance as well: as already discussed, it was associated with a titleholder's power, as the killer both demonstrated and increased this power with his act. The ideas surrounding property on the Northwest Coast are complex, and this is not the place to try to disentangle them. Yet I note that for the Kwakwaka'wakw at least, it seems to have been the case that other major property, such as canoes, could also be "killed," and indeed canoes were also sometimes destroyed at the same type of feasts as were slaves. One should not generalize from the Kwakwaka'wakw to the entire area, or even to the northern portion of the area, but this is suggestive of probably widespread notions of the nature of the items that qualify as major property.

Aside from funerals, perhaps the three most important ceremonial events for titleholders were the building of a new house, the taking of a new or additional name (title), and the erection of a commemorative post or pole (usually called totem poles in the literature). These were all occasions on which slaves were killed in the northern part of the region. Although there are some missing data, I think it safe to conclude that, except for the Nuxalk, all groups from the Kwakwaka'wakw north did kill slaves at least some of the time on these occasions. For the Nuxalk, McIlwraith explicitly denies that slaves were killed when a new house was built, but he describes one occasion when a slave of northern (Tlingit?) origin was interred under a new house post. This was done after a Nuxalk man who had been a slave in the north described this practice. McIlwraith's (1922–1924, 34) informants told him that this was done in "revenge." Although not clearly stated, the implication is that the Nuxalk did not normally kill slaves at name takings or on the erection of poles (McIlwraith 1948, 2:346–347). The Nuxalk did kill slaves at the funerals of titleholders, so that as in many other cultural practices, these northernmost Salishan speakers represent a compromise between "northern" practices and those of their more southerly linguistic confreres. Data on the use of slaves in these three ceremonies are largely missing for the Nuu-chah-nulth groups, although there is a report of slave killing at a Clayoquot name taking (Johansen 1960, 45; the original date of the source is 1791). I infer that slave killings did occur among the Nuu-chah-nulth at these types of ceremonies more often than is recognized in the sources but less frequently than was the case farther north. South of the Kwakwaka'wakw ritual slave killings are noted occasionally at "potlatches" whose exact type is unknown, but they were undoubtedly quite rare events. Not only were house-building and name-taking ceremonies less elaborate in the south, but the erection of poles was rare and often absent as a culture trait.

Slaves were also killed at important ceremonies that had a much narrower geographic distribution. The most important of these were Nuu-chah-nulth ceremonies associated with the killing of whales. The Nuu-chah-nulth (along with their neighbors and near linguistic relatives the Makah) were the only Northwest Coast peoples to actively hunt whales (all took advantage of a beached dead whale). Whaling was a titleholder prerogative and the ritual associated with it was very elaborate (Drucker 1951; 1965, 132–144). There are eighteenth-century accounts of slaves being killed during whaling rituals among both the Mowachaht (Sales 1956, 114; Wagner 1933, 160–161) and the Clayoquot.

> The first whale that was killed in a season it was their custom to make a sacrifice
> of one of their slaves the corps they laid besid a large pece of the whales head
> adorned with eagles feathers after it has lay'd their a sertain time they put it in
> a box as usual. (Howay 1941, 77–78; original date 1789)

In December 1864 Sproat (1868, 155–156) also witnessed the killing of a slave during the celebration of a "wolf dance" at Tsishaat. The most important Nuu-chah-nulth ceremonial, the so-called wolf dance, was probably the occasion of slave killings fairly regularly.

Olson (1967, 113) reports a Tongas oral tradition that recounts that a father killed two slaves in honor of his son's becoming a shaman. It is not unlikely that this happened sometimes on similar occasions among many groups in the northern part of the region.

Among at least some Nuu-chah-nulth groups, slaves were not accorded any dignities at burial but were simply thrown into the sea or the bushes. Our source on the Clayoquot whale ceremony suggests that slaves who were killed at whaling ceremonies were given the dignity of a free person's burial. Ritually killed slaves may also have been given a more dignified burial than was normal for slaves in some other groups (e.g., the Sitka Tlingit; Krause 1956, 163–164).

Slaves as Participants in Rituals

I have shown how slaves were used in various Northwest Coast ceremonies, either as sacrificial victims or as items of property to be given away. Here I describe the occasions when slaves acted as participants in some ritual or ceremony. I begin with some accounts of slave participation, when that participation was definitely not to the slave's benefit. Indeed, these events could as easily fit into the discussions of ritual killing.

Boas's Kwakiutl field notes (1896–1933, 1746–1749, A24–27) contain an account of a ceremony held at Fort Rupert where it is said that two female slaves agreed to be burned in a ceremonial display. They were told that although they would be burned to death, they would then be resurrected in four days. Their deaths were accomplished, and, with great theatrical display, four days later two Kwakiutl titleholders pretended to be resurrected from the dead.

Such impersonations were not confined to the Kwakwaka'wakw. In his reminiscences, the Tsimshian Arthur Wellington Clah (1908, 7) describes a rather elaborate ruse of a similar nature by the Gispakloats principal titleholder Legaic. The important titleholders announced that they were going to perform an important ceremony and burn all the "chiefs." About a year before this ceremony was to take place, some of the titleholders went to Tlingit country and purchased a slave who closely resembled Legaic—"get moustache, whiskers, same face"—and secretly brought him to Legaic's house. Legaic went into hiding and the slave lived among Legaic's wives and close followers as if he were the man he was impersonating. The commoners were kept at a distance from the stand-in so that they would not discover the substitution. All of the Lower Skeena Tsimshian local groups were invited to the feast. A large fire was made and the titleholders gathered around it. The common people crowded around the outside to see. The slave who looked like Legaic was burned in the fire. The slave said that if he died he would not come back, but if he did not die he would come back in a few days. The commoners ran away from the fire in considerable distress, because they saw the slave's body burning, and later the titleholders put the man's charred bones in a box. Later someone began calling inside the box. When the titleholders opened the box, Legaic stepped out. He had come back from the dead. After his resurrection there was much singing and dancing and a large feast was held. The slave's obvious cooperation in this piece of theater suggests that he, too, was convinced that the Tsimshian titleholders were capable of bringing him back from the dead.

Among most northern groups ceremonial participation seems to have been largely of this kind. Slaves, willing or unwilling, were the objects of ritual activity but had no control over the script or its performance. The Tlingit sources are particularly clear on this point. Slaves seem to have been present at ceremonies, but they could not join in the feasting. Catherine McClellan (1954, 94) cites an instance among the Taku when a slave did join in and says that the result was a war. Among the Chilkat slaves were not allowed to perform any type of ceremonial task. In the case of unusually talented slaves, pretense enabled their owners to use their talents. If a slave was a particularly skilled carver, he might carve a mask, but someone of titleholder rank was said to be the actual carver and the slave merely regarded as a "tool" (Oberg 1973, 87–88).

For most of the other northern groups, the sources have little to say about slave participation in ritual activity. For the Tsimshian, Garfield (1939) says that sometimes a favorite slave might be given the privilege of attending feasts. She gives one instance in which a slave performed minor feast duties and received small gifts for his services, but this was obviously relatively late in the nineteenth century (p. 272).

Among the Nuxalk, the Kusiut dance was one of the most widespread ceremonies. Anyone, including slaves, could be initiated into this dance. If a slave were initiated, his or her owner must give him one of the latter's own names associated with the dance (McIlwraith 1922–1924, 107–108). The Nuu-chah-nulth wolf dance has been mentioned above. This ceremonial was an elaborate piece of theater in which all of the winter village participated. The basic structure of the performance was simple. Novices (children) were kidnapped by supernatural wolves and later rescued by their kin and ritually purified. During the entire period of the ceremony many of the ordinary rules of conduct were set aside. For instance, many of the superficial marks of privilege of titleholders were not practiced. It is probably the case that even slaves had to be initiated. This means that the only noninitiates in a Nuu-chah-nulth community were small children and perhaps some non-Nuu-chah-nulth slaves. It is quite probable that even Maquinna's European slaves, John Jewitt and his companion John Thompson, were initiated into the wolf dance, even though they did not understand what was happening.[6] Probably the best interpretation of the participation of slaves in these Nuxalk and Nuu-chah-nulth ceremonies is that allowing slaves to join in these rituals recognized their humanity.[7] There is no suggestion for either group that slaves participated in other ceremonies or even that they played significant roles in either the Kusiut dance or the wolf dance.

Among the Gulf of Georgia and Puget Sound Salish, the participation of slaves in ceremonial life was also limited. Among some Salish groups, for example, the Saanich (Jenness n.d., 61) and some Puget Sound groups (Haeberlin and Gunther 1930, 75), it was sometimes possible for slaves to acquire a guardian spirit, but in at least one other group, the Twana (Elmendorf 1960, 409), slaves could not. A few groups, for example, the Lummi (Stern 1934, 73–74) and Saanich (Jenness n.d., 61), allowed slaves to participate in spirit dances. But the slave's role in religious and ceremonial life was very limited among the Salish. For the Saanich it is explicitly stated that slaves could not row canoes on ceremonial occasions (Jenness n.d., 61). But perhaps the weakness of the slave's position is best shown by the Samish case, where a man seeking a powerful guardian spirit did everything necessary to make one appear. The spirit appeared, but it gave the man only half its power, because his father was "part slave" (Haeberlin and Gunther 1930, 68). Obviously this search took place in late historic times, after slaves had been freed, but the attitude toward the spiritual powers of slaves almost certainly reflects older beliefs.

As we have seen, throughout the entire culture area slaves were generally excluded from ritual life. The few exceptions probably do no more than minimally acknowledge the slave's humanity. Nothing approaching full participation was ever possible. This is not very surprising in a region where ritual life was so firmly based on rank and privilege.

Cannibalism and Slavery

Beginning with the earliest eighteenth-century sources, cannibalism has been reported for a number of Northwest Coast groups. The historical observers usually accepted that cannibalism occurred, as did most of the ethnographers who reported it. More recently, under the influence of those who would deny the reality of cannibalism anywhere, some (e.g., Archer 1980) have denied the reality of Northwest Coast cannibalism. In the best recent treatment of the topic, Joyce Wike (1984) accepts that cannibalism was a reality and attempts to describe it and place it in its proper context in the Northwest Coast cultures where it was practiced. Her general conclusions seem reasonable to me, and I will adopt them here. That is, the consumption of human flesh, obtained from the living, from recently killed bodies, or from corpses, occurred in specific ritual contexts. The persons consuming human flesh had a *right* to do so, which was either inherited or obtained through marriage transactions. In most, perhaps all, instances human flesh was consumed to pacify the appetites of a supernatural being who during the cannibal performances infused the body of the performer.

These cannibal performances were not found throughout the culture area.

They seem to have been confined to the northern and north central part of the region. Perhaps the best known of the cannibal dancers are the Kwakwa-ka'wakw *hamatsa*. Cannibals were a part of some ritual activities among most, if not all, Kwakwaka'wakw local groups, the Northern Wakashan (Haisla and Heiltsuk), the Nuxalk, the Southern and Lower Skeena Tsimshian, the Haida, the Comox, and perhaps a few of their fellow Coast Salish groups also near the Kwakwaka'wakw and at least the northern and central local groups of the Nuu-chah-nulth. There may have been cannibal activity among some of the southern Tlingit as well.

Slaves were the major living targets of cannibals. In some instances, they seem to have been deliberately acquired so that they could be killed and eaten.[8] Individual men often sought infusion with the cannibal spirit by isolating themselves from their communities. When they returned home, they were often in a cannibalistic frenzy, needing to satiate their desire for human flesh. Some sources indicate that the most likely victim would be a slave. Among the Haida, for example, novice cannibals underwent initiation away from their villages and had to bite a piece of flesh off the first person they met on returning to the village. According to Harrison, "The chiefs, in order to save their own flesh, compelled one of the slaves to go forward and meet him" (1925, 101). Similarly, among the Heiltsuk, when a titleholder returned to the village in a frenzy and encountered a slave or a dog, it was killed (Anderson 1863, 79). And for all of our sample tribal units, where cannibalism was practiced there are ample data that slaves were killed by cannibals. Indeed, before slaves became increasingly rare as the nineteenth century wore on and before European pressure to stop killing slaves (and other persons, for that matter) was increasingly effective, purposely killed slaves were probably the major source of human flesh for cannibal performances.

Some of the most spectacular reports of cannibalism in the area are also the earliest. I refer to accounts in the eighteenth-century sources of what can be called the Mowachaht titleholder Maquinna's "cannibal feasts." Maquinna was the dominant titleholder in Nootka Sound in 1778 when James Cook and his crew made that landfall during Cook's third Pacific voyage. Maquinna, or someone holding the title, remained the dominant native figure in Nootka Sound throughout the maritime fur trade period and had encounters with many British, Spanish, American, and other ship's crews for the thirty years following this first meeting with Cook's men. We find descriptions of Mowachaht, particularly Maquinna's, cannibal practices in many of the journals and other sources relating to that period.[9] A reading of these sources could easily lead one to conclude that what was involved was not the ritual consumption of human flesh but gastronomic or even epicurean cannibalism. For instance, some of the Spanish sources consulted by Warren L. Cook (1973, 296) state that Maquinna had fattened up at least eleven young children to be killed and eaten. The sources are contradictory as to whether these cannibal undertakings were common (even monthly) or relatively rare (limited to special occasions or preparations for warfare).

The eighteenth-century Mowachaht material is important because it suggests that cannibalism was a fully developed cultural practice at the time of first European contact and because it suggests a different kind of cannibalism than is described in the nineteenth-century historical sources or in the ethnographic sources. The classic account of the origin of Northwest Coast cannibalism suggests that the hamatsa originated among the Heiltsuk and diffused via marriage, potlatching, and warfare to other northern groups (Boas 1897). Wike (1984, 240–245) argues that, although fragmentary, there is evidence to suggest that cannibal rituals date back into at least the sixteenth century. Equally important, she presents a good case that Maquinna's cannibal activities, when examined carefully, are consistent with the nineteenth-century cannibal rituals. Thus we have one rather than two kinds of Northwest Coast cannibalism. We also have a case that cannibal rituals are relatively ancient rather than relatively recent. Certainly they are not post- or protocontact, although both the diffusion of and changes in the ritual were dynamic in the nineteenth century.

Slaves and cannibals are paired, because slaves were the most important objects of cannibal appetites. When slaves became rarer and killing them more difficult, cannibals turned to ingesting corpses and to taking bites out of living fellow villagers (these victims were later compensated) and dogs. Dogs were a particularly appropriate substitute for slaves, since they are ambiguous animals and slaves have their own ambiguous status as humans.[10] We can also note one final link between the spread of cannibal ritual and slavery: war captives who had knowledge of cannibal ritual sometimes taught it to their new masters. This spread the practice, because capture in war was one legitimate way of obtaining rights to property, including ritual property. The irony of this particular form of diffusion is that what happened to one such slave teacher probably happened to others as well: Boas (1921, 1015) reports that the Nakwaktak enslaved a woman from a Nuxalk group who instructed her captor in the cannibal ceremony. The Nakwaktak then killed and ate her!

Salmon, Copper, and Slaves

The association between salmon and copper is frequently mentioned in the Northwest Coast literature. For example, in the Tsimshian myth called by Boas "Tsauda and Halus" one of the headwater streams of the Skeena is said to be a source of native copper. This happened when some chinook (spring) salmon reached the upper part of this stream and "the salmon became copper. Therefore the Indians know that there was live copper in this brook or river" (Boas 1916, 301). Later in this same myth it is told how when a young titleholder (married to the daughter of a supernatural being) spears a salmon in a certain stream it is transformed into copper. This live copper kills the young man who has caught it. His supernatural father-in-law resurrects him and teaches him how to catch the "salmon coppers or live coppers" and turn them into the ceremonial objects now known as Coppers. He becomes the first worker in copper and acquires great riches as a result (Boas 1916, 304–306). Among the Kwakwaka'wakw, there are references in myths to copper as having the smell of salmon (Widersprach-Thor 1981, 116) and Boas (1930, 185–188) notes several other identifications between salmon and copper.[11] As a final example of the salmon/copper association, McIlwraith (1948, 1:253–254) reports a Nuxalk myth about the only location where Coppers are created, a distant river far to the north of Nuxalk country. There, chiefs spear "salmon of some peculiar kind" and using heat from a fire and pounding it with a stone transform the salmon into a Copper. The link between salmon and copper does not exhaust the richness of the symbolism surrounding either copper or salmon.

Coppers and slaves are also associated. In the Nuxalk myth mentioned in the preceding paragraph, for example, when a chief attempts to spear one of the "peculiar" salmon, he "invariably" misses. He achieves success by dropping his spear, killing a slave by cutting his throat, and putting a small piece of the slave's flesh on the point of his spear. The slave's flesh makes the spear "so potent that when next the chief lunges at a salmon he transfixes it and brings it ashore" where he can transform it into a Copper as previously described (McIlwraith 1948, 1:254). Everywhere Coppers are found they are commonly valued in terms of slaves. (See chapter 7 for details.) Among the Kwakwaka'wakw, Martine Reid (in Widersprach-Thor 1981, 124–125) has clearly shown that in the last half of the nineteenth century the destruction of Coppers was substituted for the destruction of slaves on many ritual occasions. Coppers are also associated with another important war trophy, the heads of vanquished enemies. And if one accepts Reid's argument that, at least for the Kwakwaka'wakw, the shape of the Copper represents the shape of a human being, the link between the destruction of a Copper during a ritual or a rivalry potlatch in the late nineteenth century and the destruction of a slave on similar occasions earlier becomes even stronger (Widersprach-Thor 1981, 121–126; see also Jopling 1989, 15–44).

Salmon have now been linked with Coppers and Coppers with slaves. This might be taken to imply a symbolic association between salmon and slaves. The implication would be a rather weak one if other salmon/slave associations cannot be found. What will appear to be something of a digression is required, but such associations can be strongly suggested.

Throughout the northern part of the culture area deceased slaves were not normally accorded the burial usual for commoners. From the Nuu-chah-nulth and Kwakwaka'wakw north to the Tlingit most of the sources would agree with Heinrich Johan Holmberg about the treatment of slaves.

The Tlingits cremate their dead, except for their shamans or their magicians, who are laid to rest in their coffins on four high posts. Slaves may not use either type of burial, and their corpses, like those of dogs, are thrown into the sea. (1985, 23)[12]

As noted in chapter 4, when interviewed in the 1920s and 1930s a few informants claimed that slaves were given simple but "decent" burials and that their bodies were not cast out as Holmberg describes. Where there are older sources for these informants' groups, they agree with Holmberg's observations. Altogether it seems likely that throughout the northern part of the culture area the usual fate of a slave's corpse was disposal at sea unless the slave had been killed on a ritual occasion.

As far as I know, only two sources give a reason for putting the bodies of slaves into the water. Swanton (1905, 54) says of the Haida that "the bodies of slaves were thrown into the sea, for otherwise the owner thought he would never acquire any more property," and Boas's (1896–1933, 1450–1451, A5508–5509) unpublished notes contain the comment that among the Kwakwaka'wakw the bodies of slaves were "thrown into deep water. Because it is believed that if they were buried they would come back and take their master's soul."

Swanton's Haida information immediately leads us to salmon. Some form of first salmon ceremony was practiced over most of the Northwest Coast culture area. Frequently for the first run of at least some species or for fresh salmon, many groups disposed of salmon bones, offal, or both by putting them in the water. The explanation given for returning salmon bones and offal to the water is to ensure the return of the salmon next year. Salmon regenerate from the bones and offal, and should a bone not be put back in the water one of the returning salmon would be missing that part. In anger over this omission, the salmon would not return at all.

Mythological support for this is found in what Boas called the "The Prince Who Was Taken Away by the Spring Salmon," which he analyzed at length in *Tsimshian Mythology* (1916, 192–206, 770–779). There are numerous versions of this myth found throughout the culture area and in parts of the neighboring Plateau area. In brief outline, a titleholder boy somehow comes or is brought to the land of the salmon. (Salmon, in their own country, are organized into villages and so on just like human beings.) The boy is told to kill some of the salmon children for food and given instructions as to what to do so that the children may be resurrected. The boy then returns home, usually with plenty of fish for his family and community. He teaches his people the rules so that there will always be plenty of salmon. In almost every version of the myth the principal rule is that the salmon bones must be thrown into the water or into the fire. Boas notes versions of this myth or related myths that place the bones into the water for the Tlingit, the Haida, the Heiltsuk, the Nawitti, the Nuu-chah-nulth, the Squamish, the Quinault, and—on the Plateau—the Chilcotin. He notes versions that require the bones to be thrown into the fire for the Tsimshian, the Haida, and the Oowekeeno. The motif of salmon bones returned to the water is also found in Nuxalk myths (McIlwraith 1948, 2:478).

The actual practice of returning salmon bones or offal to the water is also widespread. We have reports of the practice being followed in at least some contexts for the following groups: Chilkat and Sanya Tlingit, Lower Skeena Tsimshian (bones either burned or returned to the water), Masset Haida, Heiltsuk, Nuxalk, Kwakwaka'wakw, many Nuu-chah-nulth groups, Saanich, Cowichan, Klahuse, Songish, and probably most of the Salish living around the mouth of the Fraser River.[13]

The fit is not perfect, but in general in the northern and north central part of the culture area there is a fit between the practice of returning salmon bones to the water (and the mythological explanation of the need to do this) and the disposal of the bodies of slaves by throwing them into the water. In the Coast Salish portion of the region there is good evidence of salmon bones being returned to the water but almost no information on the fate of the bodies of slaves.

It is clear that the practice of returning salmon bones or offal to the water is part of a set of practices designed to assure the recurrence of the return of the anadromous salmon. And, if salmon are not "wealth" in the sense that canoes, slaves, and important prerogatives are, bountiful salmon runs are recognized everywhere in the culture area as being of crucial importance to a community's prosperity. For most communities and kin groups they are the strategic resource of greatest consequence.

The Haida statement that slave's bodies are put into the sea to ensure continuing wealth is our most direct link between the sea as a source of wealth, salmon, and slaves. The Haida data also offer us further parallels in ideas about salmon and slaves. For his culture element distribution list, Philip Drucker interviewed both Masset and Skidegate informants. Haida culture was fairly uniform, but the lists (and other sources) do reveal that there were regional differences. Drucker's Skidegate informant said that there were no rituals associated with salmon, except for menstrual taboos, and that the bones of salmon were simply thrown away. He also said that slaves' bodies were not thrown into the sea but were given a simplified version of ordinary Haida burial. In contrast, Drucker's Masset informant reported that there was ritual treatment of salmon including the disposal of bones and offal into the water. He also stated that slaves' bodies were not buried but thrown out (Drucker 1950, 218, 280, 285–286). Adding to the contrast is the fact that Swanton's informant about the reason for the treatment of deceased slaves was probably from Masset.

There are several possible explanations for the difference between the reports of Drucker's Masset and Skidegate informants. It is possible that the Masset informant was more knowledgeable about past practice, better informed about ritual and ideology, or less influenced by what he believed to be European attitudes toward native culture. Yet Drucker (1950, 162) rated his Skidegate informant more highly. It is also possible that the two Haida groups differed in both of these areas. Arguing against that, however, is the virtually universal nature of both these traits in the northern part of the culture area. At this date the issue probably cannot be resolved. What is of greatest interest here is the parallel between the reports regarding salmon bones and deceased slaves.

Altogether, the material presented above shows the close association between salmon, copper, and slaves that is strongly suggestive of the way in which slavery was integrated into Northwest Coast culture. In addition, we are reminded that what appears obvious to outside observers—the apparently callous treatment of the dead slave—may look very different to those engaged in the practice.

9
The Scale of Slavery
on the Northwest Coast

The number of slaves present in a Northwest Coast community is important in several respects: for the owners, the number of slaves was both a reflection of and support for their power and prestige within the community and outside it; for the analyst, the number and proportion of slaves speaks to the importance of slavery on the Northwest Coast.

The study of any quantitative aspect of the population of the eighteenth- and nineteenth-century Northwest Coast is a dismal and frustrating project— frustrating because the quantitative data on population are so few and of such poor quality, dismal because we know that drastic population declines began shortly after contact and continued throughout the nineteenth century. Population destruction, largely because of disease, was a major contributor to social change throughout this era. The impact on the lives of the coast's inhabitants was often devastating. One glimpse of this impact, and its implication for the careers of many titleholders, is afforded by Paul Kane's observation of the Chinook situation.

> Their numbers have been very much reduced, and the effective power of the tribe so greatly diminished that the influence which Casenov owed to the number of his followers has correspondingly declined; his own immediate family consisting of ten wives, four children and eighteen slaves, being reduced in one year to one wife, one child and two slaves. (1855, 273)[1]

Sources of Numerical Population Data

Although what purports to be census information about several nineteenth-century Northwest Coast populations has appeared in various places, virtually all of the systematic population size information for the period before 1880 comes from a single source: the estimates and "censuses" conducted by the Hudson's Bay Company for their own purposes during the middle years of the century. The data available from these censuses, when published, has usually been partial, often inadequately or confusingly grouped, frequently inaccurately transcribed, and poorly analyzed. Therefore, what I will use here is the best and most complete source of Hudson's Bay Company Northwest Coast census information known to me—the compilation by James Douglas of the various efforts of Hudson's Bay Company employees in the 1830s and 1840s to estimate the numbers and other characteristics of all the coastal groups within their sphere of interest. This compilation appears at the beginning of January 1853 in Douglas's Private Papers (pp. 5–31 of the transcript).[2]

Douglas's discussion of the population material and various other Hudson's Bay Company sources makes it clear that, at various times in the 1830s and 1840s, officers in charge of the posts in the region were asked to supply information about the native communities in their areas of operation. The more complete inquiries supplied the following information about each community or group: name; location; name of leader; number of men, women, boys, girls, male slaves, female slaves, houses, canoes, and guns. For a few groups all of this information is reported; for many others only some of it is available. These reports are often described as "censuses," but only a few deserve the name. Examination of the reports makes it clear that most are estimates, some made during or after a visit to a community but many others based on secondhand information, usually obtained from visitors to the post. It is best to regard all of the reports as estimates, although some of the estimates are clearly much better than others. Douglas's own comment on this material is pertinent in any attempt at assessing its value.

> Census of the Indian population on the NW. Coast as far as could be ascertained collected at different times for some years back, from different sources of the best information. It is difficult to get correct information on the subject. The Tribes are often known among their neighbors by different names sometimes they bear the name of their Chief sometimes of the place where they generally reside and by other designations. But as this has been collected with great care, and much trouble it is perhaps as near the truth as can be well ascertained under existing circumstances as far as it goes. (1853, 25)

Near the posts, at least, something resembling a census enumeration sometimes took place. For example, on 21 February 1842 Roderick Finlayson at Fort Simpson reported,

> I went this morning with Pierrish to take account of the population of this place with their number of Guns; the whole appeared willing to give the information we wanted with the exception of one man, who told us to go out of his lodge that we had no business to take the number of their population alleging that the

number of deaths increased among them since their number was ascertained upon which he was told by Pierrish that we had not come to take away their property and if he said much more that he would receive what he would not like— after which he gave us the number of his family—we were not able to get through more than the half of them to day—as they will be leaving this place in a few days for the fishing station at Nass, now is the most proper time to ascertain their number.

[22 February] The whole amount to 2500 souls exclusive of several Canoes that left for Nass the number of which we have not as yet ascertained, Their number of guns 222. Pistols 14 Canoes 762, lodges 174. We found them all very willing to give their number, excepting Cachs who solicited payment for letting us know the number of his tribe. (Fort Simpson Journal 1841–1842, fols. 35–35d)

Modern-day census workers will sympathize with Finlayson—and many on the receiving end of the census takers' questions will sympathize with Cachs and the unnamed man who did not wish to participate. For at least a portion of the area a company man (James M. Yale) traveled along both sides of the Strait of Georgia collecting population data, although we cannot be sure whether he estimated or enumerated (Douglas 1853, 11–13). In other areas the man in charge is known to have made estimates, although in William F. Tolmie's case they were systematic estimates. He counted the inhabitants of the villages nearest his post (Fort McLoughlin) and used the data to obtain the average number of inhabitants per house. He then inquired of visiting natives the number of houses in their communities and used his multiplier to arrive at village population estimates (Tolmie 1963, 319).

In addition to the material in Douglas's Private Papers, I have used two other Hudson's Bay Company sources. The first of these is an 1845 census of the Stikine found in the Hudson's Bay Company Archives. This enumeration is unique in that it reports each of the variables listed above (plus the number of pistols) not merely for the Stikine as a whole but for each of eight subgroups of Stikine (probably lineage or clan groupings) as well. The data appear to be the result of a careful enumeration, but we cannot be sure. There is a version of this census in Douglas's Private Papers (1853, 25–26) that uses a different transcription for the subgroup names and lacks the names of subgroup "chiefs" and the number of pistols. There are also minor variations in many of the numbers reported. These may be transcription errors or the result of two enumerations done at slightly different times.[3] The second Hudson's Bay Company source is the Fort George District Report for 1824–1825, which includes group names, locations, leaders' names, the number of free males and females, and the number of slave males and females for twelve groups around the mouth of the Columbia River. The numbers provided are obviously estimates, being described as "the probable amount of souls in each village" (Kennedy 1824–1825, fol. 5d). An indication that at least some of the estimates are secondhand is that the name of the "principal chief" is given as "unknown" for the four groups farthest from Fort George.

The final source of numerical data used here is a "census" by Lieutenant Wehran (or Verman) of the Russian navy in the early 1860s. It covers many of the Tlingit groups (including some northern Tlingit not in Douglas 1853) and the Kaigani Haida. Wehran's data are clearly estimates and are reported by Petr A. Tikhmenev (1978, 2:403) and Ivan Petroff (1900, 99). I have used the figures in Tikhmenev.

The groups represented in these numerical estimates and censuses range from the Yakutat in the north to the Chinook in the south. Although by no means all the groups between these two are included, the entire culture area is covered. The most important omission is the Nuu-chah-nulth: although a few Nuu-chah-nulth groups are included in the Douglas material, there are no estimates for the number of slaves. The Washington coastal groups north of the Columbia River mouth (Quileute, Quinault, Makah) are also missing. The characteristics of the data for each region are discussed below.

The Slave Population as Found in the "Census" Data

Great confidence cannot be placed in the slave population data that we have to work with. But as Douglas's remarks on the information he assembled suggest, it is the best we can obtain. The quality is too low to allow definitive conclusions, but I think that some useful approximations can be made. I begin by discussing the data in six regional or "ethnic" groupings and add a discussion of the particularly important Stikine material. Next I indicate what generalizations seem justifiable as concluding hypotheses.

We have two censuses for the Tlingit, one from the mid-1840s and one from the early 1860s. The Hudson's Bay Company census has estimates for nine Tlingit groups or sets of groups and the Russian navy census contains estimates for the number of slaves for thirteen Tlingit groups. In the Hudson's Bay Company census the percentage of slaves ranges from 2.0 to 24.1 with a median percentage of 12.0; in the Russian navy census the percentage of slaves ranges from 3.8 to 12.9 with a median of 6.9. It is possible that the proportion of slaves held among the Tlingit as a whole declined during the twenty years or so between the two estimates. The median percentages of the two sets of slave estimates are significantly different (p = .03 by Mood's median test). But for the eight groups (or sets of groups) in common, six slave proportions are lower in the 1860s and only two are higher. Unfortunately, this difference is not statistically significant at conventional levels by the McNemar test for the significance of changes (p = .145). The measurable decline is marked nonetheless. Although six of the groups' *proportion* of slaves declines in the 1860s, the *number* of slaves estimated to be held by the groups common to both lists went down in only five groups. This difference, too, is not significant by the McNemar test. The Tlingit are the only communities for which we have estimates for two dates. These contradictory results mean that we cannot use inferential statistics to decide between the alternatives of a declining slave proportion between the 1840s and the 1860s and a declining proportion of slaves that began only in the 1860s or later. The data suggest to me that the decline of the majority of groups began in the 1840–1860 period.

The intergroup variation in slaveholding suggested by the Tlingit estimates is high: the range of values is 22.1 percent for the 1840s and 9.1 percent for the 1860s. Perhaps this variation is the most important contribution these censuses make to our understanding of slave numbers and proportions, a point that will be emphasized when the Stikine subgroup figures are discussed later on.

The only Haida estimate available comes from the 1860s Russian navy material, which gives 26.1 percent slaves for the Kaigani Haida. This is the highest proportion of slaves reported in a census estimate for any northern group.

The percentage of slaves can be calculated from the Douglas material for thirteen Tsimshian-speaking groups. The median percentage is 2.9. The range here is also considerable: from 1.4 to 14.0 percent, a span of 12.6 percentage points. One would expect these data to be fairly accurate since many of these groups are Lower Skeena Tsimshian who resided very near Fort Simpson for at least part of each year. (It is a Lower Skeena enumeration that Finlayson was describing in the quotation in the previous section.) There are two surprises in these data: most of the proportions of slaves reported are very low, in particular, that reported for the Kitkatla. The Kitkatla were notorious along the northern coast as slave raiders throughout the census period (see Mitchell 1981, 1984). The Kitkatla are reported as being only 4.8 percent slave, although they did hold the largest number of slaves recorded for these Tsimshian groups, thirty-five. Perhaps when the enumeration occurred, Tsibasa (the principal Kitkatla titleholder and certainly the holder of many slaves, at least at times) had recently traded off or given away many slaves (see the discussion of a Kitkatla slave raid and its aftermath in chapter 5). Or the Kitkatla slaves may have been underestimated. Or one's impression of relatively large numbers of slaves among the Kitkatla may be exaggerated. Once again, our low confidence in these data do not allow us to decide.

There are three small sets of figures for Northern Wakashan-speaking groups. Two are from Douglas's Private Papers and the other is Tolmie's 1835 diary kept at Fort McLouglin in the heart of the Northern Wakashan area. Where the Douglas figures overlap, they differ; and the Tolmie figures differ yet again. Some of these differences are important: for example, Douglas

(1853) groups the Kokwayedox, Uwitlidox, and Oyalidox together and reports 9.4 percent slaves (pp. 29–31) and 3.6 percent slaves (p. 21). Tolmie (1963, 306–307) reports 23.7 percent slaves in these three groups. This large discrepancy is made all the more puzzling by the fact that Tolmie was certainly the ultimate source for Douglas's Weletoch data. Given these contradictions, about all that can be said is that in six Northern Wakashan groups we have reports of from 1.1 to 23.7 percent slaves and that the median of the ten estimates supplied by Douglas and Tolmie is 5.3 percent.

There is information in Douglas on the number of slaves in twenty-six Kwakwaka'wakw local groups. These are estimates as the reports tend to fall into a small set of clearly rounded figures. A constant multiplier was apparently not used, however, as the number of individuals per house does exhibit some variation. Perhaps some sort of multiplier or systematic estimator was used and then the final figures were adjusted to take into account the estimator's (or some other person's) additional knowledge of some groups. The Kwakwaka'wakw range is from 1.3 to 7.2 percent slaves with a median of 5.0. Interestingly enough, the groups holding the largest number of slaves are mostly the four Lequiltok groups, the southernmost Kwakwala speakers and the ones with a reputation as feared slave raiders among the Salish speakers living south of them along the Strait of Georgia and the Fraser River (the Fort Langley Journal, for example, is full of alarms, both real and imagined, of Lequiltok raids). Unfortunately, the Lequiltok are the Kwakwaka'wakw about whom we have the least ethnographic information (although see Mauze 1984).

South of the Kwakwaka'wakw, along both sides of the Strait of Georgia and along Puget Sound and the eastern shores of the Strait of Juan de Fuca, was territory occupied by a large number of Coast Salish groups. The percent of slaves held can be calculated for sixteen of these groups from the data supplied in Douglas. Two of these (Comox and Klahuse) are included in the Kwakwaka'wakw estimates, and the others appear to be from the estimates of James Yale. For the most part the percentage of slaves reported is low. The highest report is for 17.3 percent slaves in one of six Klallam villages. In this list of villages the number of slaves is not reported for the other five. In another place in the census material Douglas reports 5.0 percent slaves for all the Klallam, who were estimated to hold sixty-three slaves. The single village was said to have held forty slaves. Unless these two reports refer to different times, one or the other must be in error. The Salish estimates range from 0.3 to 17.2 percent with a median of 3.7 percent. The Salish range suggests the sort of village-to-village variation in slaves held that was typical of the Tlingit and Tsimshian.

Finally, we have the percent of slaves reported for the mid-1820s in thirteen groups around the mouth of the Columbia River. The intergroup variation is the greatest reported, with a range of from 15.8 to 47.4 percent and a median of 20.0. That these data are certainly estimates and not based on an enumeration has already been indicated.

We have one census report that gives the details of slaves held within a single winter village, the "Census of Stekine Population 1845." Table 18 shows the proportion and number of slaves held in each of the eight Stikine kin groups reported in this census. The range of variation in both proportion of slaves held and number of slaves is very wide. The range in percent (21.6) is similar to that for the range of Tlingit interlocal group variation. This strongly suggests that in assessing the economic and other impacts of the numbers of slaves held, what we most need to know is the number of slaves held by each descent group, titleholder, or other relevant owning unit. The Stikine subgroup with ninety-three slaves (23.8 percent) in 1845 was in a much different position than the subgroups with only five or six slaves whether in terms of labor available to exploit or capital goods to trade for furs or give away at ceremonies. The leader of this group, not surprisingly, was Shakes, the principal Stikine titleholder. In the early 1840s the man who seems to have been the second-ranking Stikine titleholder was called Qualkay or Quatki in other Hudson's Bay Company sources. If this is the man called Klaquetch (the closest name in the census document), his group held only six slaves and had the lowest percentage of slaves among the Stikine. Shakes's group also owned the most guns and pistols (78) and the most canoes (89), but Klaquetch's group was second in both (43 guns and pistols, 69 canoes). Perhaps Klaquetch had just disposed of a number of slaves when the census was taken.

Although we should be careful about putting too much trust in particular figures in the population and slave estimates being discussed, we can, I think, take fairly seriously the range of variation these estimates suggest. It seems probable that over time the same group held varying numbers of slaves and that among neighboring groups at any given time some held considerably more slaves than others. I also feel confident that if we had intragroup censuses equivalent to the one for the Stikine for other groups, we would find the same kind of subgroup variation in slaveholding. I would also predict that principal titleholders would own the most slaves within each community. As will be seen, this is supported by the more qualitative estimates to be discussed below.

Regional patterning has been observed in previous chapters with respect to a number of slavery variables. Slave proportions also exhibit this kind of patterning. In keeping with other variables, the lowest percentage of slaves is in the southern, Coast Salish, region. (See table 19 for the regional summary statistics.) Most slavery variables exhibit their greatest intensity in the northern region of the culture area, with what might be called a secondary intensity at the mouth of the Columbia River. The census material reverses this trend, for the percentage of slaves reported is much higher along the lower Columbia.[4]

Table 18. Slaves Held by Stikine Tlingit Subgroups in 1845, Hudson's Bay Company Census

Subgroup	Titleholder	Percent Slave	Number of Slaves
Sik na hut ti	Kut lan	4.9	6
Te i ti tan	Kady ku ku	5.3	8
Kaske que ti	Tanuk	16.7	24
Ka as ki ti tan	Klaquetch	2.2	6
Na ni as ghe	She ekes	23.8	93
Talth queti	Kuck tenu	3.0	5
Kik seti	Kathluksh	7.1	9
Kady eti	Senuk	7.6	15
Total		10.5	166

Table 19. Summary Statistics for Percent of Slaves in Hudson's Bay Company Censuses, Mid-Nineteenth Century, by Region

	Median	Minimum	Maximum	Interquartile Range	Number of Groups
North—1840s (Tlingit, Tsimshian, Northern Wakashan)	4.8	1.4	26.1	2.8–11.8	29
Central—ca. 1850 (Kwakwaka'wakw)	5.0	1.3	7.2	2.3–5.1	26
Southern—ca. 1850 (Coast Salish)	3.7	.3	17.3	1.8–5.1	16
Extreme south—1820s (Columbia River mouth)	20.0	15.8	47.4	20.0–24.8	13

This may be partly explained by the fact that the Columbia estimates are ten to twenty years earlier than the northern estimates, for slavery certainly flourished on the Columbia under the conditions created during the maritime and early land-based fur trade periods. In addition, some of the northern estimates are surprisingly low. The Tsimshian figures considerably lower the median proportion of slaves held in the north and are not what one would have expected to find. Without the Tsimshian the northern region would have a median of 9.4 percent and an interquartile range of 3.5 to 11.4 percent. Although still not nearly as high as the Lower Columbia figures, these statistics are closer to what would be expected and also serve to distinguish the northern from the central region, something else that would be predicted from the distribution of other slavery variables.

Other Estimates of Slave Numbers

There are a few scattered attempts to assess the number or proportion of slaves in one or another of the area's communities or regions in the ethnographic or historical sources. All of these are estimates and are not based on systematic enumerations or estimates. In the case of the ethnographic estimates, they represent ethnographers' efforts to interpret statements by informants who had rarely witnessed slavery when it was flourishing. Table 20 assembles most of these estimates. George Simpson's (1847, 125) well-known 1841 estimate of one-third of the population being enslaved is not included there. It is not clear whether Simpson was referring to the Tsimshian around Fort Simpson, the Tlingit around Fort Stikine, the northern part of the culture area, or even the entire coast from the Columbia north. It is unquestionably a guess, but it was based on conversations with the Hudson's Bay Company men on the spot and Simpson's own observations. The Hudson's Bay Company had already begun to collect some systematic data on the area's native inhabitants, so that Simpson's was not a wild guess, even though it was a guess and ignored what we know to be important variation. Certainly none of the Hudson's Bay Company's censuses reported any community as one-third slaves, but Simpson was undoubtedly impressed with the number of slaves held in the region.

The other available estimates are often vague or contradictory. For example, one of the central Tlingit groups described in a general way by Kyrill T. Khlebnikov ([1861] 1976) was the Chilkat. Oberg (1973, 116), certainly a careful ethnographer with a better quantitative sense than most ethnographers who have worked on the coast, claims that Chilkat house leaders who owned ten slaves owned a large number and that most owned considerably fewer. Yet Khlebnikov's statement that twenty to forty slaves were held by "chiefs" (Oberg's house leaders) is based on observations made during the 1830s, one hundred years before Oberg went to Chilkat and while slavery

Table 20.   Estimates of Slave Population, Historical and Ethnographic Sources, Tribal
Unit Sample

Group	Estimate	Source
Yakutat	probably small	De Laguna 1972, 469
Central Tlingit	chiefs held 20 to 40 each in 1830s	Khlebnikov 1861, 32
Chilkat	never numerous—10 a large number for one owner	Oberg 1973, 116–117
Southern Tlingit	certainly less than 10%	Olson 1967, 53
Haida	"numerous" in early contact times	Harrison 1925, 40
	"a considerable number" in northern Queen Charlotte villages in 1870s	Dawson 1880, 132
Lower Skeena Tsimshian	"a small number of slaves" in precontact times	Garfield 1939, 329
	between 200 and 700 in mid-19th century	Garfield 1951, 30
Nuxalk	at times 30–40%	McIlwraith 1948, 1:158
Mowachaht	100 to 200 in 1803–1805	Jewitt 1974, 65
Central Nuu-chah-nulth	25% of males in a local group	Sproat 1868, 117
Saanich	about 16%; at no time numerous	Jenness n.d., 58–59
Puyallup-Nisqually	apparently few	Smith 1940, 47
Skagit	few in number	Collins 1974, 7
Quinault	very small proportion	Olson 1936a, 97–98
Chinook	3 villages in 1838: 24.1%, 23.7%, and 14.7%	Pipes 1934, 58

still flourished. It is probable that Oberg's informants were recalling the latter half of the nineteenth century for Krause (1956, 105) suggests that shortly before his time (the 1880s) central Tlingit chiefs were reduced to one or two slaves each.

Olson (1967, 53) says that among the southern Tlingit less than 10 percent of the population was slave, while the historical censuses suggest a modestly higher proportion. The censuses are not accurate enough to decidedly refute

Olson's interpretation of his informants' statements, but as with Oberg's informants, it is probable that late rather than early nineteenth-century circumstances are being reported.

I do not know how Garfield arrived at her 1939 statement about the "small" number of precontact slaves among the Tsimshian. She reports no strong oral tradition to that effect and the mythological material points to slaves being common in early times (e.g., Boas 1916). Her 1951 estimate about mid-nineteenth-century slaveholding says that the nine Tsimshian ranking title-holders (village "chiefs") held from 10 to 20 slaves each and that the 50 or so lineage heads owned from 2 to 10 slaves apiece. This suggests intracommunity variation in slaveholding, which has already been seen to have been important among the Stikine. It also suggests a range of slaves at midcentury of from at least 200 to as many as 700. The Hudson's Bay Company census previously discussed listed 68 slaves for these Tsimshian groups—a number already noted as being surprisingly low. Garfield's figures are more what one would expect based on Simpson's one-third estimate and, more important, the picture one gets of the number of slaves in the Fort Simpson vicinity from the Fort Simpson journals. The 1840s census should be more accurate than estimates based on ethnographic work done ninety years later, but Garfield's estimates feel right—especially since they include variation within a category of titleholder ("village chiefs" or "lineage heads") as well as differences between categories of titleholders ("village chiefs" vs. "lineage heads").

Quantitative information and economics are the weakest part of McIlwraith's excellent Nuxalk ethnography. The complete text of his estimate of slave numbers is as follows:

> Judging from conversational remarks by elderly men, it seems probable that in the old days there was a considerable slave population in every Bella Coola village, comprising at times as much as thirty to forty per cent of the total population. (1948, 1:158)

So we have an informed guess about the informed guesses of informants gleaned from their casual remarks. And the informants were either very young or, most often, not yet born when slavery was flourishing among the Nuxalk. Yet McIlwraith's estimate is at least as securely based as the other ethnographers' estimates; he is simply clearer about how he came to make it. Thirty to 40 percent seems high, yet there may have been periods when one or another Nuxalk village held that many slaves. Most probably, as McIlwraith's statement implies, the proportion was lower than that at most times.

Jewitt's discussion of Mowachaht slave numbers just after the beginning of the nineteenth century is aimed at distinguishing the number of slaves held by the leading titleholder—about 50—from the number held by other title-holders—none had more than 12—and not an overall estimate of the number or proportion of slaves. The estimate of 100 to 200 slaves is based on there being about twelve Mowachaht principal titleholders (Drucker 1950, 263); the likeliest number is about 150. Unfortunately, Jewitt does not give us a clear idea of how many Mowachaht there were. The Hudson's Bay Company census of the 1840s estimates 400 to 500 Mowachaht for that period. There was almost certainly a population decline from 1805 to the 1840s, but the figure of 500 Mowachaht would give about 30 percent slaves. Double the 1840s population in 1805 (certainly not an impossible figure) would give about 15 percent slaves. We can compare this range of estimates with Sproat's estimate of the 1860s for the various central Nuu-chah-nulth groups of 25 percent of the males in a typical group being slaves. This suggests Nuu-chah-nulth slavery was at least on a par with that in the northern part of the region.

All but one of the estimates for the area between the Wakashan speakers and the mouth of the Columbia suggest a very low number of slaves. In addition to the comments reported in table 20, the sources for many Coast Salish groups report that two or three slaves were the most held by a titleholder. Jenness (n.d.), however, estimates that the Saanich had been about 16 percent slaves. In the same section of his manuscript he says that slaves were "at no time numerous." It is hard to resolve this apparent contradiction. It reminds us of the material for the Klallam recorded in the Douglas census material: overall the Klallam (just south of the Saanich) are said to have been 5 percent slaves, while one village was reported as 17.3 percent slaves. Jenness is the most informative and careful ethnographer on Salish slavery (Elmendorf perhaps excepted), so his estimates and comments need to be taken seriously. Perhaps the most that we can say is that the numbers of slaves held by any Salish group varied considerably over time and that although usually low, sometimes a significant proportion of a community's population was slave.

The Chinook figures come from Nellie Pipes's edition of the diary of the missionary John Frost. The relevant entry in Frost's diary is dated 13 August 1840, but he explicitly states that the population figures he gives are for three Lower Columbia Chinook villages in 1838. They appear to come from a Hudson's Bay Company employee and are consistent with the Hudson's Bay Company Columbia River data from the mid-1820s.

Altogether the estimates discussed in this section are much like the census estimates treated above: although there are contradictions, more slaves were probably held in the north and central parts of the area than among the Coast Salish, but variation within and between groups and over time in slave ownership was as significant as typical slave numbers.

The Scale of Northwest Coast Slavery

A great many societies have practiced slavery. Among some it has been a minor trait, among others a very important one. In assessing the scale of slavery on the Northwest Coast, it is useful to compare the numbers and proportions of slaves held in these communities with those held in other societies. This is not easy to do as it is difficult to assemble estimates of numbers of slaves that one has confidence in. One of the most comprehensive efforts of this type known to me is Appendix C of Patterson's *Slavery and Social Death* (1982). There he gives the best estimates that he could find for the percentage of the population that was slave in a large number of what he calls "large-scale slave systems." He defines a large-scale slave system as one "in which the social structure was decisively dependent on the institution of slavery," adding that such dependence was often but not necessarily economic (1982, 353). The bulk of Patterson's cases fall into the 15 to 33 percent slave range, although some had even higher proportions of slaves.

Virtually all of the societies on Patterson's list of large-scale slave societies are organized as states and exhibit relatively high degrees of social and cultural complexity. Most of these societies would not appear to make very suitable comparisons with Northwest Coast societies, which are in so many ways classic examples of "small-scale" societies. Patterson also studied another sample of societies that offers more appropriate comparisons. He identified 66 societies in Murdock and White's 186-society Standard Ethnographic Sample as slaveholding. Three of these societies (Haida, Nuxalk, Twana) are on the Northwest Coast (and comprise all the Northwest Coast societies in the Standard Ethnographic Sample). Unfortunately, Patterson does not report estimates of proportions of slaves for most of these sixty-six slaveholding societies. He found the ethnographic and historical literature so weak on quantitative data with respect to slavery that he dropped a variable on slave numbers from his analysis of this sample (1982, 346).

Although direct comparisons of Northwest Coast societies and most of the large-scale slave systems discussed by Patterson are problematical, we can accept 15 percent slaves as an approximate threshold for large-scale slave systems. The data reviewed in earlier sections of this chapter suggest that many Northwest Coast communities fell just above or below this threshold. This is particularly true in the north (Tlingit, Haida), among the Nuu-chah-nulth, and around the mouth of the Columbia River. Elsewhere in the culture area, the percentage of slaves was probably somewhat lower, although individual communities do seem to have reached or come close to 15 percent. Our quantitative data and other estimates of slave numbers are not strong enough to be conclusive, but they do suggest that many communities on the Northwest Coast, at least in the earlier parts of the nineteenth century, did have enough slaves relative to their size to merit consideration as large-scale slave systems. This does not, of course, automatically mean that these societies were "decisively dependent on the institution of slavery," but it does mean that the probability and implications of such dependence must be given serious consideration. This will be one of the main themes of chapter 14.

In comparative terms the proportion of slaves in many Northwest Coast communities was significant. But in no slaveholding society, not even those whose populations were over half slave, were the benefits of slaveholding even approximately equally distributed among the nonslave portion of the population. Slaveholders made up only one segment of the free population, and it is they who received the greatest share of the profits of slavery. As well, there was nearly always some variation, often considerable variation, in the numbers of slaves held by different members of the slave-owning category within a community. This was the case on the Northwest Coast. Most slaves were held by titleholders, either as owners themselves or as custodians and managers for their descent group (often we cannot tell which). Commoners rarely held slaves, so that it was titleholders who most directly benefited from slave labor and the other fruits of slavery. Equally important, however, is the fact that, even within a single community, different titleholders held considerably different numbers of slaves and so were in a position to draw considerably disparate benefits from their slaves. Table 21 gives much of the information available about the numbers of slaves held by different titleholders in the tribal unit sample. These data suggest both intra- and intercommunity variation.

The best examples of intracommunity variation in slaveholding are for the Stikine, the Lower Skeena Tsimshian, the Mowachaht, and the Chinook, although there are also clear indications of sizable variation within the owning stratum for the Saanich and Quinault as well. The Stikine census already described points to considerable variation in the slaves held by different groups within a community: the largest number of slaves owned by one Stikine subgroup was $18\frac{1}{2}$ times that owned by the subgroup possessing the smallest number. Although this is the largest difference reported in the sources, the other calculable ratios of largest to smallest slaveholding are also considerable: Lower Skeena Tsimshian, 10; Mowachaht, 4; Saanich, 5; Quinault, 15; and Chinook, 6.[5] The principal titleholder in a community was often (perhaps nearly always) the owner of by far the largest number of slaves. There are clear indications of this for Shakes among the Stikine, the "village chief" among the Lower Skeena Tsimshian, Maquinna among the Mowachaht, Concomly and Casenov among the Chinook, and perhaps Edenshaw and Sditala among the Haida. Such differences in the number of slaves held meant that principal titleholders had more labor power to exploit as well as more slaves to trade for other goods or to give away or destroy at ceremonies. Titleholders both increased and maintained their positions with large numbers of slaves.

There was also interregional variation in the number of slaves held by individual owners. Although there were some exceptions, the sources for the Coast Salish indicate that few Salish titleholders owned more than two or three slaves. Among the Twana many of the titleholding stratum owned none (Elmendorf 1960, 345), a situation that was probably true in many other Salish communities as well. Among the Chinook, the Nuu-chah-nulth, and in the north at least some titleholders regularly owned many more than two or three

Table 21.   Number of Slaves Held by Owners, Tribal Unit Sample

Group	Number	Source
Yakutat	owner of 5 "very wealthy" (mid-19th century)	De Laguna 1972, 469
Chilkat	10 a large number; two "chiefs" each owned 20 in 1880s	Oberg 1973, 116–117 Olson 1967, 73
Sitka	10 slaves (1850s)	Olson 1967, 51–52
Stikine	Shakes owned about 40 a Shakes who died ca. 1920 had owned 75, his brother even more	De Laguna 1972, 470 Olson 1967, 48–51
Haida	Edenshaw owned at least 12 Sditla owned at least 10	Harrison 1925, 166 Boas 1916, 380 ff.
Lower Skeena Tsimshian	village "chiefs" 10–20, lineage heads 2–10 (mid-19th century)	Garfield 1951, 30
Fort Rupert Kwakiutl	principal Gwetla titleholder had 2 up to 7 for a titleholder recorded in marriages	Curtis 1915, 71 Boas 1921
Mowachaht	Maquinna about 50; other title-holders no more than 12	Jewitt 1974, 65
Makah	one man owned at least 12	Densmore 1924, 121
Saanich	one titleholder had 10; 2 or 3 normal	Suttles 1974, 305–306 Barnett 1939, 267
Twana	few owned more than 3	Elmendorf 1960, 345
Quinault	one titleholder about 30, most held 2 or 3	Olson 1936a, 97–99
Chinook	average titleholder 2 or 3, prin-cipal titleholders about 6; Concomly owned 10 or 12 Casenov held 18 ca. 1828	Ray 1938, 51–54 Kane 1855, 273

NOTE: Absence of entry for sample group means no information.

slaves. Such titleholders could benefit much more from slave owning than could their Salish counterparts.

Even two or three slaves could make a substantial contribution to a title-holder's wealth and to the productive capacity of his household, however. Douglas's (1853, 8) census material suggests that the typical Coast Salish household ranged in size from ten to twenty persons in the mid-nineteenth century. It is probable that titleholders' households were usually at the top of this range. Two or three slaves added into such a domestic unit were obviously a significant addition to its productive capacity. Since slaves could be exploited in ways that kin (the other members of the household) could not, the "disposable" part of the product of the slave's labor was even more significant. And if even two or three slaves could make an important difference to a unit's productive capacity, the addition of ten or even twenty slaves, as seems to have been not uncommon farther north in the culture area, was even more significant.

The number of slaves in many Northwest Coast communities was large enough to have considerable potential impact on those communities and the economic, social, and political circumstances of their owners. How this potential was realized and to what extent we can speak of the Northwest Coast societies as "large-scale slave systems" will be considered in detail when the place of slavery in Northwest Coast culture is considered in chapter 14.

Part Three

Northwest Coast Slavery
in Historical Context

10
The Antiquity of
Northwest Coast Slavery

Although there were occasional contacts with Northwest Coast people by ships from Asia for several centuries and some very indirect contacts with Europeans via overland trade for some time preceding direct contact, significant face-to-face interaction with outsiders to the culture area did not begin for the inhabitants of the Northwest Coast until the last half of the eighteenth century. The peoples of the region began to be brought into the European orbit during the 1770s, when Spanish, Russian, and British vessels and traders began to converge on the area.[1] Therefore, I will take 1770 as the end of the precontact or pre-European phase of Northwest Coast history. Thus if we are interested in the nature of the truly aboriginal practice of slavery, we must look to the decades immediately preceding 1770.

There are only two possible direct sources of information about this period: archaeology and accounts by indigenous inhabitants who were alive before contact and whose experiences were recorded after contact. Although there are certainly recorded oral traditions that contain valuable material about precontact times, I know of no accounts by Northwest Coast natives who were alive before 1770 which contain significant information about slavery and related practices they themselves witnessed. This means that the direct evidence about precontact slavery must be archaeological.

There are two additional sources of evidence that, while not direct, are important. One is the observations of outsiders during the period immediately after contact, especially in the 1770s and 1780s but including material perhaps as late as 1810. This was a period of great change in the culture area and care must be taken in interpreting this material as evidence of aboriginal practice, but there was continuity as well and these accounts are relevant to the problems of this chapter. The second source of information is that which can be gleaned from the linguistic evidence. Some inferences about aboriginal practice can be made on the basis of analysis of the vocabularies of slavery in the various languages indigenous to the region.

In this chapter, I will first describe the evidence from the three major types of sources: archaeology, eighteenth-century European accounts, and language. I will then consider what light this material throws on the problems of the origins and antiquity of slavery and whether slavery was, in fact, truly an aboriginal culture trait.

The Evidence from Archaeology

Archaeological research on the Northwest Coast has concentrated on artifacts, cultural sequences and dating, and, more recently, patterns of subsistence as represented by faunal remains. Only a few workers have attempted to look at their material in terms of what it can tell us about changes in social stratification and complexity and other features that impinge on slavery, although the first book-length treatment of Northwest Coast prehistory does include discussions of these issues (Matson and Coupland 1995). Before reviewing the evidence, I will discuss what, in principle, archaeology might be able to tell us about precontact slavery on the Northwest Coast.

In the absence of written records, I am aware of no material evidence that an archaeologist working on the Northwest Coast could recover that would conclusively show that slavery was present in a prehistoric community. No artifact known to me can be shown to be exclusively associated with slaves. Several potential lines of evidence are possible. All of these relate to burials and other treatments of human remains. Three kinds of evidence could be extracted from human remains which might tell us something about the presence of slavery prehistorically: evidence concerning the physical types present at the same time in a community; evidence about the differences in grave type and grave goods; and evidence from skeletal remains about physical conditions of life and death.

On the basis of anthropometric data collected by Franz Boas, the presence of several fairly distinctive physical types can be shown for the coast (Hall and Macnair 1972). In addition, there were several ethnically distinctive styles of head deformation practiced in the region. Thus the analysis of skeletal remains might establish that individuals not belonging to the local physical type were present in a community. The possibility that they were slaves would be one explanation for their presence. Unfortunately, we also know that inter-community marriage, especially among the elite, was common in early historic times and can explain the presence of such individuals equally as well as slavery. The physical types are spread over fairly large portions of the area, so that slaves (or in-marrying spouses) from nearby communities might well belong to the same physical type as the local inhabitants.

We know that historically in many communities slaves were not given the same burial that was accorded to those of free status (see chapters 4 and 8). The presence in the same community at the same time of carefully buried individuals and individuals who seem to have simply been "thrown out" might indicate the presence of slaves. Again, however, other explanations could be advanced—that only high-status people were formally buried or that the "thrown out" individuals had died from a particular cause—so that the presence of slavery could not be conclusively demonstrated by such a finding. Systematic differences in grave goods are often interpreted as evidence for status differentiation and stratification in prehistoric communities, but although stratification of the free and slave co-occur on the Northwest Coast, the prehistoric presence of stratification would not prove the prehistoric presence of slavery.

The physical characteristics of skeletal remains that suggest either different living conditions (such as dietary differences) or that some people died violent deaths (skull fractures from clubs, marks indicating decapitation and thus the taking of trophy heads) might strongly suggest either slavery or at least the presence of practices associated with slavery on the Northwest Coast—warfare, head-hunting, superior elite access to resources—but once more slavery is not proved.

The most comprehensive look at skeletal remains in this context is by Jerome S. Cybulski (1990, 58), the leading student of Northwest Coast archaeological skeletal remains, who has suggested that there two important systematic differences between the materials recovered from the Prince Rupert Harbour area (Tsimshian territory ethnographically) and the Strait of Georgia area (Coast Salish territory ethnographically). In the Prince Rupert Harbour sites about 40 percent of the individuals had fractures of the limbs and spine, while only about 11 percent of the Strait of Georgia region individuals had such injuries. He argues that such injuries were probably obtained in warfare. This implies a much higher incidence of fighting prehistorically in the Prince Rupert Harbour area than in the Strait of Georgia region. This is consistent with the historical and ethnographic picture. In addition, Cybulski found that there were important differences in the sex ratios of the skeletal material recovered in the two areas. For the Prince Rupert Harbour sites "interred males outnumbered females by 1.8 to 1, while in the Strait of Georgia region, the sex ratio has been more nearly equal at 1.2 to 1 over a span of 2,000 years" (Cybulski 1990, 58; see also Cybulski 1992). Cybulski suggests that a higher proportion of the female population in the Prince Rupert Harbour area were slaves, who were not buried in the same location or manner as others in these prehistoric communities. This interpretation is consistent with known burial practices and with the higher historic incidence of slavery in the Prince Rupert Harbour area when compared with the Strait of Georgia region. Cybulski's suggestions are quite reasonable, but other interpretations that do not necessarily involve slavery cannot be ruled out.

Direct evidence from archaeology does not seem very promising. There was one Northwest Coast practice, however, that could shed light on slavery. In the northern part of the culture area a slave was sometimes killed and buried beneath a new house post or a new totem pole. With some luck in preservation, evidence for human remains in such site features could reasonably be interpreted as evidence for slavery. It is true that slaves might be a historically late substitution for nonslaves in such ritual burials, but I think this possibility would appeal only to a very determined opponent of the notion of precontact slavery. Unfortunately, poor preservation conditions and dating problems mean that not finding such ritual burials cannot be interpreted as evidence for the absence of slavery. Nor could we expect to find such evidence in the central or southern parts of the culture area.

We have, then, one possible indicator of slavery (house post and totem pole burials) and several other indicators for which slavery is one of several plausible interpretations. Unfortunately, except for the materials described by Cybulski, archaeological research to date has not produced much data of any of the types described above. I know of no reports of finding house post or totem pole ritual burials.

The practice of slavery was well integrated into the ethnographically known Northwest Coast cultures. If there is strong archaeological evidence for the long-standing existence of many of the classic elements of the Northwest Coast culture type, then there is some likelihood that elements that do not leave good indicators for archaeologists to find were also present. Among the characteristic traits of Northwest Coast culture that are likely to leave their mark on the archaeological record are (1) a subsistence pattern with a strong marine focus, particularly with an elaboration of technologies for salmon fishing and marine mammal hunting; (2) a settlement pattern that includes winter villages with large plank houses and summer/fall seasonal resource exploitation sites; (3) the presence of marked social differentiation and social stratification; (4) high levels of fighting and warfare; (5) considerable intraregional trade; and (6) the distinctive Northwest Coast art style. If all of these are present in a recognizable, well-developed form in an archaeological horizon, we can say that the basic Northwest Coast culture pattern is present.

Given the present state of archaeological research in the region, the evidence is highly variable from local area to local area, but for two of the more thoroughly investigated local areas (Prince Rupert Harbour and the Strait of Georgia) the evidence suggests that between 500 B.C. and A.D. 500 early forms of what became classic Northwest Coast cultures had developed and that in both areas the succeeding five hundred-year period saw the consolidation of these developments into cultures clearly recognizable as early examples of Northwest Coast cultures similar to those known ethnographically (Fladmark, Ames, and Sutherland 1990; Mitchell 1990). Less satisfactory evidence from other parts of the region suggests that during the same period (or slightly later) the same thing was happening elsewhere on the coast (Matson and Coupland 1995). If future archaeological research confirms these findings and interpretations, then the presence for several centuries before contact of a mature Northwest Coast culture type, with stratification, warfare, and so on, will be established and the presence of slavery during this time period will be plausible, if not demonstrated.

The Linguistic Evidence

The linguistic evidence for Northwest Coast slavery is contained in the vocabularies and texts collected in the various languages of the region since contact began. There are a number of eighteenth-century vocabularies, but texts were not collected in native as opposed to European languages much before the last quarter of the nineteenth century.

Analysis of the terms associated with slaves and slavery and their use in texts can give us some clues about how well integrated into the indigenous cultures slavery was. Thus data from indigenous languages can give us some useful, if not conclusive, inferences about the antiquity of Northwest Coast slavery. Several lines of linguistic inquiry can be pursued, the most important of which is to try to determine if the term for 'slave' in the various Northwest Coast languages is a recent introduction or borrowing or has a long history.

There were more than thirty languages spoken on the Northwest Coast at the time of European contact. These can be grouped into from five to ten sets, depending on the degree of relatedness that determines which language is to be clustered with which. The two best-established and largest (in terms of number of languages) genetic groupings of Northwest Coast languages are the Wakashan and Salishan language families. No other groups of related languages in the area are as large or as widespread as these two. Therefore, the analysis that follows will concentrate on these two families.

For both Wakashan and Salishan the main questions to answer concern whether the words for 'slave' in the various languages of a family are cognate, and if so, whether this represents a common inheritance of the daughter languages from a previous ancestral language. Obviously, if it can be established that the original (proto-)language of either or both families contained a term for 'slave', this greatly enhances the argument that slavery is a long-standing culture trait in the region.

Wakashan Terms for 'Slave'

All of the members of the Wakashan language family are located on the North-west Coast, where they formed a bloc occupying the upper reaches of Doug-las Channel and Gardner Canal, the mainland shore of Queen Charlotte Sound from Price Island south, the Queen Charlotte Straits (both on the mainland and northeastern Vancouver Island), the west coast of Vancouver Island, and the Cape Flattery area of the Olympic Peninsula. There are six (Thompson and Kinkade 1990, 34) or seven (Lincoln and Rath 1980, 2–3) Wakashan languages divided into two branches. The Northern branch consists of Heilt-suk, Oowekyala, Haisla, and Kwakwala. The Southern branch is made up of Nootka, Nitinaht, and Makah. The existence of the Wakashan language family was recognized in the nineteenth century (Powell 1891; Pilling 1894), and al-though Sapir (1929) argued for a genetic relationship with the Salishan lan-guages as a part of his hypothesized Mosan family, it is now thought that Wakashan cannot be shown to be related to any other language family (Kin-kade 1990, 105).

Proto-Wakashan speakers were probably located on northern parts of the west coast of Vancouver Island at a fairly early period. The two branches sep-arated, with speakers of what became the Southern branch eventually occupy-ing virtually the entire west coast of Vancouver Island and Cape Flattery and the future speakers of the Northern branch occupying more and more of north-eastern Vancouver Island and the eastern shores of Queen Charlotte Strait, eventually moving northward into the territory they held at contact along Queen Charlotte Sound. The rugged interior terrain of Vancouver Island seems to have ensured the relative isolation of each branch from the other. Speakers of both branches probably gained ground against Salishan speakers. Archaeolog-ical research is spotty in what is probably the Wakashan speakers' Northwest Coast homeland, but what research there is suggests a Wakashan expansion during the period 500 B.C. to A.D. 300. This period is probable for the date of the split of proto-Wakashan into its Northern and Southern branches.[2]

The words for 'slave' in each of the Wakashan languages are given in ta-ble 22. According to William H. Jacobsen, Jr. (pers. com.), the words are cog-nate within the Northern and the Southern branches, but the words in the two branches are not cognate with each other. Jacobsen also states that the words are not synchronically analyzable but notes that the term for 'slave' in each branch corresponds phonologically to forms with different meanings in lan-guages in the other branch. The Northern Wakashan words correspond to Southern Wakashan forms that mean 'to cut sideways with a knife, whittle' and the Southern Wakashan words correspond to words like the Heiltsuk term meaning 'bent' (said of something rigid such as metal).[3]

I would interpret this situation to mean that the terms for 'slave' developed among Wakashan speakers after the division into two branches—but soon af-

Table 22.   *Wakashan Terms for 'Slave'*

Language	Term	Reference
Heiltsuk	q̓ák^wu	Lincoln and Rath 1980, 372
Oowekyala	q̓ak^wu	Lincoln and Rath 1980, 372
Haisla	q̓àku	Lincoln and Rath 1980, 372
Kwakwala	q̓aku	Lincoln and Rath 1980, 372
Nootka	qu·ł	Carlson, pers. com.
Nitinaht	qu·ł	Carlson, pers. com.
Makah	qułu·	Jacobsen, pers. com.

ter, before the branches developed into separate languages. This would imply that slavery developed at a similar time. This is consistent with the most plausible interpretation of current archaeological knowledge—that many of the characteristic traits of the Northwest Coast culture area were developed (or, less likely, introduced) during the period 500 B.C. to A.D. 500 and that the Wakashan began to expand out of their northwestern Vancouver Island homeland at about this time as well.[4]

Salish Terms for 'Slave'

There were more than twenty Salish languages. Most of these were spoken in the Northwest Coast culture area, but one was spoken on the Oregon coast (Tillamook/Siletz) just south of the culture area as defined here and a group of seven languages were spoken east of the Northwest Coast in the interior of British Columbia and Washington, which lies in the Plateau culture area. As might be expected from such a large language family, Salish language history is complex and only partly understood. It is even more difficult to tie language history and archaeology together than in the case of the Wakashan.

Proto-Salishans probably occupied the Fraser River delta, gradually expanding to hold the entire stretch of the protected marine environment from the southern drainage of Puget Sound, north throughout the Strait of Georgia, to perhaps even north of historic Nuxalk territory. The linguistic evidence suggests that the ancestors of the Nuxalk were the first to separate and become isolated from the main bloc of Salish speakers. Not too long after that the group(s) that became the Interior Salish (represented recently by seven languages) split off and moved into their recent Plateau environments. The next group to become relatively isolated from the main body of Salish speakers were the proto-Tsamosan speakers who were the historic occupants of the area between the southern end of Puget Sound to the Washington coast and down to the Chinookan speakers along the Columbia River. The Tillamook, although historically their territory was south of the Columbia River Chinookans, seem to have been the last to split off from the main body of Central Salish. The Central Salish were historically found from the southern end of Puget Sound (Lushootseed) north to the Fraser River delta and southeastern Vancouver Island and adjacent parts of the mainland as far north as the beginnings of Johnstone Strait.[5]

It is virtually impossible to tie the known archaeological detail into the language events outlined above. At a very general level, however, there is a plausible picture. It seems reasonable to identify the Marpole Culture Type (400 B.C.–A.D. 400) with the Central Salish at a stage in their development when they had established the "Salish" version of what was to become Northwest Coast culture. The preceding culture type in the Strait of Georgia, Locarno Beach (1200–400 B.C.), probably also represents the Central Salish at a time when the distinctive forms of Northwest Coast culture were just beginning to develop and perhaps before most of the other branches of Salish speakers had begun to become separate and distinct from the main body. It will be interesting to see, for example, if some local version of Locarno Beach will be found at appropriate time horizons in what is historic Nuxalk territory.[6]

The words for 'slave' in most of the Salish languages are given in table 23. M. Dale Kinkade (pers. com.) feels that it is possible to reconstruct a form for proto-Central Salish (*náq). This form is cognate in Comox, Sechelt, and Northern and Southern Lushootseed. Kinkade further suggests that the last part of the Squamish form is also cognate with this term. This proto-Central Salish form may also be the proto-Salish form. The latter would be the case only if the Bella Coola form is cognate with the proto-Central Salish forms, and Kinkade cautions that it may not be. Kinkade knows of no cognates for *náq in any of the Tsamosan or Interior Salish languages. He can suggest a proto-Tsamosan form (*s-yəl=qín'), which at the proto-Tsamosan level is analyzable as 'round head'. There is no prototerm for Interior Salish, although there is a term local to Northern Interior Salish and another local to Southern Interior Salish.[7]

If the form *náq is indeed proto-Salish for 'slave', then this suggests considerable antiquity for slavery among the Salish—perhaps back into Locarno times? Even the more cautious view that it is a proto-Central Salish form suggests that slavery may well have been present in the Strait of Georgia area in Marpole times. The suggestion is consistent with my interpretation that the various traits identified with the classic Northwest Coast culture type began to flourish and become integrated into a recognizable whole at about that time horizon. The inference of the relatively great time depth of the practice of slavery among the Salish is reinforced by Thom Hess's observation (pers.

Table 23. Salish Terms for 'Slave'

Language	Term	Language	Term
Bella Coola [Central Salish]	*snaax*	[Tsamosan] [Inland]	
Comox	*nán'q*	Cowlitz	*s-yəl=qín'*
Sechelt	*náq [s-k'ʷəyuc]*	Upper Chehalais	
Squamish	*s-q'ʷú'nəq*	Upper Chehalais	*s-yaqín'*
Nooksack	*sk'ʷəy'úθ*	Satsop	*s-yaqín'*
Halkomelem		[Maritime]	
Chilliwack	*sk'ʷiyəθ*	Lower Chehalis	*sy'əl'qín'*
Musqueam	*sk'ʷəyəθ*	Quinault	*dᶻəl'qín'*
Cowichan	*sk'ʷəyəθ*	Tillamook	*s-tu'tíw'at*
Nanaimo	*sk'ʷəyəθ*	[Interior Salish]	
Northern Straits		[Northern]	
Saanich	*sk'ʷəyəθ*	Lillooet	*séw't [(?) kʷíkʷinkm]*
Songish	*sk'ʷəyəs*	Thompson	*séw't*
Lummi	*sk'ʷəyəs*	Shuswap	*səsésu't*
Samish	*sk'ʷəyis*	[Southeastern]	
Klallam	*sk'wəyəc*	Okanagan	*s-kʷán=xn*
Lushootseed		Kalispel	
Northern	*s-túdəq*	Spokane	*s-kʷán=xn*
Southern	*s-túdəq*	Kalispel	*s-kʷán=xn*
Twana	*stəčəd*	Flathead	*s-kʷán=xn*
		Columbian	*'álk'ʷ=mən*
		Coeur d'Alene	*s-kʷán=xn*

NOTE: The source for all transcriptions and terms is Kinkade pers. com. The classification of Salish languages used here follows Kinkade 1990, 105.

com.) that the Lushootseed word for 'slave' has an unusual plural. He suggests it is a rare form that is associated with very old words in Lushootseed. This would imply that the word for 'slave' is also very old in the language. His suggestion is reinforced by the fact that the Lushootseed form is cognate with the proto-Central Salish (proto-Salish) form. Altogether the evidence of the Salish terms for 'slave' suggests a considerable antiquity for the practice of slavery among the Salish-speaking peoples of the coast.

The Eighteenth-Century Sources

European vessels made more than 280 visits to the North Pacific Coast of North America in the eighteenth century. Most of the Europeans who visited the area during this period encountered Native Americans at least briefly, and many left their impressions and observations in a host of journals, diaries, letters, and books. Although none of the visitors produced a comprehensive account of the native inhabitants, quite a lot of information is available on at least some aspects of late eighteenth-century Northwest Coast native life. The major sources are in Spanish and English (British and American), although valuable information can be found in Russian, German, and French sources. Erna Gunther's (1972) summary of the available information emphasizes material culture, but she does provide a useful overview.

Spanish Sources

The first Spanish contact with the peoples of the Northwest Coast culture area was in 1774 when Juan José Pérez Hernández sailed in the waters of what were to become Alaska and British Columbia and engaged in some trade with the Haida and, probably, the Mowachaht. The Spanish were very active on the Northwest Coast in the eighteenth century, although they virtually disappear from the area after 1797, having lost out to British, American, and Russian interests. The most important and useful account of the Spanish in the region is still Warren L. Cook's *Flood Tide of Empire* (1973). Cook includes an excellent discussion of the Spanish accounts of the native inhabitants of the region. A number of the accounts and reports on the various Spanish expeditions are available in translation, published and unpublished, and many of these have been used as sources for this study. There would still seem to be a vast amount of unpublished material in Mexican and Spanish archives that has not been adequately studied. The Spanish material is richest for the west coast of Vancouver Island, especially for the Mowachaht of Nootka Sound. Indeed, when Spanish and English sources are combined, we can construct a fairly good description of many aspects of late eighteenth-century Mowachaht life. In comparison, our information (in any language) on even the best described of the other parts of the culture area is very fragmentary indeed, although there is considerable useful data on the Haida and Chinook especially.

The most famous Spanish work on the area is José Mariano Moziño's *Noticias de Nutka*, based on a visit to Nootka Sound in 1792. Moziño was a botanist who spent four months there, and his description of the place and its inhabitants, the Mowachaht, is the most complete and systematic eighteenth-century account of any Northwest Coast people. It is only ninety-seven pages in the English translation and is strongest on subsistence and other easily observable activities, but it also contains useful information on the activities of the principal Mowachaht titleholder, Maquinna. Unfortunately for this study, although he recognizes the distinction between titleholders and other members of Mowachaht society, Moziño does not distinguish between commoners and slaves, designating both by the term *meschimes*.

English Sources

The English-language sources begin, of course, with the various journals associated with James Cook's third voyage to the Pacific. Cook was in Nootka Sound for four weeks in the spring of 1778. Because of the publicity generated by Cook's voyage and the quick realization in Europe and eastern North America of the potential of the fur trade (especially in sea otter skins), Nootka Sound became the first important focus of European activity in the culture area. In addition to the material in the various Cook voyage accounts, the observations of many other traders and explorers were soon added to those in the Spanish sources. No eighteenth-century English-language source is as complete as *Noticias de Nutka*, but like some of the other Spanish sources, many contain useful information on slavery. The most important and complete early source in English is not from the eighteenth century. This is John Jewitt's account (written with the help of a professional writer) of his two years as a slave among the Mowachaht from 1803 to 1805. Our single most important source on slavery in any Northwest Coast group, its value for information on the late precontact period is tempered by the fact that Jewitt was a slave twenty-five years after Cook sailed into Nootka Sound.

The first contact with the Haida was by the Spanish in 1774, but the next direct European contact with these inhabitants of the Queen Charlotte Islands was not until 1787 when George Dixon circumnavigated the islands and discovered their potential as a source of furs. After Dixon trading activity in the Queen Charlottes became intense, and a good bit of information accumulated about the Haida at the end of the eighteenth century. Yet no trader left accounts as detailed or valuable as either Moziño or the Cook chroniclers for the Mowachaht.

Although the Spanish were the first Europeans to sight the mouth of the Columbia (in 1775), the region around the mouth of this great river was not drawn directly into the fur trade orbit until 1792 when it was "discovered" by Robert Gray. For the remainder of the century a number of traders' journals provide us with information about the Chinook and their neighbors, although neither individually nor collectively do these accounts give us the detail or scope of the Mowachaht or even Haida sources.

Gradually in the 1790s other parts of the region's coasts began to be reached by European explorers and traders. But although valuable fragments of information begin to become available about many of the culture area's peoples, for no other groups do we have either the quality or the quantity of information on the eighteenth century that we do for the Mowachaht or even the less fully reported Haida and Chinook.

Other Sources

For the coasts of what is now Alaska the richest sources are in Russian. The most useful guide to Russian involvement in Alaska is perhaps Svetlana G. Fedorova (1973; see also Starr 1987). Russian involvement in the New World began in 1743 with the Bering expeditions. But, although Russian involvement in the Aleutians was considerable in the last half of the eighteenth century (with a consequent richness of Russian material on that area during the period), the Russians did not really begin to expand significantly into the Northwest Coast culture area proper until almost the end of the century. They attempted a settlement at Yakutat in northernmost Tlingit territory in 1795, but their major involvement with the Tlingit began in 1799 when they established their first base at Sitka. Thus it is for the first half of the nineteenth century that Russian sources (and Russian-sponsored sources in German) are so valuable for the Tlingit. There are French (La Pérouse, Marchand) as well as Spanish (the Malaspina expedition) and English sources for the Yakutat and Lituya Bay Tlingit, and some early nineteenth-century Russian-sponsored sources (Langsdorff, Lisiansky) provide some information about the Sitka area Tlingit just after the end of our period (1803–1806).

Was Northwest Coast Slavery an Aboriginal Practice?

The eighteenth-century evidence strongly suggests that slavery was not only present but well integrated in the various Northwest Coast cultures at the time of early contact. The linguistic evidence lends some support to this view. As we have seen, currently available information from archaeology tells us nothing directly about the presence or absence of slavery, although it does suggest that many other Northwest Coast culture traits were well established long before Europeans entered the region.

The eighteenth-century evidence is fullest for the Mowachaht, and for this Nuu-chah-nulth group we can say the following about slavery in very early contact times: prisoners of war were enslaved; there was an active trade in slaves and interested Europeans had no difficulty purchasing them; slaves were killed on several ritual occasions (including ceremonies associated with whaling); slaves performed much of the menial labor; there were special hairstyles for slaves and other external indications of differential treatment; and Mowachaht vocabulary distinguished titleholders, commoners, and slaves.[8]

Altogether this suggests that slavery was a well-established part of Mowachaht culture. But the eighteenth-century sources are very poor on numbers.

Jewitt's (1974, 65) account of the Mowachaht suggests that important title-holders held fairly large numbers of slaves, but Jewitt came twenty-five years after contact and the booming trade during the previous twenty years could have caused slaves to increase numerically.

Information about slavery is even sparser for the rest of the coast for this period. But there are mentions of slaves from all parts of the region, and what we know is consistent with both the picture for eighteenth-century Mowachaht and nineteenth-century practices.

Slavery was almost certainly a well-integrated part of traditional Northwest Coast cultures, but we can say nothing about the origin of this institution in the culture area. There are no data to indicate its time depth, where it originated in the region, or if it was a local invention or diffused from elsewhere. Although there were trade and other contacts with non–Northwest Coast neighbors and thus indirect contacts with all of aboriginal North America, as Kroeber (1923) demonstrated long ago the Northwest Coast is very different from the rest of native North America; slavery is only one of its unusual features. Although there may have been Asian influences via Alaska and Siberia, it is probable that slavery along with other distinctive Northwest Coast traits developed within the region during the thousand years (or more) preceding the intrusion of Europeans, the period that saw the gradual development of the classic Northwest Coast cultures first encountered by Europeans.

Postscript

This chapter has made what I believe to be a strong case for the antiquity of slavery in the Northwest Coast culture area. Although there is no conclusive proof, taken altogether the linguistic, archaeological, and early contact material strongly suggests that slavery was practiced by the aboriginal inhabitants of the region before contact with Europeans in the last third of the eighteenth century, probably for centuries. This view would not be accepted by all persons of aboriginal descent now living. For example, I have talked with two Nuu-chah-nulth who maintain that slavery was introduced to the west coast of Vancouver Island by the Spanish in the eighteenth century. Others would probably agree with them, although I have spoken with many more native people who do not dispute the precontact existence of aboriginal slavery. Neither of the individuals who have insisted to me that slavery was introduced by the Spanish cited specific oral traditions in support of their claims. Indeed, one of these men told me of several accounts of his own local group's enslavement of members of neighboring groups. He merely insisted that the idea had come from the Spanish. I can only respond by saying that none of the evidence known to me suggests a postcontact origin of Northwest Coast slavery or indeed that native people were uncomfortable with the idea or practice of slavery in the half century or so following contact.

11

Changes in Slavery, 1780–1880

What we know of the archaeological record on the Northwest Coast suggests gradual change during the centuries that preceded the 1770s. As with many small-scale societies previously outside the orbit of Europe, the rate of change accelerated once contact with Europeans introduced new opportunities and new constraints. Slavery was only one of the many customs and practices that underwent this increased pace of transformation.

In this chapter I consider the changes in slavery that took place between 1780 and 1880 and examine the fate of former slaves in the current century. I begin with a brief account of contact history on the Northwest Coast and a brief review of later events that had a direct impact on slavery. Then I consider the relations between the slave trade and the fur trade and examine changes in such areas as slave labor, the decline in the ritual killing of slaves, marriages between slaves and free persons, the end of slavery, and twentieth-century attitudes toward former slaves. I conclude with a summary of the material on change introduced in the previous chapters.

Before turning to contact history, a brief note on the context of Northwest Coast slavery in the wider world of the eighteenth century seems appropriate. In 1770 slavery was widespread and important—numerically, economically, and culturally—in all parts of the New World that were dominated by Europeans; there was a flourishing transatlantic slave trade; and the rhetoric about freedom in such documents as the Declaration of Independence did not apply to black slaves in what was to be the United States—witness the slaveholding clauses in the U.S. Constitution. By the 1770s there was a growing abolitionist movement in Europe and parts of the New World, but its first major success came only in 1807 when the British outlawed the slave trade. Some of the Europeans who came to the Northwest Coast in the early years of contact opposed or at least disapproved of slavery, many were indifferent to the issue, and some even willingly participated in the institution on the coast or elsewhere. Probably no European who came to the coast in the first fifty years or so of contact, even those who strongly disapproved of slavery, found the practice of slavery on the Northwest Coast odd or unusual. But one of the changes that impinged on the peoples of the culture area during their first fifty years of contact with Europeans was the growing success of the abolitionist movement in Europe and in European-controlled areas of the world.

A Sketch of Northwest Coast Contact History

There is no comprehensive or systematic treatment of the history of contact between the indigenous inhabitants of the Northwest Coast culture area and Europeans. This is partly because historical research has tended to be organized along the lines of recent, European-created, political boundaries, giving a tripartite historical literature—Alaska, British Columbia, and Washington. Even anthropological works, including those on prehistory, are usually divided up this way. Where a culture area focus has been adopted, historical issues, including contact history, have not been the primary concern. Most of the standard ethnographies of the region's groups do contain brief discussions of early contact between native and European, but these often seem to be based on the least careful and thorough research done for the entire ethnography. Even a basic framework of dates by which to order the events of native/European contact is hard to come by given the scattered references. We lack not only regional syntheses but even the basic group-by-group and sub-regional research necessary for the production of overviews. For this reason what follows is only a sketch, designed to give necessary background to understanding the changes in slavery that concern us here.

Precontact "Contact"

Before the period of European contact began, the peoples of the Northwest Coast were not completely cut off from the outside world. Although inter-community trade was probably more intense within the culture area than with groups bordering on the area, some trade networks extended beyond the culture area. For example, dentalia shells, many of which came from the west coast of Vancouver Island, are found in archaeological sites all over western North America. And many ship's crews found native people in possession of iron and copper. Some of the copper was native, obtained in trade from Alaska, just outside the culture area, but the iron and other copper came from trade to the interior—where the ultimate source was Europeans—or from the sea as drift metal. Drift metal from wrecks, of both European and Japanese vessels, had long supplied coastal communities with some iron. Sometimes wrecks brought other goods; occasionally even living Japanese sailors came ashore and were almost certainly absorbed into the local community as slaves. Trade and drift metal combined made only a modest contribution to Northwest Coast precontact material culture, but they did prepare the way for contact by making Northwest Coast natives familiar with and eager to trade for metal (Gunther 1972, 249–251; Quimby 1985; Rickard 1939).

The European Background

By the last half of the eighteenth century the North Pacific Coast of North America was the only temperate coastline not at least partially explored by Europeans. Europeans were rapidly expanding their knowledge of the landmass of North America, but the Rockies and other mountains and the Pacific Ocean had so far insulated the peoples of the Northwest Coast from direct European intrusion. This isolation ended in the 1770s, although the first steps to end it were taken earlier.

About 1750 Europe was poised to approach the North Pacific Coast. Continental North America was being settled and explored by Europeans, but most activity was occurring east of the Mississippi or in the eastern Arctic. The Spanish were, of course, well established in Mexico and parts of what later became the American Southwest, and Spanish exploration, if not settlement, of the California coast regularly reached as far north as the San Francisco area. The Russians were consolidating their hold on Siberia and were beginning to reach even farther east, to the Western Hemisphere. Spain regarded the Pacific and the shores it touched as its sphere of interest and jealously guarded its secrets. There had been British intrusions into the Pacific since the sixteenth century but no continuous British presence in the eastern Pacific. These three nations, Spain, Russia, and Britain, were the major actors in the first European forays onto the Northwest Coast.

In 1741 ships of the Russian-sponsored Bering expedition sailed in American waters, establishing the location of the northwesternmost coast of the American mainland and its relationship to Asia. Members of this expedition also brought back news of the rich potential of these waters as a source of furs. From 1743 on Russian efforts to control and exploit the coast of Alaska increased, although significant Russian intrusions into the Northwest Coast culture area proper (i.e., Tlingit territory) did not seriously begin until the last decade of the century. Russian expansion into the region was largely motivated by one of the principal attractions of the area for Europeans: furs.

The other principal attraction of the region—the search for the Northwest Passage—engaged the interest of the Spanish and the British. Europeans, especially northern Europeans, had been interested in a Northwest Passage almost since the size and extent of the North and South American continents had been realized. For if these continents were an opportunity, they were also an obstacle: there was no easy way to sail west to reach the important markets of Asia. Magellan found a water route into the Pacific by sailing around the southern end of South America, but the dream of a northwest passage and efforts to find it persisted. The Northwest Passage was still an object of interest and possibility in the eighteenth century. The Spanish did not want it found. It would make it even more difficult to control foreign intrusions into their ocean, and even Spanish efforts to find the northern route into the Pacific were not encouraged. The British had a long history of interest in finding such a route, beginning with John Cabot's voyage of 1497. When the Spanish learned of Russian activities in the far north and possible British interest in attempting to find the Northwest Passage by searching for its western end, they began to increase their activity north from California. The stage was set for the inclusion of the North Pacific Coast into the sphere of European interest and control.[1]

Contact in the 1770s

In 1774 a Spanish vessel, the *Santiago*, commanded by Pérez, reached British Columbian and Alaskan waters. There were brief contacts and some trade with an unidentified Haida group and with the Mowachaht. In 1775, nervous about Russian encroachment from the north, the Spanish sent an expedition of two ships north from the base at San Blas. The *Santiago* was captained by Bruno de Hezeta, commander of the expedition, and the smaller *Sonora* was captained by Juan Francisco de la Bodega y Quadra. The expedition's first landfall brought them into contact with the Quinault. After some initially peaceful trading there were two violent clashes during which a number of Spaniards and Quinault were killed or injured. After a few more days Hezeta sailed the *Santiago* back south along the coast and had no more significant encounters with the culture area's inhabitants. Bodega continued north in the *Sonora* and had some brief, peaceful trading encounters just north of Sitka with a few Tlingit.

In 1778 James Cook's third voyage, specially commissioned to look for the Northwest Passage, sailed into Nootka Sound. The expedition spent four weeks there in fairly intensive contact with the Mowachaht before sailing north into Alaskan waters. Cook's next contact with the indigenous inhabitants of the coast was in Prince William Sound, an ethnically complex area just to the north of the Northwest Coast culture area proper. In 1779, having previously learned of Cook's intention to explore the North Pacific Coast, the Spanish sent two warships to intercept him and protect their claims to the region. The Spanish expedition was commanded by Ignacio de Arteaga, captain of the frigate *Princesa*, with Bodega as captain of the *Favorita* and second in command. The Arteaga expedition found no traces of Cook (it did not enter either Nootka or Prince William Sound) and also convinced the Spanish that the Russians were confining their activities to the Aleutians. The failure to find traces of Cook and the false conclusion about Russian activity helped to weaken Spain's claims to sovereignty to the region. From the native point of view the most important events associated with this expedition occurred in May when the two ships stopped briefly in Bucarelli Bay on Prince of Wales Island. Initial relations with the Haida were friendly and some minor trade was carried out. Some of the crew became ill, probably with smallpox. If so, this was the time and place of this disease's introduction to the peoples of the Northwest Coast. Smallpox quickly became one of the most serious causes of depopulation in native communities.

Only seven ships on four expeditions—three Spanish and one British—are known to have contacted one or another of the peoples of the culture area during the 1770s. (Russian activity was confined largely, if not exclusively, to the region somewhat northwest of the culture area.) The Spanish gave very little publicity to their voyages, and there would be no more visits to the Northwest Coast by European vessels until a single ship came in 1785. But the British could not keep the results of Cook's voyage a secret. In addition to exploring parts of the Northwest Coast, Cook's ships had "discovered" the Hawaiian Islands. On the return visit to these islands after the Northwest Coast foray, Cook was killed. In the very short run this was the most momentous news coming out of the voyage. Some of Cook's men had traded for sea otter pelts at Nootka Sound and sold them for huge profits in China on the way home. Hoping to exploit the potential of the sea otter trade more fully after the war with its American colonies was over, the British government apparently tried to keep the news about sea otter pelt profits from leaking out by controlling all journals and diaries from the voyage after Cook's vessels reached England in 1780. But two accounts were published in 1781 and another came out in 1782; all three gave some indication of the potential of the trade. British merchant interest quickly grew, and when peace with the former American colonies came in 1783 ships rapidly began to prepare to participate in the sea otter trade.

The Beginning of the Maritime Fur Trade[2]

European traders were not the only ones keen for trade. Cook's men had found the Mowachaht very eager to obtain metal in almost any form but much less interested in other goods. Cook's crew found the Mowachaht not unskilled at trading, as did later Europeans who came to the coast seeking easy profits.

When we first Entered this Sound at about 5 PM several Canoes came of to the ships. . . . In the Canoe that first came Along side was a Man that stood up and held forth a long while. . . . [O]n his head he wore a kind of hat made of Cane and in shape resembling a buck's head; after having finished his harangue he presented it to Sale as well as several other things, which at once convinced us they were no novices at that business, in return for his hat he had a large Axe and left us quite Content. (Riou, 30 March 1778; in Beaglehole 1967, 295–296)

They are very keen traders getting as much as they could for every thing they had; always asking for more give them what you would, neither would they depend on thier own judgment but Ask the opinion of all thier friends & companions—handing what you offered them round for every one to see it, & then return it to us if they did not like it. (Bayly, Journal [p. 116]; in Beaglehole 1967, 302)

Captain James Hanna of the *Harmon* was the first to arrive to trade in Nootka Sound. Having sailed from China, he reached Vancouver Island in 1785, the only ship to do so that year. Relations with the Mowachaht quickly went sour and there was fighting and some fatalities.[3] Hanna managed to patch things up and returned to China with a good cargo of sea otter pelts. In 1786 Hanna returned to Nootka Sound, but that year he was not alone: a total of ten ships visited the coast. Most of these were British ships interested in the sea otter trade. The number of ships, most of them involved in trade, quickly increased. The peak period was 1790 to 1794, when 104 ships came to the region (Howay 1930a, 1931, 1932b, 1933, 1934).

The initial focus of the trade was Nootka Sound. But the Mowachaht's ability to supply large quantities of sea otter pelts was limited, and the captains quickly began to search out other communities with which to trade. There were also both British and Spanish government-sponsored exploring expeditions, associated with the struggle for sovereignty over the area. Spain had a strong claim to the Northwest Coast, but after the "Nootka Sound affair," which nearly led to war between Spain and Britain, the Spanish gradually pulled back from the territory of the Northwest Coast culture area, although they had ships in the area throughout the early 1790s. After 1797 no more Spanish ships were seen in Northwest Coast waters. Although ships from many nations participated in the maritime fur trade, the principal European powers during both the maritime and land-based fur trade periods now held the field—Russia, Britain, and the United States.

The Maritime Fur Trade, 1785–1825

Although furs of every type were traded, it was the sea otter that fueled the early boom in the Northwest Coast fur trade. The trade was largely a triangular one. That is, goods of interest to the inhabitants of the Northwest Coast were brought to the region from Britain or the eastern seaboard of the United States and traded for sea otter pelts and other furs. The sea otter pelts were then taken to China and exchanged for Chinese goods, which were then taken to Britain or the United States. Very large profits were possible, but these depended on completing the triangle of transactions. Frederick W. Howay (1932b, 6–8) argued (in what remains the best brief summary of the maritime fur trade period on the coast) that the Americans (primarily Bostonians) came to dominate the trade by 1800 because they did not face the monopoly restrictions on the Chinese trade that the East Indian Company successfully enforced among British traders. Without the Chinese trade the bilateral exchange of furs for European goods was not profitable enough to keep British merchants in the field.

Throughout this period the approach was from the sea. Except for a short-lived Spanish base at Nootka Sound (more concerned with sovereignty issues than with trade), there were no land posts in the culture area until the very end of the eighteenth century. And ship-based trading continued to dominate until the second decade of the next century. This meant that traders searched out native trading partners rather than that natives came to fixed points with their furs, although there were, of course, popular rendezvous spots. Even though it remained ship based, over time the style of the trade did change. In the early years, ships cruised along the coast several miles offshore and their native customers paddled out to trade. But increasing competition led to ships going into the various small harbors and coming into closer contact with native communities. The trading pattern also changed in that it went from trading "over the side" (natives remained in their canoes alongside and goods were passed back and forth over the side of the merchant ships) to the native customers expecting to come on board the trading ships to do business. At the beginning of the trade, ships spent the season (the summer months) trading and then, if they had a full cargo of furs, as sometimes happened in the early years, sailed for China. If a second season was required for a full load the ships wintered in Hawaii. Beginning about 1805, ships began wintering on the coast, carrying on their trade under difficult winter conditions. The reason was simple: increased competition and a decline in the flow of sea otter pelts. The data Howay (1930a, 1931, 1932a, 1933, 1934) assembled on ships visiting the coast suggest that ships or ships' masters rarely made more than three voyages. It was impossible for anyone to control the activities of the various merchant ships and, without a stake in permanent bases and long-term relationships, some captains and crews acted irresponsibly toward their trading partners. Relations were sometimes poor and marked with violence, and the innocent (European and native) sometimes received the retribution due others.

The demand for sea otter pelts was high, resulting in large-scale slaughter of sea otters. The pressure on the species was so great that it was hunted almost to extinction. Gradually other furs became more and more important, but none offered the spectacular profits of the sea otter. And the nature of the supply, coupled with growing European overland expansion from the east, meant that by the 1820s the maritime trade was rapidly being replaced by a land-based trade. But for most Northwest Coast peoples, the first direct contact with Europeans came during the maritime fur trade period.

The Land-Based Fur Trade

Throughout the eighteenth century almost all contact of the indigenous people with Europeans was oriented to the sea and ships. But European expansion across continental North America came closer and closer to the Pacific Coast. The approach to the North Pacific Coast was primarily due to an interest in expanding the fur trade into new and relatively untapped regions. Furs therefore remained the prime element in European/native contact, although sea otters were no longer the principal pelts sought by European traders.

The first foray onto the coast from overland came in 1793 when Alexander Mackenzie arrived at the mouth of the Bella Coola River after a journey that began at the North West Company's new post at Fort Chippewyan in what is now northeastern Alberta and went up sections of the Peace and Parsnip rivers and down sections of the Fraser and Bella Coola rivers. Ironically, Mackenzie barely missed meeting one of George Vancouver's surveying crews that was in the area about the same time. Chronologically, the next land move into the culture area was from the north. The Russians had finally begun to expand their interest into Tlingit territory. By 1796 they had established a small settlement in Yakutat Bay and, more important, in 1799 set up their first settlement at Sitka. The Tlingit destroyed this post in 1802, but the Russians reestablished it in 1804 and it became the most important European settlement in Tlingit territory for it was the political and military center of Russian activity in southeastern Alaska.

In 1805 the Lewis and Clark expedition reached the mouth of the Columbia River after an overland journey. As with Mackenzie's earlier journey, no permanent post resulted from this expedition. But fur trade posts did begin to get closer to the coast. In 1805 Fort Nelson was established by the North West Company, and in 1806 the same company founded Fort Saint James. Both of these northern British Columbia posts brought the land-based fur trade to the back door of the culture area. Fur traders on exploring expeditions began to reach the coast by various routes (Simon Fraser in 1808 via the Fraser River, David Thompson in 1811 via the Columbia River). And in 1811 the first land-based trading post was built at the mouth of the Columbia at Astoria. This post thus marked a new era in the coast's contact history. The Russian post at Sitka and the American post on the Columbia gave Europeans land bases at both ends of the culture area; now fur traders could fill in the area between as the needs of the trade and competition dictated. The maritime fur trade continued to exist into the 1820s, although after about 1810 it went into a serious decline. The land-based trade began slowly—largely because of the struggles of rival companies with each other and with free-lancers for control of the trade. In 1813 the Pacific Fur Company sold out to the North West Company and Astoria became Fort George. In 1821 the Hudson's Bay Company and the North West Company amalgamated and the establishment of the land-based fur trade on the coast began in earnest. Fort Vancouver was founded on the Columbia in 1825 and additional land bases were established over the next twenty-five years. (See fig. 8 for the founding dates and locations of some of the key posts.) The Hudson's Bay Company strove for a monopoly of the fur trade in the region. It never quite accomplished this, for the Russians remained active around Sitka and American traders remained on the scene as ship-borne competitors in at least a small way throughout the period. The land-based fur trade period did represent, however, the consolidation of European contact with the native peoples of the region. As the period drew to a close in the late 1840s and 1850s, all the peoples of the culture area were in contact with Europeans and were participants in trade. The impact of contact in the form of disease and dramatically increased death rates was also felt throughout all communities in the region.[4]

The Struggle for Sovereignty on the North Pacific Coast

Throughout the 1820s and 1830s the fur trade completely dominated European activity on the Northwest Coast, and all relations between native peoples and Europeans involved, at least indirectly, the fur trade. From the European perspective the most important local development was the establishment of the Hudson's Bay Company's near-monopoly on the fur trade between Sitka and the Columbia. From the native point of view this was very important also, as the Russians to the north and the American trading ships that visited various points along the coast were competition to the Hudson's Bay Company, forcing up both the prices of furs and the quality of goods offered in trade.

The 1840s brought increased interest from the Hudson's Bay Company in agricultural enterprises and, more significant, increasing American interest in the area as an object of settlement and immigration from the east. The European powers began to work out their political jurisdiction within the region. In 1846 the British and Americans settled on the boundary between their respective territories. In 1849 the British formally established the colony of Vancouver Island and the United States created the Oregon Territory (which included present-day Oregon and Washington). The numbers of European settlers were still small (less than 500 colonists had come to Vancouver

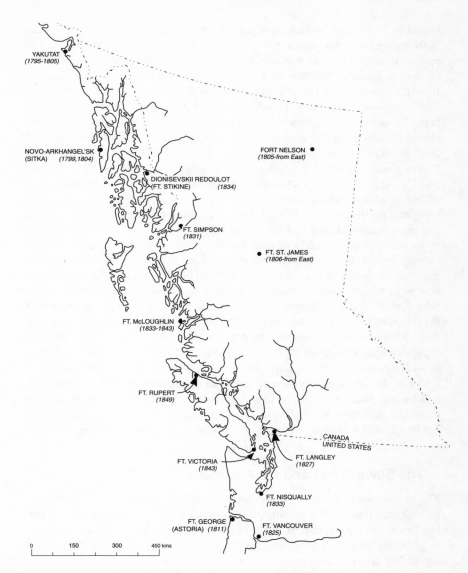

YAKUTAT
(1795-1805)

NOVO-ARKHANGEL'SK
(SITKA)   (1799,1804)

FORT NELSON
(1805-from East)

DIONISEVSKII REDOULOT
(FT. STIKINE)   (1834)

FT. SIMPSON
(1831)

FT. ST. JAMES
(1806-from East)

FT. McLOUGHLIN
(1833-1843)

FT. RUPERT
(1849)

CANADA
UNITED STATES

FT. VICTORIA
(1843)

FT. LANGLEY
(1827)

FT. NISQUALLY
(1833)

FT. GEORGE
(ASTORIA) (1811)

FT. VANCOUVER
(1825)

0   150   300   450 kms

Figure 8.   Locations and Founding Dates of Selected Key Fur Trade Posts.

Island by 1852, and the European population of what was to become western Washington State was under 1,000 in 1849), but the wave of settlement was easy to predict. The area that was to become Washington State was populous enough to become Washington Territory in 1853, and in 1858 the colony of British Columbia was formally organized on the British Columbia mainland. The growth of European population—both in permanent settlers and partici-pants in various gold rushes—was continuous. In 1867 the United States ac-quired Alaska from the Russians and the Canadian Confederation was cre-ated. In 1871 British Columbia became a province of Canada and the North Pacific Coast fell under the political and military control of the United States and Canada. The lives and institutions of the native peoples of the region would be shaped and determined to a significant degree by the policies of these two governments and their local administrations. The native peoples had not been consulted, nor had they participated in any way in the creation of these new political entities in what had been their exclusive domains only a century before. In comparison with either of the two earlier fur trade periods, the style of culture contact changed considerably. Native peoples now had to deal with both government administrations and permanent European neigh-bors whose economic interests were based on the direct European control of the resource base. The mutuality of economic interest of the fur trade days was gone. Many native institutions and practices were not acceptable to the new regime, and soon steps were taken to control and "improve" native behavior as well as to acquire the resource base. A complete account of these efforts is a part of the larger history of native/European relations in British Columbia, Alaska, and Washington in the late nineteenth and early twentieth century and cannot be attempted here. Clearly, however, slavery was a practice that would not be allowed whenever it came to the notice of political authorities.

The Slave Trade and the Fur Trade

The indigenous trade in slaves has been described in chapter 7. We can safely assume that there was a significant precontact trade in slaves. It was proba-bly "local" in nature; that is, trade in slaves, as in other items, was between neighboring groups or proximate groups. Slaves and other goods might travel significant distances, but such movements, when they occurred, would be the end result of a series of local transactions. This is supported by the earlier analysis, which suggests that slave trade connections were more widespread in late rather than early historic times. My discussion of prices implies connec-tions between the fur trade and the slave trade, as furs were often exchanged for slaves and prices are often quoted in furs or blankets. Here I describe more fully the ties between the two trades and the changes in slavery occasioned by the development of the fur trade.

Europeans in the Slave Trade

As the maritime fur trade developed, slaves became a minor part of the trade itself. While they were active in the region, the Spanish bought a number of slaves whom they took back to Mexico. They sought to purchase slaves for religious training, to save them (they bought mostly children) from slavery, and to keep them from being eaten (or so the Spanish thought was to be their fate, especially in Nootka Sound). There is also eighteenth-century evidence that some natives involved Europeans in the slave trade by hitching rides on European ships, taking along a slave or two and selling them to natives at another community when the ship came in to trade there.

There was also some direct European participation in the slave trade. At least four American ships' captains are known to have engaged in the slave trade on their own behalf. One captain, when he was unable to purchase slaves, kidnapped twelve men at the mouth of the Columbia to sell as slaves farther north (Corney 1965, 154). Slaves were not the only aspect of indigenous trade joined in by Europeans. There was a very high demand for cured elk hides (for use as armor) in various places in the northern part of the region, and many ships picked up large quantities of elk hides around the mouth of the Columbia and carried them north for resale, especially to the Queen Charlottes. As well, some ships purchased eulachon oil from the Nass River for resale in the Queen Charlottes—joining in a long-standing indigenous trade in eulachon.

The Preference for Slaves
over Trade Goods

During the maritime period, especially its first half, the trade in slaves probably played a relatively small role in the fur trade. But in the land-based fur trade era, the slave trade was important to the fur trade—at least in some local areas. By the beginning of the land-based period, native middlemen had become important. And many of these middlemen were as eager to trade furs for slaves as for European trade goods.[5] The effects of the slave trade were well described by James Douglas.

> The species of property most highly prized among the natives of Tako [Taku Tlingit] is that of slaves, which in fact constitutes their measure of wealth. . . . [S]laves being through this national perversion of sentiment, the most saleable commodity here, the native pedlars, come from as far south as Kygarnie [Kaigani Haida] with their human assortments and readily obtain from 18 to 20 skins a head for them. The greater number of these slaves are captives made in war, and many predatory excursions are undertaken not to avenge international aggressions, but simply with a sordid view to the profits that may arise from the sale of the captives taken.

This detestable traffic, and the evils it gives rise to, are subjects of deep regret to us, but we know of no remedy within our power, as we would use it were it only for the sake of our own interest, which is thereby seriously affected, as the Take [Taku Tlingit] skins are traded before our very eyes and carried off from our very door, by means of a description of property that we cannot compete in.

A few days ago a canoe from Kagarnie brought in four slaves, and a second from Stekine [Stikine Tlingit] brought one which were immediately purchased at the prices stated above. (1840, 14 July 1840)[6]

Other Hudson's Bay Company records confirm that competition with the slave trade was not confined to the post of Taku. I will return to the predatory slave raids mentioned by Douglas.

Just how serious was the competition with native slave traders? This is hard to answer, because there is no accurate count of the number of slaves traded for furs for any period. The fragmentary data for prices and numbers, however, allow some informed speculation about the probable scale and impact of the slave trade. According to Douglas, the price of a slave at Taku in 1840 was 16 to 20 beaver skins. In 1840 the Taku post trade was the equivalent of 436 beaver skins (McLoughlin 1943, 338–340). If we take 18 beaver skins as the value of a typical slave, this is equivalent to 24 slaves. In less than a week in the summer Douglas saw five slaves traded for furs at Taku, equivalent to 21 percent of the furs taken in in the six months that the post operated that year. Even if no other slaves were traded around Taku, this is a significant proportion of the post's trade. And, as Douglas makes clear, we can be certain that a good many more slaves were traded in the vicinity of Taku in that and other years. Altogether, the Hudson's Bay Company posts in the northern Northwest Coast (the area north of Vancouver Island) traded the equivalent of 7,251 beaver skins in 1840 (McLoughlin 1943, 338–340). This was equivalent to 403 slaves. Hudson's Bay Company census figures for this part of the coast at about this time suggest a Native population of at least fifty thousand, and a conservative estimate would be that 5 percent (2,500) were slaves. Thus the total value of the Hudson's Bay Company's fur returns for 1840 was worth well under 20 percent of the value of slaves held in the region. If only 10 percent of these slaves changed hands for furs, the value of the furs involved would represent well over half the 1840 fur returns. And even transactions involving a total of only one hundred slaves would represent 25 percent of the returns. Although such estimates are not conclusive and are for only one year, we do know that native middlemen traded slaves for furs on a significant scale for years, so that it is probable that the impact on the company's profits was significant.

By the 1840s the Hudson's Bay Company dominated the fur trade along most of the Northwest Coast. The major transactions involved the trade of furs for European goods and vice versa, but some Northwest Coast native people preferred to trade furs for slaves rather than for the Hudson's Bay Company's wares. Two classes of demand explain this preference for slaves: one has to do with competition in the fur trade, the other with the native demand for slaves.

Although the Hudson's Bay Company dominated the fur trade, it had not achieved the total monopoly that it desired. The Russians still operated around Sitka and to the north of Sitka, but they were not very effective competitors, and by 1840 the Hudson's Bay Company had leased locales for posts south of Sitka in Russian territory to improve their monopoly. The Hudson's Bay Company's chief competition was from American trading vessels, which were willing to outbid both Hudson's Bay Company land posts and ships for furs. Sometimes the competition was direct when the Hudson's Bay Company men and their rivals were in the same community at the same time. Always there was the threat of such competition, although with the Russian/Hudson's Bay Company agreement the Americans' position was weakened.

The impact of this competition and the natives' ability to take advantage of it can be seen from John Work's account of one incident that took place in May 1835 during a trading voyage of the Hudson's Bay Company brig *Lama* (Work 1945). When Work and the *Lama* arrived at the Nass River on May 15 they found the American ship *Europa* already there and engaging in trade. Both vessels remained on the Nass for five days. Work describes his frustration as the Natives went from ship to ship comparing prices and goods. The Americans had better-quality blankets, a key item in the trade, and the Hudson's Bay men were forced to raise their prices to meet the competition. If the Americans had superior blankets, the Hudson's Bay men had superior rum, and this helped them retain a share of the Nass trade that week.[7] As Work (1945, 41) noted, "The Indians glory in having . . . opposition and know well how to take advantage of it." To Work's great frustration, he estimated that the American captain had obtained more beavers, land otters, and martens, although he had more bears (1945, 41–43). Even in the 1840s and 1850s some competition of this type continued.

Some slave trading was probably the result of entrepreneurial enterprise— an effort to conclude a series of transactions with a profit in either furs or slaves. And where competition between the Hudson's Bay Company and American ships was likely, some native traders surely liked their chances for such profits. In addition, some energetic and ambitious titleholders may have been well placed geographically to trade with Europeans but were in control of territories poor in fur-bearing animals. Raiding and trading for slaves to trade for furs may have been a primary source of furs for such men. Tsibasa, some of whose activities have already been described, was just such a titleholder. There was also some internal demand for furs, although by the time of the land-based trade most furs ultimately reached the hands of Europeans. Only the high level of external demand for furs could have supported the local trade networks on anything like their early nineteenth-century scale.

Probably more important to the slave trade than the effect of competition among Europeans was the native demand for slaves. There was some local demand for slaves, both for their labor and for ceremonial purposes (see below). But neither this local demand nor the possibility of higher profits from competition between Europeans can completely explain the fact that the Stikine and many others often passed up European goods for slaves. The explanation lies, I think, in the fact that there was a strong native demand for slaves external to the coast.

The Trade to the Interior

According to various Hudson's Bay Company officials at Fort Simpson near the mouth of the Skeena River, the Stikine often sought slaves rather than European trade goods for their furs, because slaves were the article in greatest demand by the "Inland Indians" who traded with the Stikine and who were their principal source of furs (Fort Simpson Journal 1834–1838). These Athapaskans who sought slaves for their furs probably belonged to groups now usually called Tahltan. And, although there is less evidence in the sources, the Taku probably traded slaves to the Inland Tlingit, as did the Chilkat to the Southern Tutchone (McClellan 1975, 506).

Throughout the 1830s and 1840s, the northern trade network involved not only trade among the northern Northwest Coast peoples but also various Athapaskan groups in the interior. The network consisted in traffic in both furs and slaves. A number of coastal groups acted as middlemen, obtaining furs from inland groups and sending both European trade goods and slaves into the interior in exchange. Coastal sources (especially Hudson's Bay Company records) give good indications of the demand and direction of the trade but are vague about which interior groups were trading for slaves. Unfortunately, both the ethnographic and historical sources for these groups have little to say about the slave trade.

According to McClellan (1975, 496), most Inland Tlingit slaves were obtained in warfare, either with Tlingit or neighboring Athapaskans, although she does state that some slaves were purchased from the coast. McClellan's Tutchone informants claimed that slaves were very expensive to purchase from Tlingit traders, these traders demanding a pile of furs the height of a man as a price for one slave (McClellan 1950, 128). Rather than take this literally, I assume that this means that slaves from the coast were very expensive, so that it is not surprising that slaves were sold by the Chilkat to the "most wealthy Tutchone" (McClellan 1975, 505). Dominique Legros's research did not turn up much evidence of an extensive coast-interior slave trade among the Tutchone; rather, most Tutchone slaves seem to have been Athapaskan in origin (pers. com.). The origin of Tahltan slaves is also obscure. Teit (1906, 237) notes that a Stl'atl'imx slave was found among the Tahltan; although the most probable immediate source of this slave was the coast, we cannot be sure of this. W. P. S. Thorman (n.d.) says that according to his Tahltan informants all their slaves were Athapaskan in origin, although in another part of his notes, Tahltan recount slave raids against the Nass River Tsimshian.

Thus the interior sources offer only weak support for the flow of slaves into the interior suggested by the coastal sources. Nevertheless, I am inclined to put more reliance on the coastal sources. This is because some of the best coastal sources are contemporary with the trade whereas all the interior sources used here are from the twentieth century, collected well after the disruptions and dramatic population declines of the nineteenth century. If there was a significant flow of slaves into the interior, why did various Athapaskan groups in the interior of what is now British Columbia and the Yukon seek slaves from the coast in the 1830s and 1840s? Unfortunately, both the historical and ethnographic sources are virtually silent on this point. The cultural elaboration present in coastal communities was only weakly present in the interior if it was present at all, so that slaves would not have filled the same cultural roles that they did on the coast. I hypothesize that population losses due to smallpox and other epidemics played a major role in the Athapaskan demand for slaves from the coast.

The impact of smallpox on interior Athapaskan populations is dramatically portrayed in Thorman's (n.d.) notes on the Tahltan where his informants told of an epidemic striking in July, the midst of the fishing season, when the winter store of fish was being laid up. Entire families succumbed to the epidemic and others died of starvation in the following winter because of the shortfall in stored fish. Thorman dates this epidemic to circa 1832 and describes an equally devastating second epidemic that he dates to about 1847. James R. Gibson (1982–1983, 65) dates what are probably the same epidemics to 1835–1838 and 1862. The 1830s date fits well with the high point of the coast-interior fur and slave trade. Thus it is quite probable that slaves were in high demand as replacements for those killed by smallpox. The coastal traders' need for furs gave some interior peoples the opportunity to rebuild their populations, although these never recovered to pre-epidemic levels.

Changes in the Slave Trade

In the early nineteenth century the slave trade and the fur trade were closely linked. After the 1850s, the importance of the trade began to decline, as did slavery in general, although some transactions in slaves continued to occur. But what was the state of the slave trade before European contact and before the fur trade began to flourish? How did the slave trade change?

As discussed in chapter 10, the available data on precontact slavery are very poor. Archaeology offers little help, and we must rely primarily on information supplied by eighteenth-century observers. We do know that there was extensive trade in material items before contact, so that trade contacts through which slaves might pass certainly existed. Also, the purchase of slaves was easily effected by the Spanish very early in the contact period, suggesting that such transactions in slaves were already established. Perhaps the most that we can say about precontact slave trade is that there were almost certainly some transactions in slaves, that such transactions almost certainly involved short-distance contacts between neighbors, and that the strong external demand (from the interior) for slaves was probably a phenomenon of the fur trade period, resulting from epidemic-induced population decline.

This, however, is a conservative approach to the problem. Dell Hymes (1980, 416–417) has argued for the precontact existence, even importance, of Chinook Jargon and makes one of the key points in his discussion the importance of slavery and the slave trade along the Lower Columbia in precontact times. He assumes that the ethnographic evidence of the great importance of slavery and the slave trade among the Chinook applies to the precontact period. Unfortunately, we cannot be sure of this. Slavery and the slave trade were very important on the Lower Columbia in early historic times. In the mid-1790s, very shortly after European contact, Charles Bishop (1967, 126–127) had no difficulty distinguishing commoners from slaves, for example. It seems likely that the scale of trade of all kinds increased with contact. The extent of this increase is unclear, however. Hymes assumes a very extensive network involving the Nuu-chah-nulth and Makah as well as groups close to the Columbia River mouth. In other words, he claims that what has been identified in chapter 7 as the Columbia River network flourished at or near its full extent in precontact times. But he offers little evidence apart from ethnography done in the 1930s. He notes that in this network both slaves and dentalia flowed from the north. Before European trade goods entered the picture, there is no indication of what goods might have been moving north. (However, the brisk trade in tanned elk hides carried out by European middlemen between the Columbia River and the Queen Charlotte Islands and points north is suggestive if the Nuu-chah-nulth desired elk hides also.) This point implies that an extensive trade in slaves between the west coast of Vancouver Island and the Columbia is unlikely before contact with European traders. Nuu-chah-nulth participation in the Columbia River network in the first half of the nineteenth century was the result of the collapse of the maritime fur trade and its attendant shift of European interest away from the west coast of Vancouver Island to both the north and the south. The Nuu-chah-nulth had limited supplies of terrestrial furs and thus turned to trading slaves south to continue the flow of European trade goods into their area. This analysis is supported by a linguistic critique of Hymes's position on the antiquity of Chinook Jargon (Samarin 1986).

Thus, although the Northwest Coast slave trade was almost certainly important before contact, its early-nineteenth-century scale in both numbers and distance was probably a by-product of opportunities created by contact, particularly the fur trade.

Slave Trading, Ceremonials, and "Predatory Warfare"

The greater number of these slaves are captives made in war, and many predatory excursions are undertaken not to avenge international aggressions, but simply with a sordid view to the profits that may arise from the sale of the captives taken. (Douglas n.d.)

The slave trade was a great business with Indians who had a turn for traffic, and was resorted to by chiefs desirous of recruiting their exchange for a coming feast or the like. (Tolmie 1878)

The quote from Douglas suggests that predatory raids motivated largely by the desire to take slaves for sale were common by the 1840s. The quote from Tolmie suggests the origin of the desire for "profits" that Douglas saw in the slave trade: enhanced participation in the ceremonial activity that resulted in increased prestige and power. Here I explore the links that developed between slave and fur trading, slave raiding, and participation in the feasting complex.

Donald Mitchell (1984, 42–45) has shown that raids whose express purpose was the capture of slaves took place in all areas of the culture area and that they were relatively common during the early nineteenth century. Indeed, he is able to show that R. C. Mayne's (1862, 74) characterization of Northwest Coast warfare as a "cruel system of predatory warfare" was a particularly apt description of such nineteenth-century slave raids.

As described in chapter 5, Mitchell (1984) was able to reconstruct one such raid and its outcome in considerable detail. In this 1837 raid the Kitkatla Tsimshian raided the Nawitti Kwakwaka'wakw and traded some of the slaves they captured to the Stikine Tlingit for furs. Some of these furs were then traded by the Kitkatla leading titleholder, Tsibasa, to the Hudson's Bay Company at Fort Simpson. The goods Tsibasa traded for were given away at a major feast he hosted for the principal Lower Skeena Tsimshian titleholder, Legaic. Some months later Legaic gave a return feast for Tsibasa and his followers.

The pattern of this raid was probably common to many such raids at the time: capture of slaves; trade of at least some of the newly captured slaves for furs to other titleholders; trading of furs for European goods or other goods suitable for giving away at a feast; a large feast given by the titleholder responsible for the raid to which one or more of his principal rivals is invited; a return feast. And the cycle continues.

As is well known, one of the major purposes in giving a feast was the host's efforts to validate his claim to a title. Successful feast givers gained or at least maintained their prestige and position. The leaders who sponsored these feasts might find slaves important in their ceremonial activities in at least four ways: (1) the labor they performed could be used to help amass the large amount of goods, especially foodstuffs, needed for a feast; (2) central to most feasts were large-scale presentations of goods to specially invited elite guests—one's "rivals"—and slaves were a major value item in such "give-aways"; (3) by the early nineteenth century, items of European origin had become an important part of the goods distributed at feasts, and slaves could be traded for such goods or for furs to obtain such goods; and (4) property was not only given away but destroyed at feasts, and slaves were sometimes killed to demonstrate the wealth and power of the host. As Garfield has suggested for the Tsimshian, in the feasting context a slave might fulfill several roles within the same feast preparation.

> In addition to the slaves who were kept by wealthy families as workers and personal servants, many others were purchased as a part of the property accumulated for distribution at a potlatch. It was profitable to convert perishable or bulky provisions, goods, and even blankets into slaves when preparing for a potlatch or other public affair. A slave's labors added to the store of potlatch goods and he himself was wealth to be given away. In this fashion he paid the cost of acquiring him. (1951, 29)[8]

Garfield might also have mentioned the possibility that after his (or her) prefeast labors were completed, a slave might be killed at the feast rather than given away. And, of course, a slave might be sold to obtain other goods for feast distribution, as certainly happened before Tsibasa's 1837 feast.

By the early nineteenth century, European goods had been added to the repertoire of wealth items given away at feasts. Indeed, one suspects that by this time every titleholder needed to include some European goods among his feast gifts in order to be successful. In direct trade with Europeans, furs were the key to obtaining European goods, but, as we have seen, furs could be obtained in trade for slaves as well as trapped. And when there was a demand for slaves, titleholders like Tsibasa probably found it easier and quicker to obtain furs for the European trade via slave raiding and trading than by trapping. So the fur trade and the ceremonial system dominant in the northern and central parts of the culture area came together after European-origin goods became important parts of property distributions. And the ceremonial system encouraged raiding and trading for slaves both because of the direct contributions slaves made to feast goods and because of their potential as quick sources of furs and thus European goods. Therefore, while Hudson's Bay Company traders often complained that fighting disrupted trade and deplored slavery and the traffic in slaves, both raiding for and trading in slaves helped to maintain the flow of furs to Europe, Asia, and eastern North America.

Slave Labor

During the historic period the available evidence suggests that slaves continued to perform the tasks at which they had always worked. The coming of the fur trade expanded economic activity and slaves were sometimes employed packing furs into the interior, for example. Northwest Coast peoples had always taken furs and prepared the skins for use, but as both phases of the fur trade increased, this activity and the labor required to keep up with the demand for furs also increased. Robin Fisher (1977, 19) has suggested that the fur trade put a premium on the labor of slaves. This is a plausible hypothesis, but unfortunately no contemporary observer tells us much about the organization of the work required in the processing of skins during the fur trade period.

Later in the historic period there are also some examples of slaves being hired out as laborers. Among the Sitka in 1877, for example, some slaves were hired out to paddle canoes (Morris 1879, 324). This sort of thing probably happened more often than was realized by the Europeans who hired them.

Contact and the growing presence of Europeans in the region did, however, certainly introduce one change that affected slaves, the development of prostitution. Sexual relations between Europeans and natives began very soon after contact. Cook's men availed themselves of the sexual services of the young women of Nootka Sound as soon as possible. But they found a situation different from the relatively open and complaisant sexual mores of Polynesia. Nuu-chah-nulth women were much less willing, and most bargains for sexual favors were struck with the men who controlled the young women in question. William Bayly provided the following description of these transactions.

> Some of the officers . . . purchased the favours of some of them, but at a high price to what was generally given at any other place we have been at, for the men seemed to be rather unwilling to let them out except for something they wanted, which they could not otherwise get, & even this was practised only among the lower class of them. The better sort would not hear any thing of the kind. (Bayly, in Beaglehole 1967, 311)

David Samwell, surgeon on the *Resolution*, thought that fathers were bartering the services of their daughters (in Beaglehole 1967, 1095), but I think that Bayly's comment makes it clear that the women in question were slaves. This is confirmed by Alexander Walker's experience in 1785–1786.

Three or four poor wretches were produced for prostitution. These were the dirtiest drabs in the Village, and appeared neither to be the Wives nor Daughters of any of our acquaintances. It is probable from the unusual contempt with which they were treated, and the fatiguing offices about which they were constantly employed, that these women were Captives, taken in war, and reduced to a state of slavery. (1982, 85)

Other Europeans also thought that they were being offered the daughters of "chiefs" when in fact they were almost certainly being offered slaves. For example, in Parry Passage in 1792, a Haida titleholder offered Jacinto Caamaño a young woman. Caamaño thought this woman was the daughter of this titleholder, but she wore no labret (worn by titleholder women) and was almost certainly a slave (Caamaño 1938, 216–217).

As the fur trade developed, more and more native communities became involved in the new economy. Prostitution developed alongside the whiskey trade and other negative consequences of contact and change. By the early nineteenth century not all women engaged in prostitution were slaves, but female slaves were probably the mainstay of business. Native women as well as men exploited female slaves. When he visited the lower Columbia in 1824–1825, George Simpson noted,

Several of the Flat Head [Chinook] women at the establishment [Fort George] keep female slaves and it was the practice to allow them to be let out among the newly arrived servants [i.e., Hudson's Bay Company employees] for the purpose of prostitution; indeed the Princess of Wales (Mr. McKenzie's woman) carried on this shameful traffick to a greater extent than any other having 8 or 10 female slaves, it is however broke off although with some difficulty[,] all the women in the Fort having come to the resolution that they would not conform to this innovation as it deprived them of a very important source of Revenue. (Merk 1931, 101)

The use of female slaves as prostitutes was not confined to the southern part of the region. The Central Tlingit groups, for example, are reported by Khlebnikov ([1861] 1976, 71) to have prostituted their female slaves to Russian officials and settlers in the early part of the nineteenth century.

Female slaves remained important in prostitution at least until the 1860s. Sproat (1868, 89–92), writing of that period, says that male slaves were formerly more valuable than female slaves but that with the growth of European settlements on Vancouver Island, female slaves had become more valuable. He goes on to say that a young woman slave would be worth about thirty blankets on the northern end of the west coast of the island but would bring fifty or sixty blankets in Victoria. He also claims that there was an active trade in female slaves from the British Columbia mainland and northern parts of Vancouver Island to Victoria. Even this late in the historic period older trading patterns continued, for Sproat notes that most of the slaves sold on the west coast of the island did not go to Victoria but to the Makah on Cape Flattery. From what Sproat says, by the 1860s most of the remaining slave trade was fueled by prostitution.

Slave Destruction: The Transition from Killing to Freeing Slaves

The sources indicate that slaves were sometimes freed as an alternative to being killed on some ceremonial occasion for ten of the twenty groups in the tribal unit sample (see table A-9). We do not know for certain when the last slave was ritually killed in any of the region's communities. But for eight groups in the tribal unit sample we do have dates or approximate dates of the most recently known ritual killing. As table 24 shows, slave killings continued in some sample communities at least until about 1870, and it is probable that attempts to kill slaves at ceremonies sometimes occurred after that date. On the Queen Charlottes, for example, there seems to have been at least one failed attempt to kill a slave by the southern Haida in about 1877 (Collison 1915, 140). The last slave killing known to me—the victim is described as "an old family retainer"—occurred about 1880 at a Tlingit principal title-holder's funeral (Young 1927, 232–233).

We have even less datable information about the freeing of slaves during ceremonies. De Laguna (1972, 471) suggests that the freeing of slaves at feasts among the Yakutat were all relatively recent; that is, they occurred in the latter part of the nineteenth century, and I suspect that this was also true for most other groups in which slaves began to be freed during ceremonies. We can be reasonably sure of the timing of the transition from killing to freeing slaves for only one of the sample groups, the Sitka. The quality of information on this and other slavery topics is quite good for the Sitka because the Russians built their major base in southeastern Alaska, Novo-Arkhangel'sk, at Sitka in 1799 in the face of fierce Sitkan resistance. Most of the Russian source information on the Tlingit is about the Sitka. It was at Sitka also that the Russians could most influence Tlingit behavior, by both persuasion and force. Russian ability to interfere in things like ritual killings was probably negligible at Tlingit communities away from Russian settlements.

According to Tikhmenev (1978, 355) a slave was freed at Sitka during a funeral feast about 1804. Veniaminov (1857, 11) says that by 1837 slaves were at least sometimes freed at ceremonies, and Tikhmenev (1978, 239) claims that by about 1855 slaves were regularly ransomed to the Russians rather than killed. But we also know that slaves were ritually killed in 1842 (Krause 1956, 280). In 1868 a slave to be killed escaped to the fort. The Tlingit offered four slaves for him, suggesting that they were still serious about killing him (Teichmann 1963, 236–242). In the sequence of slave killings and

Table 24.   *Most Recent Datable Slave Killing, Tribal Unit Sample*

Group	Date	Source
Yakutat	ca. 1855	De Laguna 1972, 471
Chilkat	mid-19th century	Jones 1914, 118
Sitka	1842	Krause 1956, 280
Stikine	ca. 1870	Young 1927, 83
Haida	mid-19th century	Curtis 1916, 144
	attempt post-1876	Collinson 1915, 140
Lower Skeena	1858	Fort Simpson Journal 1855–1859,
Tsimshian		fol. 126d
Fort Rupert Kwakiutl	1868	*Daily British Colonist,*
		13 November 1868
Chinook	ca. 1850	Schoolcraft 1855, 71

NOTE: Absence of entry for sample groups means no information.

manumissions associated with the transfer of ceremonial regalia analyzed in chapter 8, Kamenskii (1985, 35) notes that the first recorded freeing of slaves occurred in the 1850s when there was a lot of pressure from the Russians to free rather than kill slaves. But as Kan indicates in his notes to Kamenskii, slave killings continued to occur in Tlingit country well into the American period, which began in 1867.

The only other group for which we can actually date the freeing of some slaves is the Stikine. The small amount of datable material suggests that the pattern was much like that at Sitka: in the beginning a slave was occasionally freed, but slaves continued to be killed and only gradually did freeing replace killing at ceremonies. In 1840 the Hudson's Bay Company men at Stikine tried to prevent a slave from being killed during a feast but were unable to do so. In the post journal they noted that the Russians sometimes achieved success by buying the slave who was to be killed (Fort Stikine Journal 1840–1842, 29 December 1840). In 1841 Simpson observed that the leading Stikine titleholder, Shakes, still killed slaves at ceremonies, while the second-ranking titleholder was inclined to follow Russian encouragement to free them instead (Merk 1931, 212–213; see also Fort Simpson Journal 1838–1840, fol. 26–26d). In December 1841, however, the Hudson's Bay Company men did persuade Shakes to free rather than kill a slave by persuading him that the Europeans would look down on him if he pursued the latter course (Fort Stikine Journal 1840–1842, 17 December 1841). But in 1848, despite the pleas of Hudson's Bay Company men, eight slaves were killed at the dedication feast for a new house (McNeill 1848, August), and we also know that slaves were killed at a funeral in 1866 (Morison 1920, 55) and that other ritual slave killings occurred about 1870 (Young 1927, 83).

The Lower Skeena Tsimshian also continued to kill slaves at ceremonies in spite of pressure from the Hudson's Bay Company men at Fort Simpson. In 1852 several slaves were to be killed at the feast dedicating a new house but were spared. We do not know whether these slaves were freed (Fort Simpson Journal 1852–1853, 53). In 1858, despite the efforts of Hudson's Bay Company men, a slave was killed (Fort Simpson Journal 1855–1859, fol. 126d).

That ritual slave killing continued so late in the historic period suggests that the question to pursue might not be, How and why did ritual slave killing cease? but, Why did ritual killing continue so long? By the 1880s slave killings were rare, but they did occasionally occur. This suggests that American and Canadian political control over the internal affairs of native communities was not complete enough to entirely prevent even such obvious defiance of European law and custom. It also suggests that the ritual system remained central not only to the religious but to the political, social, and economic life of native communities: slave killing as the ultimate destruction of property and life was too central to this ritual practice to give up easily. Native communities continued to maintain and struggle for their integrity even in the face of prolonged population loss due to disease, severe economic dislocation because of the serious curtailment of their access to the resource base, and European political and religious interference. The protracted conflict between the Kwakwaka'wakw and Canadian government and missionary authorities over the continuance of the potlatch is one of the best examples of this struggle.

This suggests that slave killings continued for so long because the ritual killing of slaves was a much more important element in Northwest Coast ritual practice than has previously been recognized. Although they served many purposes, Northwest Coast ritual feasts were above all demonstrations of power. The host demonstrated his power and by their participation the guests acknowledged it. The funeral feast was a crucial event, because it represented both the power of the deceased and the legitimate transmission of title and hence power to the heir. It is no accident that the funeral feast is the most widespread occasion in the culture area for slave killing. The ritual destruction of human life is a most dramatic and perhaps the most significant demonstration of wealth and power possible. How better for an heir to assert his claims? Slave killing was given up with reluctance, in the face of increasing outside interference and the increasing rarity of slaves.

Marriages between Slaves and the Free

According to Jenness (n.d., 61), Saanich titleholders rarely married female slaves until the nineteenth-century social breakdown began. The Saanich situation probably applies to the entire culture area. The sources indicate that for at least eight groups in the tribal unit sample marriage between slave and free was forbidden. Marriages between such persons are recorded late in the slavery period for nine of the sample units, including three where such marriages are known to have been previously forbidden (see table A-2). But even late in the nineteenth century the children of such marriages felt the stigma of their slave ancestry. The implications of this continuing stigma are discussed more fully below in the section on twentieth-century attitudes.

The End of Slavery in the Nineteenth Century

The eighteenth century and early nineteenth century were the heyday of New World plantation slavery. But even as slavery seemed to be flourishing, the abolitionist movement began to achieve results in Europe and America. The European abolitionists were, of course, primarily concerned with black slavery and with the transatlantic trade in black slaves. But their ideas, which finally triumphed in the first half of the nineteenth century, made slavery unacceptable in all contexts. This meant that as Europeans gained control over the North Pacific Coast of North America, aboriginal slavery was one of the practices that came more and more under fire from the political powers that claimed dominion there. As we shall see, however, slavery did not quickly end in Northwest Coast native communities.[9]

Slavery was abolished in the British Empire in 1834. But slaves were found in many parts of the empire until well into the twentieth century. Local realities made it difficult to end slavery, especially in its myriad indigenous forms, in a short time.[10] The attention of both the British public and the British government was on the question of black slavery in the West Indies and not on indigenous forms of slavery in less well known territories.[11] Much later, in 1865, at the end of the Civil War, the United States ended slavery.

That slavery did not end on the Northwest Coast with legal action taken by remote legislatures is shown by table 25. This gives the most recent datable slaveholding for each of the groups in the tribal unit sample for which we have such information. As can be seen, slaves were held even in the 1880s (or after) in at least six of the groups. The latest date we have for one of the Puget Sound Salish groups is the 1860s. The Saanich and Klallam dates suggest that many groups in the Strait of Georgia and Puget Sound held a few slaves in the 1860s. Some slaves were found in a few communities until about the turn of the century. In this section I consider the process of the decline of slavery from the 1830s, when it was flourishing throughout the region, until the 1880s and 1890s, when it was all but ended.

Table 25.   *Most Recent Datable Slaveholding, Tribal Unit Sample*

Group	Date	Reference
Yakutat	"about 1900"	De Laguna 1972, 470
Chilkat	1890	Schwatka 1893, 38–39
Sitka	1887, perhaps 1890	Jackson 1887, 13; Schwatka 1893, 40
Stikine	1878	Morris 1879, 87; Young 1927, 128
Haida	1880 [Alaska] late 1870s [Queen Charlottes]	Young 1927, 234 Collison 1915, 219; Dawson 1880, 132
Lower Skeena Tsimshian	post-1873	Crosby 1914, 90–91
Fort Rupert Kwakiutl	1868	*Daily British Colonist*, 13 November 1868
Mowachaht	1885	Brabant 1900, 24
Clayoquot	1885	Koppert 1930, 71
Makah	post-late-1860s	Swan 1869, 10–11
Saanich	1870s	Barnett 1955, 249–250
Klallam	1860s	Gunther 1927, 264
Lummi	1850s	Schoolcraft 1856, 703
Skagit	1850s	Schoolcraft 1856, 703
Puyallup-Nisqually	1850s	Schoolcraft 1856, 703
Twana	1860s	Elmendorf 1993, 28
Quinault	1870s	Olson 1936, 93
Chinook	1875	Ray 1938, 51–54

NOTE: Absence of entry for sample groups means no information.

European Involvement as Slaveholders

Northwest Coast slavery was certainly an indigenous institution, but some Europeans did own native slaves from time to time. I exclude from this statement the youthful slaves the Spanish purchased during the eighteenth century. I think we can accept that Spanish motivations were to prevent these children from being (as they thought) eaten at ceremonies and to take them back to Mexico for religious instruction. In any event, such Spanish purchases were immediately taken out of the region and so the Spanish played no *local* role as slave owners.

The Russians are also known to have purchased some slaves from the Yakutat in the eighteenth century (De Laguna 1972, 128, 470). Their last datable purchase was circa 1805 (De Laguna 1972, 158). They probably purchased slaves from other Tlingit groups, but I know of no documentation. Farther north, the Russians held many Aleuts and other native peoples in what was virtual slavery and the Tlingit certainly regarded the Aleuts they saw working for the Russians as Russian slaves (Veniaminov 1972, 47).

During the maritime fur trade period some ships' captains did engage in the slave trade, by purchasing or capturing a few slaves at one community and selling them elsewhere. The ships engaged in this trade that have been identified were American. The number of either ships trading slaves or slaves traded was probably small and the overall impact on Northwest Coast slavery was negligible. Such European participation in the slave trade does, however, indicate that slavery was accepted rather than disapproved of.

During the land-based fur trade period and the period of early settlement that immediately followed it, some European men are said to have purchased native women to be their wives. Contemporary observers sometimes described this as native slavery. In some of these cases what happened was the payment of brideprice by the husband to the wife's kin. As has already been described, complex economic transactions took place on the occasion of Northwest Coast marriages, especially if titleholders were involved. The European husband may not have understood exactly what he was doing when he gave goods to his prospective wife's family, but the wife he got was not his slave. In other cases it is probably true that the European man did indeed purchase a female slave to provide himself with a companion. Such a woman's previous owner would have regarded her as a slave whatever her new European "master" thought. But such purchases, while not unknown, were not common events and did not perpetuate aboriginal slavery.

One group of Europeans was accused of exploiting and maintaining native slavery in the region: employees of the Hudson's Bay Company. The 1830s and 1840s saw the founding of a number of Hudson's Bay Company posts in the culture area, each of which had one or more officers. The officers were mostly Scots or Scots Canadians. There were frequently other European employees, often French-speaking Canadians from Quebec. In addition, mixed-bloods, Iroquois, and even Hawaiians were employed in a variety of capacities. Many of the officers and other employees married (or cohabited with) local native women. As the century wore on, other employees married the daughters of these unions. One contemporary observer, William A. Slacum (1912, 191), claimed that these native wives had often been purchased, sometimes as children, by their European husbands. This claim was made in the context of more general accusations about the Hudson's Bay

Company and native slavery, and it is likely that Slacum, who knew little and understood less about native social customs, confused the payment of bride-price with the purchase of a slave.

Both Slacum (who visited the region around the mouth of the Columbia in the early months of 1837) and the Rev. Herbert Beaver (who was a missionary in the employ of the Hudson's Bay Company at Fort Vancouver from September 1836 until November 1838) claimed that Hudson's Bay Company employees at Fort Vancouver, both officers and men, owned native slaves. Beaver stated that in early 1837 at least thirty-two slaves were held by company employees—eight were said to belong to the officers, the rest to other employees (Jessett 1959, 31). Slacum (1912, 186) implies an even larger number of slaves were in the hands of Company employees, although it is likely that Beaver was Slacum's principal source of information on "native slavery." Both men acknowledged that those in charge of Fort Vancouver denied that any Company employees owned slaves. The slaves present in the fort were the property of the native wives of employees to whom, in Beaver's words, "the custom of the country concedes the right of retaining them in slavery" (Jessett 1959, 132). To both Beaver and Slacum this was specious reasoning and the Hudson's Bay Company's European employees were the actual owners of the slaves.

Slacum was an agent of the U.S. government, a sort of open "spy." He was very much in favor of U.S. sovereignty over the whole of the Oregon Territory all the way up to the 54th parallel. He was an enemy of the Hudson's Bay Company as it represented a formidable British presence in the territory, and native slavery was merely another issue on which to condemn the Company. The remarks on native people in his report show little understanding of the local situation as far as its native inhabitants were concerned.[12]

Beaver, a Church of England priest, was totally incapable of dealing with or even understanding the situation that he found at Fort Vancouver. He expected to live and be treated as he would have been had he been a parish priest in one of the more prosperous parts of rural England. He was rigid and a prig. It is fair to say that he quickly developed a hatred for Dr. John McLoughlin, who was in charge of the post. He eventually caused even those who tried hard to get along with him (McLoughlin did not try hard), like James Douglas, to lose patience. His opening statement about native slavery began, "I have seen more real slavery in the short time I have been here, than in the eight years and a half I was in the West Indies" (Jessett 1959, 20, written 15 November 1836, about two months after his arrival). He must have been remarkably unobservant while in the West Indies! It is easy to dislike Beaver and to sympathize with McLoughlin and the other residents at Fort Vancouver. And Beaver knew or cared nothing about the native inhabitants of the area. His reports to London struck a chord, however, and the issue of native slavery had to be dealt with.

By the time the governing body of the Hudson's Bay Company required a response from Fort Vancouver to Beaver's slavery charges, James Douglas was in charge of the post. His reply tacitly admits that native slaves were held by the wives of employees and perhaps by employees themselves. Douglas claims he is trying to end the practice but it is slow work. His response is worth quoting in full.

I am most anxious to second your views, for suppressing the traffic of slaves, and have taken some steps towards the attainment of that object. I regret, however, that the state of feeling among the Natives of this river, precludes every prospect of immediate extinction of slavery, unless we resort to the very objectionable plan of a forcible emancipation. With the Natives, I have hitherto endeavored to discourage the practice by the exertion of moral influence alone, carefully avoiding direct collision either with their selfish feelings or inveterate prejudices, as I do not feel justified in exposing our interests to the shock of excitement and desperate animosity which more active measures, on our part, might provoke. Against our own people, I took a more active part, and denounced slavery as a state contrary to law; tendering to all unfortunate persons held as slaves, by British subjects, the fullest protection in the enjoyment of their natural rights. I, soon after, seized a favourable opportunity, of putting the law in force, by rescuing a runaway slave boy, who had been overtaken by his pursuers and brought here for punishment. He has since enjoyed his liberty, and served the company as a free labourer. These proceedings, so clearly destructive of the principle of slavery, would have roused a spirit of resistance, in any people, who know the value of liberty; but I am sorry, that the effect has been scarcely felt here, and I fear that all my efforts have virtually failed in rooting out the practical evil, even within the precincts of this settlement. Of persons ranking as slaves, some are children of tender age, others have grown up in ignorance of every useful art, whether of civilized or savage life, by which they might have earned an independent livelihood, and all classes are so destitute and friendless, that they have, without exception, chosen the part of continuing with their present protectors. To have urged a forcible separation, in such circumstances, I must have provided them gratuitously, with food and clothing, as their spiritless labour is of no value to the Company, and I feel reluctant to turn them loose into the forest, without any means of support. The plan I now follow, of considering every person without distinction, residing on our premises as free British subjects, who may, at any time, under the Company's protection, assert the exercise of their absolute and legal rights, will greatly mitigate the evils of slavery, by operating as a security against abuse, and making affection the only bond that supports the immoral system. (James Douglas to the Governor, Deputy Governor and Committee, Hon. Hudson's Bay Company, 18th October 1838, in McLoughlin 1941, 237–238)

Douglas's response is similar to that of other officials in other locales faced with similar complaints about slavery and demands that they do something about it.[13] We can take the response as that of a realist or of an indifferent man, perhaps even an apologist for slavery. Douglas is a realist. When he wrote this dispatch he had been in the western fur trade working for the North West Company and then the Hudson's Bay Company for nineteen years, and he had been on the Lower Columbia for nine years. He was an experienced, knowledgeable man whose past and future record showed that he was good at working with native people. Of all those who worked for a long time on the coast during this period we can be surest of him as an opponent of slavery.[14] Some may judge that Douglas was overcautious, but he was not a hypocrite. The Company seems to have accepted his report.

After 1834 it was illegal for slaves to be held by British subjects. Although it is clear that, through their wives at any rate, some men employed by the Hudson's Bay Company did continue to hold native slaves, after that date the practice gradually ceased.

European Involvement as Abolitionists

Although slavery became illegal in British territory in 1834 and in all American territory in 1865, there is little evidence that either the British or the American authorities took strong steps to end aboriginal slavery on the Northwest Coast either before or after these dates. Slavery was certainly not encouraged, but there were no campaigns against native slavery like that conducted in British Columbia by both missionaries and government officials against the potlatch (see Cole and Chaikin 1990). The reason for this, I think, is that although slavery was disapproved of, it was not perceived as a serious problem or as a vital part of native life whose suppression must come about before the "civilization" of the native could proceed—unlike the potlatch, which was viewed as such an obstacle. There were at least two reasons for this: native slaves were not noticeable in the way that potlatch performances were— ordinarily it was difficult for outsiders to distinguish slaves from other native members of a community—and traditional native society was regarded as too "primitive" for slavery to be a significant institution—to the Victorians and their American counterparts slavery meant black plantation slavery above all else.

In 1869 James Swan wrote of the Makah,

> The treaty between the United States and the Makahs makes it obligatory on this tribe to free their slaves, and although this provision has not thus far been enforced, it has had the effect of securing to the latter better treatment than they formerly had. . . . And it is to be hoped that, in a few years, under the judicious plan of the treaty, slavery will be gradually abolished, or exist only in a still milder form. (1869, 10–11)

The Makah situation was probably duplicated throughout western Washington: the American authorities claimed the right to abolish aboriginal slavery, but they did not make strenuous efforts to end all individual cases of slavery in the various native communities. The more remote the community from

European settlement, the more likely that slavery lingered on, but as the nineteenth century passed, actual servitude disappeared. As we shall see below, however, the heritage of slavery continued to affect native social life for years after the institution ceased to exist.

In 1888 Niblack wrote of the situation in Alaska,

> In recent years, with the abolition of slavery and the influence of the whites, the authority of the chiefs has been very much weakened. Slaves.—On our acquisition of the Territory of Alaska in 1867 the practice of slavery received its death-blow amongst the Indians. Previously to that the Russian authorities had sought to ameliorate in some degree the hardships of this wretched class in the vicinity of Sitka, but it was still in practice when we took possession. The slave class has now gradually been absorbed into the body of the freemen and slavery is a thing of the past. (1890, 251–252)

In 1878 the missionary Hall Young had freed a number of slaves among the Stikine, "although the masters objected and often pretended to liberate their slaves while still holding them in servitude" (Young 1927, 128). In 1881 the American naval officer Henry Glass (1882) ordered seventeen slaves freed at Sitka and wrote to other Tlingit chiefs that they were to free their slaves also. And in spite of Niblack's confidence that slavery had disappeared, there are reports of slaves in Tlingit communities in the 1890s (see table 25; see also Morris 1879, 89 for reports on Tlingit groups not in the tribal unit sample). Obviously, the situation in Alaska was similar to that suggested for Washington.

In British Columbia, the authorities did not make strong efforts to suppress slavery either; rather, they seem to have hoped that it would wither away. When government officials came across a case of slavery or, especially, when a slave appealed for help in escaping his or her status, the response was to free the slave. I. V. Powell, Indian superintendent during the 1870s, for example, freed slaves who appealed to him on several occasions when he made trips to the west coast of Vancouver Island. Missionaries also denounced slavery rather than take active steps to abolish it. They seem to have accepted that, working in the remote communities of the coast, they were in a weak position to enforce their authority. William Collison, for example, certainly encouraged the Haida both to treat their slaves better and to free them. But in the 1870s he was in no position to insist; witness the frequent appearance of slaves in his book *In the Wake of the War Canoe*. His successor at the Church Missionary Society mission in the Queen Charlottes describes Powell's efforts:

> Lieutenant-Colonel Powell, when Superintendent of Indian Affairs for British Columbia, could not break down all at once the custom of slavery, but he issued an order that all the slaves had not to be called slaves but *tenas* men and *tenas klootchmen*, i.e., little men and little women.

The Haida word for slave is hal-dung-a, and the Chinook word is e-lait-e. From the day the Colonel's order was received, slavery began to decline. (Harrison 1925, 69–70)

Without taking too seriously Harrison's claim that a name change in itself brought about the decline of slavery, the passage is typical of the gradualist approach to slavery taken by those who were responsible for natives in the province, whether government official or missionary.

Although strenuous and systematic actions to end aboriginal slavery were taken by neither the American nor the Canadian political authorities, it did decline in frequency and importance throughout the last half of the nineteenth century. By 1900 there were probably no persons on the Northwest Coast actually held in bondage, although some former slaves did continue to reside with former masters—often as wives or adopted members of the family.

There were a number of causes for the decline. The most important was the cessation of warfare and the consequent end in the supply of new slaves. Warfare was something that the various governments did suppress. As well, governments, missionaries, and settlers would not assist masters in the recovery of escaping slaves. Indeed, they would normally assist the escaping slave and prevent his or her recapture. The possibilities of escape made it increasingly difficult for masters to hold onto their slaves. Swan (1869, 10–11), for example, makes it clear that even by the mid-1860s the Makah slaves who did not leave their masters for other communities were largely those who had been born in slavery in the community. The sources for no other group are this explicit, but the pattern was probably a general one. More and more European settlers lived near all but the remotest native communities, increasing the pressure on many native practices, including slavery, that were not approved or understood by Europeans.

During the last half of the nineteenth century native populations declined drastically all over the Northwest Coast, and the population nadir seems to have been reached about 1920 or shortly thereafter (see Duff 1964, 40–46). People in many communities probably found it necessary to accept slaves (or former slaves) into the social system (marriage, ceremonials) if older patterns were to continue even in modified form. By 1900 slavery seems to have been a status of the past, not the present, but as I will show below it was a status that was not forgotten and that continued to affect the lives of many native people.

Twentieth-Century Attitudes Toward Slaves and Former Slaves

As the Canadian and American authorities gradually took firmer control of the territories occupied by the aboriginal inhabitants of the region, we have seen that slavery was discouraged and then suppressed. In the last quarter of the nineteenth century in many, if not most, of the native communities marriages were occurring between former slaves and those with nonslave backgrounds. Both the ethnographic and late historical sources contain many examples. To many European observers it looked as though aboriginal slavery and its memory would soon fade away. Swan was a knowledgeable and experienced observer of the Makah when he wrote, after American control of Makah territory was well established,

> Instances are not rare where a master has married his slave woman, and a mistress has taken her slave man as her husband. The children of such connections are considered as half slave, and although some of the more intelligent have acquired wealth and influence among the tribe, yet the fact that the father or mother was a slave is considered as a stigma, which is not removed for several generations. . . . They are the hewers of wood and drawers of water. . . . Formerly it was considered degrading for a chief, or the owner of slaves to perform any labor except hunting, fishing or killing whales; . . . but since the tribe has been under the charge of an agent of the Government, and it is seen that no distinction is made between bond or free, but that both are treated alike, the old prejudice against the labor is wearing away, and the men and women, with the exception of a few among the old chiefs, are willing to engage side by side in such work as requires to be done for the agency. And it is to be hoped that, in a few years, under the judicious plan of the treaty, slavery will be gradually abolished. (1869, 10–11)

Eighty years after Swan's observations, Elizabeth Colson gave the following example of the effect of alleged slave ancestry in the same Makah community:

> When Cecil Mead as a member of the council represented the [Makah] tribe at an official celebration, charges were made that he came from slave blood and therefore had no right to represent the tribe. He retired from the council and from any further attempt at public life. (1953, 220)

Slavery had, of course, disappeared among the Makah by the 1940s, but Swan's optimism about the disappearance of the stigma of a real or alleged slave past in the family was misplaced.

The sources from the southern part of the culture area are rich in material that shows that throughout the first half of this century slave or part-slave ancestry was remembered and could be a serious social disability within many native communities. This is true despite the fact that near-disastrous population decline and other social disruptions in the last half of the nineteenth century made it increasingly difficult for even the descendants of titleholders to find spouses who were certain to have no slavery in their family backgrounds. The actual impact of real or alleged slave ancestry varies from case to case, but it always seems to be present as a potential element in native political and social life.

Writing of the 1940s G. A. Pettit says of the situation of former slaves among the Quileute,

> There is no longer a slave class among the Quileute, but the descent of a present day Quileute from an ancestor who was a slave in the days when there were slaves is not forgotten. No amount of personal effort or intrinsic worth has overcome that taint of heredity, even though the slave may have been a person of good blood and high ability from another tribe. (1950, 84)

Olson describes a case from the Quinault from the early 1930s that is much like that described above for the neighboring Quileute.

> B. M. was regarded as a chief because of his descent from chiefs. But gossip had it that his wife had slave blood in her ancestry (through her father's mother). His children are therefore referred to as skattso'ms sadjilke' (half slave) and not regarded as noble blood. This gossip, however, was retailed only by those who disliked the family. (1936, 89)

Among the Skagit the memory of slave ancestry was so shameful that it sometimes led to violence. June McCormick Collins (1974b, 128) describes two killings motivated by insults about slave ancestry. In the 1930s a man killed another over a reference to his descent from a slave (apparently the accusation was true), and somewhat earlier in the century a pair of murders resulted from the marriage of a woman to a former slave. The former slave accumulated property and "bought" the woman for his wife. The woman was eager to marry the man in spite of her family's opposition. The couple's son killed a man over being called a slave and was killed in turn by a European married to a relative of the victim's mother.

Suttles (1974, 304–305) reports that in the 1950s freedom from the taint of slavery was highly valued by all the Puget Sound and Straits Salish. Evidence of the continuing stigma of slave ancestry is also reported for the Twana (Elmendorf 1960, 326) and the Klallam (Suttles 1974, 236). Suttles (1974, 396) also describes a case among the Saanich of a man losing his titleholder status when his slave ancestry was discovered. The discovery ended his marriage, for his former upper-class father-in-law had not known of this taint when the marriage took place. Jenness's (n.d., 58) Saanich informants told him that after slavery was abolished, anyone could accumulate enough goods to give a feast and that even former slaves assumed titles. This is a description of social change and the breakdown of the old class system, but it also means that former slaves and their descendants are remembered even if they have taken titles.

The data on the situation of former slaves and their descendants is not very full for the central culture area. Boas's notes (1916–1926, 138) contain a passage that suggests that early in this century titleholders tried to avoid marriages with former slaves or their descendants because in later quarrels the children would be taunted with the words "you are nothing but half slave." And McIlwraith says this of Nuxalk attitudes toward slave ancestry in the 1920s,

> "Washing the child," during pregnancy and at birth, sufficed to cover the taint on its history, but in later years if such a person failed to continue to give ceremonies, people would again talk of his short-comings. So, too, for the child or grandchild of a mixed Bella Coola and slave marriage. As long as such an one maintained a position of importance in the community by the distribution of presents, nothing was said, but if he should fail to do so, he could be, and frequently was, insulted by having references made to his ancestry. In case of dispute or rivalry it was always a temptation to refer to such a blot, but if he had atoned for it with presents, references were considered improper. Unquestionably, memory of slave ancestry was forgotten in course of time if the line was influential, although recollections of the stigma were always carried for at least two or three generations. At the present time the most influential woman in Bella Coola, the one who had given most presents, is the granddaughter of a Smith Inlet slave. . . . No one dares insult her by mentioning her slave ancestry, but everyone knows about it and if her children should fail to hold their position, they would be open to insult on this score. (1948, 1:161–162)

I think that McIlwraith underestimated the length of time that slave ancestry would be remembered, but otherwise this account of the Nuxalk situation is probably representative of that in many other native communities as well.

For most topics on slavery, the data from the northern region of the culture area are richer than for the other regions. This is not the case for the twentieth-century circumstances of former slaves and their descendants. The information we do have is consistent, however, with the data from more southern groups. De Laguna (1972, 581) notes, for example, that in this century some people among the Tlingit continued to give away property to wash away the blemish of former slavery. Among the Yakutat, in the late nineteenth century freed slaves are often said to have been "adopted" into the family of their former owner, although the one actual case cited is that of a woman who had apparently friendly relations with her owner and his family but who when freed at the master's death immediately left the community (De Laguna 1972, 472). Among the Chilkat freed slaves who remained in the community often married nontitleholder Tlingit, but they retained the stigma of slavery, as did the offspring of these unions (Oberg 1973, 34). Olson's (1967, 53–54) discussion of slavery also implies that, at the time of his fieldwork (the 1930s, 1940s, and 1950s), in many Tlingit communities slave ancestry was a cause of shame and still brought up in quarrels. At the turn of the century to have been a slave gave a person a "bad name" among the Haida (Swanton 1905, 70), and Marianne Boelscher (1988, 60) implies that slave ancestry is still remembered by some Haida in the 1980s. Among the various Tsimshian groups slave ancestry was also a social disability earlier in this century. Garfield's (1939, 228, 274) examples of the negative effects of slave status have already been cited at length in chapter 4.

There is very little published information about attitudes toward slave ancestry after the 1940s. I have not done systematic fieldwork on the topic, but I have talked with a number of field-workers who have worked in various parts of the coast. The consensus is that while most native people are reluctant to discuss the subject of slavery with outsiders, they are indeed aware of both past slavekeeping by their ancestors and of the slave ancestry of some current members of their communities. Slave ancestry may affect a person's social or political career. It remains one of those personal characteristics that an enemy may bring up at awkward moments and is always available as a topic for gossip. For example, in one British Columbia reserve community, as recently as the 1970s, persons of slave descent lived apart from the main village. These individuals were prevented from participating in band political and social life. They might attend a band meeting, but if any of them spoke, others reminded them of their descent "from the slaves" and they were stopped from speaking further (Mooney, pers. com.).

Summary of Changes in Slavery, 1780–1880

Swan's comments about Makah treatment of slaves in the 1860s suggest that the treatment of slaves improved during the nineteenth century and provide a reason for better treatment of slaves:

> The Indians say that formerly when slaves were more numerous, and more easily obtained, they were oftener punished. Instances are related which an offender has been bound hand and foot, placed in a canoe and set adrift, while a strong east wind was blowing, which could carry him out to sea and ensure a miserable death by starvation. Others have been hung, and others tortured; but they are getting more moderate of late years, and extreme measures are seldom resorted to. (Swan 1869, 54)

Elsewhere on the coast, when the sources comment on the treatment of slaves in the latter part of the century, the condition of slaves also seems to have improved. Better treatment is claimed or strongly implied for a number of Tlingit groups, for example (see De Laguna 1972, 472; Krause 1956, 111; Schwatka 1893, 38–39; Knapp and Childe 1896, 44). But some late historical sources for the Tlingit claim that the treatment of slaves remained harsh

(Jackson 1887, 13; Jones 1914, 116–118). It is probable that treatment did, on average, improve—if only because slaves became less common toward the end of the period and because, with the presence of Europeans near many communities, it became easier for slaves to run away.

The primary source of slaves was war captives. Raids whose primary object was the taking of slaves may well have been largely a postcontact phenomenon. And as the nineteenth century went on raids for slaves began to cover longer distances. But European settlement and political control also began to increase rapidly from the 1840s on, so that after the 1860s few raids or even isolated captures were possible. Only in the remoter parts of the region, where there were few Europeans, did the taking of slaves remain possible a little longer. On his first visit to the west coast of Vancouver Island in the spring of 1874, for example, Fr. A. J. Brabant (1900, 12) found that many Nuu-chah-nulth still feared slave raids.

The precontact tasks of slaves seem to have continued throughout the historic period. It is quite probable that the fur trade increased the demand for certain kinds of work (the processing of skins) and that, as this work frequently was assigned to slaves, the demand for slaves increased somewhat. In addition, from the earliest contact of any duration (Cook at Nootka Sound in 1778), slave women were made available as prostitutes to Europeans. As native prostitution developed alongside the fur trade and into the early settlement period, many native owners, men and women, profited from putting their female slaves to work as prostitutes.

There was almost certainly a trade in slaves in precontact times. It is probable that the extent of the precontact trade networks increased and that the number of slaves involved increased as well. Prices for slaves probably increased during the nineteenth century, especially after 1850. This probably reflects both some increase in the demand for slaves and the drying up of the supply of new slaves as Europeans choked off indigenous raiding and warfare. The slave trade became linked with the fur trade by the 1830s, if not earlier. Ambitious titleholders used both the fur trade and slave raiding and trading to enhance their prestige and political careers. At least some of the intensive and frequent fighting of the 1830s to 1850s was a result of the system of "predatory warfare" that emerged from this linkage between the slave and fur trades and their contributions to the struggle to maintain prestige.

At the time of contact the most important ritual use of slaves was killing them as a part of ceremonies, especially at the funeral celebrations for titleholders. The major change during the historic period was a shift from the killing of slaves to the freeing of slaves on such occasions. Slaves could also be given away at ceremonies, but this probably occurred before as well as after contact, so that, even if the giving away of slaves increased, the most significant change was the shift from killing to manumission. Increasing European involvement in native communities and European pressure to stop ritual killings obviously played an important role. But not too much should be made of this. In the first place European power to interfere in the events within a native community was quite limited until well into the historic period. Also, ritual killings continued to occur with some frequency into the 1860s and a few occurred as late as the 1880s.

Although slavery began to change on the Northwest Coast almost from the time of European contact, it continued to flourish in its economic, social, ritual, and numerical aspects until well into the 1860s in most parts of the culture area. After that its slow decline began. Severe population losses, erosion of native control of their resource base, and increasing government, missionary, and settler interference in native life all contributed to this decline. By the 1880s slavery was all but gone.

The impact of slavery lingered on. The status of former slaves and their descendants was and is remembered. Slave ancestry continues to be a potential blight on the political and social lives of some individuals in many native communities.

Part Four

Northwest Coast Slavery
in Perspective

12
Captivity and Slavery in Aboriginal North American Cultures

The term "slave" or its equivalent in other European languages appears sporadically in the ethnographic and historical literature on many aboriginal North American peoples, but slavery is not generally regarded as a significant trait in native North America. Ethnographers of indigenous North America have not used the term with much definitional precision or with much regard for the general literature on slavery. It has been common, however, to distinguish between hereditary and nonhereditary slavery. In his various papers dealing with Native American servile statuses, William Christie MacLeod regarded this as a major distinction in North America. For example,

> Hereditary chattel slavery was a conspicuous trait of the culture of the non-agricultural North Pacific coast where it has been noted for a continuous area from the Aleutian Islands to northwestern California, inclusive. . . . In agricultural America slavery was not hereditary. Slaves were merely captive men, women, and children who were either waiting adoption or were not adopted. (1925, 375)

For MacLeod this distribution was of considerable significance.

> The writer sees *no economic or political reason for the non-existence of hereditary slavery in the agricultural southeast of North America*, considering its existence among the northwestern hunters and fishers. (1925, 379; emphasis in original)

Even earlier, H. W. Hodge, in his article in the *Handbook of American Indians North of Mexico*, recognized slavery among the peoples of the Northwest

255

Coast and some of their neighbors, and for the remainder of North America noted,

> The early French and Spanish histories, it is true, abound in allusions to Indian slaves, even specifying the tribes from which they were taken, but the terms "slave" and "prisoner" were used interchangeably in almost every instance. . . . With the exception of the area above mentioned [the Northwest Coast], traces of true slavery are wanting throughout the region N. of Mexico. In its place is found another institution that has often been mistaken for it. . . . In consequence of such warfare tribes dwindled through the loss of men, women, and children. . . . Natural increase was not sufficient to make good such losses. . . . Hence arose the institution of adoption. Men, women, and children, especially the latter two classes, were everywhere considered spoils of war. When sufficient number of prisoners had been tortured and killed . . . the rest of the captives were adopted, after certain preliminaries, into the several gentes, each newly adopted member taking the place of a lost husband, wife, son, or daughter, and being invested with the latter's rights, privileges, and duties. (Hodge 1907–1910, 599)

In the earlier literature the general consensus was that slavery, at least in a well-developed or important form, was absent in aboriginal North America, except on the North Pacific Coast. As has already been pointed out, in 1923 Kroeber not only endorsed the view that slavery was found in aboriginal North America only on the Northwest Coast but also suggested that it was one of a group of traits that set the Northwest Coast cultures somewhat apart from Native American culture more generally.

More recently in a broad comparative context, George Peter Murdock maintained the distinction between hereditary and nonhereditary slavery in his *Ethnographic Atlas* (1967) and recorded no clear examples in the North American portion of his sample of hereditary slavery outside the Northwest Coast culture area (or among its near neighbors). Murdock's codings confirm the earlier view. Unfortunately, Hodge, MacLeod, Kroeber, and Murdock did not find it necessary to define what they meant by slave or slavery.[1]

The view that slavery did not exist or was of minor significance in native North America outside the Northwest Coast continues to be held by most scholars.[2] The data for most of the continent can certainly be read that way, but there are, I think, reasons for this view that involve more than a "straightforward" interpretation of the "facts." At least since Lewis Henry Morgan, the scholarly image of Native Americans has had as one of its principal themes the egalitarian nature of native society and social life. Slavery runs counter to both late nineteenth- and twentieth-century notions of the egalitarian indigenous American. Any ambiguity in the sources about the nature of "slavery" or the importance of "slaves" will tend to be read as evidence for something more appropriate to small-scale egalitarian societies than slavery.[3] Therefore, we need to look more carefully into the possibilities of slavery elsewhere on the continent. Some of the theoretical dispositions that lead to the downplaying of Northwest Coast slavery may be at work elsewhere on the continent as well. A full survey of the topic for the remainder of North America would take another book at least the length of this one (and probably another fifteen-year research project), but the issue is sufficiently important to merit a brief look at some other parts of the continent.

As has been done for the *Handbook of North American Indians*, eastern North America is usually divided into two culture areas, the Northeast and the Southeast. MacLeod contrasted the presence of hereditary slavery on the Northwest Coast with the lack of hereditary slavery in the Southeast. For the Northeast, Hodge, MacLeod, and most other scholars have emphasized the adoption rather than the enslavement of captives. In the remainder of this chapter I will look briefly at the fate and status of captives in these two culture areas.

Captives in the Northeast

As typically delimited the Northeast culture area is not as homogeneous as is the Northwest Coast (see Driver et al. 1972; Driver and Coffin 1974). Partly for this reason I will concentrate here on the Iroquoian speakers in the culture area. Available sources suggest, however, that in terms of treatment of prisoners non-Iroquoian speakers in the area were not greatly different from the Iroquoians and it is the eventual status of prisoners that is of primary concern here. For example, if prisoners are mentioned at all in articles in the *Northeast* volume of the *Handbook of North American Indians*, it is noted that at least some were adopted, usually to replace dead relatives. This is the usual interpretation of the practice of the Iroquoian speakers. The non-Iroquoian-speaking groups specifically mentioned in the *Handbook* as adopting captives are Shawnee (Callender 1978c, 628), Fox (Callender 1978a, 642), Illinois (Callender 1978b, 676), Ottawa (Feest and Feest 1978, 777), Delaware (Goddard 1978, 220), and Western Abenaki (Day 1978, 157). The Maliseet also adopted at least some captives (Donald 1985a). The period considered here is the seventeenth and early eighteenth century, early enough for many aboriginal practices to be more or less intact.[4]

The Northern Iroquoians

The northern Iroquoians have probably occupied at least a part of the territory they held in early historic times for at least 3,500 years. Sometime after A.D. 500 they took up maize, squash, and bean horticulture, although fishing, gathering, and hunting remained an important part of their subsistence practices well into the historic period. The picture that archaeology gives us of the fifteenth-century northern Iroquoians is of modest-sized communities (a thousand or more inhabitants) subsisting on a mixture of primarily horticulture and fishing (although gathering and hunting were not insignificant, especially in some communities). Communities consisted of a group of longhouses. Each longhouse contained several independent matrifocal families whose female heads were usually matrilineally related. Community size is explained partly at least by the need for larger communities to enable more effective defense because of the frequency of intergroup conflict. Communities were grouped into sets of cooperating neighbors. People were grouped into exogamous matriclans that formed the basis for both intra- and inter-community cooperation. By the sixteenth century the northern Iroquoians began to be indirectly affected by European activities in northeastern North America. By the seventeenth century their involvement with Europeans was much more direct. This has a twofold importance for us: the pace of social change increases and Iroquoian/European relations become significant in Iroquoian affairs, so that we begin to have rich firsthand accounts recorded by European observers to supplement the archaeological record. My sketch of the northern Iroquoians and of the fate of captives among the northern Iroquoians will concentrate on the period described in these early sources, approximately 1600 to 1750. This was a period of great change and European influence, but many of the Iroquoian practices in which we are interested had their roots in the earlier pre-European period and reflect Iroquoian much more than European cultural traditions.

Fundamental to seventeenth-century northern Iroquoian society and culture was a series of divisions along gender lines. The division of labor followed gender lines quite clearly. Men cleared the fields and built the houses, hunted, fished, fought in war, and carried out public business at both the community and multicommunity level. Women gathered wild plants and firewood, planted, tended, and harvested the crops, were responsible for child care, cooked, and produced such things as pottery. Women also participated in hunting and fishing but only as processors and transporters of the catch. It was easy for European observers to regard Iroquoian women as drudges, but this was far from an accurate view of the situation of women in these societies. It is true that the Iroquoian settlement was built and governed by men, but from the Iroquoian perspective the town and its associated fields were the domain of women. The male domain was the forest and beyond. Male officeholders owed their places to women, and the women could depose them. Residence was matrilocal and the core of the longhouse was a group of mothers/sisters/daughters under the leadership of the older women. These women worked together cooperatively in the longhouse and in their fields. Men were involved in endeavors that frequently took them away from their communities, while women rarely left their home community and its fields. Men dominated intercommunity affairs and matters of public policy, but it is clear that women had significant input in these areas as well as in village affairs.

Prestige in Iroquoian society has been interpreted by most scholars as largely a matter of personal achievement. Men, for example, gained some personal prestige if they were good hunters and skilled orators. But a man's major way of obtaining prestige was through war. Success as a warrior brought men widespread recognition and approbation throughout their community. There were also titles and offices in northern Iroquoian societies, but even though many of these titles were hereditary within particular lineages, the particular man who held any individual title seems to have been chosen by the female members of the lineage on the basis of his ability and personal achievements. A titleholder could also be removed by these women. There are some suggestions in the sources that members of lineages who held rights to important titles were recognized as a kind of social elite (*agoïander* or *gens d'affaires* as French observers often called them) (Fenton 1978, 312). Iroquoian titleholders are usually described as classic examples of "chiefs" in small-scale, uncentralized societies. The material style of life of chiefs and their families was not significantly different from that of other families and individuals, and since chiefs were expected to be even more generous than other people, they often found that the demands and expectations of fellow villagers required them to distribute (or redistribute) whatever goods they might have acquired.

Iroquoian officeholders had little authority and less power. Persuasion was their principal means of accomplishing a desired end, although persuasion might be bolstered by the fact that people who had obligations to a chief should support him. Obligations and indebtedness were created by officeholders in a number of ways, but one of the principal means was through the generosity of the chief.[5]

Northern Iroquoian Warfare

There was considerable intergroup fighting among Iroquoian speakers during the seventeenth century. This is almost certainly a continuation of pre-European contact patterns, although the European presence certainly had some impact on the patterns and intensity of fighting. The stated motivation for most intergroup fighting was revenge for the death of a fellow group member at the hands of outsiders. It is almost certainly true, as Elizabeth Tooker (1964, 28) suggests, that economic motives also often played a role in initiating intergroup fighting. But the stated motivation of revenge for the death of a group member ties in, as we shall see, with the treatment of prisoners.

Most intergroup fighting was carried out by what can be termed "raiding parties," relatively small groups of men organized for a specific raid by the man who became the group's leader. As Nathaniel Knowles (1940, 152) states, the material trophies of a successful attack were scalps and captives. Casualties among the attackers blighted any success the leader could claim.

Once captives had been secured, the primary concern of the raiders was a successful return to their home community. The raiders and their new captives often had a considerable distance to travel. And the raiders expected pursuit once the relatives and friends of their victims could organize a chase. Thus they expected to have to move fast and under difficult conditions. This, in part, explains the first move of the raiders toward their new captives: the elderly, the very young, the ill, and the infirm were killed. Some of the spared captives were tortured in the course of the return to the raiders' home communities. Torture was the opening round of the highly ritualized ordeal with which most of the captives were threatened and which a number eventually underwent. The Iroquoian speakers participated in the "eastern North American torture complex" (see Knowles 1940 for the classic discussion of this). To European commentators wishing to oppose "savagery" with "civilization," this elaborate ritual activity and its associated cannibalism seemed ideal targets. But much more was involved than the opportunity to inflict pain under culturally acceptable conditions. For, among other things, these rituals provided mechanisms to allow those who had lost relatives to cope with their grief and it prepared some of the captives for absorption into their captors' households, kin groups, and society, to say nothing of the religious meanings Knowles (1940, 210-215) discusses.

It seems to have been usual for at least a few of the prisoners of each raid to be spared the full course of torture and its outcome, death. These captives were destined for incorporation into their captors' community. It should be emphasized that one of the conscious motivations of raids was to obtain captives to bring back for adoption. Thus captives were taken with two distinct purposes in mind: some were to be tortured and killed, others were to be adopted. Excepting those who from the start were clearly not suitable for adoption, the fate of the various prisoners was probably not decided until the home communities were reached. Joseph-François Lafitau (1977, 153–155) describes the ambiguous situation of captives newly brought to a community, the decision-making process of the captors, and something of the motivations behind the decision to torture and kill or adopt.[6] The community's elders decided which captives would be given to which families and the names of the deceased men and women that they were replacing. Some of these replacements would be killed out of grief or displeasure with the appearance or character of the captive, but not all of the captives could be killed for, according to Lafitau, "the obligation of replacing the dead continues to exist for the offspring in respect to their fathers' and their aunts' household until life is given a person representing the one whom they wish to resuscitate" (1977, 154).

Northern Iroquoian Captives— Adoptees or Slaves?

At least since Lafitau, the interpretation of the fate of those captives who were not tortured and killed has been that they were adopted into a family in the captor's community, usually as a replacement for a deceased family member. Thus captives who survived the early stages of captivity became members of a new society, with a well-defined place in one of its kin groups. If this long-standing interpretation is correct, then the fate of prisoners in aboriginal North-eastern North America stands in sharp contrast to their fate on the Northwest Coast. As noted at the beginning of this chapter many of the earliest sources on eastern North America do use the term "slave" in describing captives and their fate, but most authorities have agreed with Hodge and emphasized the adoption of captives, although the treatment of captives has not often been considered in any detail or depth. Recently William A. Starna and Ralph Watkins (1991) have argued that those northern Iroquoian prisoners usually regarded as adoptees were in fact slaves, according to the definition of slave and mode of analysis of slavery advocated by Orlando Patterson. In two previous publications (1985 and 1989) I have agreed with the usual interpretation of the fate of Northeastern prisoners and emphasized their incorporation as adoptees in contrast to their Northwest Coast counterparts' fate as slaves. Starna and Watkins's discussion of the issue requires a reconsideration of the position of northern Iroquoian captives in the light of the arguments and data they present.

As already noted, revenge for the death of a kinsperson was the most important public motive for warfare. Revenge was accomplished both by killing the enemy and by bringing back captives. The preference was probably for both of these outcomes. Grief might require the death of an outsider even if the relative died of natural causes and not at the hands of an enemy in war (see the Lafitau quote above). Casualties in Northeastern warfare seem to have been heavy, and after the middle of the seventeenth century epidemics also greatly reduced these populations, perhaps by up to half. The need to replace losses faster than natural increase could accomplish is often used to explain the high rate of adoption of outsiders into northern Iroquoian communities. "Since manpower was their only asset, the loss of a single person created the demand for his replacement" (Fenton 1978, 315; see also Trigger 1976, 806).[7]

In these matrilineal societies the obligation to find a replacement for the deceased did not fall on the deceased's matrilineal clansmen; rather, the father's sister could require that her brother's son organize a raid to acquire prisoners for adoption and/or torture (Fenton 1978, 311). Acquiring captives to relieve grief for the deceased (the captive as torture victim) and to replace the deceased with a living person (the captive as adoptee) was thus an important part of a man's kinship obligations to his father's matrilineage.

The scale of northern Iroquoian losses in warfare during the seventeenth century was large, particularly when considered in relative terms. When one adds to this the losses due to smallpox and other epidemic diseases, it is clear that northern Iroquoian communities did indeed need to bolster their populations if they were to remain viable. This was especially so as throughout this period all of these communities were under great pressure from both native and European enemies. The individual obligations that men had to meet the requests of their father's sisters for captives therefore also met the larger community's almost desperate need to maintain its population.

By the late seventeenth century incorporation of outsiders into northern Iroquoian communities was occurring on a large scale. In 1668, for example, Jacques Bruyas estimated that two-thirds of the Oneida were of Huron or Algonkin origin. As Bruce G. Trigger (1976, 826) points out, even if we cannot be confident of the accuracy of such statements, there is much evidence to suggest that literally hundreds of outsiders were being forcibly incorporated into northern Iroquoian societies.

What was the status of those outsiders who were incorporated into these communities? Should they be termed "adoptees," "slaves," or some other more appropriate label? This is not merely a question of nomenclature, for if we choose to call these incorporated captives slaves (or some other equally surprising term) our view and understanding of northern Iroquoian society and culture must undergo considerable revision, and the Iroquois and other northern Iroquoians as classic exemplars of kin-based, small-scale societies are seriously compromised.

Kin-based societies, especially unilineal ones, have two basic ways of recruiting new members to their constituent groups (lineages, clans, or family households): by birth (matrifiliation in the case of the northern Iroquoians) or by adoption. Marriage associates nonmembers with the kin unit but does not normally incorporate them; affines remain members of their own comparable kin unit. Recruitment by birth seems to be the preferred mechanism in virtually all such societies, but the gender balance of births is random and death at various points in the life cycle may also create personnel problems for many of the kin units in a society. Adoption is a way to turn strangers into kin. A fictive tie of kinship is created, and over time even the fictive nature of the tie may be forgotten or at least become unimportant. Adoption as a mechanism for recruiting additional kin group members varies in importance from culture to culture. In most societies it is secondary or subordinate to birth as a way to recruit kin unit members.[8]

In spite of the occurrence of the term "slave" in the seventeenth- and eighteenth-century sources, twentieth-century scholars follow these sources in regarding captives who were taken into northern Iroquoian households as adoptees. In a section entitled "Adoption," Lafitau describes his view of what was happening and shows that captives who were lucky enough to be adopted found their condition transformed:

> The condition of a captive to whom life is granted is quite hard among the Algonquin but among the Huron and Iroquois it is gentler in proportion as that of those thrown into the fire is more cruel. The moment that he enters the lodge to which he is given and where he is to be kept, his bonds are untied. The gloomy

attire which makes him appear a victim destined for sacrifice is removed. He is washed with warm water to efface the colours with which his face was painted and he is dressed properly. Then he receives visits of relatives and friends of the family into which he is entering. A short time afterwards a feast is made for all the village to give him the name of the person whom he is resurrecting. The friends and allies of the dead man also give a feast to do him honour: and, from that moment, he enters upon all his rights. If the captive is a girl, given to a household where there is nobody of her sex in a position to sustain the lineage, it is good fortune for this household and for her. All hope of the family is placed in this captive who becomes the mistress of this family and the branches dependent on it. If the captive is a man who requickens an Ancient, a man of consequence, he becomes important himself and has authority in the village if he can sustain by his own personal merit the name which he takes. (1977, 171–172)

That the adoption process was complete and that adoptees were treated as fully kin in such important matters as the rules of exogamy is illustrated by the misadventure of a well-meaning missionary who suggested that a female captive marry a member of the household to which she had been given. The proposal was rejected with horror, apparently because since she was an adopted member of the household the missionary was inadvertently proposing an incestuous marriage (Lafitau 1974, 338–339).

Trigger's (1976, 826–831) summary of the material in the Jesuit Relations relating to the fate of Huron prisoners among the Iroquois mirrors the description in Lafitau. Pierre Raddison's account of his captivity among the Iroquois in 1652–1654 also confirms Lafitau's description (Adams 1961, 1–43). Indeed, the completeness of assimilation possible is well illustrated by the plight of one Onondaga (Iroquois) leading man who had adopted two Huron women to replace his deceased sisters. He was greatly misused by these women in the Jesuits' opinion, but he was unable to punish them because now they were his sisters and public opinion supported them (Trigger 1976, 831). Morgan's (1851, 341–345) later ethnographic description of the treatment of captives is also in substantial accord with the Lafitau material presented above.

All of this material (and much more that could be cited from the Jesuit Relations) makes it easy to understand why almost all recent scholars have followed Lafitau. But Starna and Watkins (1991) argue forcefully that these "adoptees" are more accurately regarded as slaves, and a few other recent commentators have sometimes seemed to agree (e.g., Webb 1984, 254). The seeds of Starna and Watkins's position can be found in Lafitau alongside the material that supports the adoption view. For example, immediately after the paragraph quoted above, Lafitau says,

In truth, the captives, if they are wise, should remember the status in which they have been and the favour done them. They should make themselves agreeable by their complaisance. Otherwise, their fortune might change even after many years of adoption especially if the families into which they have entered are numerous and can easily do without them, but their masters, although they feel their superiority, do not make them [the captives] feel it. On the contrary, they apply themselves to persuading the latter that, being incorporated in their families, they are masters as if they were in their own and are entirely like them. Sometimes even, they are told that they are free to remain or to return to their own countries. (1977, 172)

The last part of this paragraph continues to give comfort to those holding the adoption view with its suggestion that adoptees sometimes have a choice of remaining with their new kin or returning to their former communities. It also suggests that, in Lafitau's experience, northern Iroquoians made genuine efforts to convince captives that they really were regarded as fellow kin group and community members. The beginning of this paragraph suggests, however, that no matter how long an adoptee has been living in a community, he or she must act cautiously: "otherwise, their fortune might change." This suggests that adopted kin are somewhat less than equal, although Lafitau does not indicate what this change of fortune might entail. But it should be remembered that kin group members could be banished and disowned in many Native American societies, so that adoptees among the northern Iroquoians may not have been unusually at risk of losing their status.

Lafitau also suggests the existence of more marked social divisions within Iroquoian communities than are usually described. He maintains that not only are the native-born Iroquois divided into two ranked strata ("noble families" who have rights to titles and "common people" who do not), but captives and their children form a third stratum of even less regard. It is not certain that the "captives to whom life has been granted" described in the passage on stratification means captives who have been adopted, but this is likely (Lafitau 1974, 341). If we recall Lafitau's comment that members of adopting families "feel their superiority" to adopted captives, we may begin to suspect that captive origins were difficult to live down.

Candidates for adoption into these societies were captives, people who had been taken from their home communities by violent means and forcibly marched to their fates, which they knew might be torture and death instead of adoption. And in most instances some of their fellow captives were tortured and killed as they watched. Trigger (1976, 70–73, 827) has convincingly analyzed this entire pattern of capture, torture, and adoption as a process for the incorporation of outsiders into Iroquoian communities which was usually successful.

Starna and Watkins, following Patterson, argue that we need to recognize that there are two different kinds of fictive kinship that may be present in societies that practice slavery. Fictive kin ties may be adoptive, or they may be quasi-filial (Starna and Watkins 1991, 42; see Patterson 1982, 63–65). Adoptive ties give one "all of the claims, privileges, powers, and obligations of the status he or she has been ascribed," while quasi-filial ties "are essentially expressive: they use the language of kinship as a means of expressing an authority relation between master and slave" (Patterson 1982, 63). Patterson is using the notion of quasi-filial ties to describe the common use in master/slave relationships of kin terms to express relations of authority. The master is the parent, the slave the child, mirroring what is probably the most fundamental authority relationship in all societies whether kinship based or not. This is a metaphoric use of kin terms and is not likely to mislead anyone—master, slave, or observer—for long. But Patterson is trying to get at more than metaphorical usage by his distinction. In many societies slaves are taken into households and kin groups and act as members of those groups in most instances, but their true origins and status are not forgotten and remain to disadvantage them all their lives. Such persons are often called "domestic slaves" in descriptions of some African societies. Starna and Watkins argue that seventeenth- and eighteenth-century observers and modern scholars have confused adoption and quasi-filiation among the northern Iroquoians. What has been taken as adoption was in fact usually quasi-filiation, which was the Iroquoian manner of practicing slavery.

Starna and Watkins (1991, 43) argue that however well captives who had been "adopted" were treated and however little they felt their disadvantaged origins and status, they still faced the ultimate sanction of death if they did not conform to the expectations of their "relatives." Given that many adoptees began as captives, the products of violent seizure, and remembering Lafitau's remark about changing fortunes, Starna and Watkins have a point. Northern Iroquoian adoption was frequently "forcible adoption." The question remains if it should be called slavery.

Starna and Watkins try to show that Iroquoian captives conform to each aspect of Patterson's definition of slavery and thus must be regarded as quasi-filial slaves and not as true adoptees. It is not clear if Starna and Watkins mean to imply that all those usually labeled adoptees were actually quasi-filial slaves or if they think that both true adoptees and quasi-filial slaves were present in northern Iroquoian communities. They do not discuss the possibility of true adoptees, but when Patterson makes the distinction between quasi-filial and adoptive fictive kin he remarks,

> In no slaveholding society, not even the most primitive, is there not a careful distinction drawn between the genuinely adopted outsider (who by virtue of this act immediately ceases to be an outsider) and the quasi-filial slave (who is nonetheless encouraged to use fictive kin expressions in addressing the master and other members of his family). (1982, 63)

I know of nothing in the northern Iroquoian sources that suggests such a "careful distinction" between genuine adoptees and quasi-filial slaves. It is hard to believe, however, that the situation described by Trigger and noted above where an important Onondaga man was unable to act against two of his adopted Huron sisters because public opinion would not allow a brother to deal with his sisters in such a manner represents quasi-filial slavery rather than adoption. This and much of the other evidence suggests that many "adoptions" were in fact actual adoptions. Whether some other "adoptions" are more accurately regarded as examples of quasi-filial slavery is more difficult to decide.

Perhaps the most important "condition of life" of Northwest Coast slaves was the fact that they could be killed at any time. This is true of slaves in the great majority of slave systems, and where outsiders intervened to circumscribe the master's right to kill the slave, it was usually only to ensure some order and propriety for the procedure, not to deny the master's ultimate authority over his or her slave's life. Northern Iroquoian captives were at great risk of death during the early stages of their captivity. After they had been formally assigned to a particular household as a replacement for a specific individual the risk of death was reduced, but it seems that even at this stage a mourner might decide to torture and kill a captive rather than adopt him (Lafitau 1977, 155). After adoption, the risk of death seems to have been greatly reduced, although apparently some risk remained (Trigger 1976, 827).

In discussing the conditions of life of adoptees whom they consider slaves, Starna and Watkins cite the following passage from the Jesuit Relations, in which a mother of a recently baptized Seneca woman who had just died requests that a priest baptize one of her "slaves."

> Thou didst not know her. She was Mistress here and commanded more than twenty slaves who are still with me; she knew not what it was to go to the forest to get wood, or to the River to draw water; she could not take upon herself the care of all that has to do with domestic duties. Now I have no doubt that, being at present the only one of our family in Paradise, she had great difficulty in getting used to it; for she will be obliged to do her own cooking, to go for wood and water, and to do everything with her own hands in the preparation of food and drink. Indeed, is she not to be greatly pitied at not having any one who can serve her in that place? Thou seest here one of my slaves, who is ill; I pray thee instruct her well and put her on the road to Heaven, that she may not stray from it, and that she may go and live with my daughter, to help her in all her domestic affairs. (Thwaites 1896–1901, 54:93–95; cited in Starna and Watkins 1991, 51)

This passage implies that captives worked hard at tasks of domestic drudgery, that an owner/family could hold large numbers of captives (twenty in this case), and that owners were relieved of significant amounts of work by their captives. All of this sounds reminiscent of Northwest Coast masters and slaves. Starna and Watkins (1991, 51) cite some other instances of "slave labor" among the northern Iroquoians, although they do not present a detailed analysis and on examination some of their examples turn out to involve recently taken captives rather than "adoptees." In addition to ignoring the length of captivity of "slave laborers" (pre- or postadoption), they do not analyze the material in the context of the age and gender divisions of labor of northern Iroquoian societies (i.e., was the work being performed appropriate to the age and gender of the laborer?). They also briefly discuss what are purported to be transactions in captives, although nothing like the regular and active trade in Northwest Coast slaves is described or argued for (1991, 50). Altogether, Starna and Watkins spend very little time on the economic aspects of northern Iroquoian captivity, treating both the contribution of captive labor and transactions in slaves in a paragraph each. In this they follow Patterson (1982, 21–27) who is not only uninterested in the economic side of slavery but also goes to some pains to reject property interpretations of slavery.

Although resemblances between the passage just cited from the Jesuit Relations and Northwest Coast sources have been noted, a critical difference between the fate of the "slaves" held by this Seneca family and Northwest Coast slaves should also be pointed out. In a similar circumstance (the death of an owner) in many Northwest Coast communities a slave would have been killed to accompany the master in death. All that the grieving Seneca mother is asking is that a "slave" who is apparently terminally ill be baptized so that she will soon join her mistress in paradise. It is also unfortunate that we do not know just who these twenty slaves are. Are they long-standing adoptees or recent captives?

Starna and Watkins have reinforced the thread that runs through the early sources which implies that there was more inequality in northern Iroquoian societies than nineteenth- and twentieth-century interpreters have usually recognized. They attempt to make a case that the notion of adoption is problematic when applied to northern Iroquoian captives. There was a conditional side to at least some adoptions that suggests a more servile status for some adoptees than others. Their case that northern Iroquoian adoptees are best regarded as slaves is not convincing, however. The variation that they argue is present in the status of adoptees may fall well within the range of variation in treatment that we expect to find afforded the incumbents of such a status. It is not surprising that some adopters were less than kindly disposed to the former enemy who replaced a lost loved one. Nor is it surprising that some adoptees made the transition to a new social identity more successfully and completely than others. As well, the data on northern Iroquoian adoptees spans several centuries, during which time great changes took place in all aspects of society and culture. It would not be surprising if the status and fate of adoptees changed over this period, but Starna and Watkins do not even attempt a temporal analysis of their material.

In a broader comparative context, if we look across a range of societies we will observe a great variety of servile statuses, only a few of which are usefully labeled "slave." So the question is, if some northern Iroquoian "adoptees" were in some servile status, what exactly was it like and with what other servile statuses in other societies is it best compared? Starna and Watkins convince me this question needs to be asked, but their suggested answer—that all or even some adoptees are best regarded as slaves—deserves the verdict "not proven."

Captives in the Southeast

MacLeod was one of the first to draw attention to the difference in servile statuses on the Northwest Coast and the Southeast. As already described in chapter 2, he attempted to explain the absence of hereditary slavery in the Southeast (where he thought it economically and politically possible) by reference to vague "psychological" reasons. Siegel accepted MacLeod's and others' assessment of the absence of hereditary slavery in the Southeast and tried to show that this absence made sense in the light of a functional analysis of Southeastern society and culture. As far as I know, contemporary scholars of the aboriginal Southeast continue to accept Hodge, MacLeod, and other earlier Southeastern scholars' views on the absence of significant aboriginal slavery in the culture area. Charles Hudson's *Southeastern Indians* (1976) remains the standard scholarly summary of what we know of the aboriginal inhabitants of this part of North America. He has this to say about captives:

> The fate of captives among the Southeastern Indians varied immensely. Sometimes they were adopted and treated exactly as blood kinsmen, sometimes they were put in the precarious and uncertain position of a "slave," and sometimes they were tortured to death in a most horrible manner. When captives were enslaved, it was not slavery in the economic sense as practiced by the Europeans. In a subsistence economy a slave cannot turn a profit for his master. It was rather slavery in a social sense. The captive, or "slave," belonged to the man who captured him in war. He lived in the warrior's home and thereby became another mouth to feed. He performed menial tasks, such as gathering firewoods and processing deerskins, but his primary value to his "master" seems to have been prestige—the captive was a sort of living scalp. He was not usually bound or in any way restricted in his movement around the village or its environs. But escape was not a viable option, either because he was too deep inside enemy territory to hope to make it out without being recaptured, or else because his master had taken the precaution of maiming him in some way to keep him from being able to run fast enough to elude his pursuers. His position was forever uncertain. He could be given as a gift to another master. He could be sold—or more accurately, bartered. Or for any of a number of reasons beyond his control he could be put to death, either by the swift, merciful blow of a war club or hatchet, or else by slow torture. From the earliest Spanish accounts it is clear that the Indi-

ans killed some of their captives brutally. Women and children who were taken as captives were frequently adopted and led free and relatively normal lives. But male captives, particularly the older ones who had accumulated some war honors, were frequently tortured to death in the spirit of vengeance. (Hudson 1976, 253–255)[9]

There are both striking resemblances and interesting differences between this description of the situation of captives in the Southeast and the orthodox view of Northwest Coast slavery. Both agree that "slavery" was noneconomic and social in nature, slaves being kept primarily for purposes of prestige, and this point is driven home with the claim that in a "subsistence" economy a slave is a drain rather than an economic asset to his or her master. The orthodox view of Northwest Coast slavery has already been shown to be wrong. Perhaps Southeastern aboriginal slavery might prove to have been more "economic" if the sources were carefully reexamined. An important difference, however, allies the fate of Southeastern captives with the fate of Northeastern captives and distinguishes both from the fate of Northwest Coast captives. In the Southeast prisoners are said to have had three major fates: they were tortured to death, they were adopted and integrated into their captor's household, or they became "slaves." On the Northwest Coast, except for those few who were ransomed or otherwise exchanged as a part of elite negotiations, captives became slaves. The adoption of captives has never been claimed as a significant possibility for Northwest Coast captives.

One protohistoric society on the fringe of the Southeastern culture area offers some particularly intriguing parallels with Northwest Coast societies. The Calusa of southwestern Florida and some of their neighbors were fishing, gathering, and hunting societies who appear to have been highly stratified, and general parallels with Northwest Coast societies are often noted in discussions of the Calusa.[10] Our knowledge of the Calusa depends on a few, mostly brief, largely Spanish sources for the period around the 1560s and on archaeology. After the 1560s there was little direct European contact with the Calusa and their immediate neighbors until these societies were virtually destroyed in the early eighteenth century by raids by the English and their native allies who were based in the Carolinas.

The Calusa appear to have been divided into three ranked social strata: nobles, commoners, and a group referred to as either "servants" or "slaves" and who were war captives in origin. The nobles clearly dominated Calusa ceremonial and political life, although the source of this dominance in unclear. The Calusa polity is usually described as a "chiefdom" or a "paramount chiefdom," and it seems certain that the principal officeholder of the main Calusa town also controlled, or at least dominated, a number of neighboring communities. He was able to extract tribute from these communities on a regular basis and his political control was strengthened by marriages to women from leading families in some of these towns. The Calusa population was relatively large. The principal town may have contained 1,000 or more persons, and a conservative estimate of the size of the core Calusa polity in the 1560s is 4,000 to 7,000 persons. The principal towns at least seem to have been permanent, sedentary settlements, suggesting a relatively high level of subsistence productivity.

The number, duties, and conditions of life of the slave or servant stratum are uncertain. Most, perhaps all, were originally war captives. Some captives were probably tortured and killed early in their captivity, and there seem to have been regular, small-scale sacrifices of captives. In addition, some captives might be killed on the death of a noble. It is also not known if there was an indigenous trade in captives. We do not know if captives were ever adopted by the Calusa. The fragmentary data available suggest that the Calusa servant stratum may be best described as "slaves," but we are unlikely to ever be able to say for certain.

The Calusa and their neighbors join the Northwest Coast societies as examples of "complex hunter-gatherers": societies with high levels of productivity, relatively large communities that are sedentary or at least semi-sedentary, and marriage and other social customs reminiscent of horticultural "tribal" societies rather than hunter-gatherer "band" societies. They also had a rich ceremonial life, supported by a well-developed art style. The division into three ranked strata is another similarity. Important differences between the Northwest Coast and South Florida include Calusa participation in many aspects of generalized circum-Caribbean culture and their at least marginal sharing in the eastern North American torture complex. In the area of political organization a very important difference is that while it seems certain that the Calusa and probably some of their neighbors were organized into multicommunity polities with a single head, on the Northwest Coast multicommunity polities probably did not exist.

Conclusions

In keeping with the idea of continuous area or regional studies and to provide a continentwide context for Northwest Coast slavery, this chapter has discussed some possible servile statuses found in aboriginal eastern North American societies. It has not been a comprehensive or systematic attempt to discuss servile statuses even in eastern North America, much less in all of indigenous North America. Such an attempt, while plainly needed, should await the kind of detailed studies of the topic for clusters of societies or culture areas that this book presents for the Northwest Coast. Even the brief intra–North American comparisons attempted here, however, suggest that a careful reconsideration of servile statuses in many aboriginal North American societies, and an eventual North America–wide comparison of servile statuses will greatly increase our understanding of indigenous North American cultures.

The common starting point for both the Northwest Coast and eastern North America is captives taken in intergroup fighting. The fate of these captives was clearly different in the two areas. On the Northwest Coast all captives were potentially slaves and this seems to have been the most common fate. Those who did not become slaves were ransomed by their natal kin group or were returned to their natal group as a result of peace ceremonies. Slavery was a permanent stigmatized status that was transmitted to the children of slaves, if any.

In the Northeast and Southeast captives had two, perhaps three, common fates. A significant number of captives were tortured and killed either before or shortly after they arrived in their captors' home communities. Another significant group of captives were adopted into their captors' communities and kin groups and became to some degree naturalized members of these communities. Some individuals may not have been either killed or adopted, and some of those labeled adoptees may not in fact have been fully taken into their new kin groups. Such individuals occupied some kind of servile status (or statuses) within the various eastern North American societies. If this status was stigmatized, the stigma does not seem to have been as strong as it was with slavery on the Northwest Coast and this servile status was probably not passed on to the children, if any, of this disadvantaged group of adoptees—hence the traditional label "nonhereditary slavery" in descriptions of this category of person.

The question remains as to how important this servile category was within and to eastern North American indigenous cultures. An appropriate label for this servile category also remains unclear. Starna and Watkins have recently attempted to show that for the northern Iroquoians this group should be properly understood to be slaves in the usual sense of that term. A reexamination of the ethnohistorical evidence for other eastern groups might well produce some evidence similar to that used in their case for regarding northern Iroquoian captive adoptees as slaves. In my discussion of northern Iroquoian adoptees in this chapter, I regarded their case as not proven, but it is certainly correct that the ethnohistorical evidence about servile statuses in aboriginal eastern North American cultures needs careful and detailed restudy. Such a restudy would almost certainly reveal the regular presence of indigenous servile statuses that would complicate our traditional image of the egalitarian eastern Native American. These servile statuses were almost certainly different in important respects from the status of "slave" on the Northwest Coast. Whether or not some of these eastern servile statuses are best labeled slave remains to be determined. Whatever labels scholars eventually decide on, our knowledge of how these societies worked will certainly be improved by further consideration of the problem of captives in native North America.

13
Class on the Northwest Coast

Social rank and striving for social rank is a dominant theme in all Northwest Coast cultures. In traditional Northwest Coast studies, slavery has been treated as irrelevant to an understanding of Northwest Coast rank systems. My reading of the ethnographic and historical record of the region, however, suggests that an understanding of both slavery and rank is necessary. Rank and stratification have already been touched on in various chapters, especially with regard to titleholders as owners of slaves and the ritual use of slaves, but a more comprehensive treatment is needed. This chapter reviews rank within the culture area in the context of an approach to social stratification that considers the presence of both slave and free strata. In particular, it is argued that the free populations of Northwest Coast communities were also divided into ranked strata: class as well as rank was important.

The traditional Boasian view of the culture area has denied the presence of class and emphasized rank. Although Boas and other earlier Northwest Coast scholars do sometimes use the terms "class" and "classes" in their writings, they do so casually; these terms have no particular analytical meaning or importance for them. Drucker first clearly articulated the view that rank and not class was present on the Northwest Coast and that an analysis of Northwest coast social stratification should focus on rank.

> Each society consisted not of two or more social classes, but of a complete series of statuses graded relatively, one for each individual of the group. No two individuals were precisely equal in rank. (1939, 57)

> There were no classes of statuses in Northwest Coast society. Each individual had his own particular status in the graduated series from high to low; each

person's status had its own attributes which were not quite like those of anyone else. To insist upon the use of the term "class system" for Northwest Coast society means that we must say that each individual was in a class by himself. (1939, 58)

Drucker also explicitly denied the need to consider slaves when analyzing Northwest Coast societies.

Slaves had so little societal importance in the area that they scarcely need be considered in problems relating to the social structure. "Society," in the native view, consisted of the freemen of a particular group. (1939, 55–56)

The "rank not class" view has dominated Northwest Coast scholarship since Drucker's paper. From within the Boasian tradition, Ray (1956) issued a partial challenge to this view that provoked an analysis of the Kwakwaka'wakw that sought to vindicate Drucker (Codere 1957). Soon afterward Suttles (1958) considered the case of the Central Coast Salish and concluded that two classes were present among the free, although he described the lower class as much smaller than the upper class and implied that they were of little social or economic importance. In the same paper he suggested that Drucker was probably right about "rank not class" among the Kwakwaka'wakw. Although the term "class" was sometimes casually used after this flurry of papers, Drucker's view continued to be supported. Ruyle (1973) was critical of the orthodox position and argued for classes on the Northwest Coast from a Marxist perspective. Most Northwest Coast scholars were not persuaded (see the comments published with Ruyle's paper). Irving Goldman (1975, 54) argued that not only did the Kwakwaka'wakw have classes, but Boas's material showed that the Kwakwaka'wakw thought of themselves as having classes. When John W. Adams (1981) came to review the previous twenty years of writing on the culture area he did not devote much space to the class issue and never explicitly took a position on the rank-not-class controversy, although at one point his remarks might be taken as endorsing the presence of classes among the Kwakwaka'wakw (p. 370) and he had previously labeled Gitksan social strata classes (Adams 1973). Since Adams's survey both positions have been reiterated. I argued for the class position (1985b) using Kwakwaka'wakw and Tlingit data as examples and R. G. Matson and Gary Coupland (1995, 25–28) and Kenneth Tollefson (1995, 68–70) have recently opted for classes, although other scholars continue to hold the rank-not-class position (e.g., De Laguna 1983, 74; Kan 1989, 25).

Closely associated with the emphasis on rank and denial of class is the view, also originating with Boas, that slaves are "outside" Northwest Coast society (see, e.g., De Laguna 1983, 75; Kan 1989, 25). If "outside" society means merely that they did not participate in the struggle for titles that seemed to obsess many who lived in late nineteenth-century communities and could not achieve the modest regard of their fellows to which even the lowest of the free might aspire, then this is an apt description of slaves' position in all Northwest Coast societies. Slaves were truly marginal men and women; they occupied no rung on the prestige ladder. But they were a part of traditional Northwest Coast social systems in the same sense as the working class of nineteenth-century London or the slaves of classical Athens and antebellum Alabama belonged to their respective social systems.

The earlier chapters of this book have shown the importance of slaves in many aspects of Northwest Coast culture. This chapter demonstrates that among the free in many Northwest Coast communities, the holding of important titles and their attendant economic, political, and religious prerogatives was carefully limited and retained for a distinctly defined titleholder stratum. The nature of this titleholder stratum is significant here for titleholder privileges included ownership of most slaves. Only conquest and drastic population decline seemed to open up important titles to commoners and blurred former distinctions between strata.

"Class" is used here to refer to the three strata found on the Northwest Coast. The literature on class is enormous and full of controversy, especially over definitions, and it is not possible to do it justice here. But a brief excursion into the definition of class is necessary to explain this application of the concept to strata within Northwest Coast societies, especially since most of the discussion relating to the issue on the Northwest Coast has either avoided a definition or resorted to the dictionary. Following brief consideration of the class concept, some of the ethnographic data supporting a class interpretation are presented.

The Concept of Class

The notion of class is most commonly and least controversially applied to state societies with capitalist economies, although varying definitions and modes of class analysis produce controversy over its use in analyzing even these types of societies. It is not useful to require that the notion of class be restricted to a particular sort of society by definition. We need a definition of class that does not prejudge where we will find it but that still focuses our attention on those features of class that have tended to be important in the most fruitful discussions of the subject. Briefly, class is present in a society when significant segments of that society have relatively permanent differential access to resources and/or power. In addition, a class must, in principle, be capable of biologically reproducing itself. This precludes gender or age categories from being regarded as classes.

The presence and development of classes is a matter of degree. Where classes are present we can group societies into three general types: *societies with developing or incipient classes* (class structure is still rudimentary in nature), *class-divided societies* (class is present and important but does not dominate or determine all social relationships), and *class societies* (class is present and dominates all social relationships).[1] To use Anthony Giddens's (1981, 80) phrase, in a class society class "governs the basic character of production" whereas in a class-divided society forms of social relations other than those based on class continue to play important roles in production and elsewhere. As a type, class society may well include only some of the most complex, especially capitalist, societies. The variation in the class-divided type is very great.

Northwest Coast Societies as Class-divided Societies

Most, if not all, Northwest Coast societies were class divided as defined above. Those that were not were societies with incipient classes. Identifying these societies as class divided makes a statement about the titleholder and commoner strata of these societies. Even those who regard slaves as an unimportant part of Northwest Coast communities would agree that they were seriously disadvantaged with respect to access to resources and were also marked off in other ways from free community members. The quarrel is not over the distinction between free and slave but over the nature and importance of the division, if any, in the free category. In the discussion that follows, therefore, attention will be directed to ranked divisions among those of free status.

In most Northwest Coast cultures there were three named, ranked strata, which can conveniently be translated as "titleholder," "commoner," and "slave." Of the twenty groups in the tribal unit sample, the sources indicate that fifteen definitely had names for these three strata. Two other sample units probably had the same three named categories, and the data are not good enough to decide for the remaining three (although these three did, of course, have a "slave" category). The principal problem is deciding whether there was a named commoner stratum.

Although all three named social strata were probably present in all Northwest Coast communities, stratification (class) was not a uniform phenomenon throughout the culture area. Like slavery and most other culture traits, class varied from community to community in the region. For example, there is some variation within the culture area as to how sharply the two highest categories were defined before the precipitous nineteenth-century population decline led to the blurring of such distinctions. As well, the term "titleholder" is not entirely apt for the upper stratum among some the region's groups, for example, many of the Strait of Georgia and Puget Sound Salish, where the system of titles appears very weakly developed when compared with groups in the northern and central parts of the culture area.

A thorough description and analysis of stratification on the Northwest

Coast would require another book-length volume. What can be provided in the current context are sketches of class in a few Northwest Coast cultures and an overview of the major variations in the region's class systems. As Drucker's exposition of the rank-not-class view of Northwest Coast strata is the standard account, the discussion will begin by considering stratification among his principal ethnographic subjects, the Nuu-chah-nulth.[2]

Class among the Nuu-chah-nulth

The typical Nuu-chah-nulth winter village contained several cognatic descent groups, each headed by a titleholder who was normally the patrilineal descendant of the unit's founding ancestor. Inheritance of the title was by primogeniture, and only the titleholder and his oldest siblings and oldest children were eligible to be titleholders. Younger children and especially the children of younger children were destined to be commoners. Thus each descent unit contained both titleholder and commoner members. The descent group head controlled the unit's property (fishing, hunting, and gathering loci, house sites and houses, canoes, slaves, and titles) and directed the group's economic and other activities with the assistance of his brothers and older sons. Most mundane subsistence activities were carried out by the descent group's commoner members. Titleholders monopolized sea mammal hunting, especially whaling. They were able to do so in part because of their hereditary access to the necessary ritual and practical knowledge and training.

Titleholder status among the Nuu-chah-nulth was based on the rights to property that a person had inherited. "The head chiefs, the 'real chiefs,' were those who held the most, the lower chiefs, those who owned less, and commoners were simply people who possessed none at all" (Drucker 1951, 247). The property in question is both "economic" property (such as control of resource sites) and "ceremonial" property (such as the right to perform certain dances or songs). For most Nuu-chah-nulth titleholders, the most important economic properties were the salmon streams that they controlled. Kin were granted rights to fish at assigned places on these streams, but group members used their titleholder's resource sites under strict conditions, which assured that the titleholder's ownership was publicly acknowledged.

> No one might fish on any important fishing ground until the owner formally opened the season either by ordering some men to go out to procure the first catch or the first two catches for him, or by calling on all to accompany him on the first expedition of the season. After this, men could go when they pleased. Sometime during the season, or afterward when the product had been dried, the chief sent men to collect "tribute" for him. This was nothing more or less than a tax exacted in kind for the use of his domain. . . . Informants say, "The fisherman gave all they could spare. They didn't mind giving, for they knew the chief

would give a feast with his tribute." The foodstuff collected in this fashion was always used to give a great feast, at which the giver announced it had been obtained as tribute, and explained his hereditary right to demand tribute from that place. He invariably concluded by requesting the people to remember that the place belonged to him, "to take care of it for him," though they might use it when they wished after the formal seasonal opening. (Drucker 1951, 251)

Titleholders also attempted to marry other titleholders.

> Chiefs were expected to marry women of corresponding rank, for the honor of a noble line would be tarnished by a union with someone low in the social scale. As informants put it, "Even though the children inherit all their father's (chiefly) property, they will still have a bad name; they will be half-commoner. Their children and grandchildren will be just the same." (Drucker 1951, 244)

The result of such marriages was virtual stratum endogamy. Titleholder marriages united the leading members of each Nuu-chah-nulth descent group into a network of titleholders that cut across local community and even ethnolinguistic boundaries. As Wike notes,

> Although these intermarrying well-to-do families were frequently at odds, they also had interests in common which at times united them in spite of their rivalry, placing them as a group or as individuals against the interests of the people under them. (1958, 221)

The Nuu-chah-nulth titleholder and commoner strata are classes as defined here. There is certainly differential access with respect to resources (both economic and ceremonial) and the use of stratum endogamy by titleholders strengthens the divisions between the two strata while it reinforces the common interests of titleholders as a class. But class cannot be said to dominate all social relationships. Both titleholders and commoners obtain their primary social identities as members of descent groups. That each descent group contains both commoners and titleholders illustrates both the importance of kin units in Nuu-chah-nulth society and its class-divided nature.

Class among the Kwakwaka'wakw

The principal differences between the Kwakwaka'wakw and Nuu-chah-nulth class systems lie in the more extensively developed systems of titles and secret societies (or dancing societies) among the Kwakwaka'wakw. Kwakwaka'wakw commoners also had to go through their cognatic kin unit's titleholders for access to at least some important resources. The titleholders could claim some or even all of the products of the commoner's labor at the kin group's resource sites (Boas 1921, 1333–1340). Although the Kwakwaka'wakw are not known to have gone whaling, the hunting of smaller sea mammals was also under titleholder control (Boas 1921, 174–178, 451–464, 607–608, 750–751, 1093–1104).

Customs relating to food illustrate the distinction between titleholders and commoners. Typical of Kwakwaka'wakw titleholder attitudes are the following quotes from texts collected by George Hunt.

> There are only two ways of cooking the long and short cinquefoil roots. Only this teaches the common people their low station, when it is given in a feast, for the long roots are given to the chiefs and the short ones (to the others), for only chiefs eat the long roots and the common men eat the short roots. (Boas 1921, 544)

> The hair-seal also teaches the common people their place; for chiefs receive the chest, and the chiefs next in rank receive the limbs. They only give pieces of the body of the seal to common people of the tribes. (1921, 750)

Among the Kwakwaka'wakw the practice of primogeniture for titles and cognatic membership rules for descent units also meant that descent groups contained both titleholders and commoners. The impact of birth order was enormous both on oneself and one's children.

> The fundamental principle seems to be that primogeniture, regardless of sex, entitles the first-born child to the highest rank held by one of its parents. Rank is, on the whole, determined by the order of birth, and the noblest line is the line of the first-born. The lowest in rank that of the youngest born. Hence when a father and mother are of equally high rank, the first-born child may be assigned to one *numaym* [descent group], the following to another *numaym*. In cases of equal rank of both parents the father's *numaym* has preference and to it the first-born child is assigned. . . . The Indians emphasize again and again the rule that the "house name" and the attached position and privileges can never go out of the line of primogeniture and may not be given away in marriage. . . . The inference from the general point of view of the modern Indian is that the younger lines had names of inferior rank and formed the lower classes. (Boas 1940, 360–361)

With respect to titles, Boas notes that by the late nineteenth century the number of titles exceeded the number of Kwakwaka'wakw (at least among the Fort Rupert Kwakiutl) and that as a result a single individual often held more than one title. Boas infers that the surplus of seats (titles) dates back to the 1850s. It is probable that, before the rapid decline in the Kwakwaka'wakw population, there were many more people than titles and that many people never held a title, that is, were commoners. In other words, the apparent gradation in rank from top to bottom among free Kwakwaka'wakw was created by disastrous population decline (and new economic opportunities for commoners): so many people died that the number of vacant titles allowed those with no previous claim to them to take them up, provided they could amass the wealth necessary to give the appropriate feast.

In this same publication, however, Boas explicitly endorses the rank-not-class view.

> It seems to me that the conditions among the Kwakiutl and the Nootka must have been quite similar in so far as a sharp line between the nobility and common people did not exist, that rank was rather determined by the seniority of the lines of descent. In one Kwakiutl tale, it is even stated that the youngest of five brothers "was not taken care of by his father and was like a slave or a dog." (1940, 361)

Codere (1957) used this passage from Boas as major evidence that the Kwakwaka'wakw were classless, but an examination of the full text from which Boas takes his quote suggests a different interpretation. The youngest of the five brothers was treated badly not so much because he was the youngest but because he was the fifth child. There were only four titles to inherit, so that only four children received high rank (and could transmit it to some of their children). Four was an important, even sacred, number to the Kwakwaka'wakw. This reinforces the sacred quality of rank and also points out that it does not go on forever in gradually diminishing quantity. The titleholder in the text had only so much of the quality of rank to transmit to his children. When that has been done (in this case at four) there are no more titles, no more sacred inheritance for his other children. These children are still a man's children and still members of his descent group, but from the titleholder's point of view they are like dogs or slaves, so great is the gulf between titleholder and commoner.[3]

Marriage also tended to be strata endogamous. Although Kwakwaka'wakw descent groups were not exogamous and commoners apparently frequently did marry within the descent group, titleholders attempted to marry a spouse of equal standing in another descent group. This is especially true of principal titleholders (Boas 1966, 53). Titleholders not only married into other descent groups within their winter village, they seem to have been equally likely to marry titleholders from other winter villages. Most of the marriages described in Boas's (1966, 53–76) *Kwakiutl Ethnography* are between titleholders belonging to different winter village communities, and there are many other examples in the "family histories" published in the second part of his *Ethnology of the Kwakiutl* (1921).

Class among the Coast Salish

A tripartite class system also occurs among the Coast Salish. It differs significantly from the Nuu-chah-nulth and Kwakwaka'wakw systems. Discussion is focused on the Skokomish Twana, who are included in the tribal unit sample.

The Twana recognized "three classes of people," first distinguishing between free and slave and then dividing the free into a Twana term translated by them into English as "high class" or "high priced" people versus "common people," "poor people," or "low class people" (Elmendorf 1971, 367). Skokomish Twana verbal categories make clear and rigid distinctions between "high class" and "low class" persons, but Elmendorf suggests that while rigid stereotypes of what people in these categories were like accompany informants' discussions of the meaning of the terms, when other data are considered the difference between the two is not so sharp. In many circumstances almost any free person "whose behavior did not afford grounds for disparagement" might be called by the term for "high class" persons (Elmendorf 1971, 368). But Elmendorf (1971, 368) identifies one subcategory of "high class persons" who do seem to be set apart from all other Twana: known by a special term, they were "those who had formally demonstrated their high status in an intercommunity setting."

There were three major intervillage activities that tied the various Twana communities into a complex regional system of relationships that were economic, social, and political: village exogamous marriages, the intervillage giveaway feast or potlatch, and "the secret society initiation ritual with giveaway" (Elmendorf 1971, 364). Each Twana village had a different but overlapping network of other villages involving each of these activities. The largest network involved marriage, the smallest the secret society initiation ritual.

The most active participants in these networks were the "high priced" persons,

> those who had formally demonstrated their high status in an intercommunity setting. These were the potlatch sponsors and donors whose prestige reflected on their immediate kin and household members. A connotation of this word . . . is that intercommunity recognition was necessary to attainment of [this] status. . . . [A]scription of [this] status seemed to rest on kinship connections with this limited set of intercommunally eminent individuals. (Elmendorf 1971, 368)

These high-priced persons were often described in English as "well born":

> Ideally, in order to be "well born" a Skokomish individual required parents whose status was recognized as relatively high within the free class not only within their own local community, but over the social field of that community. Further, the two parents should have been native to different villages, and both of socially eminent families in their villages of origin. Finally, the marriage of the parents, given the above circumstances, would have been contracted through a highly formalized procedure involving interfamily negotiation, payment of a bride price, and a wedding feast followed by further reciprocal donations of food and goods between the affinally related families. (Elmendorf 1971, 369–370)

A set of Twana villages formed a social network and intercommunity feast-ing was a particularly important activity of this network, but there was no ranking of communities, nor were the titleholders who attended a feast ranked as a set. There was no formalized set of seats or named positions as was fre-quently the case farther north in the culture area. Rather, the upper-class per-sons who attended a feast sat with their fellow villagers. When the gifts were given out, there was no meaning attributed to the order in which villages re-ceived their gifts, but within each village the intravillage rank of each impor-tant person was recognized in both the order of their receipt of a gift and the nature of the gift. After the "leading people" had received their gifts, the "com-mon people" received small token gifts en masse. Thus the titleholder/com-moner division was reflected at potlatches (Elmendorf 1971, 371).

Class divisions mean differential access to resources, and this is usually taken to mean access to material resources. But on the Northwest Coast the nonmaterial was also owned and controlled. Elmendorf's description of Twana intellectual culture documents more fully than is usually the case differences in access to spiritual resources.

The Twana explanation for a person's location in their social classification scheme and for the behavior that was seen to be consistent with this was the individual's "acquisition and use of personal guardian-spirit power" (Elmen-dorf 1971, 365). Twana assume that persons lacking any type of guardian spirit power "are destined to be social nullities" and that the kinds of guardian spirit powers a person possesses correlate directly to the social performance and repute of adults (Elmendorf 1971, 365).

Anyone (sometimes even a slave) could seek a guardian spirit. There were dozens, perhaps hundreds, each conveying power for success in a specific ac-tivity, and a person might receive power from more than one spirit. Most spirits appear to have been fairly egalitarian in deciding with which persons they would associate, although some specific spirits were inherited (Elmendorf 1960, 491–499). In keeping with the relatively egalitarian nature of spirit ac-quisition, most aspects of spirit power belief and practice do not occur in an intercommunity context (training, seeking a spirit, validation of possession of a particular spirit at a winter spirit dance); rather they are the concern of the individual and his or her close kin only, and so most displays of spirit powers are normally confined to the village. But there was one important ex-ception to this: a special class of guardian spirits and accompanying powers whose name is rendered into English by informants as "wealth powers" (El-mendorf 1971, 366). Elmendorf describes the relationship between "wealth powers" and high status as follows:

Wealth powers were both potent and difficult to acquire. One consistent requi-site for their acquisition was a quality of the human seeker designated by infor-mants as "good blood" or "clean blood" . . . , itself a consequence of "good

birth." This denoted an unblemished line of descent from ancestors of high status; persons not fitting this standard were known to have been rejected or refused power by *s'iyált* spirits, even when they encountered them in a vision
experience, as sometimes occurred. Thus, wealth powers presented a social se-
lection factor built into the otherwise theoretically egalitarian guardian spirit
system. (1971, 366)

Wealth powers were not exhibited or validated at winter spirit dances as
were other spirit powers, but at intercommunity feasts where their owners
gave away property. This is consistent with other demonstrations of claims to
titleholder status before one's peers from other communities.

There were important distinctions between Twana titleholders and commoners, with regard to spirit powers (wealth power), social success and prestige, access to the potlatch system and its rewards, and access to spouses.
If "resources" are taken to include spiritual power and access to social connections and opportunities, then there was certainly differential access to resources for Twana titleholders and commoners.

But the issue of differential access to material resources is not as certain,
for the data on traditional Twana resource control are thin. From their 1930s
perspective Elmendorf's informants did not describe rigid or exclusive control of resource sites, with the partial exception of some assertion of village
rights to resource loci. There is no strong evidence that titleholders could deny
commoners direct access to resource site exploitation, that commoners had to
work through titleholders who claimed rights with regard to such sites, or that
commoners owed titleholders a share of the harvest from any resource site.[4]
However, houses and house sites were owned. Such houses and sites tended
to be owned by titleholders who allowed other less important relatives to reside with them. In addition, titleholders often owned house sites at important summer resource loci, particularly important fishing stations (Elmendorf
1960, 268–270). Control of household residence may well have been one way
titleholders asserted some resource site control.

Suttles's more generalized descriptions of "class" among the Central Coast
Salish (1958, 1960; reprinted 1987) are on the whole consistent with Elmendorf's discussion, while adding a few other points of interest, including more
material on access to material resources. Although he does not indicate the
local groups involved, Suttles asserts that upper-class persons had hereditary
rights to resource sites: "exploitation of the most productive fishing and other
sites was often in the hands of certain individuals who were able to use whatever surplus might be produced" (1987, 9). Inheritance rules usually involved
primogeniture, which, as Suttles points out, limited the rights and opportunities of junior lines. The implications of primogeniture over the generations are
reflected in the use of the diminutive of the term for "younger sibling" as a
polite word for lower-class people (Suttles 1987, 10). Although those unre-

lated to resource owners were at a disadvantage, some resource exploitation, such as hunting, was available to everyone.

The idea of private property was so well developed that upper-class Coast Salish insisted that morality itself was the private property of their class: only those who had inherited knowledge of and advice about proper behavior did in fact know how to conduct themselves as moral human beings (Suttles 1987, 10–11).[5] Although Suttles includes the possession of spirit power among the attributes of upper-class Coast Salish, he does not mention specific "wealth powers" of the Twana type. Similar powers are discussed in several other Coast Salish ethnographic sources (Barnett 1955, 148; Collins 1974a, 641; see especially Haeberlin and Gunther 1930, 73) so that "wealth power" and its association with the upper class is probably not unique to the Twana but fairly widespread among the Coast Salish.

The differences, both material and nonmaterial, between upper- and lower-status families were visibly represented in many villages that were physically divided into sections for each class (Suttles 1987, 5–6). Yet, although he uses the term "class" freely in his discussion, Suttles develops a highly unusual model of the class structure to interpret the data summarized above. He suggests that Coast Salish class structure did not have the usual pyramid shape but took the form of an "inverted pear"—where the upper class greatly outnumbered the lower class. This had the effect of making the lower class insignificant except as a foil to remind upper-class children (and adults) of the folly of misbehavior.

Suttles probably depends too much on conversations with informants in the 1950s and 1960s. At that time he found that his informants all claimed membership in the upper class while ascribing low-class membership to other informants, who reversed the claimed class attributions. He treats the vocabulary of class as a kind of one-upmanship and suggests that those who were traditionally actually members of the lower class were largely the descendants of slaves and a few others who were excluded from access to productive resource sites. The ethnographic and historical data, when carefully analyzed, suggest that former slaves are largely a post-European conquest phenomena, so that they are unlikely to have been significant in traditional Coast Salish communities. The emphasis of Suttles's informants on the moral worthlessness of commoners and the notion of inherited rights to knowledge and proper behavior suggest some of the ways the Coast Salish elite justified and maintained their elite status.

To summarize: Coast Salish communities were connected in loose networks and divided into three classes, one slave and two free. The two free strata were demarcated at the level of vocabulary and stereotyped behavior, but less obviously divided in terms of actual behavior and identification. The upper class was composed of those persons who had inherited high social status and rights to resource sites and powerful guardian spirits and who had succeeded in asserting their right to titleholder status at intercommunity feasts by giving away property to titleholders from other communities. Titleholders were also expected to marry titleholders from other communities. The strength of the division between the two free classes and the relative numerical strength of each varied from community to community and within a single community over time.

Although control of strategic resource sites was often in the hands of titleholders, most free members of every Coast Salish community had access to some resource sites, if not to the most desirable ones. At the level of ideology, the various Coast Salish communities were class divided. At the level of resource access and control, the degree of control of the various community elites varied from scant to considerable. Finally, the titleholder class, and the class system as a whole, must be seen as a multicommunity phenomenon and not as part of a single community's social system. The evidence is fragmentary, but there was probably a north-south gradient in the degree of the strength of class divisions, with the northern Coast Salish communities having the more developed class systems. Elmendorf (1971, 355, 375) speculates that this may have been so and attributes it to Kwakwaka'wakw influence on the northern Coast Salish.

Class among the Lower Skeena River and Southern Tsimshian

The Lower Skeena River and Southern Tsimshian were divided into four exogamous matrilineal phratries (or clans, depending on the terminology adopted). It is probable that in traditional times each Tsimshian winter village contained resident houses of two of these phratries. The most significant social unit in traditional Tsimshian daily life was the lineage. Lineages occupied one or more houses in a winter village and also controlled their own fishing and other resource sites. House sites, the dwellings themselves, resource loci, names (titles), crests, and slaves were all lineage property that was managed by the lineage head.

In Lower Skeena River and Southern Tsimshian villages, lineages (and hence their heads) were ranked under the overall leadership of the head of the highest-ranking lineage, who is generally termed the village "chief." The political authority of such a village chief was limited even within his own community and did not extend beyond the winter village community. The village chief held "the most powerful secular name, not only in his lineage, but also in his tribe [winter village], and possesses the right to the most dangerous and powerful sacred names and spirits. Leadership in the secret society activities was a chief's prerogative" (Garfield 1939, 182).

The Tsimshian language provides labels for four ordered social strata: "real people," "other people," "unhealed people," and "slaves" (Halpin and

Seguin 1990, 275–276). Lineage heads and their immediate matrilineal relatives were "real people." They held or had strong hereditary rights to the most important names (titles). Those who had names of lesser rank and importance were "other people," and "unhealed people" were free persons who had no names (titles). Membership in the free strata cut across phratry lines.

The Tsimshian system of social stratification fits the general tripartite model of Northwest Coast class systems if we recognize both "real people" and "other people" as belonging to the titleholder class (members of both categories and only members of these categories can hold or inherit titles), "unhealed people" as commoners, and slaves, of course, as slaves. Tsimshian slaves are obviously a class, but are commoners and titleholders really two separate classes and are titleholders in fact a single class?

The Tsimshian strata are usually discussed in the ethnographic literature as if they were classes, although admittedly this is without much regard for the theoretical meaning of the term "class." Garfield (1951, 28) explicitly rejected a rank-not-class view of Tsimshian society. She is quite explicit about the way in which Tsimshian leaders operated and what their goals were.

> Inheritance of wealth in addition to the power which accompanied its acquirement and manipulation tended to set Tsimshian house heads and their heirs apart from the rest of their lineage relatives and to concentrate control of wealth in the hands of a few men. They manipulated economically valuable resources or property, directed production and other work, controlled distribution of major production, and had political authority. The heads of all lineages and houses shared these advantages and there formed a group with common interests, which were class interests. Such leaders had power to bestow hereditary names, privileges and other lineage prerogatives on relatives of their choosing. Since every bestowal must be accompanied by a potlatch, and the head controlled the people, resources and accumulations necessary for giving one, he had the power to select recipients of even hereditary privileges. A few generations of such selection concentrated the properties and prerogatives in the line of descent of older brothers and their older nephews. (1951, 26–27)

No other ethnographer of the Tsimshian (or any other Northwest Coast group) is as clear about the policies, politics, and self-interests of the activities of titleholders, but with allowances for local variation, this is probably an accurate depiction of titleholders throughout the culture area.

Titleholders certainly dominated commoners in many ways, but were there significant differences in access to resources between titleholders and commoners? Garfield says that commoners did not have access to titles and other nonmaterial prerogatives.

> The descendants of junior lines, the children of younger sisters and their daughters could not hope to succeed to positions of leadership. Their only opportunity for prestige and social participation was through the leaders of their lineages.

They helped accumulate goods for potlatches but received only insignificant gifts when invited. A substantial part of a chief's expendable wealth came from them in the form of contributions of provisions, manufactured goods and labor. (1951, 28)

The principal titleholders controlled access to membership and participation in the secret societies (Garfield 1939, 297), and in general prerogatives relating to the relations with the spirits were hereditary, with the most important privileges and relationships reserved for important titleholders.

The following passage from "The Story of Part Summer" is typical of the position of titleholders in the myths.

In those days the people of each tribe were in the habit of going for one or two days to catch salmon to be given to the chief, who was to use them in the winter; and in the winter the people would often go to the chief's house, and the chieftainess would feed them. So the people caught salmon for their chief, and the women worked for their chieftainess. They would go some days and pick berries for her. The chief and his wife did not work for themselves. The people worked for them. (Boas 1916, 278)

The distance between principal titleholders and commoners is very great in the myths, for Boas notes that "on ceremonial occasions the chief and the chieftainess do not do their own work and do not talk to the people, but have their attendants and messengers who work for them" (1916, 430). The characters of mythology are largely stereotypes and the sharply drawn picture of titleholders in the Tsimshian myths is not unlike the stereotypes of Elmendorf's Twana informants. Boas observes, however, that "the social advancement of poor boys is an ever-recurring theme in Tsimshian tales" (1916, 498). It appears that many successful social climbers were lower-ranking titleholders (other people) who successfully became real people and that "when chiefs became poor, their noble descent was remembered for a long time. . . . [O]n the other hand common people who assumed high positions were considered as intruders" (Boas 1916, 498).

According to Garfield, access to material resources was as much under the control of titleholders as access to nonmaterial resources. She states the organization of food production was in the hands of the principal titleholders of each community, who planned the seasonal movements of their own units. Chiefs delegated the work to their followers, determined how much of each type of food was to be produced, and supervised the men's work, while their principal wives supervised the women's work (Garfield 1951, 15). Taken together, the statements in Garfield's two principal ethnographic works on the Tsimshian and Boas's analysis of the mythological material strongly suggest that Tsimshian commoners gained access to resources only through and with the permission of titleholders. This is reinforced by Garfield's (1951, 14) suggestion that by the time of contact, all coastal and riverine resource sites were owned by one lineage or another.

Among the Tsimshian, marriage was exogamous with respect to the phratry but tended to be endogamous with respect to class. Marriages were regarded as alliances between lineages and considerable effort was made to obtain partners that were equal in rank. This was especially true for potential principal titleholders. It was very difficult for a child of a marriage in which the parents were of markedly different rank to escape from the rank of the lowest-ranking parent (Garfield 1939, 232). Principal titleholders in particular often sought wives of equal rank outside their winter village. As Garfield notes, "A chief gained friends and allies in other tribes [winter villages] by his own judicious marriage to daughters or nieces of other chiefs" (1951, 37). Such men also married outside the Tsimshian language area. Haida, Tlingit, and Tsimshian sources contain many references to marriages between members of all three language groups. Both the Haida and Tlingit had matrilineal clans/lineages organized into moieties. The four Tsimshian phratries were paired up with Haida and Tlingit moieties so that the rules of exogamy could be followed in cross-ethnic marriages. In analyzing some of the formal properties of these three social systems Dunn (1984, 99) has aptly characterized them as forming a system of "international matri-moieties." Titleholders from all three cultures used this system to marry and feast each other and promote titleholder solidarity.

Most of the Tsimshian data support Garfield's analysis of Tsimshian class and fit the tripartite model of class on the Northwest Coast. This view emphasizes both material and nonmaterial distinctions between the classes. The indigenous titleholder view emphasized the nonmaterial, as witnessed by a passage discovered by Marjorie Halpin in William Benyon's unpublished notes. In 1916 Joshua Tsibasa remarked to Benyon that people literally fall into the class of unhealed people from either of the upper categories by showing continuing evidence of bad character or bad behavior. A bad person's relatives may demote such a person to this class in an effort to reform him or her. It is possible for someone like this to regain upper-class status, but a bastard can never escape. A "real person" who marries a commoner wife finds that both he and his children are also commoners and, with a principal titleholder's permission, the child of slaves may be regarded as an unhealed person. As Halpin remarks, "It appears that to be an Unhealed Person was to be a deviant, essentially someone outside the social order. That is, it was less a social class, as commonly believed, than a moral condition" (1984, 60). Tsibasa makes unhealed people sound much like Suttles's version of lower-class Salish—ne'er-do-well dropouts and bad characters.

Tsibasa is the title of the leading Kitkatla titleholder, whose mid-nineteenth-century incarnation was encountered in chapters 5 and 11. Joshua Tsibasa was undoubtedly a very high-ranking Tsimshian. He reminds us that, at least in titleholder eyes, social class was about moral as well as material and ritual worth: to be a commoner was to have little moral worth anywhere in the culture area.

Class among the Tlingit

Ethnographers of the Tlingit have often explicitly endorsed the rank-not-class perspective (e.g., Olson 1967, 47), although the data are consistent with a class interpretation. Most of those who were free belonged to one of two strata: the highest class are most often labeled "nobles" in English (e.g., Oberg 1973, 41; De Laguna 1990, 213) and "commoners." De Laguna (1990, 213) describes the titleholder class as "the chiefs (headmen of clans or lineages) and their immediate relatives," and Olson (1967, 48) calls them "the persons of the very highest birth and social attainments." While Olson and De Laguna ascribe to the rank without class view of Tlingit stratification, Oberg sees the situation in definite class terms. In a discussion of the matriclan system he describes Tlingit clans as examples of classic clan solidarity, but then goes on to say,

> This clan solidarity is more apparent than real, for the element of rank is so strong that out of it crystallizes definite classes. . . . These class lines run across clan and phratry [moiety] and form a unit probably stronger than the clan itself. . . . Therefore, the *anyeti* [titleholders] in every village consists of the upper end of the two phratries, made up of the paired leading houses of the two highest clans. A member of the *anyeti* often ignores a clansman of low rank and does not speak of him as a brother, but as a man of such-and-such a house. (Oberg 1973, 41)

The marriage system also emphasizes rank and class in the same manner as among the Tsimshian: people seek spouses with a rank equal to their own, and, as Oberg (1973, 37) points out, preferential cross-cousin marriage (the ideal in all three northern cultures) helps assure the maintenance of appropriately ranked spouses for titleholders.

Tlingit clans had lineages resident in many winter village communities and many lineages were divided into sublineages ("houses") that were the daily units of production and consumption. There were titleholders and commoners within every clan and even within most lineages there were titleholder and commoner houses, so that at least at the clan level and often at the lineage level commoners were distant relatives of titleholders. The picture is complicated by the fact that a few clans were regarded as "high" or "most important" while others were regarded as "low" or "less important" (Oberg 1973, 39, 136–138; Olson 1967, 47). Commoners in high clans thought themselves superior to commoners in low clans (Olson 1967, 47), although they were still commoners.

Hereditary rights to titles and positions of leadership were controlled by titleholders, as were the crests that were displayed as paintings and carvings on totem poles, feast dishes, ceremonial regalia, and so on. That the title-holder class controlled access to material resources is less certain. Resource loci were traditionally clan property, as were house sites, but the actual exploitation of specific sites was undertaken by the house group (sublineage). As we have seen, a house might be commoner or titleholder and it is not at all certain that titleholder members of a clan exerted much control over clan resource loci that they did not directly exploit, so that at least some commoners had relatively unrestricted access to important material resources. It seems certain, however, that the titleholder lineages in a community did monopolize the best and richest resource loci (Oberg 1973, 55–64).

Although De Laguna has frequently endorsed the rank-not-class position for the Tlingit, in her role as editor of George Emmons's Tlingit ethnography she does not protest at his description of two classes among the free: a "hereditary aristocracy" and "the people in general" (Emmons 1991, 37). Emmons also provides an excellent example of Tlingit titleholder attitudes toward commoners: in 1885 when the principal titleholder of the lineage representing the Wolf moiety in Sitka married a woman of the lower class, the two principal titleholders of the opposite Raven moiety refused to attend the marriage ceremony, saying, "'No good could come of mating a chief to a clam digger'" (Emmons 1991, 38).

Class among the Nuxalk

There are almost no data on traditional Nuxalk resource control, so that nothing can be said about differential access to material resources. The available data require us to focus on possible distinctions between Nuxalk titleholders and commoners largely with regard to prerogatives and marriage.

At the time of contact the Nuxalk occupied more than twenty winter villages and were organized into cognatic descent groups that McIlwraith (1948, 1:117) termed "ancestral families." The ancestral family consists of all those who can trace their descent from a small group of first people (usually three or four brothers and sisters) who were made by the creator and sent down to occupy their ancestral village. These descent groups were not exogamous; indeed, they had a tendency toward endogamy. The most important names are those transmitted through the ancestral family from the founding ancestors of the descent group.

The Nuxalk have what are usually termed in English "chiefs." A chief holds an important ancestral name or names and related prerogatives. But, unlike the situation in most of the culture area, ancestral names are not inherited in a systematic way. In addition, although chiefs possess important ancestral names, the mere possession of such a name does not make one a chief. Rather one is a chief when one is able to distribute large numbers of valuable presents at any ceremonial occasion. Every ritual or ceremony, be it an admission into a secret society, a funeral, a marriage, a dance, or the bestowal of a name, is an occasion for the host chief to demonstrate the glory of his ancestors by giving presents. Titleholders validate their rights to titles and raise their prestige by getting witnesses to accept their use of the titles and to accept gifts on the occasion of their doing so. The gift giving is also competitive in that the recipients of such gifts should return even larger gifts on the occasion of the events that they host if they wish to retain their level of prestige (McIlwraith 1948, 1:163).

But it appears that every Nuxalk has at least one name that occurs in the ancestral family myth (McIlwraith 1948, 1:167). To become a chief on the basis of this name, the holder must make it "strong" or "bright." And this is done by the giving of generous presents on every possible occasion as described above.

To an even greater degree than in most of the rest of the region, chiefs are influential persons and not holders of political office. The principal holders of titles did form a coherent body at the village level by means of one of the Nuxalk "secret societies," the *sisaok* society. Individuals take up membership in this society by taking up sisaok names that also appear in the myths associated with ancestral families. A man or a woman takes up such a name by going into seclusion and then giving presents at the time of leaving seclusion. Additional sisaok names may be taken up by repeating the seclusion and gift giving. Only the wealthy and their children and close relatives are able to afford these name takings. A chief is not a member of the society unless he has taken up an appropriate name. It is not necessary to be a member of the sisaok in order to be a chief, but the membership of the society and the group of individuals regarded as chiefs are so similar that the Nuxalk think of the sisaok as a society of chiefs (McIlwraith 1948, 1:180–182).

Chiefs also play a major role in the other important Nuxalk secret society, the *kusiut* society. Chiefs gather at a regular meeting place to discuss the affairs of this winter ceremonial society. Nonchiefs who are important in the society may also attend these meetings, but the chiefs are always present. In particular, the initiation of new members into the kusiut society is always discussed and agreed to by such a meeting of chiefs. This meeting place is well known to community members but avoided by ordinary people out of fear and respect for the chiefs' supernatural powers as important members of the kusiut society (McIlwraith 1948, 1:177–178).

Chiefs are also associated with seals and sealing in a manner reminiscent of some other Northwest Coast groups. When a seal is killed a number of chiefs are invited to a ceremonial meal at the successful hunter's home. The more seals killed, the greater the number of chiefs invited. If many have been taken, even chiefs from other communities will be summoned. For a single small seal only the most important chiefs are asked. After cooking, the seal (or seals) is butchered and shared according to a ritual pattern. Anyone may kill a seal, but chiefs must always be invited to share the resulting meal (McIlwraith 1948, 1:176–177).

Nuxalk marriage choices are strongly influenced by considerations of prestige and with an eye to the prerogatives held by the prospective partner or, more likely among the young, their parents. A chief is inclined to look to the sons and daughters of other chiefs for a partner for his child. But Nuxalk are anxious that important prerogatives not go outside the family group, and the preferred marriage partner belongs to one's own ancestral family. McIlwraith's discussion is not detailed enough to be certain, but descent group endogamy seems to have been at least as important in marriage choice as titleholder endogamy. McIlwraith (1948, 1:374–379) does explicitly state that the tendency, at the time of his fieldwork (the early 1920s), for descent group exogamy and even ethnic group exogamy was a late nineteenth-century development.

Like titleholders on other parts of the Northwest Coast, Nuxalk chiefs held important prerogatives. But access to these prerogatives seems to have been less restricted than among most groups in the region. Population decline after contact was swift among the Nuxalk. In the late 1700s there were at least twenty-five Nuxalk villages and quite possibly as many as forty-five to sixty. Early in the nineteenth century village sites began to be abandoned due to population loss, and by the 1920s there was only one inhabited Nuxalk winter village. Titleholders died as readily of disease as did commoners and slaves. Population loss certainly loosened the grip of titleholders on many Northwest Coast communities as the nineteenth century progressed. This opened up opportunities for commoners to take up titles because of new possibilities for commoners to acquire the necessary wealth and because many titles lacked hereditary titleholders to take them up. Whether Nuxalk titleholders had lost all memory of previous hereditary control of titles by the time of McIlwraith's fieldwork in the 1920s or had never had such control must remain uncertain. Although since titleholders elsewhere did retain such memories even when their ability to continue to exercise full control ceased, it is likely that less marked class divisions existed among the Nuxalk even before population decline and massive culture change began.

The individual's ability, initiative, and luck seem to have been even more important in becoming and remaining a titleholder than elsewhere on the coast. Both inheritance of privileges and marriage alliances seem to have played a lesser role among the Nuxalk. Nevertheless, chiefs and their close relatives did form a privileged stratum within Nuxalk society, although one less distinctly separated from the mass of free men and women. More information about traditional resource control might change the picture, but the data presently available suggest that incipient classes were present in traditional Nuxalk society but that unlike the situation in many other groups on the coast, the control of prerogatives was not sufficiently in the hands of a largely hereditary titleholder elite to call Nuxalk society class divided.

Class on the Northwest Coast

The most obvious and permanent class division on the Northwest Coast was between the free and the slave. In addition, the free population in these traditional communities was usually divided into two strata, titleholders and commoners. There was differential access to resources depending on stratum membership. The data available show more distinctly the disadvantages of commoners with respect to nonmaterial resources, but there were usually material disadvantages as well. All three strata included both men and women, and age was not a criterion of stratum membership so that in principle each strata could biologically reproduce. It is doubtful that the slave stratum actually did so, but the two free strata were biologically self-sustaining, at least until severe epidemic disease-induced population decline overwhelmed many local communities in the nineteenth century. The primary social identity of members of both free strata derived from kin group rather than stratum membership. Class was present and important but did not dominate kinship.

Class was an intercommunity phenomenon. Titleholders sustained their class both reproductively and culturally through multicommunity ties and activities. Titleholders preferred to marry titleholders and also attempted to arrange titleholder marriages for their children. The usual goal was to make marriages between individuals of equal rank. Frequently this meant that titleholders went outside their local communities for a spouse. There is good evidence of intercommunity titleholder endogamy among the Nuu-chah-nulth, the various Strait of Georgia and Puget Sound Salish, the Kwakwaka'wakw, the Haida, the Tsimshian, and the Tlingit. A major focus of such titleholder marriages was the ensuring of high status for one's children. Such marriage strategies had the effect of ensuring the biological reproduction of the titleholder class. But these strategies also were a part of the social and cultural reproduction of this class. These strategies and the associated need to validate claims (through the sponsorship of feasts and ceremonies) of titleholder status before a titleholder audience drawn from other communities also created regional social networks.

These regional networks involved a range of activities and tied together large numbers of people and many communities, even though direct contact among all or even most of the participants in such networks never occurred. Titleholder marriages across community and even ethnolinguistic lines in some instances were a major element in the creation and maintenance of these networks. There were probably five major regional networks: Northern (Tlingit, Haida, Tsimshian, Haisla), Queen Charlotte/Johnstone Straits (Oowekeeno,

Kwakwaka'wakw, northern Nuu-chah-nulth, Comox), West Coast (Nuu-chah-nulth, Makah, Klallam), Strait of Georgia/Puget Sound (Coast Salish, Chemakum), and Greater Lower Columbia (Chinookans, southwestern Coast Salish, Tillamook). As Suttles (1990b, 12–14) has suggested, the external markers of participation in these regional networks included the wearing of labrets, tattoos, and style of head deformation. These markers appear to have been particularly important in the case of titleholder women. Groups along the boundaries of these networks often used the markers of both networks so that marriage partners could be found in either. The Haihais, for example, practiced the style of cranial deformation used in the Queen Charlotte/Johnstone Straits network and wore labrets as did titleholder women in the Northern network. In addition, the Haisla organized themselves into "crest groups" that resembled the matrilineal units of the north (Hilton 1990, 315, 317).

The situation with respect to class divisions in many traditional Northwest Coast communities may be described as follows. Titleholders attempted to control access to resources and other kinds of power. Slaves had no rights of access to resources. They were entirely dependent on their master's goodwill and support. Commoners stood between these two classes. As members of kin units that owned resource sites, they had rights of access by virtue of their kinship affiliations. But most commoners had to go through titleholders who controlled the use of the kin group's resource locales, and titleholders often claimed some or even all of the products of the commoners' labor at the kin group's resource site. Commoners had different (poorer) opportunities of access to all of the valued resources of their societies, not merely sites for producing food and other material goods. They were, for example, excluded from holding titles and from access to the most powerful spirits that might be sought in a spirit quest. Marriage choices also tended to be stratum endogamous. Given the importance of kinship in defining social and other relationships for two of the classes, in the terms employed here, these are class-divided societies.[6]

Not all Northwest Coast societies were class divided, and among those we can label class divided there were important variations in the strength and importance of the divisions and the way in which class was organized. The Nuxalk, for example, are almost certainly better described as having incipient classes than as being class divided. And although the Strait of Georgia and Puget Sound Salish communities were class divided, the class differences in these communities and the advantages of class membership for titleholders there were certainly considerably less than among the Nuu-chah-nulth, Kwakwaka'wakw, Tsimshian, Haida, and Tlingit. In the northern part of the culture area, Tlingit commoners may have had freer access to material resources than Tsimshian, Nuu-chah-nulth, and Kwakwaka'wakw commoners.

When the possibility of the presence of class in the culture area has been discussed by scholars much has been made of the ranking of titles and names and of the acquiring of titles by commoners in the late nineteenth and early twentieth century. The emphasis on these two points is traditional in Northwest Coast scholarship, but it is "traditional" in a more important sense: Native informants often described their societies in such terms to ethnographers. Most informants were titleholders, and this picture reflects the position of these informants within their societies. Class divides and rank unites, so that the advantage of emphasizing rank from a titleholder's perspective is obvious: it is a part of the ideology that the ruling elite uses to perpetuate itself. Mobility across class lines does not preclude class. Equally important, when commoners succeeded in taking up titles in the late nineteenth century, their success was very much the result of the devastating population declines that had occurred earlier in every Northwest Coast community. Declines often left more names and titles to be taken up than there were living people. A historical approach to class is needed on the Northwest Coast just as much as it is needed for slavery.

The intensity of class divisions appears to have varied as much as did the intensity and development of slavery. Both were most strongly developed and more important in the north and north central parts of the region (Tlingit, Haida, Tsimshian, Kwakwaka'wakw, and Nuu-chah-nulth) and much weaker in the south central and southern part of the region (Strait of Georgia and Puget Sound Salish). Slavery was also strongly developed in the southernmost part of the region among the Chinookans. The data on class among the Chinook is less than ideal, but Michael Silverstein's (1990, 541–542) interpretation of the available material is consistent with the presence of a class-divided society among the Chinookans. All of this bears out the hypothesis that the intensity of slavery and the intensity of class divisions co-vary positively. Only the Nuxalk appear to be an exception: they have "northern" slavery but only incipient classes.

14

The Place of Slavery
in Northwest Coast Culture

In this final chapter several general issues are considered. First, since the economic importance of Northwest Coast slavery has been controversial, the contributions that slaves made to the economies of their communities are reviewed. The ideology of kinship appears to be contradicted by the institution of slavery, so the next issue taken up is how slavery flourished in societies based on kinship. The next problem examined is how titleholders maintained their dominance of both commoners and slaves. The chapter concludes with a consideration of the place of slavery in Northwest Coast culture.

The Contributions of Slaves
to Northwest Coast Economies

Economic aspects of Northwest Coast slavery have already been treated in some detail in chapters 6, 7, and 11. In particular, the sections in chapter 6 on the value and significance of slave labor and in chapter 11 on the slave and fur trades deal with the issue of the importance of slavery to the Northwest Coast economies. All of that material and its analysis will not be repeated here. But it is appropriate to draw together here the principal findings and arguments on the role of slaves in these economies, especially since the economic insignificance of slavery has long been a mainstay of the orthodox view of traditional Northwest Coast cultures.

The contribution of slaves to the Northwest Coast economies must be considered in the context of the relations between master and slave. The question at issue is, What economic utility was the slave to his or her owner(s)? The most common answer in the Northwest Coast literature is "negligible." The

usual argument is that slaves were actually an economic drain on their owners, who put up with the situation for the sake of the prestige that holding
slaves brought. The implication of this view is that productivity on the Northwest Coast was so low that the work a slave performed in the subsistence area
would barely feed the slave, if it did that. This seems very unlikely. In any
"subsistence economy" most of those who perform subsistence labor produce
a "surplus" to their own subsistence needs, which is used to feed those who
cannot perform a full share of subsistence work (the young, the sick, the dis-
abled, the elderly). Relatively able-bodied slaves should have been as capable
of producing enough for their own support and a little more for the dependent
portion of the population as any other similar person in the community. At the
very least a slave should have been an economic "neutral" to his or her master,
unless he or she was somehow debarred from subsistence labor. But in chapter 6 I provide evidence that in communities throughout the culture area, slaves
did indeed perform subsistence tasks. Considerable evidence was also presented
to support the contention that masters substituted the labor of their slaves for
their own need to perform arduous subsistence and related tasks. No evidence
was found for masters working hard to "support" their slaves.

Keeping in mind that slave owners were almost always titleholders, slaves
might make economic contributions to the endeavors of their masters in at least
three ways: slaves could relieve masters of some (perhaps even all) household drudgery, freeing their time for titleholder activities, including leisure;
slaves' subsistence labors could be substituted for their masters' subsistence
labors so that communities did not suffer a loss in food production when titleholders curtailed their own subsistence activities while engaging in ceremony,
war, or other activities; and the surplus from slaves' productive labors contributed to the stock of food and goods utilized by titleholders in feasts and ceremonies. The evidence presented in chapter 6 demonstrates that slaves contributed
economically to their master's households and kin groups in all of these ways.

The labor of slaves is often described as mere drudgery, as if the drudgery
performed had no implications for the lives of masters and other nonslaves.
Slaves above all are described as hewers of wood and drawers of water, but
little attention has been paid to either the amount of time and effort involved in
these tasks or to their necessity. At all seasons, but particularly in the winter,
every household consumed a lot of firewood. Water too was in daily, year-
round demand. The substitution of slave for free labor for these tasks alone
gave masters' households significant amounts of additional time for more dignified work and for leisure.

Ethnographers of the Northwest Coast often make the point that there was
little difference in the material well-being of titleholders and others in traditional communities. There were in fact marked material advantages to being a
titleholder: higher-ranking families got the more secure, warmer, drier places
in the multifamily plank houses, and they had first call on food resources and

got the best cuts when animals such as seals were butchered and shared out, to mention but a few differences. It is probably true, however, that the extreme material differences and advantages that accrue to ruling elites in complex societies were missing. Titleholders were better off in material terms than commoners, but only somewhat so. But titleholders were better off in other ways that were of great (probably even greater) significance to participants in traditional Northwest Coast cultures, and the economic contributions of slaves helped to promote these titleholder advantages.

One of the principal purposes in giving a feast or putting on a ceremony was the host's desire to validate a claim to a title. A successful feast giver gained or at least maintained his prestige and position. From the titleholders' point of view, successful feast giving—and therefore successful validation and maintenance of titles—was probably their most important activity. Much that they undertook was directed to success in the arena of titles and feasts. Slaves in the household could contribute to titleholder ceremonial activities in four ways. First, their work helped amass the large amount of goods, including food, required for a feast. Second, large-scale distributions of goods to invited titleholder guests (who were both the host's rivals and witnesses) were the central focus of most feasts, and slaves were one of the small number of high-value items presented to the most prominent guests on the most important of such occasions. Third, not too long after European contact, goods of European origin became an important part of the goods given away at feasts, and slaves could be traded to other natives either for furs to obtain such goods or for the goods themselves. Finally, property was not only given away but destroyed at feasts, and slaves were sometimes killed to demonstrate both the wealth and the power of the host. Thus we can see that slaves might play several different roles within the context of the same feast preparation.

Overall, we can see that slaves contributed directly to the production of food and other goods that titleholders had at their disposal, contributed to titleholder leisure time, and contributed both directly and indirectly to titleholder success in contests for prestige with other titleholders. Inasmuch as commoner followers benefited from the wealth and prestige of their titleholders, slaves also contributed to the well-being of commoners.

Finally, it must be insisted that to argue that slaves were of major economic importance to Northwest Coast communities is not to argue that slaves had no other meanings, or were not important in other ways as well. One of the lessons that anthropologists have been struggling to learn and teach for a long time is that even the simplest object can be a complex entity with multiple meanings and purposes when seen and appreciated in its proper cultural context. Slaves, especially since they are human beings, are not among the simplest "objects," and when I insist on their economic importance on the Northwest Coast I am not fully describing their role and meaning in Northwest Coast cultures. Slaves' complex role in rituals and the subtle interplay of the symbolic meaning of salmon, slaves, and copper in myths and ceremonies are good examples of the noneconomic importance of slavery in the culture area.

Kinship versus Slavery
Kinship-based societies

Northwest Coast cultures are usually treated as classic examples of kinship-based societies. Lewis Henry Morgan labeled them *societas* and, based on his experience with the Iroquois, defined them as "founded upon persons, and upon relations purely personal. . . . The gens is the unit of this organization; giving as the successive stages of integration . . . the gens, the phratry, the tribe, and the confederation of tribes" ([1871] 1964, 13–14). This was contrasted with *civitas* society, which is "founded upon territory and upon property, and may be distinguished as a state" ([1871] 1964, 14). When he attempted to study economic exchange among peoples living in societies falling into Morgan's *societas* type, Marcel Mauss ([1925] 1967, 3) could not find the "simple exchange of goods, wealth and produce through markets established among individuals" which he thought characterized economic activity in early twentieth-century Europe. Rather he found that a whole range of activities, both economic and noneconomic, flowed through group relations, that is, kinship relations. In describing what he found, Mauss produced a classic description of kinship-based societies and established the Northwest Coast cultures as exemplars of this type of society.

> In these "early" societies, social phenomena are not discrete; each phenomenon contains all the threads of which the social fabric is composed. In these *total* social phenomena, as we propose to call them, all kinds of institutions find simultaneous expression: religious, legal, moral, and economic. In addition, the phenomena have their aesthetic aspect. ([1925] 1967, 1)

> It is groups, and not individuals, which carry on exchange, make contracts, and are bound by obligations; the persons represented in the contracts are moral persons—clans, tribes, and families; the groups, or the chiefs as intermediaries for the groups, confront and oppose each other. Further, what they exchange is not exclusively goods and wealth, real and personal property, and things of economic value. They exchange rather courtesies, entertainments, ritual, military assistance, women, children, dances, and feasts. . . . Finally, although the prestations and counter-prestations take place under a voluntary guise they are in essence strictly obligatory, and their sanction is private or open warfare. We propose to call this the system of *total prestations*. Such institutions seem to us to be best represented in the alliance of pairs of phratries in Australian and North American tribes, where ritual, marriages, succession to wealth, community of right and interest, military and religious rank and even games all form part of one system and presuppose the collaboration of the two moieties of the

tribe. The Tlingit and Haida of North-West America give a good expression of the nature of these practices when they say that they "show respect to each other." ([1925] 1967, 3–4; emphasis in original)

Even before Morgan produced an intellectually coherent and empirically informed analysis of kinship-based societies as a major social type, certain features of these societies were being used to contrast them with "civilized" European society. In particular, the egalitarian freedom thought to be found in such societies was frequently contrasted with the rule of hierarchy and aristocracy in Europe in discussions of the "Noble Savage" from the eighteenth-century Enlightenment on. Morgan made this contrast "scientific" and more systematically rooted in the empirical facts of Native American life in his description of the Iroquois first published in book form in 1851, but his work also contains criticisms of aristocracy and calls to return to "the liberty, equality and fraternity of the ancient gentes" [gentes equals clan in modern terminology] ([1871] 1964, 67). Since Morgan, anthropologists have largely, although not exclusively, concentrated their studies on peoples organized into societies of Morgan's societas type, that is, on kinship-based societies.

Our knowledge of how these societies actually work and of the range of variation in social and cultural practice encompassed by the category "kinship-based society" is much greater than Morgan's or even Mauss's, but the most characteristic features of these societies are still thought to be those articulated by Morgan and Mauss, including the fundamentally egalitarian nature of social units based on kinship and the presence in such societies of a system of total prestations; all Northwest Coast ethnography has certainly been influenced by this vision of such societies.[1] Within a kinship unit, relations between the unit's members are based on an ethic of sharing and reciprocity. Between equivalent kin units (family households, lineages, clans) relations are based on reciprocity, although the reciprocity may be more nicely calculated than that which prevails within the kin group. In such a society membership in a particular kinship group (and everyone in such a society belongs to one or another kin group) defines one's social identity, defines who one's friends and enemies are, assures one of access to resources (the kin group's resources), determines who one may not and who one may (or even ought to) marry, and so on. It is not always "share and share alike," but this ideal is often closely approximated and the ethic of collective, even corporate, responsibility and obligation is strong. The strength and character of the ties within the kin group can be illustrated by the fact that the kin group is not only responsible for the actions of its members but also responsible to its members should outsiders act against them. If a group member is killed or injured, the group is expected to seek whatever the locally defined appropriate redress is. And it will hold not only the offender but the offender's kin group responsible for giving this redress. In like manner, if a group member kills or injures someone, the group will both defend their member and be held responsible by the injured party's group—indeed, we might do better to say that the injured party is the victim's group rather than the individual. The strength of this internal group solidarity (at least as an ideal) can be seen by what happens when someone kills a member of his own kin group (presumably a rare occurrence). Frequently nothing happens. The kin group is both offender and offended, and although it may be obligated to seek an "eye for eye," it cannot easily act against itself and follow the injunction in St. Matthew to pluck out its own eye.

We may reduce social relations in such societies to their basics by noting that, from the perspective of any one kinship unit, there are three types of person one may encounter: ourselves (group members), those whom we marry, and strangers. Strangers are potential, often real, enemies unless some other type of relationship can be established. And even "those whom we marry" may at times be enemies also (this is certainly true on the Northwest Coast). If this is the "theory" of social categories of a kinship-based society (whether held by its members or anthropologists, or both), we can see why we do not expect to find slaves in such a society. For slaves are natally alienated and are members of no kin unit, yet they live in and are a part of the community.

Slavery as Antikinship

Slavery contradicts the idea and ethics of kinship relations, but the master/slave relation has often been seen as modeled on kinship relations. Marx and Engels, for example, identified "patriarchal" slavery with the patriarchal family, seeing the master's relationship as similar to and modeled on the father/husband's relationship with his wife and children in the earliest forms of slavery.[2] More recently, Igor Kopytoff and Suzanne Miers (1977, 7–12, 66–67) have also seen what is frequently termed "domestic" slavery in the Africanist literature as modeled on kinship relations. But I would insist that, as Paul Bohannan was one of the first to make clear, slavery negates kinship. In a general discussion of "servility," Bohannan noted,

> First of all, servile relationships are what we might call "antikinship" in analogy to antimatter. They are not merely *non*kinship (in analogy to nonmaterial), as are relationships based on contract or those established by rank. They are, rather, actively antikinship in that a slave can have no kinsmen and is connected with kinship groups by nonkinship criteria. (1963, 180; emphasis in original)

He goes on to point out that one of the clearest manifestations of the antikinship nature of slavery is the right of the master to break up elementary families of slaves.

If Bohannan is correct and slavery is not merely a nonkinship relation but an antikinship relation, then how and why could slavery flourish in kinship-based societies like those on the Northwest Coast? And flourish it did, as has been demonstrated in earlier chapters.

Dependent Labor on the Northwest Coast

Northwest Coast societies were divided into three classes (titleholder, commoner, slave). Kin groups were usually headed by titleholders, who managed the group's subsistence resources and other property. One of the principal activities of titleholders was the organization of ceremonial feasts and performances that were the focus of much attention in all Northwest Coast communities. To put on a successful feast considerable amounts of wealth—above ordinary subsistence requirements—were necessary. Titleholders managed their kin unit's resources and labor supply largely with the goal of feast-giving in mind. Titleholders gained the cooperation of commoners through the twin means of appeals to kinship reciprocity and kin group solidarity and through their control of access to the kin group's resource base. In spite of the ethic of kin group solidarity and reciprocity, this meant that commoners were to some extent dependent labor. Although kinship theory stresses egalitarian ideals of sharing and solidarity within the kinship unit, many kin-based societies contain elements of dependent labor, where ordinary group members work under the direction of the group's leader(s) at goals largely defined and determined by the leader.[3] In Northwest Coast communities there were two types of dependent labor: commoners and slaves. That both commoners and slaves were dependent labor should not be overlooked, but the differences in the kind of dependent labor involved are even more important.

Commoners labored for titleholders within a framework of kinship solidarity—a framework that both defines and exemplifies kinship relations and that, as Bohannan (1963, 181) points out, has a different basis from relationships founded on contractual arrangements, or on the rights of a person as a citizen of a state, or on the master/slave relationship. The dependence of commoners and the exploitation of their surplus by titleholders were masked by the ideology of kinship. As Drucker's Nuu-chah-nulth informants described it (1951, 272), commoners gave "help to the chief" and inferiors always "helped" superiors. Titleholders did exploit commoners, but not without offering significant returns—the ethic of sharing was real enough and commoners benefited by belonging to the kin group of a successful titleholder, sharing in his ceremonial or military successes, for example.

The dependent nature of slave labor is easier to see. In common with slavery everywhere, the slave's very life was dependent on the master. In addition, no one doubted the owner's right to all the produce of the slave's efforts. In the case of the master and the slave, the relationship was created neither by contract, nor by citizenship, nor by kinship, but by an act of forced natal alienation. To make someone a slave is not merely to deny but to destroy their kinship ties and hence their identity. This is particularly serious in a kin-based society where kinship relations predominate and indeed where there are no normal social relations outside of those created by kinship (and its extension affinity).

If someone in a traditional Northwest Coast community needed to mobilize the work of others, he (or less usually she) normally invoked kin relations and their attendant obligations. Titleholders were likely to have been able to mobilize larger numbers of workers for longer than commoners, but for everyone the kinship tie was both the basis of the request for labor and the reason for fulfilling the request. If calls to kin were not sufficient for someone's needs, there were no important nonkinship mechanisms for mobilizing labor in traditional Northwest Coast societies. Wage labor, for example, was absent. Slave owners had another source of labor power, one that was not constrained by the ethic and ideology of kinship. So slave owners had a third source of labor to add to their own labor and that of any commoner followers.

Northwest Coast Kin Unit Organization and Slavery

Northwest Coast kin units are typically described as being one of three types, which are found in three geographic blocs: in the north matrilineal descent groups (lineages, clans, and moieties) are described for the Tlingit, Haida, Tsimshian, and Haisla. A little south of these societies, the Kwakwaka'wakw, Nuu-chah-nulth, and perhaps the Nuxalk are described as having cognatic or nonunilineal descent groups (which resemble lineages but are not unilineal; Jorgensen [1980, 179] calls such units "demes"). Although cognatic, these units tended to have patrilateral biases. South of the central bloc, large- or even moderate-scale descent groups as such are usually thought to have been missing. In the southern part of the culture area groups are described as practicing bilateral "descent" and being organized into large, genealogically shallow, patrilaterally biased households.[4]

Kin unit leaders, usually titleholders, in all of these societies faced some similar problems, no matter which form of kin unit organization was found in their community. To maintain their status as titleholders each kin unit leader had to retain the unit's resource base, improve it if he could (all Northwest Coast kin unit heads seem to have been male, including the heads of matrilineal units), and compete successfully with his titleholder rivals in giving feasts that validated and demonstrated titles (names) and privileges. Exploiting the kin group's resource base, both for ordinary subsistence needs and to build up a surplus for feasting, required that the group's head maintain and manage an appropriate labor force. In the first instance, titleholders mobilized their fellow group members. The basis of such mobilization was kin group solidarity and an ethic of kinship obligation, sharing, and reciprocity plus the title-holder's control of access to the group's resources. Individualistic exploitation of resources was not the norm in any of these societies. The most important Northwest Coast resources tended to be localized and highly seasonal (salmon streams, for example, were exploited only during the annual spawning runs when the salmon returned to their natal streams after maturing in the ocean). Some seasons (the winter especially) were not particularly good for food production. Thus the need was not only to produce food but also to preserve it. Both production and preservation required considerable labor, so that labor procurement and management were an important part of a titleholder's activities. In some seasons and in some years titleholders probably needed much more labor for subsistence tasks than in others. In addition, if a titleholder planned to embark on a major feast, he might also need to add to his labor force to build up food and goods for the feast. One way to do this was to increase the size of one's kin unit. More commoners meant more workers.

Descent theorists have often argued that cognatic descent units are especially well designed for such tasks.[5] The advantage of cognatic kin units over unilineal ones is supposed to be that since large numbers of people have potential ties of group membership (through a variety of nonunilineal links), some of these ties can be activated when more members are needed or when an individual wishes to change to another group where opportunity or treatment seems likely to be better. Nonunilineal units are held to be more "flexible" and able to adjust to changing resource circumstances (or labor needs) more rapidly than unilineal units. Unfortunately, this argument overlooks the fact that unilineal kin units can also be flexible: units divide or amalgamate; individuals call on their father's matrikin unit for help (in most matrilineal societies an individual has a special relationship with his or her father's unit). There is the additional problem that the actual composition of a kin unit as a concrete unit performing tasks (examples of such activities include the members of the unit residing together or near each other, jointly performing subsistence tasks, or jointly performing rituals) is not a simple reflection of the locally prevailing descent ideology. Demographic and other variables affect who is actually living and/or cooperating with whom at any given time. Descent rules and other indigenous ideas about the way kin units ought to be composed and work are the vocabulary that people use to talk and think about the way they are organized, not empirical summaries of the actual composition of current kin units.[6]

In comparison with bilateral units or cognatic units, unilineal units have the clearest and most restrictive rules about who should and should not be a group member, but all types of kin units are capable of considerable flexibility with respect to actual group membership. In terms of flexibility, the difference is that unilineal groups, by invoking unilineal rules to recruit members, are in principle more restrictive in who can be a group member, thereby expressing a

greater concern with controlling group membership and a greater interest in
the exact determination of who should belong to what kin unit. Type of descent rule may be taken as one measure of the degree of concern in a society
with control over kin unit membership and control over persons. Unilineal rules
display the greatest concern, followed by cognatic rules. Societies with bilateral rules have the least interest in such controls, although this does not imply
a lack of interest in such matters, just less interest than in unilineal or cognatic
systems.

As stated, on the Northwest Coast we find strong unilineal systems (northern matriliny), cognatic systems (central demes or quasi-lineages), and relatively shallow bilateral systems (southern patricentric family households). The
north to south distribution of these types of kin units suggests that as we go
south in the culture area there is weaker concern with control over group membership and less concern with exactly where people belong. In a broad im-
pressionistic survey of the area's ecology and resource base, Suttles has suggested that, although the most critical food resources (fish, sea mammals) are
abundant throughout the culture area, in the north people could "rely on fewer
kinds of plants and animals and get them at fewer places and for shorter times
during the year, but in greater concentration, and with consequent greater
chance for failure" (1987, 40). David Riches (1979, 148–149) has concluded
from Suttles's characterization of these regional environmental trends that as
one moves from south to north in the area, the variety and amount of exploit-
able food plants declines and shellfish probably become more difficult to exploit, if not less important. This may mean, he suggests, that the direct subsistence contribution of women declines from south to north.[7] Riches (1979,
154, 158) treats the south to north increase in resource uncertainty as probable, if not conclusively demonstrated, and notes that the south to north shift
from bilateral to cognatic to matrilineal forms of kin group organization shows
increasing concern with "manpower" and its control. If there is an increasing
interest in the control of labor as one moves south to north in the region, one
would predict that slavery would be more important in terms of both the number and proportion of slaves and the elaboration of its practice.[8] This prediction seems borne out in a general way, although the Chinook stand out as a
southern group (the most southern in fact as the culture area is defined here)
with "northern" slavery.[9]

Another reason why there might have been an increasing interest in the
control of personnel from south to north has to do with preservation. If Suttles's characterization of resource concentration and dependability patterns are
accurate, the farther north in the region, the greater the need to preserve food
in periods of good supply. Given the usual Northwest Coast gender division
of labor, most of the work of preservation was done by women (and slaves),
so that not only did men become more important as hunters and fishers, but

women became more important because of their work in the preservation of the catch, especially since preservation of food such as salmon was probably often an even more important issue than production of food.[10] Since slaves could be employed at tasks regardless of gender appropriateness, their importance to titleholders would also increase farther north in the culture area. The use of slaves to threaten, bully, and even kill commoners also fits a pattern of an increasing need to control persons. The farther north in the region, the greater the need for titleholders to control commoners and the more useful slaves not subject to the ethics of kinship would be in assisting with such control. Once again, slaves seem to have been more frequently used as instruments of force in the familiar south to north pattern—with the usual exception of the Chinook who exhibit their familiar "northern" tendency.

Titleholder Hegemony and Slavery

In 1841 while at the Hudson's Bay Company post of Fort Stikine James Douglas wrote,

The wealth and consequence of all classes, stripling to the highest chieftains, are measured by the number of such dependents, who in many cases are kept for the mere purpose of display, are also exceeding useful as hunters and fishermen, while they constitute a bodyguard of generally faithful adherents, ready to protect their master or murder his enemies at the slightest intimation of his will without question or scruple. In fact, *Shakes the most influential Stiking* [Stikine] *chief, has no followers of his own tribe and merely a retinue of 24 slaves, who paddle his canoes, fish, hunt and perform for him every menial office, live under the same roof, and in short, uphold his cause with their ever ready swords and spears.*[11] (1841, 46; emphasis mine)

The preceding passage was analyzed in chapter 6 in the context of the importance of slave labor. Here we note the importance to Shakes of slaves as his principal body of followers, perhaps even his only close followers. For Shakes, at least at this time, slavery had virtually replaced kinship as a means of recruiting and holding dependents. Shakes's slaves are portrayed as loyal followers, whether they are doing his menial labor or his fighting. In this they do not seem to have been particularly unusual for the Northwest Coast as a whole for, as shown in chapter 4, slaves are known to have traveled with their masters, gone to war with them, and killed for them in a number of groups. Shakes's slaves were certainly not rewarded with immunity from all of the implications of slavery because of his lack of other types of immediate followers. For example, one of Shakes's slaves is said to have had slaves of his own and even his own canoe, but after he bragged that Shakes "could do nothing to him," he was killed during a ceremony (Olson 1967, 54).

Persons forced into slavery reacted in a variety of ways, although all were ashamed of their slave status. Slaves on the Northwest Coast were certainly dishonored persons, to use Orlando Patterson's phrase. Yet not all accepted their fate calmly or with resignation. As we have seen, some might hope for ransom, although only a few probably saw this hope fulfilled (most of these captives were certainly members of the titleholder class as commoners seem to have had little chance of ransom). Still others tried to escape, sometimes killing a master in the attempt, although probably only a few such attempts were ultimately successful. And we can see less overt protest in a variety of forms: the careless use of tools, lack of proper respect for the master, and so on. Indeed, some of the very traits that make up owners' stereotypes of slaves— lying, laziness, being childlike—might be seen as forms of covert resistance.

But it remains true that men like Shakes made long journeys in the company of slaves. And most of those enslaved lived out their lives as slaves without seriously challenging their status, either as individuals or in concert with other slaves. The lack of such reports is probably not due to poor data, for if one reads the literature on slavery from anywhere in the world, one is immediately struck by the rarity of genuine slave revolts. Slaves do not, as a rule, attempt to overthrow their masters. This seems a safe generalization about societies in which slavery is important, however else they may differ.[12]

Why was it that Northwest Coast slaves, however grudgingly, accepted their lot and never combined to end their common shame and servile position? A number of possible answers come to mind (or have been suggested by those with whom I have discussed this problem): slaves were mostly women or had been captured as children and were either too weak to revolt or had been brought up in slavery and thus accepted their status; the slaves in any community came from a variety of ethnic backgrounds and thus did not form a homogeneous group that would have fostered rebellion; slavers were not numerically important enough to stage a successful revolt; almost all slaves came from communities where slaves were present and so accepted that slavery was a part of their social world and that to be a slave was a shameful degradation that could not be overcome or set aside. Similar explanations have been offered for other societies. These and other reasons for the rarity of slave revolts either emphasize the practical difficulties of revolt or focus on the fact that both slaves and masters share the same values and expectations with respect to slavery, that is, that someone will be a slave and that to be a slave is a source of shame and a permanent social stigma.

It is certainly true that masters and slaves shared a common cultural framework. But such an "explanation" offers us no insight into how Northwest Coast societies worked, nor does it encourage us to explore how and why slavery was important in the area. We need a better answer than "shared values" to understand Douglas's observations about Shakes.

The Concept of Hegemony

To begin to understand the attitudes of masters and slaves toward slavery, I shall use ideas that originate in a context far removed from the late eighteenth-/early nineteenth-century Northwest Coast societies whose slave behavior I seek to explain. That context is twentieth-century Italy between the world wars, where Antonio Gramsci developed an interesting analysis of the problem of revolution in the Italian context. Gramsci meant his analysis to apply to twentieth-century states, particularly in Europe. These ideas have proved to be extremely fruitful when used in the analysis of modern societies (see, e.g., Williams 1977). Here Gramsci's ideas will be applied to societies that are still kinship based in essentials, although because of European intrusions onto the North Pacific Coast they were in transition and on the way to incorporation into states modeled on those of Europe by the middle third of the nineteenth century.[13]

Every society faces the problem of compliance. That is, at least some of the time, members must be induced to do things that do not immediately gratify their own ends and goals. There are two main ways of achieving compliance, termed by social scientists "social control" and "socialization"—useful, apparently neutral labels. Let us keep the dichotomy but use Gramscian terms, terms that introduce a more helpful emphasis for the problem here.

As Gramsci observes, the state is ultimately founded on "force," or "coercion." Force or coercion is not a free-floating entity but has a source. It operates to serve a particular set of interests—those of the ruling class. Thus we can speak of *domination*, identifying the class aspects of "social control."

But states do not run on domination alone. Anyone who thinks so is in danger of producing caricature or worse. Compliance is also produced by "consent." In the last analysis, domination will always underlie the power of the ruling class, but on a day-to-day basis consent rather than domination is the most visible means of compliance. And consent should not be dismissed as a mere disguise for, or mask of, compliance. Although domination may be the last resort of the ruling class, consent is not thereby of trivial importance. This is especially so if we recognize that consent, like coercion, is not a free-floating entity. It, too, has a source and operates to serve a particular set of interests—those of the ruling class. Thus I will speak of *hegemony*, identifying the class aspects of "socialization."

To expand briefly on the notion of hegemony: hegemony is predominance obtained by consent rather than by force. Hegemony is the exercise of intellectual leadership by a particular class. The ideas and values of that class define the cultural scene in a society. A crucial part of this definition is that the ruling class's view of the world, especially of the social world and how it works, is accepted by most members of the society as correct. And not sim-

ply correct as in "proper" or "moral" (although these too), but correct as interpretation of what the world is like. For Gramsci, hegemony is rooted in economic power: it is not simply the persuasiveness of a group's ideas but the
union of economic control and intellectual leadership that produces a ruling
class in secure control of a society.

Gramsci developed the notions of domination and hegemony to help analyze class societies, politically organized as states. The Northwest Coast societies to which his ideas are being applied were certainly not states. There was
no political integration above the local community level. Indeed, in some parts
of the region even the winter village was probably not politically unified, being
merely a coresidential set of descent groups. Gramsci's ideas are relevant because of the presence of class in most, probably all, Northwest Coast societies.

The Exercise of Hegemony by Titleholders

On the Northwest Coast, titleholders clearly exercised domination over their
slaves. Slaves were the product of violence, and beating or death were ever-
present threats. But, I argue, titleholders also exercised hegemony over their
slaves (and over commoners).[14]

All, or virtually all, of the slaves in any Northwest Coast community came
from communities where slaves were a basic part of the social order and *accepted* as such. Indeed, some slaves had been of the slave-owning class themselves. Slaves often regarded their personal status as slaves as a misfortune
but did not conceive of slavery as inequity. To become a slave was a personal,
shaming event, which also reflected badly on one's kin. But slaves were a part
of the natural social order. The degraded do not join hands with other degraded beings to throw the high from their places—especially when they accept without question that slavery is degrading, shameful. Slaves may individually escape from the psychology of slavery (which prefers slavery to
freedom) and still there are no slave revolts, because the social order remains
unchallenged. Thus it is not a particular slave's or group of slaves' acquies-
cence to slavery that explains the lack of slave revolts. It is the acceptance of
slavery as a natural part of society.

Sometimes the stain of slavery could be removed, or at least almost removed. But killing a master would not accomplish this, nor would escape.
Only the appropriate ritual feast and property presentations might accomplish
removal of the stigma. And such rituals are set firmly within a cultural order
based on titleholders/commoners/slaves. What distinguishes my argument
from the "shared cultural values" argument is that the concept of hegemony
makes it clear that the interpretation of events and social life shared by both
master and slaves was not "objective" or "neutral" but served the purposes of
the dominant, slaveholding class. Hegemony as much as domination enabled
Shakes to prowl the waters around Stikine with a force of slaves and no kin

close at hand to support him against them. It is doubtful if any Northwest Coast slave dreamed of a "world turned upside down," even when he or she wished personally to escape slavery.

The Place of Slavery in Northwest Coast Culture

In many respects the Northwest Coast culture area was quite different from the rest of Native North America. Kroeber emphasized the region's distinctiveness in his 1923 article "American Culture and the Northwest Coast," explaining the culture area's unusual character by the relative absence of traits he believed had diffused to most of the rest of Native North America from Middle America and by the presence of locally innovated traits that had diffused even to the culture area's close neighbors to only a "modest degree." Central to these differentiating local traits were what he described as "a formidable and distinctive economic complex" that included "the so-called caste stratification . . . , the extensive development of slavery as a property institution, the prestige attaching to wealth, the potlatch and credit system" (1923, 14).

In this book I have documented, described, and analyzed the "extensive development of slavery" not only as a property institution but also as an important part of Northwest Coast social, political, and ritual life. In this concluding section I will highlight the main conclusions presented in the preceding chapters and argue that Kroeber was correct about the central contribution of slavery to Northwest Coast culture as classically described.

There were a variety of servile statuses in aboriginal North America, but this status appears to have been different on the Northwest Coast. Slavery was permanent across generations and more stigmatizing and shaming, and slaves played a greater role in both the economy and the ritual system than elsewhere on the continent.

Slavery was unquestionably aboriginal and ancient on the Northwest Coast, where it probably developed as a local innovation sometime between 500 B.C. and A.D. 500 in conjunction with other traits that were also a part of the distinctive Northwest Coast culture complex. The practice of slavery changed considerably after European contact. It may even have intensified as titleholders became involved in the fur trade and used slaves more and more in their increased struggles with other titleholders for prestige and position. Titleholders used slaves as workers, followers, and especially as trade items in a growing slave trade network that paralleled fur trade activity until the last half of the nineteenth century, when the coastal fur trade collapsed and increasing European political control and settlement gradually ended both native independence and practices such as slavery.

Slaves played an important role in the traditional Northwest Coast economies. Their labor often contributed significantly to the productive capacity of the kin units that owned them. The direct economic benefits of slaveholding probably accrued largely to the titleholders who headed and managed their descent groups. Slave labor allowed them more free time for leisure, ceremonial activity, and other aspects of the titleholder style of life. At the same time slaves also contributed to the prestige of their owners: slave ownership may well have been one of the clearest signs of titleholder success. Slaves supported the ritual system by laboring to supply significant portions of the food and goods that were consumed or given away at important feasts; slaves were themselves among the most important items of value presented to rivals and witnesses at such feasts, and as ritual victims slaves demonstrated the power and capacity of their masters to take human life.

The Northwest Coast cultures are among anthropology's classic cases. Virtually every student of anthropology knows a little about the potlatch. Many others have heard of totem poles and have seen at least a few works of Northwest Coast art. One of the things that fascinates anthropologists about the traditional Northwest Coast cultures is that they are in so many ways typical of small-scale societies (what were once commonly called tribal or primitive societies) and yet they have some features that surprise and seem to contradict most generalizations and clichés about such societies: they are not egalitarian (their members are greatly concerned with rank and the privileges of rank; they practice slavery); they are greatly concerned with possessions and property (almost anything, corporeal or noncorporeal, could be and was owned); they built an elaborate material, social, and mental culture on a hunting-gathering-fishing subsistence base. That the Northwest Coast peoples could build their cultures on an extractive subsistence base causes less surprise than it once did, although they remain the principal ethnographic exception to almost all generalizations about "hunter-gatherers."

The presence of classes or at least of classlike ranked social strata is also unexpected. Classes are generally held to be found only in state societies, but on the Northwest Coast it is difficult to argue that there were any political institutions that united different communities—and even many communities may not have been political units in the usual sense. Northwest Coast titleholders are typically called "chiefs," but these individuals held names and positions in their kin units and did not really hold political office, lacking multicommunity and often even community authority—hence Kroeber's remark that in the culture area we find "privileges and honors, but not office; a status of influence, but no constituted authority" (1923, 9).

Kinship-based societies often lack political office and multicommunity political integration, but class and slavery contradict kinship as the ideological basis of social relations and contradict the lack of political integration. The great interest in possession, property, and ownership contradicts the communal views usually found in such societies, even while many other ideas and attitudes on the Northwest Coast were typical. There was no lack of contradiction, or at least apparent contradiction, in Northwest Coast cultures, yet these cultures flourished until massive outside intervention unraveled them.

When anthropologists and other outsiders think of traditional Northwest Coast cultures, some of the first things that come to mind are the rich artistic traditions, the impressive wooden houses, the potlatches, and the rich, dramatic ceremonies and performances that accompanied potlatches. All such spectacular features of these cultures were central to the seeking and reaffirmation of prestige by titleholders. Titleholders were able to undertake prestige-producing activities because they could control and manage resources and labor to produce the food and other goods and free the time needed for such activities. Fundamental to this control was the interest in possession and the notion that anything could be a possession. The concern with rank and privilege and the interest in possessions are linked. Possession could be obtained by inheritance, acquired by exchanges in the context of relationships with other titleholders, or taken by force. It is important to remember that even noncorporeal property—the right to sing a particular song, to perform a given dance, to display a certain visual representation of a supernatural being—could be obtained by killing the previous owner and thus claiming his prerogatives. The practice of slavery in the region was consistent with and a part of the intensive interest in possession: if salmon streams, clover beds, songs, dances, images, and names could be property, so could human beings.

Slaves were not a part of the system of ranking and prestige seeking in that they did not receive even the benefits that a kin unit's commoners received if a titleholder had success and they had no community standing in the eyes of the free. But they were not peripheral to Northwest Coast culture. They were present in all traditional Northwest Coast communities and carried out their prescribed tasks in these communities and in myths and tales where their appearance is as unremarkable as that of supernatural beings. They were also repositories and emblems of value: the slave's labor and its products could be completely controlled by the master, allowing titleholders an avenue other than kinship or relations with fellow titleholders to build wealth; to own a human being itself built one's prestige; to kill a slave destroyed the most valuable property and a human life—a double payoff for the titleholder who could do so. Because of the multifaceted contribution that slaves made to titleholders, because of their regular appearance in both daily community life and in myths and tales, we can see that slavery was thoroughly integrated into Northwest Coast culture. I would go further and argue that slavery was essential to Northwest Coast culture as classically observed, because only slaves made it possible for titleholders—the exemplars of Northwest Coast culture—to live and act as titleholders. In a sense MacLeod (1928, 650) was correct in suggesting that slavery was as important to Northwest Coast culture as it was to antebellum southern U.S. culture: in both areas what best and most typically represents these cultures are the lives, actions, and values of their elites, and in both regions the elites built their lives on slavery.

I believe that the material presented in this book substantiates the claims in the last paragraph that slavery was both well integrated into Northwest Coast culture and that without slavery other fundamental aspects of the culture of the region would have been much different. The core institutions, values, and traits of the region hang together as a package and that package includes slavery. But two other questions remain unanswered: Why did slavery arise on the Northwest Coast, and how does Northwest Coast slavery compare with slavery elsewhere in the world? Except for a few brief glances, I have not considered slavery elsewhere. This is because there is no general "theory of slavery" within which to frame such comparisons. I agree with Claude Meillassoux (1991, 21–22) who implied that in the absence of such a theory, comparisons of slave systems in different parts of the world and at different epochs requires a detailed knowledge of all the regions being compared. Because there is no theory of slavery, an explanation of the origins of Northwest Coast slavery must be historical, not theoretical. Slavery probably developed in the culture area long before we have any detailed knowledge of the region. Although archaeology, historical linguistics, and historical reconstruction will certainly provide us with more detail about this period of North Pacific Coast history, we are unlikely to discover enough ever to have a fully convincing history of the origins of Northwest Coast culture, including slavery.

Some of the readers of this book will not accept my claims that slavery was fundamental to Northwest Coast culture as practiced; some will even find the claim shocking and odious. In anthropology, particularly when dealing with historical subjects, one cannot "prove" such assertions by doing the equivalent of a chemistry experiment, although I think that the evidence presented in chapters 4 through 12 makes my case a strong one. To skeptics in particular I propose that when we consider the place of slavery in Northwest Coast culture, perhaps the final word should be an image, carved by a now-anonymous Kwakwaka'wakw artist: the reader is invited to look again at figure 2, "Chief carried on the back of a slave."

Tribal Unit Sample Codings on Slavery Variables

Table A-1. *Conformity to Definitional Criteria of Northwest Coast "Slaves," Tribal Unit Sample*

Group	Dispose	Destroy	Use	Inherit: Heir	Inherit: Child Is Slave	Permanent	Violence	Natal Alienation	Stigma
Yakutat	Y	Y	Y	P	Y	Y	Y	P	Y
Chilkat	Y	Y	Y	P	P	Y	Y	P	Y
Sitka	Y	Y	Y	Y	Y	Y	Y	P[a]	Y
Stikine	Y	Y	Y	P	Y	Y	Y	P	Y
Haida	Y	Y	Y	Y	Y	Y	Y	P[a]	Y
Lower Skeena Tsimshian	Y	Y	Y	P	P	Y	Y	P	Y
Nuxalk	Y	Y	Y	Y	Y	Y	Y	Y	Y
Fort Rupert Kwakiutl	Y	Y	P	?	P	Y	Y	?	Y
Mowachaht	Y	Y	Y	P	P	Y	Y	?	P
Clayoquot	Y	Y	P	P	P	Y	Y	?	P
Makah	Y	Y	Y	?	Y	Y	Y	P	Y
Saanich	Y	P	Y	Y	Y	Y	Y	Y	Y
Klallam	Y	?	Y	?	Y	Y	Y	?	A
Lummi	Y	?	Y	P	?	Y	Y	?	Y
Skagit	Y	?	P	?	Y	Y	Y	P	Y
Puyallup-Nisqually	Y	Y	Y	Y	P	Y	Y	?	Y
Twana	Y	Y	Y	Y	Y	Y	Y	Y	Y
Quileute	Y	Y	Y	P	P	Y	Y	P	Y
Quinault	Y	P	Y	P	Y	A	Y	?	Y
Chinook	Y	Y	Y	P	P	A	Y	P	Y

NOTES:
   Y = yes; P = probable, inference or based on generalized source or source for nearly identical nonsample neighboring group; A = ambiguous; ? = missing information.
   [a]Ransom by consanguines in captor's group sometimes occurred.

313

Table A-2.   External Signs of Slave Status, Tribal Unit Sample

Group	Degrading Burial	Poor Sleeping Quarters	Can "Marry" Slave	Can "Marry" Free	Labret	Cranial Shaping	Short Hair	Slave Names
Yakutat	Y	Y	Y	?	?	X	?	?
Chilkat	Y	?	Y	N	N	X	?	?
Sitka	Y	?	?	?	PN	X	?	?
Stikine	Y	?	PY	?	PN	X	?	?
Haida	A	Y	Y	N	?	X	?	?
Lower Skeena Tsimshian	Y	Y	Y	N	PN	X	PY	?
Nuxalk	N	?	Y	L	X	?	?	?
Fort Rupert Kwakiutl	Y	?	Y	N	X	?	?	?
Mowachaht	Y	?	Y	?	X	PY	Y	PY
Clayoquot	N	?	Y	?	X	PY	PY	PY
Makah	Y	?	Y	N/L	X	?	?	?
Saanich	N	?	Y	L	X	A	PY	Y
Klallam	?	Y	Y	L	X	N	PY	?
Lummi	?	?	Y	?	X	?	Y	?
Skagit	?	?	Y	N/L	X	?	?	?
Puyallup-Nisqually	?	Y	?	L	Y	N	N	?
Twana	Y	?	Y	N	X	?	Y	Y
Quileute	?	?	?	L	X	?	?	?
Quinault	Y	?	Y	L	X	A	?	Y
Chinook	Y	Y	Y	N/L	X	N	?	Y

NOTE:

Y = present; N = absent; P = probable, inference or based on generalized source or source for nearly identical nonsample neighboring group; A = ambiguous; X = trait not practiced; L = late in slavery period; ? = missing information.

Table A-3.   Demographic Characteristics of Slaves, Tribal Unit Sample

Group	Preference for Women and Children as Slaves	Sex Ratio of Slaves Identified in Sources	Sex Ratio of Slaves in Census	Titleholders Enslaved
Yakutat	Y	63	104	?
Chilkat	?	20	117	?
Sitka	Y	80	98	Y
Stikine	?	18	69	Y
Lower Skeena Tsimshian	Y	65	?	Y
Haida	Y	80	100	Y
Nuxalk	Y	75	?	Y
Fort Rupert Kwakiutl	Y	100	?	?
Mowachaht	Y	77	?	Y
Clayoquot	Y	125	?	Y
Makah	?	77	?	Y
Saanich	Y	43	?	Y
Klallam	Y	33	?	?
Lummi	Y	100	?	?
Skagit	?	200	?	?
Puyallup-Nisqually	Y	33	?	Y
Twana	?	75	?	?
Quileute	Y	120	?	Y
Quinault	?	90	?	Y
Chinook	Y	66	143	Y

NOTE: Y = present; ? = missing information.

Table A-4.   Slave Behavior, Tribal Unit Sample

Group	Slaves Attempt Escape	Slaves Travel with Masters	Slaves Accompany to War	Slaves Kill for Masters	Slaves Kill Masters	Minor Rebellions
Yakutat	Y	Y	?	?	?	Y
Chilkat	?	Y	Y	Y	?	?
Sitka	Y	Y	?	?	?	Y
Stikine	Y	Y	Y	Y	?	?
Lower Skeena Tsimshian	Y	Y	?	Y	?	Y
Haida	Y	Y	Y	?	Y	?
Nuxalk	Y	?	Y	?	Y	Y
Fort Rupert Kwakiutl	?	Y	Y	Y	Y	?
Mowachaht	P	Y	Y	Y	?	Y
Clayoquot	P	Y	?	?	?	?
Makah	Y	?	Y	Y	Y	Y
Saanich	Y	?	N	?	?	?
Klallam	Y	?	?	?	?	?
Lummi	Y	?	?	?	Y	?
Skagit	Y	?	?	?	?	?
Puyallup-Nisqually	N	Y	?	?	?	?
Twana	Y	?	?	?	?	?
Quileute	?	Y	Y	?	?	?
Quinault	?	Y	?	Y	?	Y
Chinook	?	Y	Y	Y	?	Y

NOTE: Y = present; N = absent; P = probable, inference or based on generalized source or source for nearly identical nonsample neighboring group; A = ambiguous; ? = missing information.

Table A-5. Conditions after Slavery, Tribal Unit Sample

Group	Ransom Attempted	Stigma After Return	Cleansing Ceremony	Property Given Away
Yakutat	Y	Y	P	P
Chilkat	P	Y	Y	Y
Sitka	Y	Y	P	P
Stikine	Y	Y	P	P
Lower Skeena Tsimshian	Y	Y	Y	Y
Haida	Y	Y	?	Y
Nuxalk	Y	Y	Y	Y
Fort Rupert Kwakiutl	Y	Y	Y	Y
Mowachaht	Y	P	?	Y
Clayoquot	Y	P	?	Y
Makah	Y	Y	?	P
Saanich	Y	Y	?	P
Klallam	Y	A	?	?
Lummi	Y	Y	?	P
Skagit	Y	Y	?	?
Puyallup- Nisqually	Y	Y	?	?
Twana	Y	Y	?	Y
Quileute	P	Y	?	?
Quinault	Y	Y	?	?
Chinook	P	Y	?	?

NOTE: Y = present; P = probable, inference or based on generalized source or source for nearly identical nonsample neighboring group; A = ambiguous; ? = missing information.

Table A-6.   Subsistence Tasks of Slaves, Tribal Unit Sample

	Subsistence Task					
Group	Pick Berries	Collect Shellfish	Dig Roots	Fish	Hunt	Preserve Food
Yakutat	?	?	?	?	?	Y
Chilkat	Y	Y	Y	Y	Y	Y
Sitka	Y	?	?	Y	?	?
Stikine	?	Y	?	Y	Y	?
Lower Skeena Tsimshian	?	?	?	Y	?	Y
Haida	?	?	?	Y	?	?
Nuxalk	?	?	?	Y	Y	?
Fort Rupert Kwakiutl	PY	?	PY	?	Y	?
Mowachaht	Y	?	?	Y	?	PY
Clayoquot	PY	?	?	?	?	PY
Makah	?	?	?	Y	?	Y
Saanich	Y	Y	Y	Y	Y	Y
Klallam	Y	Y	Y	Y	?	?
Lummi	?	?	?	?	?	?
Skagit	?	?	?	?	?	?
Puyallup-Nisqually	?	?	?	?	?	?
Twana	Y	?	Y	Y	Y	Y
Quileute	?	Y	Y	?	?	Y
Quinault	Y	?	Y	Y	Y	?
Chinook	?	Y	Y	Y	Y	?

NOTE: Y = yes; N = no; P = probable, inference or based on generalized source or source for nearly identical nonsample neighboring group; ? = missing information.

Table A-7. Household Tasks of Slaves, Tribal Unit Sample

Group	Carry Water	Child Care	Cook	Fetch Wood	House Servant	Serve Food
			Household Task			
Yakutat	Y	Y	?	Y	Y	?
Chilkat	Y	Y	Y	Y	Y	Y
Sitka	?	PY	?	Y	?	Y
Stikine	?	?	?	?	Y	?
Lower Skeena Tsimshian	?	Y	Y	Y	Y	Y
Haida	Y	Y	Y	Y	Y	Y
Nuxalk	Y	?	?	Y	?	Y
Fort Rupert Kwakiutl	PY	?	PY	PY	Y	PY
Mowachaht	Y	?	Y	Y	?	PY
Clayoquot	PY	?	?	PY	?	PY
Makah	Y	?	?	Y	?	?
Saanich	?	?	Y	Y	Y	?
Klallam	Y	?	?	Y	Y	?
Lummi	?	?	?	?	?	?
Skagit	?	?	?	?	?	?
Puyallup-Nisqually	?	?	?	?	Y	?
Twana	Y	Y	Y	Y	?	Y
Quileute	?	?	?	Y	?	?
Quinault	Y	?	Y	Y	?	?
Chinook	Y	?	?	Y	?	?

NOTE: Y = yes; N = no; P = probable, inference or based on generalized source or source for nearly identical nonsample neighboring group; ? = missing information.

Table A-8.   Miscellaneous Tasks of Slaves, Tribal Unit Sample

	Task					
Group	Accompany on Travels	Carry Burdens	Go on Raids	Lookout/ Watchman	Messenger	Paddle Canoes
Yakutat	?	Y	?	?	?	?
Chilkat	Y	Y	?	Y	Y	Y
Sitka	?	Y	Y	?	Y	?
Stikine	?	Y	Y	?	Y	Y
Lower Skeena Tsimshian	?	Y	?	Y	Y	Y
Haida	?	Y	Y	?	?	Y
Nuxalk	?	?	Y	?	?	?
Fort Rupert Kwakiutl	Y	?	PY	?	PY	Y
Mowachaht	Y	?	Y	?	PY	PY
Clayoquot	?	?	?	?	PY	Y
Makah	?	?	Y	?	?	?
Saanich	?	?	?	?	?	Y[a]
Klallam	?	?	?	?	?	?
Lummi	?	?	?	?	?	?
Skagit	?	?	?	?	?	?
Puyallup- Nisqually	?	?	?	?	?	?
Twana	?	?	?	?	?	?
Quileute	?	Y	Y	?	?	?
Quinault	?	?	?	?	?	?
Chinook	?	?	?	?	?	Y

NOTES:
    Y = yes; N = no; P = probable, inference or based on generalized source or source for nearly identical nonsample neighboring group; ? = missing information.
    [a]But not on ceremonial occasions or in war.

Table A-9.   *The Use of Slaves in Ceremonies, Tribal Unit Sample*

Group	Title-holder's Funeral	New House	New Pole	Name Taking	Cannibal Initiation/ Dance	Peace Ceremony	Girl's Puberty Ceremony	"Pot-latches"
Yakutat	K/F	K	?	F	X	G	?	K/F
Chilkat	K/F	K	K	?	X	G	(F)	K/F/G
Sitka	K/F	K	?	(K)	X	?	?	K/F/G
Stikine	K	K/(G)	K	K/F	X	K	?	K/F/G
Haida	K/F	K	K	G	K	K/G	?	K/F/G
Lower Skeena Tsimshian	K/F/G	K	K/F/G	(K)/G	K	G	(K/G)	K/G
Nuxalk	K/F	N	?	?	K	?	?	G
Fort Rupert Kwakiutl	K/F	(K/G)	(K/G)	(K)	K	K	?	K/(G)
Mowachaht	(K/F/G)	?	?	?	K	?	?	K/G
Clayoquot	SK/SF	?	?	K	K	?	?	(G)
Makah	K	?	?	?	?	?	?	?
Saanich	?[a]	?	?	?	X	?	?	?[a]
Klallam	?[a]	?	?	?	X	?	?	?[a]
Lummi	?[a]	?	?	?	X	?	?	?[a]
Skagit	?[a]	?	?	?	X	?	?	?
Puyallup-Nisqually	K	?	?	?	X	?	?	?
Twana	N	N	N	N	X	?	?	?
Quileute	SK	?	?	?	X	?	?	?
Quinault	SK	?	?	?	X	?	?	?
Chinook	K	?	?	?	X	G	?	?

NOTES:

F = freed; G = given away; K = killed; N = no; S = sometimes; X = ceremony absent; ? = missing information; / = or; ( ) = strong inference.

[a]But neighboring group in same linguistic grouping did practice this trait.

Tribal Unit Sample
Identification and References

Note: In many places in the text, especially in the tables showing the coding of variables, exact references for groups in the tribal unit sample are not cited. The following list gives the sources of information about slavery for each member of the tribal unit sample.

CHILKAT: Four Northern Tlingit-speaking winter villages at the north end of Lynn Canal. The principal ethnography is Oberg 1973.

Slavery sources: Crosby 1914; De Laguna 1972; Drucker 1950; Glave 1892a, 1892b; Howay 1930b; Jones 1914; McClellan 1950, 1975; Muir 1915; Oberg 1943, 1973; Olson 1967; Petroff 1900; Schwatka 1893; Shotridge 1921, 1928; Wood 1882; Young 1915.

CHINOOK: Often called the Lower Chinook. As used here the term encompasses the numerous villages of Chinookan speakers who lived along the Columbia River and the mouths of its tributaries from the Willamette River west to the Pacific Ocean. There was certainly pre- and early contact variation among these communities, but neither the historical nor the ethnographic sources allow systematic distinctions. The best overall treatment, though brief, is Silverstein 1990.

Slavery sources: Bishop 1967; Boas 1894, 1901; Clarke 1905; Colvocoresses 1852; Connolly 1824–1825; Corney 1965; Cox 1957; Dennis 1930; DeSmet 1847; Dunn 1844; Gary 1923; Jacobs 1959; Kane 1855; Kennedy 1824–1825; Lee and Frost 1968; Lockley 1928; McLoughlin 1941; Merk 1931; Parker 1967; Powers 1902; Ray 1938; Rollins 1935; Ross 1969; Ruby and Brown 1976; Santee 1932; Schoolcraft 1853; Scouler 1905; Slacum 1912; Smith 1901; Strong 1893; Swan [1857] 1956; Willoughby 1886; Work 1842–1844; Wyeth [1833] 1970.

CLAYOQUOT: An early postcontact amalgamation of a number of Nootkan-speaking groups on Kennedy Lake and Clayoquot Sound, Vancouver Island. The principal ethnographic account is Drucker 1951.

Slavery sources: Brabant 1900; Colnett 1940; Curtis 1916; *Daily British Colonist* (16 September 1865); Deveraux 1890–1896; Drucker 1950, 1951; Howay 1941; Jacobsen [1884] 1977; Jewitt 1974; Johansen 1960; Koppert 1930a, 1930b; Mooney n.d.; Powell n.d.; Sapir and Swadesh 1955; Sproat 1868.

FORT RUPERT KWAKIUTL: Originally four winter villages of Kwakwala speakers who resided together in historic times near the Hudson's Bay Company post at Fort Rupert on northeastern Vancouver Island. Although Franz Boas collected and published a voluminous amount of ethnographic material on the "Fort Ruperts," he produced no comprehensive ethnographic account. The closest such accounts are Boas 1966 and Curtis 1915.

Slavery sources: Boas 1892, 1895a, 1896–1933, 1897, 1916–1931, 1921, 1935, 1966; Curtis 1915; *Daily British Colonist* 1858–1890; Drucker 1950; Healey n.d.; Helmcken 1975; Hunt 1926–1928; Jacobsen [1884] 1977; Mayne 1862; Moffat 1857–1867; Poole 1872; Tolmie 1963.

HAIDA: There were at least twenty traditional Haida winter villages. Most were on the Queen Charlotte Islands, although at least three were on the southern portion of Prince of Wales Island. There were six, later four, dialectical and geographic groupings of Haida villages. There were cultural differences at least at this grouping level, but only a few can be reconstructed on the basis of available information. There is no single dominant ethnographic account. The most important is probably Swanton 1905, although Dawson 1880 and Curtis 1916 are also important.

Slavery sources: Barbeau 1950; Bishop 1967; Boas 1892, 1896–1933, 1916, 1916–1931, 1932; Chittenden 1884; *Church Missionary Intelligencer* 1856–1885; Collison 1915; Crosby 1914; Curtis 1916; *Daily British Colonist* 1858–1890; Dawson 1880; Douglas 1840; Drucker 1950; Fleurieu 1801; Fort Simpson Journal 1834–1838, 1838–1840, 1852–1853, 1855–1859; Fort Simpson (Nass) Journal 1840; Fort Stikine Journal 1840–1842; Garfield 1939; Hamilton Log 1809–1819; Harrison 1925; Howay 1941; Ingraham 1971; Jackman 1978; Lopatin 1945; Martin 1849; Morison 1920; Oberg 1943; Parker 1967; Petroff 1900; Poole 1872; Reynolds 1970; Sanger 1970; Simpson 1831–1832; Storie et al. 1973a, 1973b, 1973c; Swanton 1905; Teit 1906; Work 1842–1843, 1842–1844, 1843, 1844, 1945; Wrangel 1965; Young 1927.

KLALLAM: The Klallam spoke a Salish language and occupied about a dozen winter villages along the southern shore of the Strait of Juan de Fuca from the Hoko River to Port Discovery Bay. The most important ethnographic source is Gunther 1927.

Slavery sources: Brown n.d.; Elmendorf 1960; Fort Langley Journal 1827–1830; Grant 1857; Gunther 1925, 1927; Haeberlin and Gunther 1930; Martin 1849; Schoolcraft 1856; Simpson 1830; Suttles 1958, 1974; Vancouver [1798] 1967.

LOWER SKEENA TSIMSHIAN: There were ten Coast Tsimshian-speaking winter villages on the lower Skeena River below the Skeena River canyon. The major ethnographic sources are Garfield 1939 and Boas 1916.

Slavery sources: Barbeau 1940, 1950; Boas 1912, 1916; Boas et al. 1923; *Church Missionary Intelligencer* 1856–1885; Collison 1915; Crosby 1914; *Daily British Colonist* 1858–1890; Drucker 1950; Dunn 1844; Fort Simpson Journal 1834–1838, 1838–1840, 1841–1842, 1852–1853, 1855–1859, 1859–1862, 1863–1866; Garfield 1939, 1951; Jackson 1880; MacFie 1865; McIlwraith 1948; Martin 1849; Moeller 1966; Swanton 1905; Work 1842–1843, 1945.

LUMMI: These are Straits Salish speakers who occupied two principal winter villages in the San Juan Islands. The major ethnographic source is Stern 1934.

Slavery sources: Schoolcraft 1856; Stern 1934; Suttles 1958, 1974.

MAKAH: The Makah speak a Wakashan language closely related to Nootka. In precontact times they occupied five winter villages in the vicinity of Cape Flattery on the southern side of the entrance to the Strait of Juan de Fuca. There is no overall traditional ethnography. Swan 1869 is perhaps the most useful single source. Colson 1953 is excellent but focuses primarily on reservation life in the 1940s.

Slavery sources: Bishop 1967; Colson 1953; Curtis 1913, 1916; Densmore 1924; Drucker 1951; Gunther 1942; Holmberg 1985; Irvine 1921; Jacobsen [1884] 1977; Jewitt [1815] 1975; Johansen 1960; Kane 1971; Kenyon 1975; Olson 1936; Owens 1985; Reynolds 1970; Sapir and Swadesh 1955; Scouler 1841, 1905; Singh 1966; Sproat 1868; Swan 1869; Wagner 1933.

MOWACHAHT: The Mowachaht are most frequently encountered in the ethnographic literature as Moachat. Two Nootkan-speaking winter villages resided together at a single summer village. They were located in Nootka Sound, Vancouver Island, which was Capt. James Cook's first landfall on the North Pacific Coast of North America and the first focal point of European activity in the area, resulting in a rich eighteenth-century historical record. The principal ethnographic account is Drucker 1951.

Slavery sources: Beaglehole 1967; Bell 1914; Brabant 1900; Cook 1973; Curtis 1916; Drucker 1951; Jacobsen [1884] 1977; Jewitt [1815] 1975; Meares [1790] 1967, 1933; Moser 1926; Moziño 1970; Sales 1956; Sproat 1868; Wagner 1933; Walker 1982.

NUXALK: The Nuxalk are known in the historical and ethnographic literature as the Bella Coola. There were certainly over twenty traditional Nuxalk winter villages in the Bella Coola River valley and nearby South and North Bentick Arm and Dean Channel. Their inhabitants spoke a Salish language usually termed Bella Coola. The principal ethnographic source is McIlwraith 1948.

Slavery sources: Boas 1892, 1898–1933; Drucker 1950; Fort Simpson Journal 1852–1853; Kopas 1970; McIlwraith 1922–1924, 1948; Mackenzie 1931; Tolmie 1963.

PUYALLUP-NISQUALLY: These speakers of Southern Lushootseed occupied winter villages at the mouths of the Puyallup and Nisqually rivers north and south of what is now Tacoma, Washington. The principal ethnographic source is Smith 1940.

Slavery sources: Haeberlin and Gunther 1930; Kane 1971; Martin 1849; Ray 1938; Schoolcraft 1856; Smith 1940.

QUILEUTE: The Quileute spoke a Chimakuan language and occupied several winter villages on the Quillayute and Hoh rivers on the western coast of Washington State. The most important ethnographic source is Curtis 1913.

Slavery sources: Andrade 1928, 1931; Curtis 1913; Farrand 1897, 1919; Frachtenberg 1921; Indian Claims Commission 1958b; Owens 1985; Pettit 1950; Ray 1938; Reagan 1929; Reagan and Walters 1933; Singh 1966.

QUINAULT: The Quinault spoke a Salish language and occupied a number of winter villages on the Queets, Quinault, and Copalis rivers on the central Pacific coast of Washington State. The major ethnographic source is Olson 1936.

Slavery sources: Bishop 1967; Curtis 1913; Dennis 1930; Farrand 1897; Farrand and Kahnweiler 1902; Indian Claims Commission 1958a, 1958c; Olson 1936; Sapir and Swadesh 1955; Singh 1966; Swan [1857] 1956.

SAANICH: These Straits Salish speakers had three principal winter villages on the Saanich Peninsula on the southeastern tip of Vancouver Island. Unfortunately unpublished, the principal ethnographic account is Jenness n.d. (written 1935).

Slavery sources: Barnett 1939, 1955; Jenness n.d.; Suttles 1958, 1974.

SITKA: These Northern Tlingit speakers occupied a winter village on Baranof Island. The Russians built a fort and settlement there in 1799 and rebuilt it as Novo-Arkhangel'sk in 1804 after the Sitka and their allies destroyed it. This was the principal Russian base in Tlingit country. The principal ethnography is Krause 1956 (originally published in 1885).

Slavery sources: Beardslee 1882; Belcher 1843; Boas 1892; De Laguna 1972; Emmons 1991; Fort Simpson Journal 1834–1838, 1852–1853; Glass 1882, 1890; Hodge 1907–1910; Holmberg 1985; Jackson 1887; Jones 1914; Kotzebue 1830; Krause 1956; Lisiansky [1814] 1968; Lutke 1839; Martin 1849; Morice 1894; Morris 1879; Olson 1967; Petroff 1900; Schwatka 1893; Swanton 1908, 1909; Teichmann 1963; Tikhmenev 1978; Veniaminof 1857; Veniaminov 1972; Wood 1882.

SKAGIT: The Skagit spoke Northern Lushootseed, a Salish language, and occupied winter villages on Whidbey Island in Puget Sound. The principal ethnography is Collins 1974b.

Slavery sources: Collins 1974b; Fort Langley Journal 1827–1830; Martin 1849; Schoolcraft 1856; Suttles 1974.

STIKINE: The Stikine were Southern Tlingit speakers and occupied a winter village on the mainland across from Wrangel Island. The Russian-American Company and the Hudson's Bay Company both built trading forts nearby for access to the area around the Stikine River circa 1840. There is no single major ethnographic source focusing on the Stikine.

Slavery sources: Barbeau 1950; Boas 1892; Census of Stikine Population 1845; Corser 1940; *Daily British Colonist* 1858–1890; De Laguna 1972; Douglas 1840, 1841, 1853; Fort Simpson Journal 1834–1838, 1838–1840, 1841–1842; Fort Stikine Journal 1840–1842; Gordon 1880; Jackson 1880; Krause 1956; Merk 1931; Morison 1920; Morris 1879; Olson 1967; Petroff 1900; Schoolcraft 1856; Simpson 1847; Swanton 1909; Tikhmenev 1978; Tolmie 1963; Veniaminov 1972; Work 1842–1843, 1945; Young 1927.

TWANA: The Twana spoke a Salish language and occupied nine small winter villages on the Hood Canal just west of Puget Sound. The principal ethnography is Elmendorf 1960.

Slavery sources: Elmendorf 1960, 1993.

YAKUTAT: The Yakutat were the northernmost Tlingit group. Although largely Tlingit in language and culture by the late eighteenth century, the earlier inhabitants of the Yalutat Bay area were Eyak speakers and some Yakutat Tlingit were Tlingitized descendants of this Eyak population. There were at least two traditional winter villages. The principal ethnography is De Laguna 1972.

Slavery sources: Abercrombie 1884; Bancroft 1886; Birket-Smith 1953; Birket-Smith and De Laguna 1938; De Laguna 1952, 1972; Emmons 1991; Hrdlichka 1930; Khlebnikov 1835; Kotzebue 1830; Krause 1956; Petroff 1900.

Notes

Introduction

1. For an overview of the current ideas about hunter-gatherers discussed here, see the editors' sections of Burch and Ellanna 1994.

1. An Overview of Northwest Coast Cultures

1. The locations of some of the more important geographic features are shown on figure 1. Figure 4 gives the locations of many of the most frequently mentioned groups and communities.

2. The best general book-length descriptions of the culture area are still Drucker 1955 and 1965. The latest compendium of information on the area is volume 7 of the *Handbook of North American Indians* (1990). There are some gaps in its coverage, and its individually authored articles are of uneven quality. Particularly useful ones will be noted as appropriate.

3. Useful, brief descriptions and analyses of the environment from the perspective of aboriginal use can be found in Jorgensen 1980 and Suttles 1990a.

4. The one group for whom ocean-based resources ranked first was the only one to take significant amounts of salmon in salt water.

5. Pottery vessels were absent in the culture area.

6. For Northwest Coast economies, see Mitchell and Donald 1988. There is still no good, comprehensive overview of the social organization of the culture area.

7. For a good overview of Northwest Coast art, see Holm 1990.

8. The best overall treatment of the potlatch remains Barnett [1938] 1968.

2. The Study of Northwest Coast Slavery

1. A. L. Kroeber also touched on our topic. His views have already been discussed in chapter 1.

2. I also omit discussion of my previous publications on the topic and those of my colleague Donald Mitchell.

3. MacLeod, Averkieva, Siegel, and Ruyle all cite Nieboer, but only MacLeod provides a serious critique of Nieboer's analysis of Northwest Coast materials. Siegel is primarily interested in criticizing Nieboer's theory of slavery, and Ruyle, while giving brief attention to some aspects of the theory, cites Nieboer as an authority for facts about Northwest Coast slavery.

4. Nieboer's identification of the subsistence mode of particular groups is often inadequate or even wrong. He also sometimes muddles his group identifications. This is partly because he indiscriminately relies on good sources (such as Boas 1897) and notoriously unreliable ones (such as Bancroft 1875). From here on I will omit further consideration of Nieboer's empirical findings. There is no point in correcting them. Nieboer did correctly recognize that the Northwest Coast peoples (and a few of their neighbors) practiced slavery and that this had to be explained in the context of a general lack of slavery among foragers. It is his theoretical argument that interests us now.

5. He uses only published sources.

6. The relatively small number of citations of Russian ethnographic and historical sources suggests that she did not do extensive archival research looking for unpublished or obscure material.

7. Functionalism's assumptions and methodology are at least as inadequate and problematical as those of positivism. This is not the place to rehearse this long-standing debate in anthropology and the other social sciences. For a discussion of the problems of functionalism, see Hempel 1959 and Jarvie 1965.

8. Averkieva should certainly be regarded as a Northwest Coast expert, but her location (the Soviet Union), her principal language of publication (Russian), and her theoretical framework (Soviet Marxism) have all marginalized her with respect to mainstream Northwest Coast scholarship.

3. Methods and Sources

1. For a demonstration and analysis of variation within the culture area in one domain, technology and material culture, see Donald and Mertton 1975; and for variation in other domains, see Jorgensen 1980.

2. This is not altogether a criticism of the ethnographers who have worked on the Northwest Coast. Often, by the time an ethnographer arrived in an area, depopulation and rapid culture change meant that even if detailed village-by-village information had been sought it would not have been available.

3. Strictly speaking, Horatio Hale, who was a member of Charles Wilkes's United States Exploring Expedition in 1841, was the first professional ethnologist to work in the area, but his material is superficial and fragmentary and his publications are really more representative of the transition from traveler's/explorer's accounts than of ethnography as it developed in the last half of the nineteenth century.

4. By "European" here and elsewhere I mean persons of European cultural background, whether they come from Europe proper or one of its overseas extensions in North America or elsewhere. "European" is far preferable to "white," whose racial (and racist) overtones are worse than any confusion likely to result from the use of the term "European."

5. To make matters even more complicated in this case, George M. Dawson visited the Queen Charlotte Islands in 1878. His interests were primarily geological, but his visit resulted in an important ethnographic source on the Haida, "On the Haida Indians of the Queen Charlotte Islands" (included in Dawson 1880). Collison, who was active on the Charlottes then, had several discussions with Dawson about the Haida at that time. Collison and Harrison had both almost certainly read Dawson's account when they wrote their own books.

6. For more on museums and collecting for museums on the Northwest Coast, see Lohse and Sundt 1990 and especially Cole 1985.

7. For more on the image of the indigenous Americans in European thought and this image's influence on descriptive and scientific writings about Native Americans, see Donald 1990, 145–148, and the references cited therein.

8. In the eighteenth century it was not uncommon for the aboriginal inhabitants of lands newly "discovered" by Europeans to be called "Indians." The indigenous inhabitants of both the Pacific Islands and Australia were sometimes referred to as Indians, for example.

4. Slaves and Masters Described

1. For the definition of slavery and its relations to other forms of unfree labor, I have found Archer 1988 helpful, especially the essay by Robin Blackburn.

2. The Eyak, occupying territory just north of the Yakutat, were in the transition zone between the Northwest Coast and Subarctic culture areas. Birket-Smith and De Laguna's description of Eyak slavery suggests that it was a less elaborate version of Tlingit slavery.

3. There are brief references in other contemporary ship's logs to what is probably the same incident.

4. For a discussion of the Jewitt narrative as an example of the "captivity narrative" genre, see Donald 1985a.

5. There may be more to casting a slave's body into the water than meets the outsider's eye. I discuss this possibility in chapter 8 when the link between slaves and Coppers is discussed.

6. For many Northwest Coast groups short hair was a sign of mourning.

7. Simpson's remarks were made in the journal he kept during 1824 and 1825. Although he may have intended that they be seen by some others, they were not written for publication or public consumption.

8. The reader is reminded that slavery was legal in the United States until the Thirteenth Amendment to the U.S. Constitution was ratified in December 1865.

9. I deal here only with the demographic characteristics of slaves. The problem of slave numbers is treated in detail in chapter 9.

10. The sex ratio is calculated by dividing the number of males by the number of females and multiplying by 100. Thus sex ratios of less than 100 show a preponderance of females, while sex ratios of greater than 100 show a preponderance of males.

11. The context of this quote is a discussion of the use of spirit power by slaves against masters.

12. On the characteristics and character of slaves in the American South, see Elkins 1976, 81–88 and Genovese 1974.

13. It is worth noting that ten blankets was about the price of a slave in the Fort Simpson area in the late 1830s.

14. To produce the desired head shape the skulls of infants were bound in various ways, so that pressure was applied to the growing skull and it developed the intended form. These head deformations were permanent. There were three major types and several intermediate forms in the culture area. Because the various forms had a clear geographic distribution, a good idea of an adult's area of origin could be obtained from the shape of her or his skull. The practice ceased over the course of the last half of the nineteenth century. The most accessible discussions of Northwest Coast cranial deformation and its probable status as a social and cultural marker are Cybulski 1990, 52–53 and Suttles 1990b,13–14.

15. Kwakwaka'wakw descent groups were not exogamous.

16. In addition, he published a Nuxalk myth about events that took place among the Heiltsuk that suggests the same attitude as Drucker describes for Northern Wakashan speakers. In this myth, some of the women married to a titleholder with supernatural powers "became almost his slaves, as their families were unable to rebuy them" (McIlwraith 1948, 1:524).

17. All of the northern groups are matrilineal.

5. The Production of Slaves

1. Those who enslaved themselves because of poverty or debt are a possible exception.

2. For descriptions of such patterns, see McIlwraith 1948, 2:340–344 for the Nuxalk; Boas 1966, 105–119, for an overly ritualized view of the Kwakwaka'wakw; or Donald 1987, 164–167, for a general discussion.

3. On the complex question of the motivations and causes of warfare on the Northwest Coast, see Donald 1987, 166, and Ferguson 1984.

4. This section has benefited from and draws on Mitchell 1984.

5. This was written in 1827 to an American missionary by a "respectable ship master" who had experience on the North Pacific Coast. The missionary's informant is almost certainly drawing on experiences as a fur trader in the northern part of the culture area.

6. Slave Labor

1. A partial exception is Viola Garfield, who, commenting favorably on Oberg's dissertation, pointed out the need for much more information on many areas of Northwest Coast economics. And, even in the paper containing her assessment of Oberg, Garfield (1945) was primarily interested in the control of productive resources and says little about the organization of production or work.

2. Although the risk varied somewhat with the season, people on their own were always subject to more danger, including from passing enemies, than were people in groups.

3. Among some Straits Salish speakers (including the Lummi and Saanich) reef net fishing was an important salmon procurement technique. In the late nineteenth cen-

tury nonkin were included among those hired to work the reef nets. The use of nonkin on hired crews before that time is not documented.

4. The Nuu-chah-nulth local groups and the Makah were the major active whalers in the culture area, although all the region's groups took advantage of a beached whale. A few of the Makah's Olympic Peninsula neighbors did some whaling, but it was a minor activity learned from the Makah (Drucker 1955, 16).

5. Girls' puberty rites were widespread in western North America. The classic discussion is Driver 1941. Some fairly elaborate version of these rites, especially for the daughters of titleholders, was practiced in all Northwest Coast societies.

6. The economic value of slaves has been suggested before; see MacLeod 1928 and, more recently, Ruyle 1973.

7. Krause spent December 1881 through April 1882 in the Central Tlingit area of Alaska. His book records both his firsthand observations and his gleanings from the nineteenth-century sources.

8. Even the ecological rethinking of the potlatch during the 1960s focused primarily on arguments about variation in the resource base, on one hand, and exchange and distribution (or redistribution), on the other. How people were organized and motivated, as workers, to produce for feasting was largely ignored. See the references cited in note 10 below.

9. A thorough discussion of the problem of how to decide that a society is based on slave labor can be found in G. E. M. de Ste. Croix 1981 (esp. pp. 52–55). I return to this issue in chapter 9.

10. See, for example, Suttles 1960, 1962, 1968; Piddcocke 1965; Donald and Mitchell 1975; Schalk 1977, 1979; and Langdon 1979.

11. The most accessible account of Northwest Coast fishing is Stewart 1977, which also contains some good material on fish preservation (see esp. pp. 135–147).

7. Transactions in Slaves

1. One other crew member (an Aleut) was traded south and was recovered on the Columbia River by an American ship in 1809.

2. An alternative path is possible. The northern Nuu-chah-nulth might have traded slaves to Kwakwala-speaking groups on northeastern Vancouver Island. There were certainly Kwakwaka'wakw/Nuu-chah-nulth contacts, and Nuu-chah-nulth held Salish and Kwakwaka'wakw slaves, but almost all Nuu-chah-nulth slaves of known origin were Nuu-chah-nulth and there is no evidence of slaves being traded into Nuu-chah-nulth territory from the south. Altogether, the relative isolation of the west coast of Vancouver Island makes it unlikely that important links between the two networks crossed Nuu-chah-nulth territory.

3. I have tended to use "price" and "value" indiscriminately, but at times it is useful to distinguish "price," what was actually handed over in exchange for a slave in a transaction, from "value," the stated equivalent of a slave in something else or the stated number of slaves something is said to be worth.

4. It is usually claimed that they were made of either native copper or of copper obtained from Europeans. All of the Coppers tested so far, however, were manufactured of copper of non-native origin (Couture and Edwards 1964; Jopling 1989, 74–98; Widersprach-Thor 1981, 127). For this and other reasons Martine Reid may well

be correct in suggesting that Coppers may be postcontact phenomena (Widersprach-Thor 1981, 112–113). Symbolically, Coppers are intimately associated with and, in some senses, represent human life. Indeed, Reid has argued that the destruction of Coppers replaced the killing of slaves at ceremonies during historic times (Widersprach-Thor 1981). See chapter 8 for further discussion of this issue.

5. Emmons worked among the Tlingit in the 1880s and 1890s, so his "old people" could easily have witnessed events in the 1840s and 1850s and perhaps even in the 1830s.

6. The term "brideprice," although encountered most frequently in African ethnography, is the standard anthropological term for significant prestations made by the groom's kin to the bride's kin. The goods handed over are usually thought of as compensation to the bride's kin group for her loss. The imputation that somehow the bride is being "sold" is incorrect.

8. Slaves and Ritual

1. Although these occasions are often called "potlatches" in the literature, I prefer and will use the term "feast" here.

2. In earlier drafts I often used the term "sacrifice" in connection with ritual slave killings on the Northwest Coast. Further reflection led me to conclude that "sacrifice" has too many connotations in anthropology, theology, and religious studies to be used casually. Without attempting a judgment of how indigenous concepts fit into various theoretical notions of sacrifice, I have opted for what I hope are more neutral phrases, such as "ritual killing."

3. This account is based on Kamenskii 1985, 35–37. The original date of publication was 1906.

4. Note that she was not returned to the Haida.

5. For revenge and other motives of Northwest Coast warfare, see Donald 1987 and the references cited therein.

6. Philip Drucker has a good discussion and analysis of this ceremony (1951, 386–443; see esp. pp. 387–391).

7. In 1864 Robert Brown attended a potlatch given by the Sheshaht for the Opetchesaht. The poorest and last presents given out (an old blanket and a very small string of ornaments) went to a small slave boy. "While these small gifts were being given and received, a sort of murmur of appreciation was heard among the Seshahts, especially from the women; but the Opetchesahts seemed rather to dislike it, as lowering to the dignity of the free-born recipients of presents" (Hayman 1989, 167).

8. For example, while attending a winter dance ceremony at Oowekeeno, a Nakwaktak hamatsa purchased a female slave from his hosts, then killed and ate her (Curtis 1915, 238–239).

9. There is a full discussion of the sources in Cook 1973 and in Wike 1984, whose conclusions about Maquinna are largely accepted here.

10. See Amos 1984 for a discussion of the ambiguous status of the dog in Northwest Coast culture.

11. Goldman (1975, 115, 117, 178, 226) also demonstrates many salmon/copper linkages among the Kwakwaka'wakw.

12. Holmberg was in Alaska in 1850–1851. His main exposure to the Tlingit was in the Sitka area. The Tlingit and Tsimshian groups cremated their dead. The other groups being discussed here used box internments (in burial houses, on the tops of posts, in caves) or graves.

13. The sources for the information about practice are Barnett (1939, 238), Boas (1921, 609–613), Drucker (1950, 284–286; 1951, 175–176), and Gunther (1926, 1928). The first salmon ceremony and related ideology regarding salmon have not been extensively studied since Gunther. There is now enough additional material to warrant another systematic analysis.

9. The Scale of Slavery on the Northwest Coast

1. The year was probably 1829.

2. A typed transcript of the original is available in the Provincial Archives of British Columbia. This greatly facilitates using the data, but the transcript is poorly or confusingly done in places and some information in the original does not appear in the transcript. Therefore, serious analysis of this material requires a comparison of the original and the transcript. My use of this source has benefited greatly from having access to a corrected version of the transcript, made by Donald Mitchell as a result of such a comparison. The analysis to be presented later has benefited greatly from discussions with Mitchell and from his 1985 paper on slave numbers, although we sometimes interpret the Douglas papers differently on minor points and the results of our analyses are somewhat different.

3. The Douglas Private Papers version appears in Petroff (1900, 97), but with so many transcription errors that it should not be used.

4. The difference between the Columbia percentages and those for the other three regional groupings is statistically significant, $p = .001$ by Mood's median test.

5. In the case of the Mowachaht, especially, this is certainly an understated difference.

10. The Antiquity of Northwest Coast Slavery

1. In chapter 11, on changes in slavery in the historic period, I discuss the history of contact in some detail.

2. For a summary of the language history, see Thompson and Kinkade 1990, 47; and for an archaeological interpretation, see Mitchell 1988, 282–285.

3. William H. Jacobsen, Jr., very kindly answered my queries about Wakashan language history and suggested the analysis contained in the preceding paragraph. He is not responsible for the inferences in the paragraph that follows.

4. It is also reasonably consistent with Swadesh's (1954, 361–362) glottochronological estimate of twenty-nine centuries for the split in Wakashan.

5. This summary of probable Salishan linguistic prehistory is based on Thompson and Kinkade 1990, 33–38, 45, 47. On the basis of the linguistic evidence (especially the reconstruction of proto-Salish terms for plants and animals), Kinkade (1991) makes a good case for a Fraser River to Skagit River coastal homeland for the proto-Salish.

6. See Mitchell 1990, 340–348, 357–358, for a summary of the archaeological material on which these speculations are based.

7. M. Dale Kinkade very kindly answered my queries about Salish language history. The information and analysis in the preceding paragraph is only a portion of the extensive information that he sent me. He is not responsible for the speculations in the paragraph that follows.

8. This summary is based on a reading of all the eighteenth-century sources on Mowachaht available to me; see especially Beaglehole 1967; Bell 1914; Haswell n.d.; Sales 1956; Wagner 1933. Also see Cook 1973 (esp. pp. 190, 313–314).

11. Changes in Slavery, 1780–1880

1. For the Russian interest in Alaska, see Fedorova 1973; for Spanish activity (and inactivity), see Cook 1973; for British interest in the Northwest Passage, see Williams 1962. The irony of the Northwest Passage is that, unlike so many other geographic myths, it does exist. But it is too far north to be commercially useful.

2. The most recent and comprehensive treatment of the maritime fur trade on the North Pacific Coast of North America is Gibson 1992.

3. The fault seems to have lain with Hanna, not Maquinna and the Mowachaht; see Cook 1973, 101.

4. For a brief account of some aspects of contact during the land-based fur trade period, see Fisher 1977, 24–48. The demographic consequences are more systematically spelled out in Boyd 1990.

5. For an account of one native middleman, the Lower Skeena Tsimshian Legaic, and his activities, see Mitchell 1983.

6. James Douglas was personally strongly opposed to slavery, but it was also the case that by 1840 British subjects and British companies could not legally participate in slave trading.

7. As late as 1825 it was Hudson's Bay Company policy not to sell liquor to natives, but by 1830 it was necessary to do so to compete with American trading ships like the *Europa* (McLoughlin 1941, lxx, 312–313).

8. The Chilkat are also known to have acquired additional slaves for use before and at feasts (Oberg 1973, 116–117).

9. I will concentrate on Britain, the United States, and Canada for these were the political regimes that controlled the region in the later nineteenth century. Spain was not a factor after the 1790s and, although Russia retained Alaska until 1867, Tlingit slavery ended in an American, not a Russian, political climate.

10. For example, the British public was shocked in the 1920s to learn that many slaves were still held in the Sierra Leone Protectorate—the hinterland of the colony founded by British abolitionists in the eighteenth century as a home for freed African slaves. Thousands were finally freed in the twenties (see Grace 1975), but my own field research indicates that in remote parts of northern Sierra Leone some slaves were held as late as 1940.

11. Even the abolition of black slavery in the British West Indies was not, of course, simply a matter of declaring slavery legally at an end and seeing it disappear overnight. For a good summary of the protracted struggle to bring slavery to an end in the

West Indies, see Davis 1984, especially his well-named chapters "British Emancipation: A Deceptive Model," parts 1 and 2 (pp. 168–226).

12. For more on Slacum and his mission, see Leary 1975.

13. I have read very similar statements, for example, in early twentieth-century reports by British colonial officials on domestic slavery in the Sierra Leone Protectorate. See the quotations in Grace 1975.

14. Douglas is often described as a "Scotch West Indian," having been born in British Guiana of a "Creole" mother and a Glaswegian father. For a brief account of Douglas's life, see Ormsby 1972.

12. Captivity and Slavery in Aboriginal North American Cultures

1. Nieboer, who did define slavery, also found no slavery outside the North Pacific Coast on the North American continent. Unfortunately, we cannot use his findings as evidence of a lack of slavery in the remainder of North America because of his poor control of the ethnographic material.

2. Leaving aside the point that many still hold slavery to be unimportant on the Northwest Coast also.

3. For an extended discussion of the scholarly image of the "egalitarian Indian" and its implications, see Donald 1990.

4. This is also a period rich in written sources. See, for example, the discussion of sources on the Huron for this period in Tooker (1964, 3–8). I am not an expert in Northeastern ethnography. Therefore, what follows is the result of a highly focused look into secondary sources (such as Trigger 1976 and Tooker 1964) and some excursions into the primary sources such as the Jesuit Relations and others that are cited as appropriate.

5. This sketch of northern Iroquoian society is based on Fenton 1978 and Trigger 1990.

6. Lafitau is a significant primary and secondary source. As a Jesuit missionary he worked among the Iroquois from 1712 until 1717. He was also familiar with the reports of various Jesuit missionaries among the Huron and other natives in the region during the seventeenth century. These reports, usually known as the Jesuit Relations, are our single most important source on the seventeenth-century northern Iroquoians. Lafitau's principal work, *Moeurs des sauvages ameriquains comparees aux moeurs des premiers temps*, is a rare book. Fortunately, the Champlain Society edition, edited by William Fenton and Elizabeth Moore, is more accessible. The editorial work by Fenton, an Iroquois expert, and Moore, an expert on eighteenth-century French, is superb.

7. Trigger (1990, 75) notes that although the Huron valued children highly, births were widely spaced and many children did not live to adulthood. Perhaps various northern Iroquoian practices minimized natural population increase, making these societies particularly vulnerable to population losses due to warfare or epidemic disease. Hodge, previously quoted, advances the same population crisis explanation for the adoption of captives.

8. In this chapter I am using the term "adoption" in the same manner as the older northern Iroquoian and Northeastern literature—uncritically, as if it were an unproblematic term in cross-cultural contexts. This is also true of Starna and Watkins's usage.

They do raise questions about northern Iroquoian adoptions, suggesting that what they claim were northern Iroquoian slaves have been mislabeled adoptees, but they do not explore how we ought to use the term "adoption" in an aboriginal North American context. For some indications of the ways in which the concept of adoption is not transparent or unproblematic in cross-cultural contexts, see, for example, Goody 1969 and Goody 1971, 1982 (esp. pp. 6–34). Any definitive work on the fate of Northeastern captives will have to analyze the local notions of adoption much more thoroughly than has been done in the past.

9. For more on Southeastern warfare patterns and its motivations and the Southeastern natives' participation in the eastern North American torture complex already described for the northern Iroquoians, see Hudson 1976, 239–257. Note that in the index to Hudson's book, "slavery: Indian" has eleven entries, all referring to the enslavement of natives by Europeans. The passage cited above appears in the index only under "captives."

10. The most accessible modern discussions of the Calusa are Goggin and Sturtevant 1964, Marquardt 1988, and Widmer 1988. My treatment of the Calusa relies on these three publications.

13. Class on the Northwest Coast

1. This particular typology of societies with class was worked out with the help of Giddens' discussion of Marx's ideas about social evolution (1981, 76–81). The terminology in particular is adapted from that discussion.

2. Joyce Wike's analysis (1958) of Nuu-chah-nulth social stratification is very similar to this one. She provides additional ethnographic material to support the picture presented here.

3. The use of the number four and certain other features of the text suggest that the tale is an exemplary one and not about an actual incident.

4. However, some of the remarks in texts collected by Elmendorf (1993) can be interpreted as indicating titleholder control over salmon weirs (p. 10), the division of a beached whale (p. 27), and elk hunting (p. 99).

5. Various Coast Salish groups had ceremonies to wash away the stain of slavery from former slaves who managed to return to their natal communities. These "cleansing rites" (as Suttles translates the indigenous term) were the property of certain families and were used only on behalf of family members. Control and knowledge of these rites were restricted by primogeniture, keeping these rites in the hands of their upper-class owners (Suttles 1987, 10).

6. In a discussion of "estates and castes" Jérôme Rousseau (1978) has broadened the notion of estate from its original historical application (largely with respect to European feudalism) in much the same way as I have done with class here. In doing so he classifies the Northwest Coast societies (along with many others) as having estates. Obviously I have found focusing on class more fruitful, but we both make the point that the three strata found in Northwest Coast societies are profound and important divisions within these societies and that the difference between titleholders and commoners was neither gradual nor superficial.

14. The Place of Slavery in Northwest Coast Culture

1. For a modern anthropological overview and analysis of the type of society Morgan and Mauss attempted to describe, see Sahlins 1968.

2. The writings of Marx and Engels do not contain a systematic or lengthy treatment of slavery in any form, including "patriarchal" slavery. Some followers of Marx and Engels have used the scattered remarks and insights found in various of their works (see, e.g., Engels 1942, 50–52; Marx 1965, 122–123; Marx 1966, 332; Marx and Engels 1964, 38–39) as a basis for considerable discussion of patriarchal slavery. As briefly discussed in chapter 2, one of Averkieva's principal goals as a Soviet scholar writing in the 1930s was to establish that Northwest Coast slavery was patriarchal in character.

3. Dependent labor based on gender and age—wives working for husbands, young men working for lineage elders—is widespread in kin-based societies; for West African examples, see Meillassoux 1981.

4. Riches 1979 includes a summary of the usual characterizations of Northwest Coast kin units, although this essay also contains a number of insights and hypotheses that lift his discussion above mere ethnographic summary. See also Jorgensen's (1980, 174–192) discussion in the context of western North America.

5. However, the argument has tended to focus on resource fluctuation and the need to reduce group size or shift group membership in times of privation, rather than on fluctuating labor needs; see Sahlins 1957, for example.

6. For an overview of descent theory as it relates to these issues, see Scheffler 1974. On the specific point of descent as "ideology" and the relation of descent rules to the actual composition of descent groups, see Sahlins 1965.

7. Riches's suggestions are based on Suttles's very general and undocumented characterization of Northwest Coast environments. No one has produced the detailed systematic analysis of Northwest Coast ecology and resources that will allow proper testing of Suttles's hypotheses. Schalk (1979, 57) has also argued that there is a general decline in the importance of gathering as one goes north along the coast. Unfortunately, Schalk's apparently more empirically based study depends on Murdock's *Ethnographic Atlas* codings, which can easily be shown to be too unreliable to use for these variables (Mitchell and Donald 1988, 307).

8. Riches's (1979, 152–153) comes to a similar conclusion.

9. The patterning of most of the slavery variables discussed in chapters 4 through 8 fits the predicted pattern better than the demographic data do. The demographic data are, however, problematic (see chapter 9).

10. If female labor is increasingly important, one might also predict that the incidence of polygyny would also increase from south to north (although polygyny was largely a titleholder prerogative), but the only effort known to me to estimate the incidence of polygyny for the Northwest Coast does not support this prediction very well (Jorgensen 1980, 454).

11. Douglas was an experienced and acute observer of the coastal native scene, having been on the coast since early 1830. He is not likely to have confused a commoner with a slave, and we can be confident that Douglas correctly recognized Shakes's attendants for what they were, slaves.

12. For discussion of the rarity of slave revolts in a broad context, see Finley 1980, 110–111, 114–115.

13. The following discussion of Gramsci's ideas is based primarily on Gramsci 1971, but I also found Adamson 1980 and Femia 1981 helpful.

14. Titleholders also exercised domination over commoners, although in a somewhat milder and less consistent fashion than over slaves. One of the tasks titleholders sometimes set slaves was the bullying and even on occasion the killing of commoners.

References

Abercrombie, W. R.

1884   Report of a supplementary expedition into the Copper River Valley, Alaska. In *Compilation of Narratives of Explorations in Alaska.* Pp. 381–408. Washington, D.C.: U.S. Government Printing Office.

1900   Alaska: 1898 Copper River exploring expedition. In *Compilation of Narratives of Explorations in Alaska.* Pp. 563–591. Washington, D.C.: U.S. Government Printing Office.

Adams, A. T.

1961   *The Explorations of Pierre Esprit Radisson.* Minneapolis: Ross and Haines.

Adams, John W.

1973   *The Gitksan Potlatch: Population Flux, Resource Ownership and Reciprocity.* Toronto: Holt, Rinehart and Winston.

1981   Recent ethnology of the Northwest Coast. *Annual Review of Anthropology* 10: 361–392.

Adamson, Walter L.

1980   *Hegemony and Revolution: A Study of Antonio Gramsci's Political and Cultural Theory.* Berkeley and Los Angeles: University of California Press.

Amos, Pamela

1984   A little more than kin and less than kind: The ambiguous Northwest Coast dog. In *The Tsimshian and Their Neighbors of the North Pacific Coast*, ed. Jay Miller and Carole M. Eastman, 292–395. Seattle: University of Washington Press.

Anderson, Alexander C.

1863   Notes on the Indian tribes of British North America and the Northwest Coast. *Historical Review* 7: 73–81.

339

Andrade, M. J.
    1928   Quileute ethnology notes: D notebook. Philadelphia: American Philo-
                sophical Society Library.
    1931   *Quileute texts*. Columbia University Contributions to Anthropology, vol.
                12.
Archer, Christon I.
    1980   Cannibalism in the early history of the Northwest Coast: Enduring myths
                and neglected realities. *Canadian Historical Review* 61: 453–479.
Archer, Leonie, ed.
    1988   *Slavery and Other Forms of Unfree Labour*. London: Routledge.
Averkieva, Julia
    [1941] 1966 *Slavery among the Indians of North America*. Trans. G. R. Elliot. Vic-
                toria, B.C.: Victoria College.
Bancroft, Hubert H.
    1875   *The Native Races of the Pacific States of North America*. Vol. 1: *Wild
                Tribes*. New York: D. Appleton.
    1886   *History of Alaska 1730–1885*. San Francisco: A. L. Bancroft.
Barbeau, C. Marius
    1940   Old Port Simpson. *Beaver* 271(2): 20–23.
    1950   *Totem Poles*. Bulletin (119) of the National Museum of Canada, Ottawa.
    1958   *Pathfinders in the North Pacific*. Caldwell, Id.: Caxton Printers.
Barnett, Homer G.
    1938   The nature of the potlatch. *American Anthropologist* 40: 349–358.
    [1938] 1968 *The Nature and Function of the Potlatch*. Eugene: University of Ore-
                gon Press.
    1939   Culture element distributions: IX, Gulf of Georgia Salish. *University of
                California Anthropological Records* 1(5): 221–295.
    1955   *The Coast Salish of British Columbia*. Eugene: University of Oregon Press.
    1957   *Indian Shakers: A Messianic Cult of the Pacific Northwest*. Carbondale:
                Southern Illinois University Press.
Beaglehole, J. C., ed.
    1967   *The Journals of Captain James Cook on His Voyages of Discovery; the
                Voyage of the "Resolution" and "Discovery," 1776–1780*. Cambridge: Hak-
                luyt Society.
Beardslee, L. A.
    1882   *Reports of Captain L. A. Beardslee, U.S. Navy, Relative to Affairs in
                Alaska and the Operations of the USS Jamestown Under His Command
                While in the Waters of That Territory*. Washington, D.C.: U.S. Govern-
                ment Printing Office.
Belcher, Sir Edward
    1843   *Narrative of a Voyage around the World Performed in Her Majesty's Ship
                Sulphur, During the Years 1836–1842*. Vol. 2. London: Henry Colburn.
Bell, Edward
    1914   A New Vancouver Journal. *Washington Historical Quarterly* 5(2): 129–
                137, (3): 215–224, (4): 300–308.

Birket-Smith, Kaj, and Frederica De Laguna
    1938   *The Eyak Indians of the Copper River Delta, Alaska.* Copenhagen: Levin and Munksgaard.
Bishop, Charles
    1967   *The Journals and Letters of Captain Charles Bishop on the North-West Coast of America, in the Pacific and New South Wales 1794–1799.* Cambridge: Cambridge University Press.
Blackburn, Robin
    1988   Slavery: Its Special Features and Social Role. In *Slavery and Other Forms of Unfree Labour,* ed. Leonie Archer, 262–279. London: Routledge.
Boas, Franz
    1889   Linguistics, III Tsimshian. On the northwestern tribes of Canada. General report on the Indians of British Columbia. *Report of the British Association for the Advancement of Science.* Pp. 877–889.
    1892   The Bilqula. Physical characteristics of the tribes of the North Pacific Coast. Seventh report on the north-western tribes of Canada, 1891. *Report of the British Association for the Advancement of Science.* Pp. 408–449.
    1894   *Chinook Texts.* Bureau of American Ethnology Bulletin no. 20. Washington, D.C.
    1895a   Fifth report on the Indians of British Columbia. Tenth report on the north-western tribes of Canada, 1895. *Report of the British Association for the Advancement of Science.* Pp. 522–592.
    1895b   *Indianische Sagen von der nordpacifischen Kuste Amerikas.* Berlin: A. Asher.
    1896–1933 Kwakiutl materials. Boas Collection 372, microfilm rolls 21 and 22, item W1a.3. Philadelphia: American Philosophical Society.
    1897   The social organization and secret societies of the Kwakiutl. *Report of the United States National Museum for 1895.* Pp. 371–738. Washington, D.C.
    1901   *Kathlamet Texts.* Bureau of American Ethnology Bulletin no. 26. Washington, D.C.
    1910   *Kwakiutl Tales.* Columbia University Contributions to Anthropology, vol. 2.
    1912   *Tsimshian Texts (New Series).* Publications of the American Ethnological Society, vol. 3.
    1916   *Tsimshian Mythology.* Bureau of American Ethnology, Thirty-First Annual Report, 1909–1910. Washington, D.C.
    1916–1926 Kwakiutl ethnographic material. Boas Collection 372, roll 2, item 28. Philadelphia: American Philosophical Society.
    1916–1931 Kwakiutl ethnographic notes. Boas Collection 372, roll 2, item 29. Philadelphia: American Philosophical Society.
    1921   *Ethnology of the Kwakiutl.* United States Bureau of American Ethnology Annual Reports, 35, part 1 and 2. Washington, D.C.
    1928   *Bella Bella Texts.* Columbia University Contributions in Anthropology, vol. 5.

1930   *The Religion of the Kwakiutl Indians*. Columbia University Contributions to Anthropology, vol. 10.

1932   *Bella Bella Tales*. Memoirs of the American Folklore Society, vol. 25.

1935   *Kwakiutl Culture as Reflected in Mythology*. Memoirs of the American Folklore Society, vol. 28.

1940   The social organization of the Kwakiutl. In *Race, Language, and Culture*, 356–369. New York: Free Press.

1946   Kwakiutl ethnographic texts with translation. Boas Collection 372, roll 23, item Wla.19. Philadelphia: American Philosophical Society.

1966   *Kwakiutl Ethnography*. Chicago: University of Chicago Press.

Boas, Franz, et al.

1923   Salish texts. Boas Collection 372, rolls 2 and 3, item 33. Philadelphia: American Philosophical Society.

Boelscher, Marianne

1988   *The Curtain Within: Haida Social and Mythical Discourse*. Vancouver: University of British Columbia Press.

Bohannan, Paul

1963   *Social Anthropology*. New York: Holt, Rinehart and Winston.

Boyd, Robert T.

1990   Demographic history, 1774–1874. In *Handbook of North American Indians*. Vol. 7: *Northwest Coast*, ed. Wayne Suttles, 135–148. Washington, D.C.: Smithsonian Institution Press.

Brabant, A. J.

1900   *Vancouver Island and Its Mission, 1874–1900*. Hesquiat, B.C.

Brown, Robert

n.d.   Memoir on the geography of the interior of Vancouver Island. Victoria: Provincial Archives of British Columbia.

Burch, Ernest S., Jr., and Ellanna, Linda J., eds.

1994   *Key Issues in Hunter-Gatherer Research*. Oxford: Berg.

Caamaño, Jacinto

[1792] 1938 The journal of Jacinto Caamano. *British Columbia Historical Quarterly* 2: 189–222, 265–301.

Callender, Charles

1978a   Fox. In *Handbook of North American Indians*. Vol. 15: *Northeast*, ed. Bruce G. Trigger, 636–647. Washington, D.C.: Smithsonian Institution Press.

1978b   Illinois. In *Handbook of North American Indians*. Vol. 15: *Northeast*, ed. Bruce G. Trigger, 673–680. Washington, D.C.: Smithsonian Institution Press.

1978c   Shawnee. In *Handbook of North American Indians*. Vol. 15: *Northeast*, ed. Bruce G. Trigger, 622–635. Washington, D.C.: Smithsonian Institution Press.

Census of Stekine Population

1845   Hudson's Bay Company Archives B209/2/1 to 4. Winnipeg: Provincial Archives of Manitoba.

Chittenden, Newton H.

1884   *Hyda Land and People: Official Report of the Exploration of the Queen*

Charlotte Islands for the Government of British Columbia. Victoria: Queen's Printer.

Clah, Arthur Wellington
1908   Reminiscences of Arthur Wellington Clah of the Tsimpshean Indian Nation. WMS.AMER.140(70). London: Wellcome Institute for the History of Medicine Library.

Clarke, S. A.
1905   *Pioneer Days of Oregon History.* Cleveland: Arthur H. Clark.

Codere, Helen
1950   *Fighting with Property.* American Ethnological Society Monographs, vol. 18.
1957   Kwakiutl society: Rank without class. *American Anthropologist* 59: 473–486.

Cole, Douglas
1985   *Captured Heritage: The Scramble for Northwest Coast Artifacts.* Vancouver: Douglas & McIntyre.

Cole, Douglas, and Ira Chaikin
1990   *An Iron Hand Upon the People: The Law Against the Potlatch on the Northwest Coast.* Vancouver: Douglas & McIntyre.

Collins, June McCormick
[1946] 1974a A study of religious change among the Skagit Indians, western Washington. In *Coast Salish and Western Washington Indians IV.* Pp. 619–763. New York: Garland.
1974b   *Valley of the Spirits: The Upper Skagit Indians of Western Washington.* Seattle: University of Washington Press.

Collison, William H.
1915   *In the Wake of the War Canoe.* London: Seeley, Service.

Colnett, James
1940   *The Journal of Captain James Colnett Aboard the "Argonaut" from April 26, 1789 to November 3, 1791.* Toronto: Champlain Society.

Colson, Elizabeth
1953   *The Makah Indians.* Manchester: Manchester University Press.

Colvocoresses, George M.
1852   *Four Years in a Government Exploring Expedition Under the Command of Captain Charles Wilkes.* New York: Cornish, Lamport.

Connolly, William
1824–1825 Western Caledonia Report 1824/25. Hudson's Bay Company Archives MS B188/e/3. Winnipeg: Provincial Archives of Manitoba.

Cook, Warren L.
1973   *Flood Tide of Empire: Spain and the Pacific Northwest, 1543–1819.* New Haven: Yale University Press.

Corney, Peter
1965   *Early Voyages in the North Pacific, 1813–1818.* Fairfield, Wash.: Ye Galleon Press.

Corser, H. P.
1940   *Totem Lore of the Alaska Indians and the Land of the Totem.* Wrangell, Alaska: Walter C. Waters.

Couture, A., and J. O. Edwards
  1964   *Origin of Copper Used by Canadian West Coast Indians in the Manufac-*
              ture of Ornamental Plaques. National Museum of Canada, Bulletin no.
              194: 199–219.
Cox, Ross
  [1831] 1957 *The Columbia River*. Norman: University of Oklahoma Press.
Crosby, Thomas
  1914   *Up and Down the North Pacific Coast by Canoe and Mission Ship*. To-
              ronto: Missionary Society of the Methodist Church.
Curtis, Edward S.
  1913   *The North American Indian*. Vol. 9. Norwood, Mass.: Plimpton Press.
  1915   *The North American Indian*. Vol. 10. Norwood, Mass.: Plimpton Press.
  1916   *The North American Indian*. Vol. 11. Norwood, Mass.: Plimpton Press.
Cybulski, Jerome S.
  1990   Human biology. In *Handbook of North American Indians*. Vol. 7: *North-*
              west Coast, ed. Wayne Suttles, 52–59. Washington, D.C.: Smithsonian
              Institution Press.
  1992   *A Greenville Burial Ground: Human Remains and Mortuary Elements in*
              British Columbia Prehistory. Ottawa: Canadian Museum of Civilization.
Davis, David Brion
  1984   *Slavery and Human Progress*. New York: Oxford University Press.
Dawson, George Mercer
  1880   *Report on the Queen Charlotte Islands, 1878*. Montreal: Dawson Brothers.
  1887   *Notes and Observations on the Kwakiool People of the Northern Part of*
              Vancouver Island and Adjacent Coasts. Transactions of the Royal Soci-
              ety of Canada, vol. 5, no. 2: 63–98.
Day, Gordon M.
  1978   Western Abenaki. In *Handbook of North American Indians*. Vol. 15:
              Northeast, ed. Bruce G. Trigger, 148–159. Washington, D.C.: Smithso-
              nian Institution Press.
De Laguna, Frederica
  1952   Some dynamic forces in Tlingit society. *Southwestern Journal of Anthro-*
              pology 8: 1–12.
  1972   *Under Mount St. Elias: The History and Culture of the Yakutat Tlingit*.
              Washington, D.C.: Smithsonian Institution Press.
  1983   Aboriginal Tlingit sociopolitical organization. In *The Development of Po-*
              litical Organization in Native North America, ed. Elisabeth Tooker, 71–
              85. Proceedings of the American Ethnological Society. Washington, D.C.,
              1979.
  1990   Tlingit. In *Handbook of North American Indians*. Vol. 7: *Northwest*
              Coast, ed. Wayne Suttles, 203–228. Washington, D.C.: Smithsonian In-
              stitution Press.
Dennis, E. F.
  1930   Indian slavery in the Pacific Northwest. *Oregon Historical Quarterly* 31:
              69–81, 181–195, 285–296.
Densmore, Frances
  1924   *Field Studies of Indian Music*. Smithsonian Miscellaneous Contributions,
              vol. 76, no. 10: 119–127.

DeSmet, P. J.

1847   *Oregon Missions and Travels over the Rocky Mountains in 1845 and 1846.* New York: Edward Dunigan.

Devereaux, John Francis

1890–1896 Correspondence on the location of the ship "Tonquin." Victoria: Provincial Archives of British Columbia.

Domar, E.

1970   The causes of slavery. *Journal of Economic History* 30: 18–32.

Donald, Leland

1983   Was Nuu-chah-nulth-aht (Nootka) society based on slave labor? In *The Development of Political Organization in Native North America*, ed. Elisabeth Tooker, 108–119. Proceedings of the American Ethnological Society. Washington, D.C., 1979.

1984   The slave trade on the Northwest Coast of North America. *Research in Economic Anthropology* 6: 121–158.

1985a   Captive or slave? A comparison of northeastern and northwestern North America by means of captivity narratives. *Culture* 5: 17–23.

1985b   On the possibility of social class in societies based on extractive subsistence. In *Status, Structure and Stratification: Current Archaeological Reconstructions*, ed. Marc Thompson, Maria Teresa Garcia, and François Kense, 237–244. Calgary: University of Calgary Archaeological Association.

1987   Slave raiding on the North Pacific Coast. In *Native Peoples, Native Lands*, ed. Bruce Cox, 161–172. Ottawa: Carleton University Press.

1989   Paths out of slavery on the aboriginal North Pacific Coast of North America. *Slavery & Abolition* 10: 1–22.

1990   Liberty, equality, fraternity: Was the Indian really egalitarian? In *The Invented Indian*, ed. James A. Clifton, 145–168. New Brunswick, N.J.: Transaction Publishers.

1995   Review of *Indian Slavery in the Pacific Northwest* by Robert H. Ruby and John A. Brown. *Journal of American History* 82: 187–188.

Donald, Leland, and Jacquelyn Mertton

1975   Technology on the Northwest Coast: An analysis of overall similarities. *Behavior Science Research* 10: 73–100.

Donald, Leland, and Donald H. Mitchell

1975   Some correlates of local group rank among the southern Kwakiutl. *Ethnology* 14: 325–346.

Douglas, James

1840   Diary of a trip to the Northwest Coast, April 22 to October 2, 1840. Victoria: British Columbia Provincial Archives.

1841   Diary of a trip to the Northwest Coast. Victoria: British Columbia Provincial Archives.

1853   James Douglas Private Papers, 2d ser. B20/1853: 5–31. Victoria: Provincial Archives of British Columbia.

n.d.   Indian population and statistics: Notes on traditions and populations of the Indians of the Northwest Coast. F/1/D75. Victoria: Provincial Archives of British Columbia.

Driver, Harold E.

1941   Culture element distributions: XVI, Girl's puberty rites in western North America. *University of California Anthropological Records* 6: 21–90.

Driver, Harold E., et al.

1972   Statistical classification of North American Indian ethnic units. *Ethnology* 11: 311–339.

Driver, Harold E., and J. Coffin

1974   Statistical classification of North American Indian ethnic units from the Driver-Massey sample. In *Comparative Studies by Harold E. Driver and Essays in His Honor*, ed. Joseph G. Jorgensen, 225–228. New Haven: HRAF Press.

Drucker, Philip

1939   Rank, wealth, and kinship in Northwest Coast society. *American Anthropologist* 41: 55–65.

1940   Kwakiutl dancing societies. *University of California Anthropological Records* 2(6): 201–230.

1950   Culture element distributions: XXVI, Northwest Coast. *University of California Anthropological Records* 9(3): 157–294.

1951   *The Northern and Central Nootkan Tribes.* Bureau of American Ethnology Bulletin no. 144. Washington, D.C.

1955   *Indians of the Northwest Coast.* New York: Natural History Press.

1958   *The Native Brotherhoods: Modern Intertribal Organizations on the Northwest Coast.* Bureau of American Ethnology Bulletin no. 168. Washington, D.C.

1965   *Cultures of the North Pacific Coast.* Scranton, Penn.: Chandler.

1983   Ecology and political organization on the Northwest Coast of America. In *The Development of Political Organization in Native North America,* ed. Elisabeth Tooker, 86–96. Proceedings of the American Ethnological Society. Washington, D.C., 1979.

Drucker, Philip, and Robert F. Heizer

1967   *To Make My Name Good: A Re-examination of the Southern Kwakiutl Potlatch.* Berkeley: University of California Press.

Duff, Wilson

1964   *The Indian History of British Columbia: The Impact of the White Man.* Anthropology in British Columbia, Memoir no. 5.

Dunn, John

1844   *History of the Oregon Territory.* London: Edwards and Hughes.

Dunn, John Asher

1984   International matri-moieties: The North Maritime Province of the North Pacific Coast. In *The Tsimshian, Images of the Past: Views for the Present,* ed. Margaret Seguin, 99–109. Vancouver: University of British Columbia Press.

Elkins, Stanley

1976   *Slavery, a Problem in American Institutional and Intellectual Life.* 3d ed. Chicago: University of Chicago Press.

Elmendorf, William W.
  1960   *The Structure of Twana Culture.* Research Studies, Monographic Supplement no. 2. Pullman: Washington State University.
  1971   Coast Salish ranking and intergroup ties. *Southwestern Journal of Anthropology* 27: 353–380.
  1993   *Twana Narratives: Native Historical Accounts of a Coast Salish Culture.* Seattle: University of Washington Press.
Emmons, George T.
  1911   *The Tahltan Indians.* University of Pennsylvania Anthropological Publications no. 4.
  1991   *The Tlingit Indians.* Edited by Frederica De Laguna. Vancouver: Douglas & McIntyre.
Engels, Friedrich
  1942   *The Origin of the Family, Private Property and the State.* New York: International Publishers.
Farrand, L.
  1897   Quinault ethnographic and field notes. Boas Collection 372, roll 48, item S2a.1. Philadelphia: American Philosophical Society.
  1919   Quileute tales. *Journal of American Folklore* 32: 251–279.
Farrand, L., and W. S. Kahnweiler
  1902   Traditions of the Quinault Indians. *American Museum of Natural History Memoirs* 4: 77–132.
Fedorova, Svetlana G.
  1973   *The Russian Population in Alaska and California.* Kingston: Limestone Press.
Feest, Johanna E., and Christian F. Feest
  1978   Ottawa. In *Handbook of North American Indians.* Vol. 15: *Northeast,* ed. Bruce G. Trigger, 772–786. Washington, D.C.: Smithsonian Institution Press.
Femia, Joseph V.
  1981   *Gramsci's Political Thought: Hegemony, Consciousness, and the Revolutionary Process.* Oxford: Clarendon Press.
Fenton, William N.
  1978   Northern Iroquoian culture patterns. In *Handbook of North American Indians.* Vol. 15: *Northeast,* ed. Bruce G. Trigger, 296–321. Washington, D.C.: Smithsonian Institution Press.
Ferguson, R. Brian
  1984   A re-examination of the causes of Northwest Coast warfare. In *Warfare, Culture, and Environment,* ed. R. Brian Ferguson, 267–328. Orlando: Academic Press.
Finley, Moses I.
  1980   *Ancient Slavery and Modern Ideology.* New York: Viking.
Fisher, Robin
  1977   *Contact and Conflict: Indian-European Relations in British Columbia, 1774–1890.* Vancouver: University of British Columbia Press.

Fladmark, Knut R., Kenneth M. Ames, and Patricia D. Sutherland

1990   Prehistory of the northern coast of British Columbia. In *Handbook of North American Indians*. Vol. 7: *Northwest Coast*, ed. Wayne Suttles, 229–239. Washington, D.C.: Smithsonian Institution Press.

Fleurieu, C. P.

1801   *Voyage Round the World, Performed during the Years 1790, 1791, and 1792*. London: Longmans and Rees.

Ford, Clellan S.

1941   *Smoke from Their Fires: The Life of a Kwakiutl Chief.* New Haven: Yale University Press.

Fort Langley Journal

1827–1830 Victoria: Provincial Archives of British Columbia.

Fort Simpson Journal

1834–1838 Hudson's Bay Company Archives, B201/a/3. Winnipeg: Provincial Archives of Manitoba.

1838–1840 Hudson's Bay Company Archives, B201/a/4. Winnipeg: Provincial Archives of Manitoba.

1841–1842 Hudson's Bay Company Archives, B201/a/6. Winnipeg: Provincial Archives of Manitoba.

1852–1853 Hudson's Bay Company Archives, B201/a/7. Winnipeg: Provincial Archives of Manitoba.

1855–1859 Hudson's Bay Company Archives, B201/a/8. Winnipeg: Provincial Archives of Manitoba.

1859–1862 Ms A/C/20Si. Victoria: Provincial Archives of British Columbia.

1863–1866 Hudson's Bay Company Archives, B201/a/9. Winnipeg: Provincial Archives of Manitoba.

Fort Simpson (Nass) Journal

1840   Hudson's Bay Company Archives, B201/a/5. Winnipeg: Provincial Archives of Manitoba.

Fort Stikine Journal

1840–1842 Hudson's Bay Company Archives, B209/a/1. Winnipeg: Provincial Archives of Manitoba.

Frachtenberg, L. H.

1921   The ceremonial societies of the Quileute Indians. *American Anthropologist* 23: 320–352.

Fried, Morton H.

1967   *The Evolution of Political Society*. New York: Random House.

Garfield, Viola E.

1939   *Tsimshian Clan and Society*. Publications in Anthropology no. 7. Seattle: University of Washington.

1945   A research problem in Northwest Indian economics. *American Anthropologist* 47: 626–630.

1951   The Tsimshian and their neighbors. In *The Tsimshian: Their Arts and Music*, ed. Marian W. Smith, 5–70. Publications of the American Ethnological Society, no. 18. New York: J. J. Augustin.

Gary, George H.
1923   Diary of Reverend George H. Gary—II. *Oregon Historical Quarterly* 24: 153–185.
Genovese, Eugene
1974   *Roll, Jordan, Roll: The World the Slaves Made.* New York: Pantheon.
Gibson, James R.
1982–1983 Smallpox of the Northwest Coast, 1835–1838. *BC Studies* 56: 61–81.
1992   *Otter Skins, Boston Ships, and China Goods.* Montreal: McGill-Queen's University Press.
Giddens, Anthony
1981   *A Contemporary Critique of Historical Materialism.* Berkeley and Los Angeles: University of California Press.
Glass, Henry
1882   Report of U.S. naval officers cruising Alaska waters. Pt. 1, 11 October 1880–June 1881; Pt. 3, 14 November 1818–10 January 1882. U.S. Serial Set no. 2027; American State Papers; U.S. Exec. Doc. 81; 47th Cong., 1st sess.
1890   *Naval Administration in Alaska.* Proceedings of the United States Naval Institute no. 1.
Glave, E. J.
1892a   Pioneer packhorses in Alaska, 1: The advance. *Century Illustrated Monthly Magazine.* Pp. 671–682.
1892b   Pioneer packhorses in Alaska, 2: The return to the coast. *Century Illustrated Monthly Magazine.* Pp. 869–881.
Goddard, Ives
1978   Delaware. In *Handbook of North American Indians.* Vol. 15: *Northeast,* ed. Bruce G. Trigger, 213–239. Washington, D.C.: Smithsonian Institution Press.
Goggin, John W., and William C. Sturtevant
1964   The Calusa: A stratified nonagricultural society. In *Explorations in Cultural Anthropology,* ed. Ward H. Goodenough, 179–220. New York: McGraw-Hill.
Goldman, Irving
1975   *The Mouth of Heaven.* New York: John Wiley & Sons.
Goody, Esther
1971   Forms of pro-parenthood: The sharing and substitution of parental roles. In *Kinship,* ed. Jack Goody, 331–345. Harmondsworth: Penguin Books.
1982   *Parenthood and Social Reproduction: Fostering and Occupational Roles in West Africa.* Cambridge: Cambridge University Press.
Goody, Jack
1969   Adoption in cross-cultural perspective. *Comparative Studies in Society and History* 11: 55–78.
Gordon, Daniel M.
1880   *Mountain and Prairie: A Journey from Victoria to Winnipeg, via Peace River Pass.* Montreal: Dawson Brothers.

Grace, John
    1975   *Domestic Slavery in West Africa, with Particular Reference to the Sierra Leone Protectorate, 1896–1927.* London: Frederick Muller.

Gramsci, Antonio
    1971   *Selections from the Prison Notebooks.* New York: International Publishers.

Grant, W. Colquhoun
    1857   Description of Vancouver Island. *Journal of the Geographical Society* 27: 268–320.

Green, Jonathan S.
    1915   *Journal of a Tour on the North West Coast of America in the Year 1829.* New York: Chas. Fred. Heartman.

Gunther, Erna
    1925   Klallam Folk Tales. *University of Washington Publications in Anthropology* 1: 113–170.
    1926   Analysis of the first salmon ceremony. *American Anthropologist* 28: 605–617.
    1927   Klallam ethnography. *University of Washington Publications in Anthropology* 1: 171–314.
    1928   Further analysis of the first salmon ceremony. *University of Washington Publications in Anthropology* 2(5): 129–173.
    1942   Reminiscences of a whaler's wife. *Pacific Northwest Quarterly* 33: 65–69.
    1972   *Indian Life on the Northwest Coast of North America as Seen by the Early Explorers and Fur Traders During the Last Decades of the Eighteenth Century.* Chicago: University of Chicago Press.

Haeberlin, Hermann, and Erna Gunther
    1930   The Indians of the Puget Sound. *University of Washington Publications in Anthropology* 4: 1–84.

Hall, Roberta L., and Peter L. Macnair
    1972   Multivariate analysis of anthropometric data and classifications of British Columbia natives. *American Journal of Physical Anthropology* 37(3): 401–409.

Halpin, Marjorie
    1984   Feast names at Hartley Bay. In *The Tsimshian, Images of the Past: Views for the Present*, ed. Margaret Seguin, 57–64. Vancouver: University of British Columbia Press.

Halpin, Marjorie M., and Margaret Seguin
    1990   Tsimshian peoples: Southern Tsimshian, Coast Tsimshian, Nishga, and Gitksan. In *Handbook of North American Indians*. Vol. 7: *Northwest Coast*, ed. Wayne Suttles, 267–284. Washington, D.C.: Smithsonian Institution Press.

Hamilton Log
    1809–1819 Salem, Mass.: Essex Institute.

Harrison, Charles
    1925   *Ancient Warriors of the North Pacific.* London: H. F. & G. Witherby.

Haswell, Robert
n.d.   A voyage around the world on board the ship *Columbia Rediviva* and
            Sloop *Washington* in 1787–1789. Victoria: Provincial Archives of British
            Columbia.
Hawthorn, Audrey
1979   *Kwakiutl Art*. Seattle: University of Washington Press.
Hayman, John, ed.
1989   *Robert Brown and the Vancouver Island Exploring Expedition*. Vancou-
            ver: University of British Columbia Press.
Healey, Elizabeth
n.d.   History of Alert Bay. Victoria: Provincial Archives of British Columbia.
Helmcken, John S.
1975   *The Reminiscences of Doctor John Sebastian Helmcken*. Vancouver: Uni-
            versity of British Columbia Press.
Hempel, Carl G.
1959   The logic of functional analysis. In *Symposium on Sociological Theory*,
            ed. N. Gross, 271–307. New York: Harper and Row.
Hill-Tout, Charles
1907   *The Far West: The Home of the Salish and Dene*. London: Archibald
            Constable.
Hilton, Susanne F.
1990   Haihais, Bella Bella, and Oowekeeno. In *Handbook of North American
            Indians*. Vol. 7: *Northwest Coast*, ed. Wayne Suttles, 312–322. Washing-
            ton, D.C.: Smithsonian Institution Press.
Hodge, Frederick Webb, ed.
1907–1910 *Handbook of American Indians North of Mexico*. Bureau of American
            Ethnology Bulletin no. 30. Washington, D.C.
Holm, Bill
1990   Art. In *Handbook of North American Indians*. Vol. 7: *Northwest Coast*,
            ed. Wayne Suttles, 602–632. Washington, D.C.: Smithsonian Institution
            Press.
Holmberg, Heinrich Johan
1985   *Holmberg's Ethnographic Sketches*. Fairbanks: University of Alaska Press.
Howay, Frederick W.
1930a   *A List of Trading Vessels in the Maritime Fur Trade, 1785–1804*. Pro-
            ceedings and Transactions of the Royal Society of Canada, 3d ser., 24,
            sec. 2. Pp. 111–134.
1930b   The attempt to capture the brig *Otter*. *Washington Historical Quarterly*
            21: 179–188.
1931   *A List of Trading Vessels in the Maritime Fur Trade, 1795–1804*. Pro-
            ceedings and Transactions of the Royal Society of Canada, 3d ser., 25,
            sec. 2. Pp. 117–149.
1932a   *A List of Trading Vessels in the Maritime Fur Trade, 1805–1814*. Pro-
            ceedings and Transactions of the Royal Society of Canada, 3d ser., 26,
            sec. 2. Pp. 43–86.

1932b   An outline sketch of the maritime fur trade. *Annual Report of the Canadian Historical Association for 1932:* 5–14.

1933   *A List of Trading Vessels in the Maritime Fur Trade, 1815–1819.* Proceedings and Transactions of the Royal Society of Canada, 3d ser., 27, sec. 2. Pp. 119–147.

1934   *A List of Trading Vessels in the Maritime Fur Trade, 1820–1825.* Proceedings and Transactions of the Royal Society of Canada, 3d ser., 28, sec. 2. Pp. 11–49.

Howay, Frederick W., ed.

1941   *Voyages of the "Columbia" to the Northwest Coast, 1787–1790 and 1790–1793.* Boston: Massachusetts Historical Society.

Hrdlicka, Ales

1930   Anthropological survey in Alaska. *Bureau of American Ethnology Annual Reports* 46: 19–374.

Hudson, Charles

1976   *The Southeastern Indians.* Knoxville: University of Tennessee Press.

Hunt, George

1926–1928 Kwakiutl ethnographic materials. Boas Collection 372, microfilm roll 22, item Wla.15. Philadelphia: American Philosophical Society.

Hymes, Dell

1980   Commentary. In *Theoretical Orientations in Creole Studies*, ed. Albert Valdman and Arnold Highfield, 389–423. New York: Academic Press.

Indian Claims Commission

1958a   Appendix to docket 155 and docket 242: The Quileute tribe of Indians and the Quinaielt tribe of Indians. *American Indian Ethnohistory, Indians of the Northwest: Coast Salish and Western Washington Indians* 2. Pp. 205–400. New York: Garland.

1958b   Commission findings on the Coast Salish and western Washington Indians. Docket no. 155: Quileute tribe of Indians. *American Indian Ethnohistory, Indians of the Northwest: Coast Salish and Western Washington Indians* 5. Pp. 202–235. New York: Garland.

1958c   Commission findings on the Coast Salish and western Washington Indians. Docket no. 242: Quinaielt tribe of Indians. *American Indian Ethnohistory, Indians of the Northwest: Coast Salish and Western Washington Indians* 5. Pp. 236–251. New York: Garland.

Ingraham, Joseph

1971   *Joseph Ingraham's Journal of the Brigantine "Hope."* Barre, Mass.: Imprint Society.

Irvine, Albert

1921   How the Makah obtained possession of Cape Flattery. *Indian Notes and Monographs* 6: 5–11.

Jackman, S. W., ed.

1978   *The Journal of William Sturgis.* Victoria, B.C.: Sono Nis Press.

Jackson, Sheldon

1880   *Alaska and Missions on the North Pacific Coast.* New York: Dodd Mead.

1887   *Alaska: Its People, Villages, Missions and Schools.* New York: Woman's Executive Committee of Home Missions of the Presbyterian Church.

Jacobs, Melville
1959   *Clackamas Chinook Texts, pt. 2.* Indiana University Research Center in Anthropology, Folklore and Linguistics Publications no. 11.

Jacobsen, Johan Adrian
[1884] 1977 *Alaskan Voyage 1881–1883.* Chicago: University of Chicago Press.

Jarvie, I. C.
1965   Limits to functionalism and alternatives to it in anthropology. In *Functionalism in the Social Sciences,* ed. Don Martindale, 18–34. Philadelphia: American Academy of Political and Social Science.

Jenness, Diamond
n.d.   The Saanitch Indians of Vancouver Island. Victoria: Provincial Archives of British Columbia.

Jessett, E., ed.
1959   *Reports and Letters of Herbert Beaver, 1836–1838.* Portland, Ore.: Champoeg Press.

Jewitt, John R.
[1815] 1975 *Narrative of the Adventures and Sufferings of John R. Jewitt While Held as a Captive of the Nootka Indians of Vancouver Island.* Edited by Robert Heizer. Ballena Press Publications in Archaeology, Ethnology and History no. 5.
1974   *The Adventures and Sufferings of John R. Jewitt, Captive among the Nootka 1803–1805.* Toronto: McClelland and Stewart.

Johansen, Dorothy O., ed.
1960   *Voyage of the Columbia Around the World with John Boit, 1790–93.* Portland, Ore.: Beaver Books.

Jones, Livingston F.
1914   *A Study of the Thlingets of Alaska.* New York: Fleming H. Revell.

Jopling, Carol F.
1989   *The Coppers of the Northwest Coast Indians: Their Origin, Development, and Possible Antecedents.* Transactions of the American Philosophical Society, 79, pt. 1.

Jorgensen, Joseph G.
1974   On continuous area and worldwide studies in formal comparative ethnology. In *Comparative Studies by Harold E. Drover and Essays in His Honor,* ed. Joseph G. Jorgensen, 195–203. New Haven: HRAF Press.
1980   *Western Indians: Comparative Environments, Languages, and Cultures of 172 Western Indian Tribes.* San Francisco: W. H. Freeman.

Kamenskii, Anatolii
1985   *Tlingit Indians of Alaska.* Fairbanks: University of Alaska Press.

Kan, Sergei
1989   *Symbolic Immortality: The Tlingit Potlatch of the Nineteenth Century.* Washington, D.C.: Smithsonian Institution Press.

Kane, Paul
1855   The Chinook Indians. *The Canadian Journal* 3: 273–279.
1971   Wanderings of an artist among the Indians of North America. In *Paul Kane's Frontier,* ed. J. Russell Harper, 47–159. Toronto: University of Toronto Press.

Kennedy, Alexander
    1824–1825 Report, Fort George District, Columbia Department, 1824–25. Hudson's Bay Company Archives MS B76/e/1: Winnipeg: Provincial Archives of Manitoba.
Kenyon, Susan
    1975   *Rank and Property among the Nootka.* Canadian Ethnology Service, National Museum of Civilization, Ottawa.
Khlebnikov, Kyrill T.
    1835   *Baranov, Chief Manager of the Russian Colonies in America.* Kingston, Ont.: Brown & Martin.
    [1861] 1976 *Colonial Russian America, Kyrill T. Klebnikov's Reports 1817–1832.* Portland: Oregon Historical Society.
Kinkade, M. Dale
    1990   History of research in linguistics. In *Handbook of North American Indians.* Vol. 7: *Northwest Coast,* ed. Wayne Suttles, 90–106. Washington, D.C.: Smithsonian Institution Press.
    1991   Prehistory of the native languages of the Northwest Coast. In *Proceedings of the Great Ocean Conferences.* Vol. 1: *The North Pacific to 1600.* Pp. 140–158. Portland: Oregon Historical Society Press.
Knapp, Frances, and Rheta Louise Childe
    1896   *The Thlinkets of Southeastern Alaska.* Chicago: Stone & Kimball.
Knauft, Bruce M.
    1987   Reconsidering violence in simple human societies: Homicide among the Gebusi of New Guinea. *Current Anthropology* 28: 457–500.
Knowles, Nathaniel
    1940   The torture of captives by the Indians of eastern North America. *Proceedings of the American Philosophical Society* 82(2): 155–225.
Kopas, Cliff
    1970   *Bella Coola.* Vancouver: Mitchell Press.
Koppert, Vincent A.
    1930a   *Contributions to Clayoquot Ethnography.* Anthropological Series no. 1. Washington, D.C.: Catholic University of America.
    1930b   The Nootka family. *Primitive Man* 13: 49–55.
Kopytoff, Igor, and Suzanne Miers
    1977   African 'slavery' as an institution of marginality. In *Slavery in Africa: Historical and Anthropological Perspectives,* ed. Suzanne Miers and Igor Kopytoff, 3–81. Madison: University of Wisconsin Press.
Kotzebue, Otto von
    1830   *A New Voyage Round the World in the Years 1823, 24, 25, and 26.* London: Henry Colburn & Richard Bentley.
Krause, Aurel
    1956   *Tlingit Indians of Alaska.* Seattle: University of Washington Press.
Kroeber, A. L.
    1923   American culture and the Northwest Coast. *American Anthropologist* 25: 1–20.
Lafitau, Joseph-François
    1974   *Customs of the American Indians Compared with the Customs of Primi-*

tive Times. Vol. 1. Edited by William N. Fenton and E. L. Moore. Toronto: Champlain Society.

1977   *Customs of the American Indians Compared with the Customs of Primitive Times.* Vol. 2. Edited by William N. Fenton and E. L. Moore. Toronto: Champlain Society.

Langdon, Steve

1979   Comparative Tlingit and Haida adaptation to the west coast of Prince of Wales Archipelago. *Ethnology* 18: 101–119.

Leary, David T.

1975   Slacum of the Pacific 1832–37: Background of the Oregon report. *Oregon Historical Quarterly* 76: 118–134.

Lee, D., and J. Frost

[1844] 1968   *Ten Years in Oregon.* Fairfield, Wash.: Ye Galleon Press.

Lincoln, Neville J., and John C. Rath

1980   *North Wakashan Comparative Root List.* Mercury Series, Ethnology Service Papers no. 68. Ottawa: National Museum of Man.

Lisiansky, Urey

[1814] 1968   *A Voyage Round the World, in the Years 1803, 4, 5, & 6.* New York: Da Capo.

Litke, Fredric

1987   *A Voyage Around the World 1826–1829.* Vol. 1: *To Russian America and Siberia.* Kingston, Ont.: Limestone Press.

Lockley, Fred

1928   *History of the Columbia River Valley from the Dalles to the Sea.* Chicago: S. J. Clarke.

Lohse, E. S., and Frances Sundt

1990   History of research: Museum collections. In *Handbook of North American Indians.* Vol. 7: *Northwest Coast,* ed. Wayne Suttles, 88–97. Washington, D.C.: Smithsonian Institution Press.

Lopatin, Ivan A.

1945   *Social Life and Religion of the Indians in Kitimat, British Columbia.* Los Angeles: University of Southern California Press.

Lutke, Frederic

1839   *Voyage autour du monde . . . dans les annees 1826, 1827, 1828 et 1829.* Paris: Fumin Didot Freres.

McClellan, Catherine

1950   Culture change and native trade in southern Yukon Territory. Ph.D. dissertation, University of California.

1954   The inter-relations of social structure with northern Tlingit ceremonialism. *Southwestern Journal of Anthropology* 10: 75–96.

1975   *My Old People Say: An Ethnographic Survey of Southern Yukon Territory.* National Museums of Canada Publications in Ethnology no. 6.

MacFie, Matthew

1865   *Vancouver Island and British Columbia.* London: Longman, Green.

McIlwraith, T. F.

1922–1924   *Bella Coola Notes.* Ottawa: National Museum of Civilization, Ethnology Division.

1948   *The Bella Coola Indians*. Toronto: University of Toronto Press.

MacKenzie, Alexander

1892   Descriptive notes on certain implements, weapons, etc. from Graham Island, Queen Charlotte Islands, B.C. *Proceedings and Transactions of the Royal Society of Canada* 9, sec. 2. Pp. 45–59.

Mackenzie, Alexander

1931   *Alexander Mackenzie's Voyage to the Pacific Ocean in 1793*. Chicago: Lakeside Press.

MacLeod, William Christie

1925   Debtor and chattel slavery in aboriginal North America. *American Anthropologist* 27: 370–380.

1927   Some social aspects of aboriginal American slavery. *Journal de la Société des Américanistes* 19: 123–128.

1928   Economic aspects of indigenous American slavery. *American Anthropologist* 30: 632–650.

1929   The origin of servile labor groups. *American Anthropologist* 31: 89–113.

McLoughlin, John

1941   *The Letters of John McLoughlin from Fort Vancouver to the Governor and Committee, First Series, 1825–38*. London: Hudson's Bay Record Society.

1943   *The Letters of John McLoughlin from Fort Vancouver to the Governor and Committee, Second Series, 1839–44*. London: Hudson's Bay Record Society.

McNeill, W. H.

1848   Letter to Sir George Simpson from Ft. Stikine, 26 August 1848. Hudson's Bay Company Archive D5–22 fol. 567–571. Winnipeg: Provincial Archives of Manitoba.

Marquardt, William H.

1988   Politics and production among the Calusa of South Florida. In *Hunters and Gatherers*. Vol. 1: *History, Evolution and Social Change*, ed. Tim Ingold, David Riches, and James Woodburn, 161–188. Oxford: Berg.

Martin, R. M.

1849   *Hudson's Bay Territories and Vancouver's Island*. London: T. & M. Boone.

Marx, Karl

1965   *Pre-capitalist Economic Formations*. New York: International Publishers.

1966   *Capital*. Vol. 3. Moscow: Progress Publishers.

Marx, Karl, and Friedrich Engels

1964   *The German Ideology*. Moscow: Progress Publishers.

Mason, Otis T.

1896   Influence of environment upon human industries or arts. *Annual Report of the Smithsonian Institution for the Year 1895*. Pp. 639–665. Washington, D.C.

Matson, R. G., and Gary Coupland

1995   *The Prehistory of the Northwest Coast*. San Diego: Academic Press.

Mauss, Marcel

[1925] 1967 *The Gift*. New York: W. W. Norton.

Mauze, Marie
 1984   Enjeux et jeux du prestige des Kwagul méridionaux aux Lekwiltoq (côte
           nord-ouest du Pacifique). Thèse pour le doctorat de troisième cycle. Paris:
           Ecole des Hautes Etudes en Sciences Sociales.
Mayne, Richard Charles
 1862   *Four Years in British Columbia and Vancouver Island: An Account of
           Their Forests, Rivers, Coasts, Gold Fields and Resources for Colonisa-
           tion.* London: John Murray.
Meares, John
 [1790] 1967 *Voyages to the Northwest Coast.* Amsterdam: Da Capo.
 1933   *The Memorial of John Meares to the House of Commons Respecting the
           Capture of the Vessels in Nootka Sound.* Ed. N. B. Pipes. Portland, Ore.:
           Metropolitan Press.
Meillassoux, Claude
 1981   *Maidens, Meal and Money: Capitalism and the Domestic Community.*
           Cambridge: Cambridge University Press.
 1991   *The Anthropology of Slavery.* Chicago: University of Chicago Press.
Merk, Frederick, ed.
 1931   *Fur Trade and Empire: George Simpson's Journal.* Cambridge, Mass.:
           Harvard University Press.
Mitchell, Donald
 1981   Sebassa's men. In *The World Is as Sharp as a Knife: An Anthology in
           Honour of Wilson Duff,* ed. Donald N. Abbott, 79–86. Victoria: British
           Columbia Provincial Museum.
 1983   Tribes and chiefdoms of the Northwest Coast: The Tsimshian case. In
           *The Evolution of Maritime Cultures on the Northeast and the Northwest
           Coasts of America,* ed. Ronald J. Nash, 57–65. Burnaby, B.C.: Simon
           Fraser University.
 1984   Predatory warfare, social status, and the North Pacific slave trade. *Eth-
           nology* 23: 39–48.
 1985   A demographic profile of Northwest Coast slavery. In *Status, Structure,
           and Stratification: Current Archaeological Reconstructions,* ed. M. Thomp-
           son, M. T. Garcia, and F. J. Kense, 227–236. Calgary: Proceedings of the
           Sixteenth Annual Conference of the Archaeological Association of the
           University of Calgary.
 1988   Changing patterns of resource use in the prehistory of Queen Charlotte
           Strait, British Columbia. In *Prehistoric Economies of the Pacific North-
           west Coast,* ed. Barry L. Isaac, 245–290. Greenwich, Conn.: JAI Press.
 1990   Prehistory of the coasts of southern British Columbia and northern Wash-
           ington. In *Handbook of North American Indians.* Vol. 7: *Northwest Coast,*
           ed. Wayne Suttles, 340–358. Washington, D.C.: Smithsonian Institution
           Press.
Mitchell, Donald, and Leland Donald
 1988   Archaeology and the study of Northwest Coast economies. In *Prehistoric
           Economies of the Pacific Northwest Coast,* ed. Barry L. Isaac, 293–351.
           Greenwich, Conn.: JAI Press.

Moeller, Beverly B.
    1966   Captain James Colnett and the Tsimshian Indians, 1787. *Pacific Northwest Quarterly* 57: 13–17.

Moffat, Hamilton
    1857–1867 Fort Rupert Letter Book. A/B/20/R2A. Victoria: Provincial Archives of British Columbia.

Mooney, Kathleen A.
    n.d.   Interview with Chief Charles Jones of Pacheenaht, August 1978.

Morgan, Lewis Henry
    1851   *League of the Ho-de-no-sau-nee, Iroquois.* Rochester, N.Y.: Sage & Brother.
    [1871] 1964 *Ancient Society.* Cambridge, Mass.: Belknap Press.

Morice, A. G.
    1894   *Notes Archeological, Industrial, and Sociological on the Western Denes.* Transactions of the Royal Canadian Institute no. 4, pt. 1.

Morison, C. F.
    1920   Reminiscences of the early days of British Columbia 1862–1876, by a pioneer of the Northwest Coast. Add. MSS, EB M82. Victoria: Provincial Archives of British Columbia.

Morris, William Gouverneur
    1879   *Report upon the Customs District, Public Service and Resources of Alaska Territory.* Washington, D.C.: U.S. Government Printing Office.

Moser, Charles
    1926   *Reminiscences of the West Coast of Vancouver Island.* Victoria, B.C.: Acme Press.

Moziño, J. M.
    1970   *Noticias de Nutka: An Account of Nootka Sound in 1792.* Seattle: University of Washington Press.

Muir, John
    1915   *Travels in Alaska.* New York: Houghton Mifflin.

Murdock, George Peter
    1967   *Ethnographic Atlas: A Summary.* Pittsburgh: University of Pittsburgh Press.

Niblack, Albert P.
    1890   The Coast Indians of Southern Alaska and Northern British Columbia. *Annual Report of the Smithsonian Institution, 1887–1888.* Pp. 225–386. Washington, D.C.

Nieboer, H. J.
    1910   *Slavery as an Industrial System: Ethnological Researches.* The Hague: Martinus Nijhoff.

Oberg, Kalervo
    1934   Crime and punishment in Tlingit society. *American Anthropologist* 36: 145–156.
    1943   A comparison of three systems of primitive economic organization. *American Anthropologist* 45: 572–588.
    1973   *The Social Economy of the Tlingit Indians.* Seattle: University of Washington Press.

Olson, Ronald L.

1936   *The Quinault Indians.* University of Washington Publications in Anthropology no. 6.

1967   *Social Structure and Social Life of the Tlingit in Alaska.* University of California Anthropological Records no. 26. Berkeley: University of California.

Ormsby, Margaret A.

1972   Douglas, Sir James. In *Dictionary of Canadian Biography* 10: 238–248. Toronto: University of Toronto Press.

Owens, Kenneth N., ed.

1985   *The Wreck of* Sv. *Nikolai: The Narrative of Timofei Tarakanov, translated from the 1874 Russian edition, and the narrative of Ben Hobucket, a Quileute oral tradition.* Portland: Oregon Historical Society.

Parker, Samuel

1967   *Journal of an Exploring Tour Beyond the Rocky Mountains, under the Direction of the A.B.C.F.M. Performed in the Years 1835, 37, and 38.* Minneapolis: Ross and Haines.

Patterson, Orlando

1982   *Slavery and Social Death: A Comparative Study.* Cambridge, Mass.: Harvard University Press.

Petroff, Ivan

1900   The population and resources of Alaska, 1880. In *Compilation of Narratives of Explorations in Alaska.* Pp. 53–284. Washington, D.C.: U.S. Government Printing Office.

Pettit, G. A.

1950   *The Quileute of La Push, 1775–1945.* University of California Anthropological Records no. 14.

Piddcocke, S.

1965   The potlatch system of the southern Kwakiutl: A new perspective. *Southwestern Journal of Anthropology* 21: 244–264.

Pilling, James C.

1894   *Bibliography of the Wakashan Languages.* Bureau of American Ethnology Bulletin no. 19. Washington, D.C.

Pipes, Nellie B., ed.

1934   Journal of John Frost, 1840–43. *Oregon Historical Quarterly* 35: 50–73, 139–167, 235–262, 348–375.

Poole, Francis

1872   *Queen Charlotte Islands.* London: Hurst and Blackett.

Powell, I. W.

n.d.   Diaries and Notes. AE P87 P87, vols. 1–7. Victoria: Provincial Archives of British Columbia.

Powell, John Wesley

1891   Indian linguistic families of America north of Mexico. *Bureau of American Ethnology, 7th Annual Report.*

Powers, K. N. B.

1902   Across the continent seventy years ago. *Oregon Historical Quarterly* 3: 82–106.

Quimby, George
  1985   Japanese wrecks, iron tools, and prehistoric Indians of the Northwest
            Coast. *Arctic Anthropology* 22(2): 7–15.
Ray, Verne F.
  1938   *Lower Chinook Ethnographic Notes.* University of Washington Publica-
            tions in Anthropology, vol. 7, no. 2. Seattle: University of Washington.
  1956   Rejoinder. *American Anthropologist* 58: 165–170.
Reagan, A. B.
  1929   Traditions of the Hoh and Quillayute Indians. *Washington Historical
            Quarterly* 20: 178–189.
Reagan, A. B., and L. V. W. Walters
  1933   Tales from the Hoh and Quileute. *Journal of American Folklore* 46: 297–
            346.
Reynolds, Stephen
  1970   *The Voyage of the New Hazard.* Fairfield, Wash.: Ye Galleon Press.
Riches, David
  1979   Ecological variation on the Northwest Coast: Models for the generation
            of cognatic and matrilineal descent. In *Social and Ecological Systems,*
            ed. R. Ellen and P. Burnham, 145–166. London: Academic Press.
Rickard, T. A.
  1939   The use of iron and copper by the Indians of British Columbia. *British
            Columbia Historical Quarterly* 3: 25–50.
Rohner, Ronald P., and Evelyn C. Rohner
  1970   *The Kwakiutl: Indians of British Columbia.* New York: Holt, Rinehart and
            Winston.
Rollins, Phillip A., ed.
  1935   *The Discovery of the Oregon Trail, Robert Stuart's Narratives.* New York:
            Eberstadt.
Ross, Alexander
  [1849] 1969 *Adventures of the First Settlers on the Columbia River.* New York:
            Citadel Press.
Rousseau, Jérôme
  1978   On estates and castes. *Dialectical Anthropology* 3: 85–95.
Ruby, Robert H., and John A. Brown
  1976   *The Chinook Indians.* Norman: University of Oklahoma Press.
  1993   *Indian Slavery in the Pacific Northwest.* Spokane: Clark.
Ruyle, Eugene R.
  1973   Slavery, surplus and stratification on the Northwest Coast: Ethnoenerget-
            ics of an incipient stratification system. *Current Anthropology* 14: 603–
            631.
Sahlins, Marshall
  1957   Differentiation by adaptation in Polynesian societies. *Journal of the Poly-
            nesian Society* 66: 291–300.
  1965   On the ideology and composition of descent groups. *Man* 65: 104–107.
  1968   *Tribesmen.* New York: Prentice-Hall.

Ste. Croix, G. E. M. de
  1981   *The Class Struggle in the Ancient Greek World, from the Archaic Age to the Arab Conquest*. London: Duckworth.
Sales, Fr. Luis
  1956   *Observations on California, 1772–1790*. Los Angeles: Glen Dawson.
Samarin, William J.
  1986   Chinook Jargon and pidgin historiography. *Canadian Journal of Anthropology* 5: 23–34.
Sanger, David
  1970   The archaeology of the Lochnore-Nesikep locality, British Columbia. *Syesis* no. 3, Suppl. 1.
Santee, J. F.
  1932   Comcomly and the Chinooks. *Oregon Historical Quarterly* 31: 271–278.
Sapir, Edward
  1929   Central and North American languages. In *Encyclopaedia Britannica*. 14th ed. Pp. 138–141. London.
Sapir, Edward, and Morris Swadesh
  1939   *Nootka Texts: Tales and Ethnological Narratives*. Philadelphia: Linguistic Society of America.
  1955   *Native Accounts of Nootka Ethnography*. Indiana University Research Center in Anthropology, Folklore, and Linguistics, Publications no. 1.
Schalk, Randall F.
  1977   The structure of an anadromous fish resource. In *Theory Building in Archaeology*, ed. L. R. Binford, 207–249. New York: Academic Press.
  1979   Land use and organizational complexity among foragers of northwestern North America. In *Affluent Foragers: Pacific Coasts East and West*, ed. S. Koyama and D. H. Thomas, 53–75. Senri Ethnological Studies.
Scheffler, Harold
  1974   Kinship, descent and alliance. In *Handbook of Social and Cultural Anthropology*, ed. John J. Honigmann, 747–793. New York: Rand McNally.
Schoolcraft, Henry R.
  1853   *Information Respecting the History, Condition and Prospects of the Indian Tribes of the United States: Collected and Prepared Under the Direction of the Bureau of Indian Affairs*. Philadelphia: Lippincott, Grambo.
  1856   *Information Respecting the History, Condition and Prospects of the Indian Tribes of the United States: Collected and Prepared Under the Direction of the Bureau of Indian Affairs*. Philadelphia: J. B. Lippincott.
Schwatka, Frederick
  1893   *A Summer in Alaska*. St. Louis: J. W. Henry.
Scouler, John
  1841   Observations on the indigenous tribes of the North-West Coast of America. *Journal of the Royal Geographical Society* 11: 215–250.
  1905   Journal of a voyage to North West America. *Oregon Historical Quarterly* 6: 54–76, 159–205, 276–289.
Shotridge, Louis
  1921   Tlingit woman's root basket. *Museum Journal* 12: 162–178.
  1928   The emblems of the Tlingit culture. *Museum Journal* 19: 350–377.

Siegel, Bernard J.
  1945   Some methodological considerations for a comparative study of slavery. *American Anthropologist* 47: 357–392.
Silverstein, Michael
  1990   Chinookans of the Lower Columbia. In *Handbook of North American Indians*. Vol. 7: *Northwest Coast*, ed. Wayne Suttles, 533–546. Washington, D.C.: Smithsonian Institution Press.
Simpson, Aemilius
  1830   Untitled Report of 1828 Expedition to Puget Sound. Hudson's Bay Company Archives. Winnipeg: Provincial Archives of Manitoba.
  1831–1832 Log of Dryad. Hudson's Bay Company Archives, MS C 1/218. Winnipeg: Provincial Archives of Manitoba.
Simpson, George
  1847   *Narrative of a Journey around the World.* London: Henry Colburn.
Singh, Ram Raj Prasad
  1966   *Aboriginal Economic Systems of the Olympic Peninsula Indians, Western Washington.* Sacramento Anthropological Society Papers no. 4.
Slacum, William A.
  1912   Slacum's report on Oregon, 1836–7. *Oregon Historical Quarterly* 13: 175–224.
Smith, Marian W.
  1940   *The Puyallup-Nisqually.* Columbia University Contributions to Anthropology no. 32.
Smith, Silas B.
  1901   Primitive customs and religious beliefs of the Indians of the Pacific Northwest Coast. *Oregon Historical Quarterly* 2: 255–265.
Sproat, Gilbert Malcolm
  1868   *Scenes and Studies of Savage Life.* London: Smith, Elder.
Starna, William A., and Ralph Watkins
  1991   Northern Iroquoian slavery. *Ethnohistory* 38: 34–57.
Starr, S. Frederick, ed.
  1987   *Russia's American Colony.* Durham: Duke University Press.
Stern, Bernhard J.
  1934   *The Lummi Indians of Northwest Washington.* Columbia Contributions to Anthropology no. 17.
Stewart, Hillary
  1977   *Indian Fishing: Early Methods on the Northwest Coast.* Vancouver: J. J. Douglas.
Storie, S., et al.
  1973a   Bella Bella stories. Victoria: Provincial Archives of British Columbia.
  1973b   Klemtu Stories. Victoria: Provincial Archives of British Columbia.
  1973c   Oweekano Stories. Victoria: Provincial Archives of British Columbia.
Strong, J. C.
  1893   *Wah-Kee-Nah and Her People.* New York: G. P. Putnam's Sons.
Suttles, Wayne
  1958   Private knowledge, morality, and social class among the Coast Salish. *American Anthropologist* 60: 497–507.

1960   Affinal ties, subsistence, and prestige among the Coast Salish. *American Anthropologist* 62: 296–305.

1962   Variation in habitat and culture on the Northwest Coast. *Proceedings of the 34th International Congress of Americanists*. Pp. 522–537. Vienna.

1968   Coping with abundance: Subsistence on the Northwest Coast. In *Man the Hunter*, ed. Richard B. Lee and Irvin DeVore, 56–68. Chicago: Aldine.

1973   Comment on Eugene E. Ruyle, *Slavery, Surplus, and Stratification on the Northwest Coast. Current Anthropology* 14: 622–623.

1974   The economic life of the Coast Salish of Haro and Rosario straits. *Coast Salish and Western Washington Indians* no. 1. Pp. 41–512. New York: Garland.

1987   *Coast Salish Essays*. Seattle: University of Washington Press.

1990a   Environment. In *Handbook of North American Indians*. Vol. 7: *Northwest Coast*, ed. Wayne Suttles, 16–29. Washington, D.C.: Smithsonian Institution Press.

1990b   Introduction. In *Handbook of North American Indians*. Vol. 7: *Northwest Coast*, ed. Wayne Suttles, 1–15. Washington, D.C.: Smithsonian Institution Press.

Suttles, Wayne, and Aldona C. Jonaitis
1990   History of research in ethnology. In *Handbook of North American Indians*. Vol. 7: *Northwest Coast*, ed. Wayne Suttles, 73–88. Washington, D.C.: Smithsonian Institution Press.

Swadesh, Morris
1954   Time depths of American linguistic groupings. *American Anthropologist* 56: 361–364.

Swan, James G.
[1857] 1966 *The Northwest Coast*. Fairfield, Wash.: Ye Galleon Press.

1870   *The Indians of Cape Flattery, at the Entrance to the Strait of Fuca, Washington Territory*. Smithsonian Contributions to Knowledge no. 16. Washington, D.C.: Smithsonian Institution.

Swanton, John R.
1905   *Contributions to the Ethnology of the Haida: The Jesup North Pacific Expedition*. Memoirs of the American Museum of Natural History no. 8, pt. 1. New York.

1908   Social condition, beliefs, and linguistic relationship of the Tlingit Indians. *Annual Report of the Bureau of American Ethnology*, 26: 391–485.

1909   *Tlingit Myths and Texts*. Bureau of American Ethnology Bulletin no. 39.

Teichmann, Emil
1963   *A Journey to Alaska in the Year 1868: Being a Diary of the Late Emil Teichmann*. New York: Argosy-Antiquarian.

Teit, James A.
1906   *The Lillooet Indians*. Memoirs of the American Museum of Natural History no. 4, pt. 5.

Thompson, Laurence C., and M. Dale Kinkade
1990   Languages. In *Handbook of North American Indians*. Vol. 7: *Northwest Coast*, ed. Wayne Suttles, 30–51. Washington, D.C.: Smithsonian Institution Press.

Thorman, W. P. S.
    n.d.   Notes on the Tahltan. Victoria: Provincial Archives of British Columbia.
Thwaites, Reuben Gold, ed.
    1896–1901 *The Jesuit Relations and Allied Documents*. Cleveland: Burrows Broth-
                ers.
Tikhmenev, Petr A.
    1978   *A History of the Russian-American Company*. 2 vols. Seattle: University
                of Washington Press.
Tollefson, Kenneth D.
    1995   Potlatching and political organization among the Northwest Coast Indi-
                ans. *Ethnology* 34: 53–73.
Tolmie, William F.
    1878   *History of Puget Sound and the Northwest Coast*. Berkeley: Bancroft
                Library, University of California.
    1963   *The Journals of William Fraser Tolmie: Physician and Fur Trader*. Van-
                couver, B.C.: Mitchell Press.
Tooker, Elizabeth
    1964   *An Ethnography of the Huron Indians, 1615–1649*. Bureau of American
                Ethnology Bulletin no. 190.
Trigger, Bruce G.
    1976   *The Children of Aataensic: A History of the Huron People to 1660*. Mon-
                treal: McGill-Queen's University Press.
    1990   Maintaining economic equality in opposition to complexity: An Iro-
                quoian case study. In *The Evolution of Political Systems*, ed. Steadman
                Upham, 119–145. Cambridge: Cambridge University Press.
Vancouver, George
    [1798] 1967 *Voyage of Discovery to the North Pacific and Around the World*. Am-
                sterdam: Da Capo.
Veniaminof, Ivan
    1857   The Russian Orthodox Church in Russian-America from 1793 to 1853.
                H/G/In7. Victoria: Provincial Archives of British Columbia.
Veniaminov, Innokentii
    1972   The condition of the Orthodox Church in Russian America: Innokentii
                Veniaminov's history of the Church in Alaska. *Pacific Northwest Quar-
                terly* 63: 41–54.
Wagner, H. R.
    1933   *Spanish Explorations of the Straits of Juan de Fuca*. Santa Ana, Calif.:
                Fine Arts Press.
Walker, Alexander
    1982   *An Account of a Voyage to the North West Coast of America in 1785 and
                1786*. Vancouver: Douglas & McIntyre.
Watson, James L.
    1980   Slavery as an institution: Open and closed systems. In *Asian and African
                Systems of Slavery*, ed. James L. Watson, 1–15. Oxford: Basil Blackwell.
Webb, Stephen Saunders
    1984   *1676: The End of American Independence*. New York: Alfred A. Knopf.
Widersprach-Thor, Martine de
    1981   *The Equation of Copper*. Papers from the Annual Congress, 1979 Cana-

dian Ethnology Society, National Museum of Man, Mercury Series no. 78. Pp. 112–130.

Widmer, Randolph J.
  1988   *The Evolution of the Calusa: A Nonagricultural Chiefdom on the South-west Florida Coast.* Tuscaloosa: University of Alabama Press.

Wike, Joyce
  1958   Social stratification among the Nootka. *Ethnohistory* 5: 219–241.
  1984   A reevaluation of Northwest Coast cannibalism. In *The Tsimshian and Their Neighbors of the North Pacific Coast,* ed. J. Miller and C. M. Eastman, 239–254. Seattle: University of Washington Press.

Williams, Glyndwr
  1962   *The British Search for the Northwest Passage in the Eighteenth Century.* London: Longmans.

Williams, Raymond
  1977   *Marxism and Literature.* Oxford: Oxford University Press.

Willoughby, Charles
  1886   Indians of the Quinaielt Agency, Washington. *Annual Report of the Board of Regents of the Smithsonian Institution,* pt. 1: 267–282.

Wood, C. E. S.
  1882   Among the Thlinkets of Alaska. *Century Magazine* 24: 323–339.

Work, John
  1842–1843 Fort Simpson Journal, May 1842 to June 1843. A/B/20/Si2.1. Victoria: British Columbia Provincial Archives.
  1842–1844 Fort Simpson Correspondence—1842 through 1844. A/B/20/Si2. Victoria: Provincial Archives of British Columbia.
  1843   Correspondence to Sir George Simpson. Hudson's Bay Company Archives D5/8 fol. 572–573. Winnipeg: Provincial Archives of Manitoba.
  1844   Correspondence to Sir George Simpson. Hudson's Bay Company Archives D5/12 fol. 396–399. Winnipeg: Provincial Archives of Manitoba.
  1945   *The Journal of John Work, January to October, 1835.* Archives of British Columbia, Memoir no. 10. Victoria, B.C.: King's Printer.

Wrangel, F. P. von
  1965   The inhabitants of the Northwest Coast of America. *Arctic Anthropology* 6: 5–21.
  1980   *Russian America: Statistical and Ethnographic Information.* Kingston, Ont.: Limestone Press.

Wyeth, John B.
  [1833] 1970 *Oregon; or, a Short History of a Long Journey.* Fairfield, Wash.: Ye Galleon Press.

Young, S. Hall
  1915   *Alaska Days with John Muir.* New York: Fleming H. Revell.
  1927   *Hall Young of Alaska, an Autobiography.* New York: Fleming H. Revell.

Index

Note: Page numbers in italics refer to figures.

367

176; capture of slaves by, 107, 108; census of, 186; concubinage in, 116; European contact with, 217, 218; first salmon rites of, 179, 180–81; freeing of slaves by, 93, 244; gambling in, 117; marriage customs of, 292; matrilineal descent of, 24, 302; peace-making ceremonies of, 162–63; potlatches of, 163; price of slaves in, 152; ritual slave-killing in, 86, 235; scale of slavery in, 194; shamans in, 164; slave participation in ritu-als of, 127; slave raiding by, 116; slaves from, 108, 147; slave trade with, 142–44; source materials on, 58, 210, 211, 324; statements about slaves in, 84; status of for-mer slaves in, 249; status of slaves in, 92, 93, 120; tobacco cultivation by, 20; treat-ment of dead slaves in, 76; in tribal unit sample, 52, 53; warfare by, 106; wergild payments in, 162. *See also* Cumshewa; Kaigani; Masset; Rose Spit Haida; Skedans; Skidegate
Haihais: cranial deformation in, 94, 293; debt enslavement in, 118; marriage customs of, 98, 293
Haisla: cannibalism in, 176; excluded from tribal unit sample, 53; marriage customs of, 98, 293; matrilineal descent of, 24, 302; slave trade with, 144. *See also* Kitimat
Haisla language, 206
Hale, Horatio, 328n3
Halkomelem Salish ethnic groups: excluded from tribal unit sample, 53; slave labor in, 136; slaves from, 106; slave status in, 93
Halpin, Marjorie, 287
Handbook of American Indians North of Mexico (Hodge), 255–56
Handbook of North American Indians, 15, 257, 327n2
Hanna, James, 219
Harrison, Charles, 58, 176, 244–45
Head-hunting, 65, 112, 178
Healey, Elizabeth, 136
Hegemony, definition of, 307–9
Heiltsuk: cannibalism in, 176, 177; cranial de-formation in, 94; escape of slaves from, 99; excluded from tribal unit sample, 53; first salmon rites of, 179, 180; gambling in, 117; Kwakwaka'wakw killing of, 104; marriage customs of, 98; patrilateral descent of, 24; price of slaves in, 149; slave trade with, 143, 144. *See also* Kokwayedox; Oyalidox; Uwitlidox; Weletoch
Heiltsuk language, 206
Henya (Tlingit), wergild payments in, 162
Hess, Thom, 208–9
Hezeta, Bruno de, 217
Hides, trading of, 26, 225, 230

Historical materialism, Soviet, 45
Historical sources: bias in, 57, 60–61; descrip-tion of, 56–57; of early contact period, 210–12, 215–24; independence of, 58–60; on slave trade, 140. *See also* Source materials
Hodge, H. W., 255–56, 257, 261, 268
Holmberg, Heinrich Johan, 178–79
Housing: construction rituals, 171–72; de-scription of, 2, 22, 23; manufacture of, 122, 127
Howay, Frederic W., 220
Hudson, Charles, 268–69
Hudson's Bay Company: censuses by, 183–84, 190, 192, 193; exploitation of slaves by employees of, 240–43; fur trade by, 222, 226–27; historical sources from, 57, 60, 140
Huna (Tlingit), ritual slave-killing in, 166–68, 169
Hunt, George, 59, 278
Hunter-gatherers: slavery among, 42; subsis-tence strategy of, 1–3, 5, 17, 20–21
Hunting technology, 20. *See also* Head-hunting; Seals: hunting of; Whales: hunt-ing of
Huron, captives from, 262, 263, 266
Hymes, Dell, 230

Illinois, treatment of captives in, 257
"Indian Slavery in the Pacific Northwest" (Dennis), 41
Indian Slavery in the Pacific Northwest (Ruby and Brown), 41
Inequality. *See* Class; Social stratification
Infanticide, 117
Informants: availability of, 63; bias of, 57, 64, 65–66; characteristics of, 61–62; as ethno-graphic sources, 9–10, 51, 58–60, 61, 201; independence of views of, 58–60
Inland Tlingit, slave trade with, 228
Intergroup fighting, 27, 33, 103–4. *See also* Warfare
Intergroup relations. *See* Political organization
Interior Salish ethnic groups, linguistic evi-dence from, 207, 208
Interviewing. *See* Informants
Iron, trade in, 215–16
Iron-working, 22
Iroquoian-speaking ethnic groups, treatment of captives in, 257–68, 271
Ivory carving, 31

Jacobsen, William H., Jr., 206
Jenness, Diamond: on Coast Salish population size, 193; on Saanich labor organization, 132; on Saanich marriage customs, 237; on Saanich master-slave relations, 80; on

Sproat, Gilbert Malcolm, 56; on Nuu-chah-nulth labor organization, 134; on Nuu-chah-nulth population size, 193; on Nuu-chah-nulth ritual killing of slaves, 172; on price of slaves, 156; on prostitution, 234–35

Squamish (Central Coast Salish): annual round of, 21; enslavement of orphans by, 119; first salmon rites of, 180; slave trade with, 144–45

Squamish language, 208

Starna, William A., 261, 263, 264–68, 271

Stekine. See Stikine

Stern, Bernhard J., 119

Stikine (Tlingit): capture of slaves by, 107–8; census of, 184, 188; debt enslavement in, 118; economic value of slaves in, 128; master-slave relations in, 89; non-ritual freeing of slaves in, 244; non-ritual slave-killing in, 80–81; potlatches of, 163; price of slaves in, 154; ransoming of slaves by, 96; ritual killing or freeing of slaves in, 86, 169, 236–37; scale of slavery in, 195; self-enslavement in, 118; slave labor in, 127, 131; slave ownership in, 195; slave raiding by, 116; slaves from, 120; slave trade with, 114, 142, 154, 228, 231; source materials on, 326; in tribal unit sample, 52, 53

Stl'atl'imx (Lillooet), slave trade with, 144–45, 229

Straits Salish language cluster, 106

Stratification. See Class; Social stratification

Subsistence strategies: of Northwest Coast cultures, 1–3, 17, 20–21, 122; and slavery, 42–43

Suttles, Wayne: on economic system, 5; on food/resource distribution (potlatches), 3, 133; on marriage networks, 293; on Northwest Coast resource base, 133, 304; on slavery, 40; on social ranking, 4, 273, 282–83; on status of former slaves, 247

Swadesh, Morris, 159

Swan, James G., 56, 79, 124, 243, 245, 246, 249

Swanton, John R., 179, 180

Tahltan (Athapaskan-speaking), slave trade with, 144, 228–29

Taku (Tlingit): slave participation in rituals of, 174; slave trade with, 142, 154, 225–26, 228

Tarakanov, Timofei, 74–75

Task specialization, 123

Technology. See Hunting technology; Iron-working; Toolmaking; Woodworking technology

Teit, James A., 144–45, 229

Textiles, 23, 31

Theology. See Ceremonialism; Religion

Thompson, David, 221

Thompson, John, 113, 174

Thompson ethnic group. See Nlak'pamux

Thorman, W. P. S., 229

Tikhmenev, Petr A., 185, 235

Tillamook-speaking ethnic groups, linguistic evidence from, 207, 208

Titleholders. See Elite; Masters

Tlingit ethnic groups: art of, 30; burial of slaves in, 178–79; cannibalism in, 176; capture of slaves by, 107–8; census of, 185–86, 191–92; clothing of, 23; debt enslavement in, 118–19; escape of slaves in, 99; European contact with, 217, 221; first salmon rites of, 179; freeing of slaves by, 244; housing of, 23; marriage customs of, 288, 289, 292; matrilineal descent of, 24, 302; peace-making ceremonies in, 162; price of slaves in, 154, 156; ritual slave-killing in, 77, 90, 170, 174, 235; Russian sources on, 45; scale of slavery in, 194; slave labor in, 130–31, 135, 136; slavery in, 249, 329n2; slaves from, 108, 147; slave trade with, 142–44, 154, 240; social stratification in, 288–89, 293; source materials on, 212; status of former slaves in, 96–97, 248, 249; tobacco cultivation by, 20; warfare by, 106. See also Angoon; Central Tlingit ethnic groups; Chilkat; Henya; Huna; Inland Tlingit; Sanya; Sitka; Southern Tlingit ethnic groups; Stikine; Taku; Tongas; Yakutat

Tollefson, Kenneth, 273

Tolmie, William F., 184, 186, 187, 231

Tongas (Tlingit): capture of slaves by, 107–8; peace-making ceremonies in, 162; ritual killing of slaves by, 172; wergild payments in, 162

Tooker, Elizabeth, 259

Toolmaking, 122

Totem pole rituals, 171, 172

Trade networks, 26. See also Eulachon oil, trading of; European trade goods; Furs: trade in; Metal: trade in; Slave trade

Treachery, against slaves, 120

"Tribal" societies, 2, 310

Trigger, Bruce G., 262, 263, 264, 266

Tsamosan-speaking ethnic groups, linguistic evidence from, 207–8

Tsetsaut (Athapaskan-speaking), slaves from, 109

Tsibasa (Sabassa) (Kitkatla leader), 114, 186, 227, 231, 232, 287

Tsibasa, Joshua, 287

Tsimshian: archaeological evidence of, 203–4; art of, 30; capture of slaves by, 107, 108–9; census of, 186, 190, 192; concubinage in,

Compositor: Prestige Typography
Text: 10/12 Times Roman
Display: Helvetica
Printer: Thomson-Shore
Binder: Thomson-Shore